Superintending Democracy

Series on Law, Politics, and Society

Lichfield
The U.S. Army on Trial
Jack Gieck

Murder, Culture, and Injustice
Four Sensational Cases in American History
Walter Hixson

Superintending Democracy
The Courts and the Political Process
Christopher P. Banks and John C. Green, eds.

The University of Akron Press
Akron, Ohio

Superintending Democracy

The Courts and the Political Process

Edited by Christopher P. Banks and John C. Green

Art on pages ii and 251 by Chip Bok

Library of Congress Cataloging-in-Publication Data

    Superintending democracy: the courts and the political process / edited by
Christopher P. Banks and John C. Green. — 1st ed.

      p.   cm. — (Series on law, politics, and society)

    Includes index.

    ISBN 1-884836-72-0 (alk. paper)

    1. United States. Supreme Court. 2. Political questions and judicial power—United
States. 3. Election law—United States. 4. Campaign funds—Law and legislation—
United States. 5. Law and politics. I. Banks, Christopher P. II. Green, John Clifford,
1953– . III. Series.

    KF8742 .S55   2001

    342.73'07—dc21   2001000480

For Zachary and

Samantha Banks

and

Brendan and

Darcy Green

Contents

Figures and Tables

Preface

THE ROLE OF THE UNITED STATES SUPREME COURT in superintending the electoral process is a topic that has been inadequately studied by social scientists. This book, which emerged from a dialogue that was generated from a 1998 conference in Akron, Ohio, exploring the nexus between law and politics,[1] investigates the impact of the Court's judicial decision making on key political resources and actors that are central to American politics. These cases involve political corruption, campaign finance, patronage, political parties, redistricting, and representation. The diverse and provocative essays presented here illustrate that law is inherently political, and that American politics is greatly influenced by what goes on in the Marble Temple. For this reason, each author makes a contribution to the study of law and courts, and American politics.

There are many colleagues and friends from The University of Akron community who have made this book possible. We are very grateful for the support for this project by our colleagues at the law school, especially its Dean, Richard Aynes, and Professors Wilson Huhn and William Rich. We also appreciate the efforts and contributions made by Professor David Louscher, the Chair of the Department of Political Science, and our other departmental colleagues, such as Professors Steven Brooks, Richard Farmer, William Lyons, Katherine Hinckley, Jesse Marquette, and Marion Miller. Several persons at the Ray C. Bliss Institute of Applied Politics were important as well, including Holly Harris-Bane, Kimberly Havercamp, and Jennifer Zap. We would also like to thank the anonymous reviewers of the manuscript, as well as Henry J. Abraham, John Blakeman, Stephen Bragaw, and Nancy Kassop for their support. A special word of thanks and praise goes to retired Chief Judge of the U.S. Court of Appeals for the

District of Columbia, Abner J. Mikva, and Thomas J. Moyer, Chief Justice of the Ohio Supreme Court, for participating in the dialogue that prompted this collection. We would also like to the thank contributors for their generosity, goodwill, and patience, as well as the University of Akron Press (as well as its editor, Michael J. Carley, and its production coordinator, Amy Petersen) for its support in publishing the book. Last but hardly least, we owe a great debt to our spouses and families. Their love and support is the foundation upon which this book stands.

CHAPTER 1

Superintending Democracy

Introduction

Christopher P. Banks and John C. Green

THE AMERICAN POLITICAL SYSTEM is in a precarious position as the twenty-first century begins. Public confidence in government is at an all-time low and shows no immediate signs of improving. Many observers complain that the political process is unresponsive to the public interest, and all too responsive to an array of special interests. Calls for reform and renewal dominate political discourse, and yet they are regularly rebuffed in legislatures and litigation. Partly as a consequence, many citizens have become apathetic, abandoning all kinds of political participation, while others have become alienated to the point of incivility and violence. Widespread discontent grips American democracy, even as democratic ideals triumph around the world.

As the 2000 campaign for President between George W. Bush and Al Gore well illustrates, the federal courts—especially the United States Supreme Court—are deeply enmeshed in this discontent. Lawyers and judges, along with politicians, are counted among those most responsible for the present failings of the political process. Thus, and because there is no clear separation between law and politics, the judiciary is at the center of the debate over reforming and renewing American democratic institutions. This debate raises a critical question: what role do—and should—courts play in regulating the electoral process?

The essays in this book explore this question from a variety of perspectives, including legal theory, political science, and applied politics. The authors consider the impact of court decisions on the regulation of political resources and political actors, for good or for ill. Many go a step further, indicating how the judiciary can improve upon its own record and the present situation. Taken together, these essays outline the ways the courts superintend American democracy.

Superintending Democracy. According to the *Oxford English Dictionary*, a superintendent is one who oversees, directs, guides, manages, or supervises an institution. The word comes from the Latin prefix *super*, used in the sense of being "on top of" or "over," and the verb *intend*, as in "to apply oneself to do something, to endeavor, to strive" and "to design or express, to mean." Thus, superintending is the act of directing an institution from above to achieve a specific purpose. This theme underlies the chapters in this book: the judiciary oversees democratic institutions and does so with the goal of furthering democratic purposes.

This kind of superintendence is inevitable in the American political system. Since *Marbury v. Madison* (1803),[1] the judiciary, led by the Supreme Court, has become the chief interpreter of the U.S. Constitution, the foundation for laws that govern the political process. If nothing else, the judiciary is required to judge the constitutionality of the laws affecting political resources and actors, and beyond that, it often involves itself in the broader debates that transpire over the limits of democracy in a republican form of government, where institutional power is shared and the people reign supreme. This is because, as Professor David O'Brien forcefully reminds us, "[t]he judiciary fulfills an important albeit limited role as an auxiliary precaution against both the abuse of governmental power by a tyrannical minority and the excesses of majoritarian democracy."[2] Thus, the courts are central to the ongoing struggle to preserve the key values of order and liberty that allow democratic institutions to function legitimately and effectively.

Such superintending is fraught with irony. After all, the courts are not, strictly speaking, democratic institutions, and they frequently exercise their power to interpret the Constitution in a countermajoritarian fashion. However, undemocratic decision-makers can be critical in preventing excesses on the part of democratic institutions. Majoritarian institutions can produce outcomes that undermine majority rule; such a "tyranny of the majority" can be especially problematic when it perverts the laws governing political resources and actors, reducing the ability of the political process to correct itself. Thus, an unelected judiciary superintends electoral institutions.

How does the judiciary play this role? Extensive debate surrounds this issue, and is well illustrated by the "political question" doctrine of the Supreme Court. The Court has often ruled that cases involving the law of political resources and actors were not justiciable, and thus beyond its jurisdiction, because they involved matters that were more properly decided by the "political" branches of government.[3] In recognizing a political question, the Court exercises its power to superintend democracy: it chooses to defer to the legislature or executive on a particular matter rather than intervene directly. Under such circumstances, the Court has, in effect, rendered a judgment about the proper scope of powers that can be exercised by the legislative and executive branches in a particular area of the law.[4]

Although the political question doctrine has a long history, it has been defined in different ways at different times, some restricting and some expanding the Court's jurisdiction over democratic institutions.[5] A good example of the former is Justice Felix Frankfurter's argument in *Colegrove v. Green* (1946)[6] that the Court should avoid the "political thicket" of state representation and apportionment. He expressed concern over the Court's lack of competence and the absence of effective remedies in matters where the democratic political process could successfully resolve the controversy.[7] A much different conclusion was reached by Justice Tom Clark in *Baker v. Carr* (1962),[8] arguing that a *failure* of the political process necessitated judicial review of state representation and apportionment.[9]

Once the Supreme Court determines that it has jurisdiction over a case regarding political resources or actors, the Court then must decide the degree of intervention it will exercise. In some cases, the Supreme Court has interceded deeply into the workings of the political process, essentially substituting its own judgments for those of legislatures and executives. At other times, courts have intervened less, largely deferring to the judgments of the other branches of government. Either way, the consequences of judicial action or abstention are profound. On the one hand, the judiciary risks a loss of legitimacy and influence when it delves too deeply into the political thicket, thus making it unwise for courts to interfere with the political process. Conversely, though, perhaps the risk is greater if the court opts out of the political process because

Figure 1.1. Heuristic Model of Judicial Superintendence of Political Democracy

| | | Level of Judicial Intervention | |
		Micro-management	Macro-management
Target of Judicial Action	Political Resources	High Intervention (with Resources)	Low Intervention (with Resources)
	Political Actors	High Intervention (with Actors)	Low Intervention (with Actors)

then it is merely avoiding tough questions of democratic practice and reform.

It is crucial, then, to consider the extent to which the judiciary superintends democracy. Figure 1.1 offers a simple heuristic model of the ways the Supreme Court has played this role. The figure has two dimensions: the degree of judicial intervention by the Court ("high" and "low") and whether the law in question pertains to political resources or political actors. These dimensions produce four ideal types of superintendency.

We have labeled the upper left-hand box "micromanagement of the political resources." Here the Court makes detailed rulings regarding political resources and the process in which they are used; a good example is *Buckley v. Valeo* (1976) on campaign finance (see chapters 3 and 4). The lower left-hand box is labeled "micromanagement of political actors." In such cases, the Court makes detailed rulings regarding actors and the structure in which they operate; a good example is the Court's rulings on political parties (see chapter 7).

We labeled the upper right-hand box as "macromanagement of political resources." Here the Court makes general rulings regarding political resources and the process in which they operate; a good example is campaign finance regulation before 1976 (see chapter 2). The lower right-hand box is labeled the "macromanagement of political actors." In such cases, the Court makes general rulings regarding political actors and the structure in which they operate; a good example is *Timmons v. Twin Cities Area New Party* (1997) on the "fusion" ballots (see chapter 8).

The actual superintending of democracy is, of course, vastly more complex than these four ideal types and the application of the types to cases is not mutually exclusive. But this oversimplification is a useful way of thinking about how the judiciary superintends political resources and actors in the name of expanding or limiting democratic tendencies under a republican regime in America.

Superintending Political Resources. Political resources are critical to elections, a hallmark of democratic politics. Money, time, speech, and ultimately votes, are all essential to the "rule of many." Not surprisingly, the use of political resources in elections has been the subject of extensive regulation by state and federal governments. The essays in Part I of the book consider the role of courts in three areas: political corruption, campaign finance, and the drawing of electoral districts.

Political scientist Christopher P. Banks sets the tone for the book in chapter 2 by analyzing the U.S. Supreme Court's decisions in political corruption cases. Corruption of the political system is a serious threat to democracy because it can undermine the constitutional foundations and diminish public support of the government. In order to preserve the integrity of the democratic process, legislatures and executives regulate the use of political resources. Yet such efforts are inherently controversial because anticorruption statutes often pose a threat to individual liberty. Banks describes the Court's activity in three areas: political influence, campaign finance, and the integrity of the electoral process. The political influence cases, and to a lesser extent, the electoral integrity cases, have been characterized by macromanagement of political resources. Campaign finance cases show two patterns. Prior to 1976, the Court by and large practiced macro-management of political resources. However, beginning with *Buckley v. Valeo* in 1976, the Court shifted to micromanagement of political resources. This significant case is the subject of the next three chapters.

In chapter 3, attorneys John C. Bonifaz, Gregory G. Luke, and Brenda Wright of the National Voting Rights Institute attack *Buckley* because it supports unlimited spending in elections. To these authors, unrestricted spending—along with the guiding maxim of *Buckley* that "money is speech"—is a serious threat to the democratic process because it undermines public confidence in elections, increases the danger of actual political corruption, and interferes with the governing duties of our elected representatives. For these reasons and others, Bonifaz, Luke, and Wright assert that the time has come to revisit *Buckley*. An appropriate response, in their view, would be for the Court to allow campaign finance reforms that limit campaign expenditure and, in effect permit the Court to macromanage political resources.

In chapter 4, law professor Joel M. Gora, who also acted as cocounsel for the plaintiffs in the *Buckley* ruling, strongly defends the decision as a landmark of political freedom. For Gora, *Buckley* correctly invalidated expenditure limitations enacted by the Congress because they restricted political speech. Working from the premise that the people (and not the government) have the sole power to control political expression, Gora quickly dismisses the notion that government could impose limits on spending for the purpose of equalizing monetary resources in campaigns. Achieving that sort of equal opportunity is not only impracticable, Gora maintains, but it also threatens core values of the First Amendment. Instead, he suggests reform options that would expand political opportunities without limiting political speech. His argument suggests that *Buckley* is an example of judicial micromanagement of political resources.

In chapter 5, attorney Trevor Potter, a former commissioner and chairman of the Federal Election Commission, discusses the effects of *Buckley* with regard to disclosure of campaign finance information. After observing that disclosure is the most popular kind of campaign finance regulation, Potter notes that the Court has left unanswered many constitutional questions about its scope. In the face of the Court's inconsistent and often unpredictable approach to this topic, Potter offers a useful four-part test to analyze the constitutionality of disclosure legislation. In doing so, he reveals the micromanagement of political resources that characterizes *Buckley*.

In chapter 6, political scientist Barbara Perry considers an area notorious for the micromanagement of political resources, namely, the drawing of legislative districts and the distribution of political power to parties. After noting that representation can be conceptualized both descriptively and substantively, Perry briefly surveys the recent history of voting rights legislation and its impact on the creation of majority-minority districts, which prevent minority vote dilution and strengthen minority voting power. Although these districts increase minority representation in the spirit of the 1965 Voting Rights Act, Perry suggests that their existence presents a number of complex moral and political questions that divide the civil rights and legal communities. While the Court's attempt to draw an acceptable line between race-neutral and race-conscious gerrymandering is sure to generate additional judicial conflict and continue to cause controversy, Perry concludes that one should not expect any less when the Supreme Court intervenes in the political thicket.

Superintending Political Actors. Political actors are, quite literally, where the action is in the political process. It is hardly surprising, then, that there are extensive federal and state laws defining the appropriate behavior of political parties, candidates, and officeholders. It is this legal framework that typifies the "rule of the many." The essays in Part II consider the role of courts in affecting the legal conduct of three types of political actors: political parties, independent counsel, and organized groups engaged in voting rights litigation.

Political scientist John C. Green begins this section in chapter 7 with a survey of Supreme Court decisions that regulate the structure and operation of political parties. He argues that the Supreme Court has developed a "right to party" for party members. In the last thirty years, the Court has used the concept of associational rights to reduce substantially the scope of state regulation of parties, which in turn has given greater autonomy to party officials and their supporters. This new jurisprudence is much different than before, when the courts generally deferred to state party regulations on the grounds of maintaining the integrity of the electoral process. Advocates of "responsible parties" applaud this line of cases since it has given parties more leeway for engaging in responsible behavior. But ironically, the right to party has encouraged the development of "service parties," a new and notoriously irresponsible form of party organization. This situation has arisen because the new right to party has not been accompanied by new standards of responsibility for party officials. These cases are good examples of micromanagement of political actors.

In chapter 8, political scientist David K. Ryden makes a similar argument regarding *Timmons v. Twin Cities Area New Party* (1997), the Supreme Court decision that upheld state prohibition—and provision—of fusion ballots, where candidates can be nominated by more than one party. *Timmons* is a good example of macromanagement of political actors, and in this case, the Court deferred to state authorities. Ryden is critical of this decision on the grounds that it inappropriately supported the two-party system against minor parties. He asserts that the Court abdicated its responsibility to act as a guardian of representative government. This duty requires that the Court develop and aggressively apply a party-oriented theory of jurisprudence that takes into account the complexity of political representation. In this sense Ryden may be advocating judicial micromanagement of political actors.

In chapter 9, political scientist David M. O'Brien presents a less critical view of the Court in a review of decisions on political patronage. After acknowledging that the Supreme Court's rulings after 1976 appeared to substantially curtail patronage, he demonstrates that the time-honored tradition of rewarding the party faithful with the spoils of political victory largely remains intact. Somewhat wryly, O'Brien states the Court's initial decision in *Elrod v. Burns* (1976) to restrict the practice at all is indeed ironic, if for no other reason than recognizing that federal judgeships are classic patronage appointments. He argues that *Elrod* and subsequent decisions did not substantially restrict the practice of patronage nor significantly weaken the two-party system. Here the Court practiced macromanagement of political actors, requiring reasonable standards for patronage appointments rather than eliminating them wholesale.

The last three chapters shift perspective with regard to political actors. In chapter 10, political scientist Katy J. Harriger analyzes the operation of the independent counsel statute.[10] As she explains, the appointment of special counsels and the legal duties they perform in investigating public corruption are supposed to be apolitical in scope and application. However, her analysis of the Iran-Contra and Whitewater affairs reveals the limits of the law in constraining politics, which belies the notion that such investigations are immune from political considerations. Special counsels are appointed and supervised by judges, and their activities are mostly directed at courts, making them a special case of micromanagement of political actors.

In chapter 11, political scientist Steven C. Tauber evaluates the impact of interest group litigation on the judiciary by reviewing the impact of the NAACP Legal Defense Fund (LDF) on protecting minority voting rights. He finds that the LDF has had considerable influence on the Supreme Court with regard to overturning state laws and enforcing federal voting rights statutes. This influence is especially noteworthy in light of the conservative shift of the judiciary in recent times. Here interest group litigation has prompted the Court to engage in micromanagement of political actors.

The last chapter, written by Banks, examines the best, if not most controversial, illustration of courts superintending the electoral process. In *Bush v. Gore*

(2000), the U.S. Supreme Court decided the 2000 presidential race by stopping the recount of disputed ballots in Florida, a ruling that had the effect of awarding the state's twenty-five electoral votes—and the presidency—to George W. Bush. As Banks observes, the ruling reflects a judicial choice that allowed the Court to micromanage the behavior of political actors such as the Florida Supreme Court and other state election officials. Yet, he notes, the Court's involvement in the campaign also increased the risk that the federal Supreme Court might appear to be politically illegitimate, something that could have been avoided by using the political question doctrine.

Taken together, these essays raise serious questions about the judicial superintendency of democracy. Does the presence of political corruption permit courts to assume a special role in superintending the electoral process? Has the judiciary done more harm than good by entering into the political thicket and deciding these types of cases? Should courts intervene in the political process and assume the role of the faithful guardian of constitutional rights? Or should they defer to the political branches in these matters? By not deferring, are courts overstepping their judicial authority? Is it possible for the third branch of government to reconcile political accountability with individual freedom in the American democracy? And what is the policy impact of judicial decisions that regulate campaigns and elections? Learning the answers to these questions is crucial to resolving the discontent that grips American politics at the dawn of a new century. The scholarship contained herein is a starting point for making that discovery.

PART I

Superintending Political Resources

CHAPTER 2

The United States Supreme Court's Response to American Political Corruption

The Failure of Constitutional Law or the
Success of Republican Liberty?

Christopher P. Banks

> As there is a degree of depravity in mankind which requires a cer-
> tain degree of circumspection and distrust, so there are other quali-
> ties in human nature which justify a certain portion of esteem and
> confidence. Republican government presupposes the existence of
> these qualities in a higher degree than any other form. Were the
> pictures which have been drawn by the political jealousy of some
> among us faithful likenesses of the human character, the inference
> would be that there is not sufficient virtue among men for self-gov-
> ernment; and that nothing less than the chains of despotism can
> restrain them from destroying and devouring one another.
>
> —James Madison, *The Federalist Papers*

WHILE A MAJORITY OF AMERICAN CITIZENS may agree "corrup-
tion is truly a staple of our Republic's existence,"[1] few would probably
appreciate that the Founding Fathers were acutely aware of the threat
that corrupt government posed to the health of republican institutions. The founders knew that the antithesis of corruption, namely
civic virtue, was a vital element of republicanism and the quest to secure political freedom. The colonists declared their independence in
large part because they concluded that a corrupt monarch and an increasingly tyrannical Parliament were destroying the English Constitution. Indeed, Sir Robert Walpole's (1721–42) intrigue and his control over the Parliament were forever linked with the corruption of
rotten boroughs, patronage, the imposition of higher taxes, multiple
officeholders, and the presence of standing armies. Critics of England
thought that "Everywhere . . . there was corruption—corruption technically, in the adroit manipulation of Parliament by a power-hungry

ministry, and corruption generally, in the self-indulgence, effeminizing luxury, and gluttonous pursuit of gain of a generation sunk in new and unaccustomed wealth."[2] Counseled by the writings of radical Whigs and John Locke, but also mindful of the demise of ancient republics, the American revolutionaries feared that English corruption would soon infect their country and undermine democratic equality, political representation, and natural rights.[3]

After the revolution, the lack of virtue in government helped James Madison construct the constitutional theory that he brought to Philadelphia in 1787. He concluded that personal ambition and self-interest in state governments threatened the public weal. As he observed shortly before the Constitutional Convention in "The Vices of the Political System of the U. States," the parochialism of state politics led to the passage of mutable laws that were unjust, serving the interests of dominant factions at the expense of the public good. The solution to bad government, he reasoned, was to create a large, extended republic that would diffuse the power of the majority and help build a consensus toward achieving what is best for society. As historian Jack Rakove put it, "At some point, Madison reasoned, the 'enlargement of the sphere' of the republic would offset the regression in civic virtue that he associated with the sway of dominant interests or passions among the multitude." Accordingly, Madison's "entire program of constitutional reform," including "his ideas of federalism, representation, and the separation of powers," mirrors "his disillusion with the failings of state legislators and citizens alike."[4]

By 1787, therefore, a consensus emerged among the Framers that a constitutional republic had to be built upon institutional checks that guarded against self-interest and relied less on abstract and idealistic notions of civic virtue.[5] Citizens, particularly those operating in small republics, could not be trusted to legislate for the common good. As table 2.1 illustrates, the United States Constitution included a variety of organizational and procedural features to control ambition. These structural provisions were the result of the Framers' fears of corrupt government. Without them, political liberty was in jeopardy because the government would be subject to corruption, such as dependency (or unbalanced government, where the executive improperly influences legislative behavior), cabal, patronage, unwarranted influence, intrigue, and bribery.[6] These parchment barriers are also significant because they are the legal framework by which the nation's highest federal court superintends the political process.

Table 2.1. Select Provisions of the U.S. Constitution Relating to Preventing Corruption or Preserving Institutional Integrity

Constitutional Text	Constitutional Purpose	Principal Branch	Corruption or Integrity Interest
Article I, Sec. 3	U.S. Senate to conduct impeachment trials	Legislature	Preventing cabal and exertion of influence upon Congress
Article I, Sec. 5, cl. 2	Internal "in house" punishment of legislators	Legislature	Preserving rule of law; preserving integrity and fidelity of Congress
Article I, Sec. 6, cl. 1	Legislative immunity through speech or debate	Legislature	Preserving integrity and fidelity of Congress
Article I, Sec. 6, cl. 2	Prohibition of multiple office holding	Legislature	Preventing cabal, influence, or bribery; preserving integrity, fidelity
Article I, Sec. 9	Prohibition of presents, emoluments, titles, offices	Legislature	Preserving integrity, fidelity of Congress; preventing external (foreign) influence or bribes
Article II, Sec. 1	Election of the president (Electoral College)	Executive	Preventing cabal or exertion of influence upon electors
Article II, Sec. 4	Impeachment of the president	Executive	Preventing treason, bribery, high crimes or misdemeanors
Article III, Sec. 1	Life tenure of judges (with good behavior)	Judiciary	Preserving integrity, fidelity of courts
Amendment 7	Jury trial in criminal (and minor civil) matters	Judiciary	Preserving integrity of judicial process

Sources: James D. Savage, "Corruption and Virtue at the Constitutional Convention," *Journal of Politics* 56 (1992): 174–86; John T. Noonan, Jr., *Bribes* (New York: Macmillan Publishing Company, 1984): 428–35.

POLITICAL CORRUPTION AND THE U.S. SUPREME COURT

As it did during the framing of the U.S. Constitution, corrupt behavior in politics has greatly influenced constitutional doctrine. Its presence can be felt even when it is not directly at issue in an appeal, as the landmark opinion of *Fletcher v. Peck* (1810) suggests. The famous "Yazoo" case began when the Georgia legislature agreed to convey 35 million acres of land in the Yazoo River territory (located now in Mississippi and Alabama) to four companies (with investors who were prominent members of government) for $500,000, or a penny and a half an acre. In return, the companies sold back to the legislators a portion of the land for about $1,000. When the facts surrounding the corrupt land grant were discovered, an outraged public voted all but two members from the 1795 legislature out of office in 1796. Shortly thereafter, the new legislature rescinded the fraudulent conveyance.

However, before legislative nullification many of the Yazoo tracts were sold to purchasers like Robert Fletcher, who bought his land from John Peck with a warranty of good title. In an effort to clear his title, Fletcher sued Peck in federal court, where Fletcher lost. On appeal, Chief Justice John Marshall affirmed the lower court's decision by ruling that the state law rescinding the 1795 land grant violated the Contracts Clause, or Article I, Section 10, of the U.S. Constitution. In an important case involving the economic liberty and private property rights, the Court held that state government had no power under the Constitution to impair the private land contract between Fletcher and Peck.[7]

Although the legal issue in *Fletcher* did not ostensibly concern corruption, clearly the case never would have been the subject of a federal appeal but for the bribery of the 1795 Georgia legislature. In this sense corruption was the factual predicate for giving the U.S. Supreme Court the opportunity to declare, for the first time, that a state law ran afoul of the federal constitution.[8] Corruption was thus the vehicle for the Court to condone implicitly the Georgia legislature's original fraud in 1795 and, more subtly, to reject what the Georgia voters did in response to a notorious political scandal in 1796. Because the federal government assumed from Georgia the responsibility of settling many of the problems associated with the Yazoo debacle, *Fletcher* inadvertently handed "the Yazoo claimants a new stick to beat on Congress" when, as titleholders under the original land grant, they sought compensation from the national government. In this light it is easy to see why George M. Troup, the U.S. congressman from Georgia, denounced *Fletcher* on the floor of the House as a ruling that only shows that "the Representatives of the people may corruptly betray the people."[9]

As *Fletcher* implies, the judicial reaction to cases pertaining to political corruption often has unintended effects that are quite controversial. It also invites a number of inquiries about the extent to which government misfeasance influences the Court's role in superintending democracy. Does the simple existence of corruption create more agenda opportunities for the Court to superintend the political process? If so, how has the Court taken advantage of them and what has been their impact on public policy? Or, since the Supreme Court is inherently an undemocratic institution, has the judicial response to corruption brought the Court too much into the political thicket and weakened its institutional legitimacy? In a related fashion, has Supreme Court decision making led to unintended consequences that frustrate attempts by the political branches to prevent corruption?[10]

In order to explore these issues further, the Court's response to political corruption is analyzed by reviewing a sample of published opinions from the U.S. Supreme Court between 1789 and 1999.[11] The sample covers a broad range of corrupt political behaviors involving all three branches of government on both the national and state levels. Specifically, the cases touch upon three broad areas of corruption: (1) cases involving political influence, which represent 48% of the sample, and include bribery and conflict of interest cases; (2) campaign finance cases, which comprise 27% of the sample; and, (3) cases implicating the integrity of the electoral process, which consist of 25% of the sample and relate to issues of ballot control, patronage, and direct democracy movements.

Examining the cases yields a greater understanding about the heuristic model (figure 1.1) referred to in chapter 1 as well as the Court's role in superintending American democracy. In certain types of appeals—such as in cases of political influence, pre-1976 campaign finance, and integrity of the ballot and franchise—the Supreme Court generally has opted to interfere less with political resources and actors, thus macromanaging political affairs. With other subject matter, however, the Court has taken a more aggressive, micromanaging approach, as illustrated by its judicial behavior in post–1976 campaign finance appeals, certain patronage cases, and legal disputes involving direct democracy and the regulation of political parties.

POLITICAL INFLUENCE CASES

Thomas Jefferson once said "[t]he whole art of government consists in the art of being honest."[12] In that 48% of the sample involves facts or legal issues relating to political influence, it seems more realistic to say that the lack of honesty in government is a persistent problem. Tables 2.2 and 2.3 indicate that this category of misfeasance broadly encompasses appeals typically raising factual or legal issues of bribery (25%) and conflict of interest (23%).[13] In both sets of cases, the Court most often wielded its judicial authority by enforcing the moral choices and legal sanctions that were imposed through the statutory prohibitions at issue. For example, in two-thirds of the bribery cases (67%) the Court affirmed the defendants' conviction. In the remaining appeals, a favorable outcome was reached on the basis of a constitutional violation or an erroneous lower court ruling.[14] An identical pattern emerges in the conflict of interest cases where the Court enforced a negative ruling against the litigant in almost two-thirds of the appeals (64%); and, for the balance of the cases, the Court often recognized the litigant's constitutional rights or, on occasion, upset a lower court error.[15] In both types of cases, then, the Court condoned the use of a sanction against corruption in nineteen of twenty-nine appeals, or 66% of the time. In seven of ten of the remaining cases where the litigant received a favorable ruling, the Court did so by holding that government violated the litigant's constitutional rights under either the Speech or Debate Clause, the Qualifications Clause, the Fourteenth Amendment's Due Process Clause, or the First Amendment.[16]

Political influence cases underscore rival interpretations of key phrases in the U.S. Constitution by ideologically opposed members of the Court. Appeals raising the issue of whether corrupt legislators can claim legislative immunity (from the judicial process) under the Speech or Debate Clause (Art. I, Sec. 6) are illustrative.[17] These appeals generate internal conflict on the Court because they implicate the "proper" scope and application of the separation of powers principle: that is, legislators engaging in illegal behavior claim that the Speech or Debate Clause stops the Court from using its authority to sanction conduct that occurs during the legislative process, even if the representative breaks the law. Interpreting what the clause means as a matter of constitutional law thus compels the Court to consider, on grounds of separation of powers, whether the judiciary ought to inquire into affairs that are inherently political. While taking an active role may allow the Court to punish the culpable politician, it also invites the criticism that the judiciary is meddling in the legislative process. Conversely, though, while staying out of the political thicket may show respect for separation of powers, it also has the potential to bar the judiciary from making a corrupt legislator accountable under the rule of law. As the next case shows, sometimes the Court tries to draw a line that is wavy, at best, in attempting to reconcile these competing interests and defending its construction of what the Speech or Debate Clause means.

Table 2.2. Cases Involving Allegations of Bribery

Case	Constitutional Issue(s)	Facts	Main Legal Issue/Holding
In re Green (1891)	None	Attorney alleged judge was bribed	Court without power to vacate order disbarring attorney for making allegations in pleadings
Burton v. U.S. (1906)	Separation of powers; Fifth Amendment double jeop.	Senator accepted money to persuade Postmaster that corporation not defrauding government	Senator's rights not violated because U.S. Senate enjoys power to police its own members; no double jeopardy violation
U.S. v. Russell (1921)	None	Attorney corrupted juror in trial	Lower court properly construed statute against defendant and conviction upheld
U.S. v. Hood (1952)	None	Illegal contributions to state party committee in exchange for getting federal appointments	Statute applies to selling of influence in anticipation of jobs and offices being created
U.S. v. Shirey (1959)	None	Defendant offered money to political party in exchange for using influence to get appointment	Statute prohibits making donation to "person" of "influence"
Osborn v. U.S. (1966)	Fourth Amendment	Lawyer convicted of trying to bribe juror in Jimmy Hoffa trial	Evidence properly admitted at trial; no constitutional violation
U.S. v. Brewster (1972)	Speech/Debate Clause	Senator accepted bribe	No legislative immunity
Helstoski v. Meanor (1979)	Speech/Debate Clause	Congressman took bribes in exchange for passing laws helping aliens to remain in country	Grand jury properly heard evidence of legislative acts; no legislative immunity
U.S. v. Helstoski (1979)	Speech/Debate Clause	Congressman took bribes in exchange for passing laws helping aliens to remain in country	Legislative immunity bars hearing references to past legislative acts as evidence in bribery prosecution
U.S. v. Gillock (1980)	Speech/Debate Clause	State senator bribed in exchange for blocking extradition and passing laws granting licenses	No legislative immunity created that bars hearing evidence of legislative acts
Dennis v. Sparks (1980)	None	State court judge and private parties allegedly conspired to bribe judge in civil action	Civil rights action can proceed against private parties who conspired with judge that has judicial immunity
Brown v. Hartlage (1982)	First Amendment	Candidate "bought" votes by promising to lower salaries of local commission if elected	State legislation burdens political speech and violates First Amendment
McCormick v. U.S. (1991)	None	State legislator did not report campaign contributions in exchange for influence	Hobbs Act conviction overturned where legislator not held to extort payments under color of official right
Evans v. U.S. (1992)	None	State board commissioner did not report campaign contribution in exchange for influence	Conviction upheld because affirmative act of inducement is not an element of Hobbs Act crime
Bracy v. Gramley (1997)	Fourteenth Amendment Due Process (fair trial)	Convicted felon sought habeas because sentencing judge later convicted for taking bribes and "fixing" murder convictions	Judge biased against defendant who was convicted after trial in order to deflect suspicion that judge was taking bribes in other cases

Source: Lexis on-line search (April 24, 1997).

Table 2.3. Cases Involving Allegations of Conflict of Interest

Case	Constitutional Issue(s)	Facts	Main Legal Issue/Holding
Bartle v. Nutt (1830)	None	Public agent made fraudulent contract with government to profit self in rebuilding fort	Court will not enforce fraudulent private contract benefiting public agent
Marshall v. Baltimore & Ohio (1850)	None	Citizen/lobbyist sought money owed under contract with railroad to secure right of way	Lobbyist cannot recover on special contract made in secret for lobbying services and contingent fee
Trist v. Child (1874)	None	Executor sought payment of claim under contract to procure by lobbying passage of legislation	Executor cannot enforce private contract claim that is fraudulently made and against public policy
Meguire v. Corwine (1879)	None	Ex-government official used inside knowledge to obtain prize property in control of government	Plaintiff cannot collect prize on basis of contract that is fraudulently made and against public policy
Hazelton v. Sheckells (1906)	None	Promise to convey land based on expectation that government will pass law to build hall of records on land to be sold	Contract void and against public policy where contingent compensation for obtaining favorable legislation part of consideration
U.S. v. Carter (1910)	None	Army captain/engineer made corrupt contract with contractors that benefited self and contractors	Army captain/engineer as public agent must account for profits made under corrupt contract that presented conflict of interest
Mammoth Oil Co. v. U.S. (1927)	None	Government officials entered into corrupt oil and gas lease with corporation	Fraudulent oil and gas lease/contract void and against pubic policy
Near v. Minnesota (1931)	First Amendment	Press exposed corruption of mayor and police and their illegal association with gangsters	Statute violates First Amendment as prior restraint where publication exposing corruption censored
U.S. v. Harriss 1954)	First . Amendment	Lobbyists failed to report contributions designed to influence passage of legislation	Federal Regulation of Lobbying Act does not violate First Amendment since Congress can reasonably require disclosure
U.S. v. Miss. Valley Generating Co. (1961)	None	Private banker had conflict of interest by also representing government in business transaction	Contract invalid on statutory grounds of conflict of interest
U.S. v. Johnson (1966)	Speech/ Debate Clause	Congressman conspired with savings and loan association to use influence to dismiss mail fraud indictments	Speech or Debate Clause bars inquiry into congressman's speech favorable to bank that was part of conspiracy and a conflict of interest
Powell v. McCormack (1969)	Qualifications, Speech/ Debate Clause	Illegal salary payments made to congressman's spouse and other corrupt activity by Representative	Congress has no power to oust duly elected congressman from taking seat; no immunity under Speech or Debate Clause; case is justiciable
Crandon v. U.S. (1990)	None	Lump-sum payment given to private sector workers entering government service to compensate for loss of income	Workers not subject to criminal prohibition giving supplemental compensation from private party before entering governmental service
U.S. v. National Treasury Employees Union (1995)	First Amendment	Career civil servants challenged honoraria ban for making speeches and writing articles	Statutory ban preventing federal employees from getting honoraria violates First Amendment

Source: Lexis on-line search (April 24, 1997). U.S. v. Johnson (1966) was added as a result of the Court's discussion about controlling precedent in U.S. v. Brewster (1972). See table 2.2.

In *U.S. v. Brewster* (1972), for example, the Court decided if the provision prevented a former senator from being prosecuted for allegedly accepting a bribe and using his influence to help obtain favorable postal rate legislation. In his opinion for the Court, Chief Justice Warren Burger (a moderate to conservative jurist) held that no immunity exists because the speech or debate provision only bars the executive or judicial branches from examining conduct pertaining to the legislative process or, alternatively, the motivations behind the conduct at issue. In *Brewster,* Burger stated that the government could prove its case under a narrowly drawn bribery statute without taking into account why, or how, the senator voted on postal legislation. For Burger, this conclusion had the effect of allowing the government to prosecute Senator Brewster while, at the same time, respecting the principle of separation of powers. In this sense, the decision not to immunize Brewster under the clause did not needlessly drag the courts into the political fray and upset the delicate balance of power envisioned by the Framers when they created a tripartite form of government. Instead, the ruling promoted honest representation in government (by punishing corruption) and preserved the Framers' intent of extending the privilege to only those acts occurring in the "regular course of the legislative process."[18]

Yet, dissenting justice William Brennan (a liberal jurist) countered that the holding disturbed the "principles of legislative freedom" underlying the Speech or Debate Clause and upset established precedent. Only six years earlier, Brennan observed, the Court ruled in *U.S. v. Johnson* (1966) that Article I, Section 6 barred any extracongressional inquiry into why a senator delivered a speech that was generally favorable to loan companies in a conspiracy-to-defraud (the government) prosecution. For Brennan, *Johnson* correctly recognized that the clause gave legislators a broad immunity since it was intended to be constitutional security against (as Justice John Harlan put it) "possible prosecution by an unfriendly executive and conviction by a hostile judiciary."[19] As such, *Johnson* respects separation of powers and prevents the judiciary making any sort of inquiry into the senator's acts or motives. Moreover, to do otherwise threatens legislative independence by wrongfully permitting the Court to take away from Congress the responsibility of disciplining one of its own members. As Justice Brennan thundered at the end of his dissent,

The Framers' judgment was that the American people could have a Congress of independence and integrity only if alleged misbehavior in the performance of legislative functions was accountable solely to a Member's own House and never to the executive or judiciary. The passing years have amply justified the wisdom of that judgment. It is the Court's duty to enforce the letter of the Speech or Debate Clause in that spirit. We did so in deciding *Johnson*. In turning its back on that decision today, the Court arrogates to the judiciary an authority committed by the Constitution, in Senator Brewster's case, exclusively to the Senate of the United States. Yet the Court provides no principled justification, and I can think of none, for its denial that *United States v. Johnson* compels affirmance of the District Court. That decision is only six years old and bears the indelible imprint of the distinguished constitutional scholar who wrote the opinion for the Court. *Johnson* surely merited a longer life.[20]

Although Justice Byron White (who did not participate in *Johnson*) declined to join Justice Brennan's opinion, he shared Brennan's view that Congress, and not the Court, ought to discipline a senator for corrupt behavior. Unlike his senior colleague, though, White charged that the Court ignored the "realities of the American political system" by not realizing that representatives often make promises to constituents to enact favorable laws on the basis of campaign contributions. With this in mind, White preferred to grant Speech or Debate Clause immunity in situations where the executive uses a criminal statute as a weapon to control a legislative process that presumes influence will be gained through the exchange of money. Hence, while the "Speech or Debate Clause does not immunize corrupt Congressmen," White concluded that the Court had no business judging this political matter because the Clause clearly "reserves the power to discipline in the Houses of Congress."[21]

The contentious debate between Chief Justice Burger and Justice Brennan over the proper interpretation of Article I, Section 6 stems from differences in the policy preferences of a Court whose membership changed significantly between the *Johnson* and *Brewster* rulings. *Johnson's* principal holding, which broadly applied the legislative privilege to the conspiracy count of the indictment, was written by Justice John Harlan near the end of the Warren Court (1954–69) and enjoyed the support of all of the justices who participated in the case.[22] By the time *Brewster* was handed down in the Burger Court (1969–86), only Justices Brennan, Douglas, Stewart, and White and remained on the bench. While Justice White joined Brennan and Douglas in dissent in *Brewster*, Justice Stewart switched his position and helped to solidify the five-justice majority by joining Chief Justice Burger and Justices Thurgood Marshall, Harry

Blackmun, Lewis Powell, and William Rehnquist. Presumably the emerging judicial philosophy of the Burger Court had an effect in causing an abrupt switch
in legal policy. In other words, reexamining (and overruling) precedent in light
of a rapidly changing Court membership is part of what Justice William O.
Douglas termed "constitutional flux" and is a regular feature of the judicial politics of the high court.[23]

This debate also illustrates that the Court's discussion of the scope and
meaning of the clause does not always occur when a representative seeks to
claim immunity for issuing reports or communicating speeches that are delivered during the course of legislative activity. Scholars attach constitutional
meaning, therefore, to the Court's interpretation of the clause when members
try to protect themselves from legal liability when they convey a controversial
political message in the course of legislative affairs.[24] Notwithstanding the constitutional significance of this "informing function," the foregoing cases reveal
that political corruption ironically can sometimes form the constitutional basis
for protecting congressmen from their own misdeeds with, no less, the help of
the nation's highest judicial tribunal. The double irony, of course, is that the
original purpose of the Speech or Debate Clause was to safeguard the legislature from an overbearing (and perhaps corrupt) executive branch, and not to
insulate a corrupt legislator from the rule of law.

CAMPAIGN FINANCE CASES

Until 1972, national and state efforts to regulate money in political elections
were typically described in terms of corruption and virtue. In 1829, New York
enacted legislation called "An Act to Preserve the Purity of Elections," which
generally forbade anyone from making money contributions to elections. The
Credit Mobilier scandal (1872–73), which involved building a transcontinental
railroad through corporate greed and political graft, popularized the notion
that corporate donors were innately corrupt. Shortly thereafter, Congress
passed the Tillman Act (1907), which prohibited campaign contributions from
corporations and national banks to federal campaigns, and the Publicity Act
(1910), a law requiring post election disclosure of receipts and expenditures of
national party committees in congressional (House of Representatives) elections. The latter statute was amended a year later and, among other things, required preelection disclosure and extended the act's coverage to Senate elec-

tions. The amendment also established, for the first time, spending limits for federal elections.[25] Specifically, the 1911 amendments to the Publicity Act imposed a $5,000 limit on House campaign expenditures while, for Senate races, spending was limited to $10,000 or the amount established by state law, whichever was less.[26] Between 1911 and 1972 (and in light of scandals like Teapot Dome and Watergate), the rhetoric of corruption was used as the basis of sundry legislation that placed stricter controls on the way in which individuals, political action committees (PAC), and labor unions either contributed or spent money in national campaigns. Some of this legislation, like the Federal Corrupt Practices Act of 1925 (revising spending limits and requiring all multistate political committees and all congressional candidates to report certain contributions), was a response to major national scandals, such as Teapot Dome. Other laws were aimed at minimizing conflict of interest or the influence that labor had on elections. The Hatch Act of 1939 (or the Clean Politics Act), for example, forbade federal employees from soliciting political contributions. The War Labor Disputes Act of 1943 and the Labor Management Relations Act of 1947 prohibited labor unions from using their treasury funds to make contributions to candidates for federal office.[27]

These campaign finance laws did not prevent increased campaign spending over time, especially with the advent of candidate-centered politics and the electronic media. In the early 1970s the Federal Corrupt Practices Act was repealed and replaced by the 1971 Federal Election Campaign Act (FECA). The FECA was principally designed to combat perceived increases in campaign spending, and its 1974 amendments were a specific reaction to the financial abuses associated with the Watergate scandal. Shortly after the 1971 law went into effect, for example, the data gathered from the act's new disclosure requirements revealed that total campaign spending increased from $300 million in 1968 to $425 million in 1972. After the Watergate scandal broke, however, the emphasis shifted to preventing the type of illegal contributions and political dirty tricks that characterized President Nixon's second run for office. Thus, by substantially strengthening the disclosure, spending, and contribution provisions of the 1971 law, the 1974 amendments refocused campaign finance regulation.[28]

The 1974 amendments revolutionized campaign finance by permitting presidential candidates to receive public funding (through matching funds) while simultaneously controlling the influence of money on congressional races with expenditure and contribution limits. In addition, the amendments created more stringent disclosure requirements for federal election candidates and gave a new independent agency, the Federal Election Commission, the power to enforce compliance with all of the act's provisions. Before the new amendments even had a chance to operate in an election, the United States Supreme Court handed down *Buckley v. Valeo,* a landmark 1976 per curiam ruling that created an "analytic divide" in the constitutional law pertaining to the modern regulation of political money.[29]

Buckley serves as a convenient (and necessary) point of departure for understanding the Court's impact on campaign finance before and after 1976. Tables 2.4 and 2.5 collect cases that deal with the regulation of political money. Sixteen cases, or 27% of all corruption cases in the sample, are represented. Of these cases 10% relate to the pre-*Buckley* period. The balance, or 17%, account for the Court's decision-making afterwards (including *Buckley*). As table 2.4 reveals, before 1976 the Court entertained only a handful of political money cases that raised First Amendment concerns. These cases also emphasize the basic issue of whether Congress enjoys broad constitutional authority to regulate elections, and especially whether aggregated wealth is a legitimate threat to political equality and perhaps then a valid basis for regulation.[30] In this fashion the judicial language in the cases manifest key elements of doctrine that appear later in *Buckley* and ultimately become the First Amendment principle that states that money is, for constitutional purposes, equivalent to the expression of political speech. At the same time, this tenet becomes a major source of criticism as the Court struggles after *Buckley* to find a defensible and coherent rationale for its campaign finance jurisprudence.

In the first half of the twentieth century, Congress's authority to regulate elections under Sections 4 and 5 of the first Article of the U.S. Constitution was tested in the context of campaign spending. Under Section 4 each state had the constitutional duty to prescribe the time, place, and manner of holding elections for federal senators and representatives; yet, except as to the place of choosing senators, "Congress may at any time by Law make or alter such Regulations."[31] Section 5 commands that "Each House shall be the Judge of the Elections, Returns and Qualifications of its own Members."[32] In *Newberry v. U.S.* (1921), a candidate for U.S. Senate, Truman H. Newberry, was convicted under

Table 2.4. Regulation of Money in Political Election Cases Before 1976

Case	Principal Constitutional Issue(s)	Principal Holding	Controlling Governmental Interest (As Identified in Opinion for Court)
Newberry v. U.S. (1921)	Art. I, Sec. 4 (time, place, and manner of elections); 17th Amendment; Art. I, Sec. 5 (judging elections, returns, and qualifications)	Congress has no power under Federal Corrupt Practices Act to limit campaign expenditures by candidate in state nominating primary for U.S. Senate seat	Preventing Congress from exceeding its delegated authority to regulate the manner of holding elections; not impinging upon state power to regulate primary for nominating U.S. Senators; preserving Congress's power to judge the elections, returns, and qualifications of its own members, and protecting against corruption in state nominating process
Barry v. U.S. (1929)	Art. I, Sec. 5; Art. I, Sec. 1 (judging elections, returns, and qualifications)	Congress has constitutional power to compel attendance of witness in investigation of validity of U.S. Senate election where excessive campaign contribution made in state nominating primary	Preserving power of Congress to investigate corrupt practices in senatorial primary election and judge the elections, returns, and qualifications of its own members
Burroughs and Cannon v. U.S. (1934)	Art. I, Sec. 1 (appointment of electors)	Congress has power under Federal Corrupt Practices Act to require disclosure of contributions made to political committees who try to influence the election of presidential electors	Preserving the purity of presidential and vice presidential elections; affirming Congress's power to safeguard election from the improper use of money to influence the result; preserving general government against impairment or destruction, whether threatened by force or corruption
U.S. v. Congress of Industrial Organizations (1948)	1st Amendment (speech, press, assembly)	Indictment dismissed under Federal Corrupt Practices Act charging labor union and its president with illegally spending general union funds to publish a weekly periodical supporting political candidate (no opinion expressed on constitutionality)	Strengthening the bar against the misuse of aggregated funds gathered into the control of a single organization from many individual sources; minimizing the influence of labor unions over elections through monetary expenditures
U.S. v. International Union (1957)	1st Amendment (speech, press, and assembly)	Indictment sustained under Federal Corrupt Practices Act charging labor union with illegally using union dues to sponsor commercial television broadcasts supporting election of congressional candidates (no opinion expressed on constitutionality)	Preserving the integrity of the electoral process by guarding against the deleterious influence that money will have on federal elections where labor unions or corporations exercise control over large aggregations of capital; preventing the use of corporate or union funds to influence the public at large to vote for a particular candidate or a particular party
Pipefitters v. U.S. (1972)	1st, 5th, 6th, and 17th Amendments; Art. I, Sec. 2 (appointment of electors)	Unions can make political contributions under 1971 Federal Election Campaign Act if given voluntarily from segregated fund (no opinion expressed on constitutionality)	Preventing the corroding effect of money employed in elections by aggregated powers; protect minority interests from overbearing union leadership

Source: Lexis on-line search (April 24, 1997). Pipefitters (1972) was added as a result of reading cases in the full sample of cases generated by Lexis.

a federal statute for spending more than federal and state law permitted in a primary race against his opponent, Henry Ford. While a majority voted to reverse the conviction, an evenly divided Court (4–4) agreed with Newberry's argument that Congress did not have the constitutional power to regulate primary elections, which also meant that it could not criminally prohibit congressional candidates from making excessive campaign expenditures in state nominating primaries. In reasoning that candidate selection is not part of the power to hold an election, Justice James C. McReynolds ruled that the states retained some control over primaries because the Framers did not intend Congress to have unlimited power to regulate the electoral process. The Court in *Newberry*, then, refused to defer to the legislative judgment that the corruptive influence of money is best deterred through criminal prohibitions that limit spending under the 1911 amendments to the Publicity Act.[33]

Congress's authority to regulate elections was challenged again a few years later in *Barry v. U.S.* (1929). There, the Supreme Court held that Congress enjoys broad power under Section 5 of Article I to investigate (by obtaining witness testimony through compulsory process) whether a senatorial seat was, in effect, bought in 1927 with excessive campaign contributions.[34] Moreover, in a ballot fraud case that did not directly concern the regulation of political money, in *U.S. v. Classic* (1941) the Court overruled the narrow (if not politically naive) ruling in *Newberry* by stating that Congress has the power under Article I, Section 4 to regulate primaries whenever the states were an integral part of the electoral process.[35] A fair reading of *Newberry, Barry,* and *Classic,* then, establishes that Congress has paramount authority under the Constitution to control allegedly corrupt activities pertaining to political elections and, implicitly, the concomitant ability to determine what role money plays in campaigns.

That the Court was more prone to respect the policy choices of Congress in dealing with corruption in campaign finance cases is suggested by the remaining pre-*Buckley* cases in table 2.4. At issue in *Burroughs and Cannon v. U.S.* (1934) was whether the 1925 Federal Corrupt Practices Act ran afoul of the Constitution by requiring disclosure of contributions by political committees that were trying to influence the selection of presidential and vice presidential electors. In upholding the act's constitutionality, the Court affirmed Congress's power under Article I, Section 2 to preserve the purity of national presidential elections. "To say that Congress is without power to pass appropriate legislation to safeguard such an election from the improper use of money to influence the result," Justice George Sutherland wrote for the majority, "is to deny to the nation in a vital particular the power of self protection." For Sutherland, "Congress, undoubtedly, possesses that power, as it possesses every other power essential to preserve the departments and institutions of the general government from impairment or destruction, whether threatened by force or by corruption."[36] Significantly, Sutherland looked to *Ex Parte Yarbrough* (1884) to support his rationale, where the Court during Reconstruction refused to grant a writ of habeas corpus to several members of the infamous Ku Klux Klan who were convicted of illegally conspiring to intimidate a black man from exercising his right to vote. *Yarbrough,* suggested Sutherland, aptly illustrates that a republican government must have sufficient power to thwart not only lawless violence, but also corruption associated with "the free use of money in elections, arising from the vast growth of recent wealth" in some parts of the United States. *Burroughs* therefore conceded that the national legislature had the requisite constitutional power to protect the sanctity of presidential elections. And, perhaps more importantly, the opinion strongly implies that Congress (and not the judicial branch) has the inherent discretion to choose the means by which that end will be achieved.[37]

The volatile mixture of aggregated wealth, politics, and the First Amendment right of expression emerged as a point of contention in two other cases, *U.S. v. Congress of Industrial Organizations* (1948) and *U.S. v. International Union United Automobile, Aircraft, and Agricultural Implement Workers of America* (1957). In each case the Supreme Court determined if the federal government could indict labor unions under the Federal Corrupt Practices Act for allegedly using general treasury funds to pay for a weekly periodical *(CIO)* or television advertisements *(International Union)* that communicated the unions' support for a political candidate. While the Court reached dissimilar results in dismissing *(CIO)* and sustaining *(International Union)* the indictments, the opinions expose fundamental differences in dealing with the question of how to best strike a balance between the competing interests of curbing political corruption and protecting free expression. In abstaining from ruling on the constitutionality of the provision outlawing corporate or labor spending in federal elections, the Court in *CIO* used the act's legislative history to show that Congress did not clearly intend to classify as a prohibited expenditure the costs of publishing a weekly periodical that is only disseminated to union members. The Court thus dismissed the indictment, since the act's history disclosed that while Congress was sensitive to the pernicious influence that corporate or labor money had on elections, it was also acutely aware that the prohibition might not withstand a First Amendment challenge under the facts described in the indictment.[38]

Justice Wiley Rutledge, concurring in the result only, added that the Court should have addressed the constitutional issue and struck down the statute as a violation of the First Amendment. In language that is a harbinger of what the Court would later do in *Buckley*, Rutledge argued that any advantage to the democratic process in banning the expenditures is outweighed by the loss of hearing diverse political views. Rutledge specifically disavowed the notion that government could suppress the "bloc sentiment" of labor unions through a law that is not narrowly tailored to meet the aim of reducing the impact a wealthy organization has in the political arena. In recognizing that "unions can act and speak today only by spending money," the concurring justice suggested not only that money is highly protected First Amendment political speech, but also that it is irrelevant if a well-funded group enjoys a disproportionate influence in politics. As Rutledge stated: "If therefore it is an evil for organized groups to have unrestricted freedom to make expenditures for directly and openly publicizing their political views and information supporting them . . . it does not follow that it is one which requires complete prohibition of the right because it is not essential to correction of the evil, whether it be considered corruptive influence or merely influence of undue or disproportionate political weight."[39]

Shortly thereafter the Court revisited the question of prohibiting expenditures by labor unions in *International Union*. This time, however, the Court confronted the First Amendment issue and upheld, in a 6–3 decision, the amended Federal Corrupt Practices Act as a valid exercise of congressional power. In stark contrast to Justice Rutledge's concurrence in *CIO*, Justice Felix Frankfurter's majority opinion used the act's legislative history to state that Congress knew that "money is the chief source of corruption," especially in the hands of wealthy corporations and labor unions. Instead of perceiving that it is the Court's duty to act as a faithful guardian of political liberty, Frankfurter held that the judicial branch is obligated to defer to legislation that reasonably seeks to fight the corruptive influence that spending has on politics. Consequently, and over the

strenuous objection of the dissent, Frankfurter distinguished the Court's holding in *CIO* and sustained the indictment alleging that a labor union broke the
law when it used union dues to sponsor commercial broadcasts of advertisements supporting the election of a congressional candidate. As Frankfurter reasoned, allowing the prosecution to go forward is the best means to preserve the
integrity of the electoral process.[40]

The Supreme Court also had the opportunity to decide the issue of whether
labor unions can be criminally prosecuted for violating the 1971 Federal Election Campaign Act. Since the FECA prohibited unions from making a contribution or expenditure in connection with a federal election, Pipefitters Local
Union No. 562 and three of its officers were convicted in federal court of conspiring to violate the act by requiring members to contribute to a fund that was
used, in part, to support the union's political activities. In *Pipefitters Local Union
No. 562 v. United States* (1972) the Court held that a union does not break the
law by spending money from a segregated account (i.e., one that separates its
monies from union dues and assessments) that was voluntarily funded with
the knowledge that the donations were earmarked for political purposes, if
members could refuse to contribute without fear of reprisal. For Justice Brennan and the rest of the Court's majority, the legislative history of the act indicated that Congress did not intend to attach a criminal sanction to situations
where the decision to donate to a political fund is not coerced and remains the
voluntary choice of the union's membership. As Brennan explained, the volun-
tariness of the contribution is determinative because Congress was most concerned about protecting minority interests inside the union; but it was not as
interested in ameliorating the impact of aggregated wealth on elections, at
least if the money is freely secured from individual members and it is not coming from the general union treasury. Still, since the Court reversed the convictions on grounds that made the disposition of the constitutional issues premature, the Court declined to address the argument that the FECA contravened
the petitioner's constitutional rights.[41]

The most significant pre-1976 cases show the Court's tendency to analyze
corruption from the standpoint of preserving the integrity of American elections. In this way, the Court deferred to the judgment of legislative majorities
in trying to regulate money and its impact. This pattern is especially conspicuous in the *CIO, International Union,* and *Pipefitters* cases, where the Court in

each opinion chose not to address the constitutionality of the congressional legislation that was at issue. Moreover, the Court did not draw any precise lines by defining corruption, since its discussion of the concept was vague and presented only in the context of acknowledging the government's interest in preserving electoral sanctity. In most cases the Court simply yielded to the policy choices made by the elected representatives by reaffirming Congress's constitutional power to maintain a virtuous political system and, in the end, effectuate broad democratic ideals.[42]

Beginning with *Buckley v. Valeo* (1976), the Supreme Court charted a new course for subsequent campaign finance decisions by using a relatively narrow conception of corruption to evaluate the constitutionality of the government's interest in regulating political money under the 1974 amendments to the Federal Election Campaign Act. There, in a per curiam decision that included five other separate opinions, the Court recognized that Congress had a compelling interest under the First Amendment to limit contributions, but not expenditures. Contribution restrictions were justified because politicians must be prevented from exchanging political favors for large individual contributions (actual corruption) or, simultaneously, destroying confidence in government by creating an appearance of corruption stemming from the possibility that they will be improperly influenced in a "regime of large individual contributions" (appearance of corruption). Statutory ceilings on contributions (along with disclosure and reporting requirements) protect the integrity of the electoral process without placing an impermissible burden on political debate and discussion.[43]

But, whereas controlling the amount of political money contributed to a campaign slightly impedes a donor's expressive activity, *Buckley* reasoned that expenditure limits directly abridge "the quantity of expression by restricting the numbers of issues discussed, the depth of their exploration, and the size of the audience reached," since "virtually every means of communicating ideas in today's mass society requires the expenditure of money." The government's interest in preventing the reality or appearance of corruption also does not outweigh the high priority given to preserving the quantity and diversity of political speech. To illustrate, the Court said that the act's limits on independent (i.e. uncoordinated with a candidate) spending only restrict expenditures expressly advocating the election or defeat of a specific candidate. As a result, such limits cannot realistically meet the goal of preventing corruption since they cannot stop unlimited spending or political quid pro quos from occurring in any other situation beyond the restricted category. Moreover, since independent political spending is not coordinated with a specific candidate or his campaign, there is little chance for the candidate to control the expenditure and use it as a basis for a quid pro quo. Therefore, while restrictions on independent spending have little impact in curbing corruption, they greatly inhibit the robust and free discussion of diverse political ideas.[44]

Even though the distinction between contributions and expenditures is a key aspect of *Buckley*'s per curiam rationale, the ruling is also significant in rejecting other interests that government has in monitoring the corruptive influence of political money. Working from the premise that "restrict[ing] the speech of some elements of our society in order to enhance the relative voice of others is wholly foreign to the First Amendment," the Court dismissed the notion that the Constitution required an equal playing field in terms of wealth and the ability it has to influence electoral outcomes by striking down the disparate spending limits imposed by the act. Stating that the "First Amendment denies government the power to determine that spending to promote one's political views is wasteful, excessive, or unwise," the Court rejected the claim that government has an interest in curbing the escalating costs of political elections. In short, as long as the Court treated the act of campaign spending as a form of highly protected speech, the government has little power to constrain spending under any type of corruption hypothesis.[45]

As table 2.5 indicates, the free speech and association elements of the First Amendment are virtually the exclusive basis for asserting that the regulation of political money is unconstitutional in all of the cases that came to the Court after *Buckley*. Notably, the distinction between limits on political giving and spending is applied in eight of the nine cases identified.[46] In five of those eight appeals the Court struck down expenditure limits four times *(First National Bank of Boston, National Conservative Political Action Committee, Massachusetts Citizens for Life, and Colorado)* and upheld them once *(Austin)*. In the remaining three cases limits on contributions were upheld twice *(California Medical Association* and *National Right to Work)* and struck down once *(Citizens Against Rent Control/Coalition for Fair Housing)*. As many critics are quick to point out, these findings suggest that the distinction *Buckley* established between contributions

Table 2.5. Regulation of Money in Political Election Cases After 1976

Case	Principal Constitutional Issue(s)	Principal Holding	Controlling Governmental Interest (As Identified in Opinion for Court)
Buckley v. Valeo (1976)	1st Amendment (speech, association)	In congressional elections Congress can limit contributions; but it cannot limit independent expenditures	Preventing reality or appearance of corruption by limiting large contributions to prevent political quid pro quo from officeholders and avoiding appearance of improper influence
First National Bank of Boston v. Bellotti (1978)	1st Amendment (speech); 14th Amendment (Equal Protection Clause)	State legislature cannot prohibit expenditures by business corporations that are made to influence electorate in voting on ballot issue in referenda elections	Preserving integrity of electoral process; sustaining active, alert responsibility of citizen in democracy for wise conduct of government; preserving citizen's confidence in government; preventing corruption in candidate elections; preventing coercion of shareholders holding minority political views
California Medical Association v. Federal Election Commission (1981)	1st Amendment; 5th Amendment (Equal Protection Clause)	Congress can impose $5,000 limit on campaign contributions by unincorporated associations to multicandidate political committees	Preventing reality or appearance of corruption of political process by reducing chance individuals and unincorporated associations will evade statutory contribution limits; protecting integrity of contribution restrictions upheld in Buckley
Citizens Against Rent Control/ Coalition For Fair Housing v. City of Berkeley (1981)	1st Amendment (association, speech)	City cannot impose $250 limit on contributions to unincorporated association formed to support or oppose ballot measures submitted to a popular vote	Preventing reality or appearance of corruption by limiting large contributions; preventing corruption in candidate elections; identifying sources of support/opposition in ballot measures to preserve voters' confidence in referenda and preserve integrity of political system
Brown v. Socialist Workers '74 Campaign Committee (1982)	1st Amendment (association, speech)	State legislature cannot compel disclosure of campaign contributors/recipients of expenditures of minor political party that is/will be harassed	Enhancing voter knowledge of candidate's interests and allegiances; deterring corruption; enforcing contribution limits; misuse of campaign funds
FEC v. National Right to Work Committee (1982)	1st Amendment (association, speech)	Congress can limit solicitation of campaign contributions paid into segregated fund from nonmembers of nonprofit corporation	Ensuring large aggregations of wealth amassed by special advantages of having corporate form do not incur political debts from legislators aided by contributions; preventing coercion of shareholders holding minority political views
FEC v. National Conservative Political Action Committee (1985)	1st Amendment (association, speech)	Congress cannot impose $1,000 limit on independent expenditures by political action committee in presidential election	Preventing reality or appearance of corruption in regard to uncoordinated expenditures (even if large) made by PACs

Table 2.5.   *(Continued)*

Case	Principal Constitutional Issue(s)	Principal Holding	Controlling Governmental Interest (As Identified in Opinion for Court)
FEC v. Massachusetts Citizens for Life (1986)	1st Amendment (speech)	Congress cannot prohibit independent expenditures made from general treasury fund by a non-stock, nonprofit, ideologically oriented corporation in publishing pro-life newsletter	Prevents corruption associated with potential for unfair deployment of wealth for political purposes; corrosive influence of concentrated corporate wealth on electoral process; prevent coercion of shareholders holding minority political views
Austin v. Michigan State Chamber of Commerce (1990)	1st Amendment (speech); 14th Amendment (Equal Protection Clause)	State legislature can prohibit non-profit corporation from making independent expenditures to pay for political advertisement in state elections except through segregated fund	Reality or appearance of corruption by reducing corrosive and distorting effects of immense aggregations of wealth accumulated with help from corporate form and that have little or no correlation to the public's support for the corporation's political ideas, and which will be used to influence unfairly the outcome of elections
Colorado Republican Federal Campaign Committee v. FEC (1996)	1st Amendment (speech)	Congress cannot impose limit on independent expenditures by state political party using radio ads to attack political opponent	Reality or appearance of corruption associated with independent party expenditures

Source: Lexis on-line search (April 24, 1997).

and expenditures is problematic.[47] In that *Buckley* can be read as drawing a clear line between permissible contribution limits and impermissible spending limits based on a corruption rationale, its progeny belies the notion that any such clear line exists. And, for at least some *Buckley* opponents, upholding contribution but rejecting spending limits mistakenly ignores the reality that unfettered spending (especially by special interests) has a corruptive influence on electoral outcomes and diminishes any chance for achieving competitive races.[48] The fuzziness with which the Court has applied *Buckley,* when combined with the potentially deleterious consequences of its application in the rough and tumble of American politics, arguably means that the distinction between contributions and expenditures (and its anticorruption rationale) loses much of its analytical force, which in turn may diminish its ability to be a legitimate constitutional principle that reasonably facilitates the ordering of legal expectations.

Four cases, *Citizens Against Rent Control/Coalition for Fair Housing v. City of Berkeley* (1981), *Austin v. Michigan State Chamber of Commerce* (1990), *Colorado Republican Federal Campaign Committee v. Federal Election Commission* (1996), and *Nixon v. Shrink Missouri Government PAC* (2000), illustrate the difficulty the Court has had in trying to rely upon corruption as a principled and coherent justification for regulating campaign finance. In *Citizens Against Rent Control/ Coalition for Fair Housing,* the Court invalidated a city ordinance imposing a $250 campaign contribution limit to political committees that were formed to support or oppose ballot measures. In drawing off *First National Bank of Boston* (1978), where business corporations were held to have the same right of political expression that individuals did in ballot elections, the Court reiterated the view first suggested in *Buckley* that the risk of individual, or quid pro quo, corruption is only present in candidate elections. Since "referenda are held on issues, not candidates for public office," the Court concluded that there was no justification for limits on contributions since candidates cannot be influenced with large contributions in elections where issues are submitted to a popular vote. By stating that money loses its deleterious impact in popular initiatives but not in candidate-centered elections, the Court incorporated another distinction into the constitutional analysis that makes *Buckley*'s narrow quid pro quo definition superfluous in regulating political money in grassroots American politics.[49]

The different impact that money has as a source of political influence in referenda and candidate elections is also difficult to reconcile with *Austin v. Michigan State Chamber of Commerce* (1990), a ruling that upheld limits on corporate campaign speech by expanding the Court's usual narrow definition of corruption. Shortly before *Austin,* the Court nullified an attempt by Congress to cabin political spending when it struck down a $1,000 limit on independent expenditures by political action committees in *Federal Election Commission v. National Conservative Political Action Committee* (1985). In *National Conservative Political Action Committee,* Justice William Rehnquist's opinion for the Court specifically adhered to the *Buckley* formulation of corruption by defining it as "a subversion of the political process," where "[e]lected officials are influenced to act contrary to their obligations of office by the prospect of financial gain to themselves or infusions of money into their campaigns." "The hallmark of corruption," he continued, "is the financial *quid pro quo:* dollars for political favors."[50] Yet in *Austin,* the Supreme Court identified a "different type of corruption in the political arena" and held that government has a compelling interest in diminishing "the corrosive and distorting effects of immense aggregations of wealth that are accumulated with the help of the corporate form and that have little or no correlation to the public's support for the corporation's political ideas." In explicitly affirming the danger that corporate wealth poses in the political system, *Austin* therefore embraces what *Buckley* explicitly denied in formulating an individualistic definition of corruption, namely that regulating wealth to enhance the speech of others is "wholly foreign to the First Amendment."[51] Moreover, as the disparate case holdings (and accompanying diverse anticorruption rationales) listed in table 2.5 imply, *Austin* is persuasive evidence that the Supreme Court will continue to act as a "perpetual policeman" in campaign finance cases by using a variety of factual distinctions to mark the uncertain boundaries of permissible regulation of political money under the First Amendment.[52]

For example, two decisions from the Rehnquist Court (1986–) in 1996 and 2000, *Colorado Republican Federal Campaign Committee v. Federal Election Commission* and *Nixon v. Shrink Missouri Government PAC,* indicate that *Buckley* is likely to remain a controversial, if not misapplied, precedent that will only produce more judicial conflict and uncertainty for federal courts and reformers alike in subsequent appeals. In *Colorado Republican Federal Campaign Committee,* a badly fractured Court employed the *Buckley* distinction between contributions and expenditures to establish the broad principle that political parties may spend an unlimited amount of money in a congressional election if the expenditures at issue are independent, or uncoordinated, with the candidate or campaign. Although Justice Stephen Breyer's plurality opinion noted that there was a real possibility that political parties could evade individual contribution limits by using donations as independent expenditures, it did not find any "special dangers of corruption" that are compelling enough to restrict uncoordinated party spending.[53]

The 6–3 ruling in *Shrink Missouri Government PAC,* moreover, turned back the constitutional challenge (on First and Fourteenth Amendment grounds) of a candidate for state auditor and a political action committee who argued that the state of Missouri impermissibly set a contribution limit ($1,075) that was too low for meaningful participation (or success) in the electoral process. In upholding the statute, the Court, through Justice David Souter, rejected the claim that there was insufficient proof that the appearance or reality of corruption was a compelling interest that justified the low contribution limit. For Souter and the rest of the majority, *Buckley* (and, in part, *Colorado Republican Federal Campaign Committee*) did not require Missouri to present evidence of real harm or corruption to establish that the limits were necessary; and neither did it fix in law a limit below which legislatures could not regulate.[54]

Unquestionably *Colorado Republican* and *Shrink Missouri Government PAC* illustrate that the Court's management of campaign finance regulation raises the question of the Court's proper judicial role in a political system that values certain democratic ideals such as equality, political participation, and representation. While, for some, the Court's interventionism in the political process threatens these underlying norms and principles, defenders of the Court maintain that it is necessary for the judicial branch to step into the political thicket to protect basic political freedoms under the First Amendment that might be taken away by a dominant legislative majority.[55] Moreover, despite their relatively straightforward application of *Buckley*'s anticorruption rationale, for several reasons *Colorado Republican* and *Shrink Missouri Government PAC* also offer an uncertain vision of what the Court will do in this area of jurisprudence in the future.

First, in a manner that is reminiscent of the Court's struggle to define obscenity between 1957 and 1973, *Colorado Republican* offers little guidance as to controlling legal precedent since the plurality could not produce an opinion for the Court where five Justices agreed on the controlling rationale.[56] The Court's ruling in *Shrink Missouri Government PAC* is analogous, since each of the three dissenters (Justices Anthony Kennedy, Antonin Scalia, and Clarence Thomas) argued that *Buckley* is bad law and ought to be overruled; and, in his concurrence (joined by Justice Ruth Bader Ginsburg) Justice Stephen Breyer suggested that *Buckley* may "den[y] the political branches sufficient leeway to enact comprehensive solutions to the problems posed by campaign finance," which may necessitate that the Court revisit the validity of the landmark decision in the future.[57] Indeed, whereas in *Colorado Republican* Justice Clarence Thomas asserted that *Buckley*'s distinction between political spending and giving should be rejected because it lacks "constitutional significance,"[58] in *Shrink Missouri Government PAC* Justice Kennedy maintained that it is "our duty to face up to adverse, unintended consequences flowing from our prior decisions" and reject *Buckley* because it has created "covert speech," or expression that (through soft money and funding unregulated issue advocacy) "forced a substantial amount of political speech underground" in an attempt to evade contribution limits.[59]

Second, apart from the destabilizing effect that *Buckley* has on the Court's post-*Buckley* jurisprudence, *Colorado Republican* left open a critical issue as to whether coordinated expenditures of political parties are subject to regulation under the First Amendment, a question that it will decide in the 2000–2001 term. Indeed, in the second round of the *Colorado Republican* litigation, the district court and the Tenth Circuit have already decided that Congress cannot limit such expenditures.[60] Third, as *Colorado Republican, Shrink Missouri Government PAC,* and the rest of *Buckley*'s earlier progeny suggest, one could plausibly conclude that "[a]fter *Buckley*, campaign finance regulation [has] survived in a form that no legislature ever voted to create and, one may surmise, no legislature would ever have voted to create."[61] Accordingly, unlike the propensity of earlier Courts (pre-1976) to defer to Congress and affirm the validity of campaign finance legislation, after *Buckley* there is little doubt that the Supreme Court has continued to put itself at the forefront of making policy choices about the proper role that money plays in America.

CASES ON THE INTEGRITY OF THE ELECTORAL PROCESS

Much of the genius of the principal architect of the United States Constitution flows from the recognition that democracy is a threat to republicanism. Consequently, the framing document does not advocate direct democracy or the creation of democratic institutions such as political parties.[62] As James Madison explained in "Federalist No. 10," factional rule and the ascendancy of dominant groups pursuing narrow interests threatened to undermine any effort to create a virtuous, representative republic. In "Federalist No. 51," he underscored the same point by describing the need for creating a constitutional framework that prevented one branch from accumulating too much power at the expense of securing republican liberty. Although popular sovereignty helps to keep government in check, precisely because "men are not angels," Madison concluded that "experience has taught mankind the necessity of auxiliary precautions." As a result, the principles of separation of powers, federalism, and the various checks and balances in the Constitution are there to "enable the government to control the governed" and then "oblige it to control itself."[63]

Yet, the currents associated with democratic popular control of government are very much a part of making our elected representatives politically accountable for their actions. Even though the U.S. Constitution was originally designed to reduce factional influence and curb tyrannical majorities, the citizenry has taken advantage of the basic freedom of association in the First Amendment by forming political parties in order to achieve popular electoral objectives. The rise of political parties, though, has laid the foundation for perpetuating the type of corruption that ironically once served as the impetus for American independence and the creation of auxiliary precautions in the Constitution. Over time parties have been the objects of progressive reform (i.e., civil service primaries) but also, in part, the cause of legislative entrenchment, political patronage, voter alienation, and direct democracy movements.[64]

As tables 2.6 through 2.8 reveal, these elements of the political system have been at the center of several legal challenges before the nation's high court. Table 2.6, a collection of ballot and franchise cases that comprise 8% of the sample, demonstrates that the Supreme Court acts much the way it did in using its authority to reaffirm violations of the criminal law in bribery and political influence cases (see tables 2.2 and 2.3). Also present in these early cases is the Court's propensity to interpret Congress's power to regulate the time, place, and manner of elections broadly (often at the expense of state power). All five cases firmly ratified the notion that Congress must have the ability to punish those who violate electoral norms and procedures with the enforcement of a criminal sanction. With the help of the nation's high court, the concept of political corruption became an indirect accomplice to extending the national government's power over individuals and the states, thereby maintaining the sanctity of the electoral process.

For example, in *Ex Parte Siebold* (1879), Congress's power to superintend elections and secure their "purity" is described as "fundamental" and "necessary to the stability to our frame of government" in light of the "violence, fraud, corruption, and irregularity which have frequently prevailed" in the na-

Table 2.6. Cases Involving Protecting the Integrity of the Ballot and Franchise

Case	Constitutional Issue(s)	Facts	Main Legal Issue/Holding
Ex Parte Siebold (1879)	Art. I, Sec. 4 (time, place, and manner of elections)	Judges of election convicted under federal Enforcement Act for stuffing ballot boxes during city elections sought habeas corpus	Denied habeas by holding that Congress has concurrent (but paramount) constitutional power to regulate national elections where states play an important role
Ex Parte Yarbrough (1884)	Art. I, Sec. 8 (necessary and proper clause); Art. 1, Sec. 4 (time, place, and manner of elections); 15th Amendment	Ku Klux Klan members convicted for impeding black man's exercise of franchise sought habeas corpus	Denied habeas by holding that Congress has implied and express power to protect elections an the right of the franchise
Ex Parte Coy (1888)	None	Inspectors of election convicted for ballot tampering in election pertaining to congressional seat sought habeas corpus	Denied habeas by holding that federal court had jurisdiction to try and convict defendants under federal law even though the state at center of their election interference
U.S. v. Classic (1941)	Art. I, Sec. 2 (appointment of electors); Art. I, Sec. 4 (time, place, and manner of elections)	Commissioners of elections in state primary prosecuted for ballot tampering under federal law	States are given wide discretion under U.S. Constitution in formulating a system for the choice of electing representatives for Congress, including congressional primaries held in states
U.S. v. Saylor (1944)	None	Defendants prosecuted for ballot tampering in state election held for purpose of filling U.S. Senator seat	Statute prohibits making donation to "person" of "influence"

Source: Lexis on-line search (April 24, 1997).

tion's recent history. Preserving the integrity of elections and the republican form of government is characterized in similar terms when the Court, in *Ex Parte Yarbrough* (1884), upheld the convictions of several Klansmen who beat up a black man trying to vote. There, Justice Samuel F. Miller said:

That a government whose essential character is republican, whose executive head and legislative body are both elective, whose most numerous and powerful branch of the legislature is elected by the people directly, has no power by appropriate laws to secure this election from the influence of violence, of corruption, and of fraud, is a proposition so startling as to arrest attention and demand the gravest consideration. If this government is anything more than a mere aggregation of delegated agents of other States and governments, each of which is superior to the general government, it must have the power to protect the elections on which its existence depends from violence and corruption. If it has not this power it is left helpless before the two great natural and historical enemies of all republics, open violence and insidious corruption.[65]

This idea of using constitutional principles to protect the integrity of congressional elections is also illustrated well by *U.S. v. Classic* (1941), an important case holding that Congress's authority under Article I, Section 4 extends to regulating primary elections in the states since they are a key part of selecting federal candidates. Writing this holding into constitutional law therefore enabled the Court to conclude that qualified voters in the Louisiana primary had the right to have their votes counted in an election primary that was tainted by corruption.[66]

While table 2.6 touches upon broader concerns of federalism, the last two sets of cases address particular challenges to the practice of patronage (table 2.7) and the specific claims by parties and citizens to be free from regulation controlling ballot initiatives and other campaign activities (table 2.8). Patronage cases represent 10% of the total sample of corruption cases. With the exception of *United Public Workers of America v. Mitchell* (1947), these cases arguably can be collectively described as a judicial assault upon the traditional right of political parties in a democracy to dispense the spoils of victory to the party faithful. From another perspective, though, they only represent the Court's vindication of democratic values that, at their core, favor a broad recognition of political participation and expression under the First Amendment. As a result, the judicial conflict in the patronage cases after 1976 centered on whether the Court should use its power to restrict patronage in public employment because dispensing the spoils of victory by the party invariably meant a loss of basic individual freedom for the employee.[67]

Historically the Supreme Court and the rest of the judiciary showed little enthusiasm for treating patronage dismissals as a First Amendment problem. The judicial acknowledgement that they presented a difficulty of free expression did not emerge until 1976, when *Elrod v. Burns* was decided. Before then, courts either refused to assign to the employee a constitutionally protected interest or, alternatively, denied relief because the employee waived any legal protection by virtue of assuming the risk of initially taking a patronage job. Precedent, in short, settled the issue early on by declaring that a person who lived by the political sword could also die by it without having any legal re-

Table 2.7. Cases Involving Political Patronage and Partisan Activity by Public Employees and Independent Contractors

Case	Constitutional Issue(s)	Facts	Main Legal Issue/Holding
United Public Workers of America v. Mitchell (1947)	1st, 5th, 9th, 10th, and 14th Amendments (Due Process)	Federal employees prosecuted for violating Hatch Act, which barred them from engaging in certain political activities	Court upheld Hatch Act as reasonable exercise of congressional power to regulate partisan conduct of federal employees in the interest of promoting integrity and efficiency in government
Elrod v. Burns (1976)	1st and 14th Amendments (Due Process)	Non–civil service employees fired by newly elected sheriff after local election	Patronage dismissals violate political belief and association rights under the First Amendment
Branti v. Finkel (1980)	1st Amendment	Assistant public defender terminated from employment on the basis of his political beliefs and partisan affiliation	Patronage dismissals made solely on the basis of partisan affiliation violate political belief and association rights under the First Amendment
Rutan v. Republican Party of Illinois (1990)	1st Amendment	Public employees denied promotions, transfers, recalls, and/or hirings on basis of partisan affiliation	Patronage promotions, transfers, recalls, and/or hirings on basis of partisan affiliation violate public employees' First Amendment rights of political belief and association
O'Hare Truck Service, Inc. v. City of Northlake (1996)	1st Amendment	Independent contractor removed from list of companies that provide towing services for city in retaliation for supporting opponent in mayor's race	Protections of *Elrod* and *Branti* extend to case where government retaliates against an independent contractor or regular provider of services for exercise of rights of political association or political allegiance under First Amendment
Board of County Commissioners, Wabaunsee County, Kansas v. Umbehr (1996)	1st Amendment	Commissioners terminated the contract of trash hauler in retaliation for criticizing county board	First Amendment protects independent contractors from termination of at-will government contracts in retaliation for their exercise of freedom of speech

Source: Lexis on-line search (April 24, 1997).

course.[68] Moreover, the Court seemed more inclined to defer to the legislative choices effectuated through progressive reform (which was in part an effort to curb the type of corruption associated with machine politics and the incentive-through-reward patronage system) and the movement towards a merit-based civil service system. In *United Public Workers of America,* for example, the Court rejected a First Amendment claim of federal employees and deferred to Congress by upholding the Hatch Act, legislation that restricted the political activities of federal employees by mandating their dismissal if they engaged in prohibited political management and campaigning.[69]

Yet as table 2.7 reveals, beginning with *Elrod* and continuing to *O'Hare Truck Service, Inc. v. City of Northlake* (1996) and *Board of County Commissioners, Wabaunsee County, Kansas v. Umbehr* (1996), the Court has actively defended the First Amendment claims of public employees (and independent contractors) who have had their employment negatively affected by the patronage decisions of their bosses (or those with political power).[70] As political scientist David O'Brien argues in surveying the Court's jurisprudence in this area, there are many possible explanations for why there was a shift in the Court's thinking in the patronage cases after 1976. One reason he mentions—that the changing membership of the bench has altered its constitutional politics and led to a grudging acceptance of the underlying *Elrod* precedent—seems particularly persuasive.[71] In any event, even though political corruption is not often discussed in any depth in these cases, it is clear that its presence increased judicial conflict on the high bench, particularly in *Elrod, Branti v. Finkel,* and *Rutan v. Republican Party of Illinois.*[72] In a fashion analogous to what has transpired in the post-*Buckley* campaign finance cases, corruption has also indirectly caused the Supreme Court to use the First Amendment as the right of choice to manage the electoral process more closely. In doing so, it is worth considering the claims of Justice Powell *(Elrod)* and Justice Antonin Scalia *(Rutan)* that the Court's interference in the political thicket has severely restricted patronage and decreased the salutary impact that parties have on American democracy.[73]

Table 2.8, consisting of cases involving direct democracy and the regulation of political parties (7% of the sample), presents yet another feature of the Court's work. In general, they pertain to claims that government is threatening First Amendment freedoms by wrongfully regulating political parties or impeding a citizen's right to put issues on a ballot for voter consideration. In *Eu v. San*

Francisco County Democratic Central Committee (1989), the Supreme Court addressed whether a party's internal organization is subject to extensive state regulation. The California Elections Code prohibited the official governing bodies of political parties from endorsing candidates in party primaries. Other provisions controlled the structure and membership of those entities, imposed term limits of office for the state central committee chair, and required that the chair rotate between residents living in northern and southern California. After finding that these regulations burdened speech and association rights, Justice Thurgood Marshall's opinion for a unanimous bench rejected the state's argument that the ban of party endorsements is necessary to safeguard primary voters from confusion and undue influence. Citing *Buckley* (1976), Marshall held that nothing in the record illustrated that California's ban met the objective of regulating the information flowing between political associations and their members in order to stop fraud or corruption. Marshall likewise struck down the rest of the statutory restrictions because California did not have a compelling interest in *directly* regulating internal party affairs, at least insofar as to preserve the integrity of the electoral process and guarantee that elections are fair and honest. Put differently, while some state control is permissible to ensure openness and fairness, a "State cannot substitute its judgment for that of the party as to the desirability of a particular internal party structure, any more than it can tell a party that its proposed communication to party members is unwise."[74]

The balance of the cases identified in table 2.8 concern whether legislatures could use the prevention of corruption as a justification for burdening the free speech and association rights of citizens engaging in some form of direct democracy through campaign activities connected to initiatives, referenda, and ballot measures. *McIntyre v. Ohio Elections Commission* (1995) gives one answer. There, Justice John Paul Stevens held for the Court that Ohio's "blunderbuss approach" to prohibiting the distribution of anonymous literature expressing opposition to a proposed school tax levy is a content-based regulation that did not serve the governmental interest of preventing fraud. Justice Antonin Scalia (with Chief Justice William Rehnquist joining in the opinion), however, dissented. Rather than burdening core political speech, Scalia viewed the state law requiring disclosure of the identity of the pamphleteer as an "established legislative practice" that improves the quality of the electoral process.

Table 2.8. Cases Involving Direct Democracy and Regulation of Political Parties

Case	Constitutional Issue(s)	Facts	Main Legal Issue/Holding
Meyer v. Grant (1988)	1st Amendment (speech)	State legislation made it a crime to pay petitioners who circulated petition to get enough signatures of qualified voters to put issue on ballot election	Petitioners' right to engage in political speech violated under the First Amendment
Eu v. San Francisco County Democratic Central Committee (1989)	1st & 14th Amendments (speech, association)	State legislation prohibited primary endorsements by official governing bodies of political parties; also regulated various internal organizational procedures of political parties	State legislation's ban on making primary endorsements violates speech and association rights of political parties under First Amendment; restrictions on the organization and composition of official governing bodies, and other restrictions, burden association rights under First Amendment
McIntyre v. Ohio Elections Commission (1995)	1st Amendment (speech)	Parent/taxpayer fined for distributing campaign literature opposing a proposed school tax levy because it did not have name/address of person or campaign official issuing the literature	State law prohibiting the distribution of anonymous campaign literature abridges the freedom of speech under the First Amendment
Buckley v. American Constitutional Law Foundation (1999)	1st Amendment (speech)	State legislation regulated ballot initiatives by requiring disclosure of identity of paid petitioners who circulated petitions to garner signatures	State law violates right to political speech under the First Amendment

Source: Lexis on-line search (April 24, 1997). Buckley v. American Constitutional Law Foundation (1999) is added because of the Court's discussion of Meyer v. Grant (1988) as controlling precedent.

Notably, in echoing Justice Byron White's views contained in his disagreements with the underlying principles of Buckley's (1976) progeny, Scalia dissented too because he believed that the Court (all six unelected members of it who joined in the majority) had no business questioning the wisdom of "real-life experience of elected politicians" in drafting the law. On balance, therefore, McIntyre registers polar views about when government can reasonably burden speech and association in trying to regulate the dissemination of campaign literature in a school tax referendum.[75]

The Rehnquist Court evaluated the constitutionality of ballot initiative restrictions in Buckley v. American Constitutional Law Foundation (1999), a ruling that invalidated Colorado's attempt to control the possibility of corruption occurring in the ballot initiative process. The decision was handed down in light of *Meyer v. Grant* (1988), where the Court also struck down Colorado legislation that prohibited compensation for individuals who circulated petitions as a violation of free speech. In spite of *Meyer,* however, the state afterwards, in 1993, regulated the process even more, since citizens were complaining that there were too many initiatives and that the petition process itself was too commercialized. As a result, *American Constitutional Law Foundation* arose from the state's attempt to temper the abuses flowing from a loosely regulated initiative process that was increasingly manipulated by commercial interests.[76]

Consequently, in *American Constitutional Law Foundation,* a number of plaintiffs interested in deregulating the initiative process challenged Colorado law as a violation of free speech and association. The law at issue imposed a number of requirements on those who sought to garner enough signatures to place an issue on the ballot. Specifically, the regulations required that petition circulators be registered voters; that they wear identification badges indicating whether they were paid or volunteers; and that they file reports with state officials indicating the identity of the paid petition circulators and how much they were paid. Treating petition circulation as highly protected political speech, the Court struck down the provisions by applying exacting scrutiny and holding that Colorado's legislation does not meet the claimed objective of maintaining the integrity of the ballot initiative process.

Justice Ruth Bader Ginsburg, in writing the opinion for the Court, rejected Colorado's arguments that the regulations were necessary in order to promote greater administrative efficiency, prevent fraud, and inform voters about key political issues. Although it left intact that part of the regulatory scheme that mandated disclosure of the names of initiative sponsors and the amount of money they spent in gathering support for the initiatives, the Court said that identifying the names of paid circulators and the amount of compensation they receive is unconstitutional because it does not pose a risk of political quid pro quos that are normally associated with candidate elections.[77] By invoking the same standard of review used in *Buckley v. Valeo* (1976), the Court thus signaled that laws restricting certain aspects of the ballot initiative process are not always going to get the type of greater judicial deference that is ordinarily afforded to other kinds of state laws that control access to the ballot.

The decision also implies that the Court will not discourage the very real possibility that commercial interests will dominate the process by which citizens try to make their own laws through ballot initiatives, a form of direct democracy. As dissenting Chief Justice William Rehnquist lamented, "The ironic effect of [*American Constitutional Law Foundation*] is that, in the name of the First Amendment, it strikes down the attempt of a State to allow its own voters (rather than out-of-state persons and political dropouts) to decide what issues should go on the ballot to be decided by the State's registered voters." Moreover, the chief justice suggested that the majority opinion would do little to prevent the initiative process from becoming increasingly influenced by out-of-state professional firms that have plenty of money to impose their nationwide business objectives on the state.[78] In this light, the effect of the ruling is comparable to the 1976 campaign finance decision in *Buckley v. Valeo*, where the Court's interpretation of the First Amendment has (among other things) led to increased spending and further cooptation of the political system by incumbents and special interest groups with money. Perhaps, then, Justice Byron White was right when he said that the Supreme Court's holding in *Buckley v. Valeo* proceeds from "the maxim that '[m]oney talks.'"[79]

CONCLUSION

As a judicial institution the U.S. Supreme Court is not a self-starter, so it must wait for a new generation of political corruption cases to fill its docket. Especially in the aftermath of President Bill Clinton's impeachment it is plausible to think that "[t]he boundaries of what constitutes corruption and misconduct in public life have been redrawn to include a lot more private conduct."[80] If so, it will be interesting to see if the Court's response to corruption go beyond the types of cases considered in this study and begin to include those involving private acts that previously were beyond the scope of the Court's work.

The inevitability of hearing more diverse cases in the future illustrates that the Court's agenda opportunities—and its concomitant ability to superintend the political process—are closely tied to the fear of political corruption in our rights-conscious society. How the Court resolves cases raising the issue is thus significant, because its rulings ultimately mirror a collective judgment about what the Court believes is the proper conception of the judicial role in a system of separated powers and representative government. Also, measuring the Court's response to the problem of corruption allows for an assessment about whether the Court is acting legitimately in superintending the political process.

Still, presupposing the existence of virtuous qualities in men is not always an easy thing to do in a political system that is characterized by self-government and designed, in large part, to overcome the weakness of man. As a result, it is sometimes necessary for the Court to use its judicial authority to protect liberty in those instances when humans fail miserably in the effort to preserve the ideals underlying republican government. In this light, it is plausible to believe that the Court's jurisprudence in political corruption cases reflects, in part, the success or failure of republican government. For when the Supreme Court steps into the political thicket, as it invariably does in corruption cases, the fate of republican liberty often hangs in the balance. It is precisely because the stakes are so high that the Court must be careful in striking an acceptable balance between the lesser of two evils. In many political corruption cases, the Court must decide between allowing the legislature to make anticorruption laws with impunity or, instead, reject what the legislature has done and run the risk of becoming an unwitting ally of corruption by perpetuating it through the rule of law.

In spite of this dilemma, and keeping in mind that courts are not necessarily in the business of getting *in front of* a policy problem (as a legislature should), it is important to recognize the social impact of the Court's decision making in corruption cases. From this perspective the rulings of the Supreme Court have produced judicial and political conflict, along with some unintended consequences. Despite the best intentions of the political branches, as political scientist Larry Sabato and journalist Glenn Simpson once said, "Oddly, the Constitution may sometimes guarantee that the law fails."[81] At least in part, the results of this study support that conclusion.

For example, the bribery and political influence cases reveal that the Supreme Court uses its power to punish those who engage in a narrow definition of corrupt behavior. More often than not the Court defers to the legislative choice about what is the best means to protect society by simply enforcing the criminal law against the corrupt politician. Using the law as a coercive sanction in this context is probably the least controversial exercise of judicial authority, since most would probably agree that corrupt politicians (along with anyone else) need to be punished when they break the criminal law.

Yet the cases in the remaining two categories are more controversial and it is more difficult to agree that the Court's decision making has produced a positive benefit for society, at least in practical terms. Clearly the line that the Court has drawn in the post-*Buckley* campaign finance cases has been blurry at best, since the expenditures/contribution distinction is hard to apply consistently in cases involving complex facts. Justice White, one of the few on the bench to have hands-on political experience, went so far as to claim that the *National Conservative Political Action Committee* ruling "again transformed a coherent regulatory scheme into a nonsensical, loophole-ridden patchwork."[82] Regardless of whether Justice White is correct or not, it is clear that the Court's inconsistency in the regulation of political money cases makes it very difficult for litigants to order their legal expectations. More significantly, the confusion generated from the Court's judicial opinions makes the lower federal courts, by default, carry the burden in trying to make sense of what the Court is doing, which only depletes finite judicial resources and wastes time. Moreover, reducing the definition of corruption to quid pro quo terminology has increased the likelihood of judicial intervention by the high court, since it must continually address the unanswered questions that were raised in *Buckley*. At the same time, however, changing the definition later (as the Court did in *Austin* by formulating a "new corruption" standard) creates even more hardships for those trying to comprehend the Court's work.

Apart from the doctrinal incoherence that characterizes *Buckley* and its progeny, the basic *Buckley* principle that treats expenditures as a form of expression and not conduct (i.e., money is speech) has the unintended effect of allowing political spending to increase to unprecedented levels. In no small measure the problem has been exacerbated by wealthy special interest groups (and the political parties and candidates themselves) who spend more in American politics and, in the process, flaunt any contribution limits and, perhaps, corrupt the system more. While the corrosive influence of money is debatable, the Court's jurisprudence has not ameliorated its impact; nor has it equalized the financial ability to compete amongst vying political candidates or parties that continually confront the obstacles of incumbency and massive political war chests; and it has not retarded the public perception that money buys votes. Of course, all of these contumacious problems that infect the American political system cannot fairly be dumped at the front door of the Marble Temple. Yet the judiciary cannot escape the reality that its decision making has, in part, caused reformers to blame the Court for making the diseased American republic sicker.[83]

The problem of unintended consequences has also made its mark in affecting core democratic values as well. With the arguable exception of *Austin,* the Court has been less than receptive to promoting equality (in terms of imposing spending limits) among competing groups and individuals that struggle for power in the political arena with disproportionate financial resources. Apart from campaign finance, in an analogous fashion the Court in *Buckley v. American Constitutional Law Foundation* used the First Amendment to protect, perhaps inadvertently, the commercialized interests that threaten to capture the ballot initiative (or direct democracy) process in the states. At the same time, the Court's work in patronage cases also illustrates that the Court has arguably weakened political parties and impeded their ability to act as organizations that further democratic ideals. As a result, perhaps Justices Powell and Scalia are correct in suggesting that the Court's antipatronage rulings have driven a stake in the heart of political parties and their ability to serve as an important link in the chain of representation existing between the governing and the governed.

Even so, in the end it is important to recognize the wisdom of Alexander Hamilton's words when he implicitly referred to the justices of the United States Supreme Court as "faithful guardians of the Constitution."[84] This study has demonstrated that the Court has used its power of judicial review to protect core values in the Bill of Rights (particularly the First Amendment) in the political corruption cases. One need look no further than to *Eu v. San Francisco County Democratic Central Committee* or to *FEC v. Massachusetts Citizens for Life* and *McIntyre v. Ohio Elections Commission* as evidence to support that view. From this perspective, it is rather unremarkable that the Supreme Court generates great controversy when it chooses to walk into the political thicket. After all, in many ways it remains one of the last lines of defense in challenging arbitrary rule and protecting republican liberty, a Madisonian goal that few can dispute is always worth achieving, even in spite of the principle of unintended consequences.

CHAPTER 3

A Legal Strategy for Challenging
Buckley v. Valeo

John C. Bonifaz, Gregory G. Luke, and Brenda Wright

IN ITS 1976 RULING IN *Buckley v. Valeo,* the United States Supreme
Court sanctioned a system of unlimited campaign spending in federal
elections. Since that ruling, this nation has witnessed an explosion of
campaign spending. The 1996 election cycle marked the most expensive election in U.S. history, with congressional and presidential candidates spending a total of more than $2 billion. The 2000 election
cycle is expected to far surpass that total, setting a new spending
record at more than $3 billion. Campaign spending has also dramati-
cally risen in state and local elections across the country.[1]

Unlimited spending poses a serious threat to our democratic
process. It undermines public confidence in our elections and in our
democratic institutions. It presents an increased danger of actual corruption as large contributors dominate the financing of public election campaigns. It places enormous time pressures on officeholders
running for reelection, interfering with their ability to carry out their
governing duties. It enables candidates with wealth or access to
wealth to drown out the voices of lesser-funded candidates and their
supporters. It violates the promise of political equality.[2]

The time has come to revisit *Buckley v. Valeo*. The facts and circumstances of unlimited campaign spending have dramatically changed
since the *Buckley* ruling. They now demonstrate the necessity for campaign spending limits to protect the integrity of our electoral process.
New facts now require a new review. As the Supreme Court has stated:
"In constitutional adjudication as elsewhere in life, changed circum-

stances may impose new obligations, and the thoughtful part of the Nation could accept each decision to overrule a prior case as a response to the Court's constitutional duty."[3]

And there are signs that the wall is crumbling. As the result of *Nixon v. Shrink Missouri Government PAC* (2000), a U.S. Supreme Court ruling reaffirming the constitutionality of campaign contribution limits, four justices are now on record stating that *Buckley* may need to be revisited on the spending limits question. As Justice Anthony Kennedy said, "For now, however, I would leave open the possibility that Congress, or a state legislature, might devise a system in which there are some limits on both expenditures and contributions." Justice Stephen Breyer, joined by Justice Ruth Bader Ginsburg, expressed a similar thought by stating: "Suppose *Buckley* denies the political branches sufficient leeway to enact comprehensive solutions to the problems posed by campaign finance. If so, like Justice Kennedy, I believe the Constitution would require us to reconsider *Buckley*." And Justice John Paul Stevens, who has previously called for a revisitation of *Buckley* concurred in conveying the point that: "Money is property; it is not speech."[4]

This chapter will highlight the emergence of a new legal movement for challenging *Buckley*. It will present the arguments developed in several test cases in jurisdictions that have sought to revisit the constitutionality of campaign spending limits by enacting and defending mandatory spending limits. These beginning efforts—from the cities of Cincinnati, Ohio, and Albuquerque, New Mexico, to the State of Vermont—have been launched with the recognition that legal reform may be a long-term project.

In 1937 and again in 1951, the Supreme Court upheld the poll tax as constitutional.[5] A fee charged to voters in order to vote did not, the Court found, violate the Equal Protection Clause of the Fourteenth Amendment. In 1966, the Court reversed its prior rulings. In the landmark case of *Harper v. Virginia Board of Elections,* the Court held that "the Equal Protection Clause is not shackled to the political theory of a particular era. . . . Notions of what constitutes equal treatment for purposes of the Equal Protection Clause *do* change."[6] This chapter is presented in the spirit of *Harper. Buckley* may stand today. But it cannot stand the test of time.

THE *BUCKLEY* RULING

In 1974, in the wake of the Watergate scandal, the United States Congress enacted a set of amendments to the Federal Election Campaign Act (FECA) (first enacted in 1971) which many regarded as "the most comprehensive reform legislation [ever] passed by Congress concerning the election of the President, Vice-President, and members of Congress."[7] The amendments created limits on contributions to a candidate for federal office and expenditures in support of such a candidacy. Under the new FECA provisions, an individual could contribute no more than $1,000 to a federal candidate in a primary or general election, and political action committees were limited to $5,000 contributions per primary or general election. The amendments also set limits on overall campaign expenditures, on expenditures by candidates from personal or family resources, and on "independent" expenditures (expenditures made on behalf of a candidate but not in coordination with the candidate's campaign). In addition, the amendments created a scheme for the public financing system of presidential campaigns, required reporting and disclosure of contributions and expenditures above certain levels, and established the Federal Election Commission to administer and enforce the federal campaign finance laws.

Soon after its passage, an unlikely coalition of plaintiffs (including then U.S. Senator James Buckley [R-N.Y.], presidential candidate Eugene McCarthy, philanthropist Stewart Mott, the Conservative Party of the State of New York, the Mississippi Republican Party, the Libertarian Party, and the New York Civil Liberties Union) filed suit in federal court challenging the new FECA amendments as unconstitutional on First and Fifth Amendment grounds. With respect to the provisions limiting campaign contributions and expenditures, the plaintiffs argued that "limiting the use of money for political purposes constitute[d] a restriction on communication violative of the First Amendment, since virtually all meaningful political communications in the modern setting involve the expenditure of money."[8]

The FECA amendments included a special provision for expedited judicial review of any constitutional challenge to the reform legislation.[9] The provision required the district court presiding over such a challenge to certify immediately all questions regarding the constitutionality of the legislation to the U.S. court of appeals for the circuit involved and further required that the appellate court hear the matter sitting en banc. The provision effectively prevented the possibility of any trial at the district court level and any development of a full factual record to be weighed in the determination of the constitutionality of the laws under challenge. Because of that provision, the only "facts" available for the Supreme Court's eventual consideration in *Buckley* were those stipulated to by the parties, without a trial or significant discovery.

In a per curiam opinion, an eight-judge panel of the U.S. Court of Appeals for the District of Columbia Circuit (hearing the case en banc), upheld, with one exception, the substantive new provisions of FECA. In analyzing the First Amendment issues presented in the case, the court held that the FECA provisions regulating campaign contributions and expenditures were regulations of conduct, not speech. It found that Congress had "a clear and compelling interest in safeguarding the integrity of elections and avoiding the undue influence of wealth."[10] The court stated: "It would be strange indeed if, by extrapolation outward from the basic rights of individuals, the wealthy few could claim a constitutional guarantee to a stronger political voice than the unwealthy many because they are able to give and spend more money, and because the amounts they give and spend cannot be limited."[11]

Because of the truncated litigation process mandated by FECA, the case reached the Supreme Court for argument only thirteen months after FECA was enacted. The Court issued a lengthy but unsigned opinion, with numerous concurrences and dissents that must be carefully added and subtracted to determine the Court's holding on different aspects of the FECA regulations. Six of the eight participating members of the Supreme Court, not all applying the same reasoning, affirmed the appellate court's ruling upholding FECA's limits on campaign contributions, finding that such limits were justified by the sufficiently important governmental interest of preventing corruption and the appearance of corruption in the electoral process.[12] Seven justices voted to strike down the campaign spending limits as violative of the First Amendment. The First Amendment, the Court ruled, protected the right of candidates for federal office to engage in unlimited campaign spending.

Justice Byron White, the only member of the *Buckley* Court to have worked in a federal election campaign, issued a strong dissent to the ruling on spending limits. "[E]lections are not to turn on the difference in the amounts of money that candidates have to spend," wrote Justice White. He continued: "The Court nevertheless holds that a candidate has a constitutional right to spend unlimited amounts of money, mostly that of other people, in order to be elected. The holding is not that federal candidates have the constitutional right to purchase their election, but many will so interpret the Court's conclusion in this case. I cannot join the Court in this respect."[13]

THE LEGAL MOVEMENT TO REVISIT *BUCKLEY*

In the twenty-four years since *Buckley,* the ruling has generated significant dissent within and outside of the legal community. More than two hundred constitutional scholars from across the nation have signed a statement calling for the reversal of *Buckley*'s prohibition on spending limits. The attorneys general for twenty-six states and the secretaries of state or chief election officers for twenty-one states have gone on record seeking to overturn the ruling.[14] Members of Congress have introduced eleven bills since 1976 that would establish campaign spending limits for federal elections and set the stage for revisiting *Buckley.*[15] Thirty-eight U.S. Senators have supported the call for the reversal of the ruling. The White House and the U.S. Justice Department have also announced their interest in supporting a test case for revisiting *Buckley.*[16] Editorialists around the country have joined the call for a new look at the constitutionality of spending limits.[17]

Sparking this growing support for revisiting *Buckley* are a series of state and local initiatives to halt the spiraling influence of money in elections by enacting and defending limits on campaign spending. The case that has received the most attention to date is *City of Cincinnati v. Kruse,* the first test case since *Buckley* to address directly the question of the constitutionality of campaign spending limits in legislative elections. Although the Supreme Court declined, without comment, to hear Cincinnati's appeal of a lower court ruling enjoining the limits, the case has had a significant impact in the support it has generated for revisiting *Buckley.* It also generated a significant concurring opinion in the U.S. Court of Appeals for the Sixth Circuit which recognized, for the first time, that *Buckley* need not be read as a per se ban on all spending limits and that state or local jurisdictions might be able to justify such limits based on new compelling interests not addressed by the *Buckley* Court in 1976. Examination of the *Kruse* case therefore provides an important starting point for understanding the legal and factual issues involved in the movement to revisit *Buckley.* Its lessons will have continued application in future anticipated cases defending spending limits in Vermont, New Mexico, and elsewhere.[18]

Kruse v. City of Cincinnati

In July 1995, following twenty months of study and deliberation, the Cincinnati City Council enacted limits on campaign expenditures in city council elections. The city council set the limits at the level of three times the annual salary for a city councilmember, a level of approximately $140,000. In enacting these limits, the city council recognized the Supreme Court's ruling in *Buckley*, but found that new facts and circumstances associated with campaign spending in its local elections demonstrated the necessity for spending limits. In March 1996, John R. Kruse, an unsuccessful city council candidate, his political committee, and two financial contributors filed suit in federal district court in Cincinnati, challenging the limits on *Buckley* grounds. The city retained the National Voting Rights Institute as special counsel to defend the limits.

Throughout the litigation, the plaintiffs contended that *Buckley* stands for the proposition that all campaign spending limits are per se unconstitutional. The facts, the plaintiffs argued, do not matter. In so doing, the plaintiffs stipulated at the summary judgment stage to any and all facts that the city introduced into the record in its defense of the ordinance. This record included the following facts:

• In the past several election cycles, the City of Cincinnati witnessed a dramatic rise in the cost of Cincinnati city council campaigns. The highest candidate expenditure for a winning campaign increased by more than 480 percent, rising from $75,000 in 1989 to $362,000 in 1995.

• The rise in the overall cost of Cincinnati city council races has caused a corresponding rise in the influence of wealthy donors in Cincinnati's elections. From 1991 to 1995, one-third of 1 percent of the metropolitan area's population provided more than $3.9 million in campaign contributions to city council candidates, amounting to nearly 70 percent of all the money raised by those candidates.

• The public perception in Cincinnati, shared by an overwhelming majority of Cincinnati residents, is that "large campaign contributors wield undue influence on the political system." That same overwhelming majority state that "[t]he amount of money in election campaigns has caused [them] to lose a great deal of faith in the political system." Cincinnati residents "firmly believe that their own and others' level of trust in the integrity of the political system has been eroded by the amount of money in politics."

• The rising costs of Cincinnati's city council campaigns causes city councilmembers to spend increasing amounts of time raising money for the next election, which interferes with their responsibilities for governing the city. This consequence of unlimited campaign spending further has fueled the erosion of public confidence in Cincinnati in its local election process and in its local government.

• The system of unlimited campaign spending in Cincinnati city council elections has caused a "blackout" phenomenon with respect to television advertising time. The policy of local television broadcasters in Cincinnati is to sell television advertising spots on a first-come, first-served basis. Because there is a limited supply of the most valuable advertising spots available on local television, city council candidates with significant quantities of campaign funds early in a campaign season have been able to pre-empt effectively the right of other, less-well-funded candidates to purchase such advertising time.

• Candidates for Cincinnati city council can run a viable campaign spending less than $140,000, the limit set by Cincinnati's ordinance. Of the nine winning Cincinnati city council candidates in the 1995 elections, four won election spending less than $140,000, including one who spent only $33,000 and a challenger candidate who spent $97,000.

Based on this record, the city argued that its limits were justified by the compelling governmental interest in preventing corruption and the appearance of corruption in the local election process, freeing its elected officials from the pressures of fund raising so as to ensure that they are able to carry out their representative duties without interference, and preventing some city council candidates from blocking other candidates' access to key television advertising time. In opposing the plaintiffs' motion for summary judgment, the city further argued that this factual record was sufficient, at a minimum, to demonstrate new facts and circumstances warranting a trial at which the district court could properly weigh the evidence showing the necessity of the limits.

In April 1998, a three-judge panel of the United States Court of Appeals for the Sixth Circuit affirmed the district court's January 1997 ruling granting the plaintiffs' motion for summary judgment and denying the city its opportunity to prove its case at trial. A majority of the Sixth Circuit panel held that, under *Buckley*, Cincinnati's campaign spending limits were per se unconstitutional regardless of what the record might show about the impact of unlimited campaign spending. The panel further ruled that, were it to consider the factual record, the City had not demonstrated that spending limits were necessary to prevent corruption and the appearance of corruption in the electoral process. The panel held that Cincinnati could not rely on the twenty-two years of federal election experience with contribution limits since *Buckley* to demonstrate that such limits working alone are insufficient to assure the integrity of the electoral process. The majority acknowledged that the time a candidate must spend raising money for her campaign "detracts an officeholder from doing her job," but it nonetheless ruled that the interest in reducing the time elected officials spend on fundraising "cannot serve as a basis for limiting campaign spending."[19]

U.S. District Judge Avern Cohn issued a concurring opinion. While joining the majority's affirmance of the District Court's ruling, Judge Cohn disagreed with the majority's reading of *Buckley* with respect to campaign spending limits: "The Supreme Court's decision in *Buckley* . . . is not a broad pronouncement declaring all campaign expenditure limits unconstitutional. It may be possible to develop a factual record to establish that the interest in freeing officeholders from the pressures of fundraising so they can perform their duties, or the interest in preserving faith in our democracy, is compelling, and that campaign expenditure limits are a narrowly tailored means of serving such an interest."[20]

In September 1998, Cincinnati filed a petition for certiorari before the Supreme Court. In its petition, the city argued that the Sixth Circuit ruling conflicts with *Buckley*. In the alternative, the city argued that, if the Sixth Circuit correctly read *Buckley* to hold all campaign spending limits per se unconstitutional, *Buckley* should now be overruled. The following two sections provide an overview of the city's arguments that its campaign spending limits ordinance was narrowly tailored to serve compelling state interests and thus was consistent with the First Amendment.

The Compelling Governmental Interest in Preventing Corruption and the Appearance of Corruption Justifies Campaign Spending Limits

In *Buckley,* the U.S. Supreme Court upheld congressional limits on campaign contributions in federal elections as justified by the sufficiently important governmental interests of preventing corruption and the appearance of corruption.[21] The *Buckley* Court specifically cited the dangers associated with public perception of corruption, holding that: "Congress could legitimately conclude that the avoidance of the appearance of improper influence 'is also critical . . . if confidence in the system of representative Government is not to be eroded to a disastrous extent.'"[22]

The Court nevertheless rejected the necessity of expenditure limits, expressing its faith, based on the record before it, that the contribution limits alone would be sufficient to address such governmental interests. While the appellate court had ruled that "the expenditure restrictions are necessary to reduce the incentive to circumvent direct contribution limits,"[23] the Supreme Court found: "There is no indication [in the record] that the substantial criminal penalties for violating the contribution ceilings combined with the political repercussion of such violations will be insufficient to police the contribution provisions."[24]

This pivotal passage from *Buckley* unambiguously reveals that a key empirical judgment—drawn from the record—ultimately determined the constitutionality of the congressional campaign spending limits. For what if the record in *Buckley* had established that the "substantial criminal penalties" and the "political repercussion" were not sufficient to "police the contribution provisions"? Clearly, *Buckley* leaves the door open for a different factual record that would justify the need for campaign spending limits. The argument that campaign spending limits are a necessary concomitant to contribution limits was rejected by the *Buckley* Court only as a *matter of fact*.

The Cincinnati record presented new facts and circumstances demonstrating the necessity for campaign spending limits to address the city's interest in preventing corruption and the appearance of corruption in the electoral process. John Deardourff, a public opinion researcher with more than thirty years of experience, documented a pervasive public perception of corruption in Cincinnati with respect to the city council election process. The city demonstrated, through Mr. Deardourff's affidavit, that this crisis in public confidence in Cincinnati with respect to the political system is directly tied to unlimited campaign spending. Cincinnati residents "firmly believe that their own and others' level of trust in the integrity of the political system has been eroded by the amount of money in politics." An overwhelming majority of Cincinnati residents agreed with the statement, "The amount of money in election campaigns has caused me to lose a great deal of faith in the political system." The record in Cincinnati thus demonstrated that public confidence in the system of representative government in Cincinnati has been "eroded to a disastrous extent," and that contribution limits alone were insufficient to address this public perception of corruption.

The city also presented crucial expert testimony that "the rise in the overall cost of city council races *has caused* a rise in the influence of wealthy donors in the City's elections, with such donors increasingly dominating the campaign fundraising process." From 1991 to 1995, one-third of 1 percent of the metropolitan area's population provided more than $3.9 million in campaign contributions to city council candidates, amounting to nearly 70 percent of all the money raised by those candidates. The *Buckley* Court did not hear this type of critical evidence linking unlimited campaign spending with a corresponding rise in the influence of wealthy donors in elections.[25]

Like Cincinnati, the nation as a whole has witnessed the harmful impact of unlimited campaign spending in elections, despite the existence of contribution limits for federal elections. In the twenty-five years since *Buckley,* the federal election experience has demonstrated that contribution limits will not, alone, sufficiently address corruption and the appearance of corruption in the electoral process.

Recent public opinion polls confirm that citizens on all sides of the political spectrum perceive both actual and potential corruption in government under the current system of unlimited campaign spending. Notably, in a 1996 poll taken directly after the November elections, Americans ranked the "power of special interest groups in politics" second only to "international terrorists" when asked to identify "major threats" to the future of the country. The same poll revealed that the percent of people who feel the country is "losing ground" in its effort to fight political corruption has grown steadily over recent years.[26]

In a 1997 survey of the public's views on the impact of money in politics, 66% of respondents deemed the excessive influence of political contributions on elections and government policy a "major problem." Sixty-five percent identified as another "major problem" the conflict of interest that occurs when politicians make decisions about issues of concern to those who fund their campaigns while 71% cited the good people being discouraged from running for office by the high cost of campaigns.[27]

In a February 1997 Gallup poll for CNN–USA Today, 53% of voters said that "campaign contributions influence the policies supported by elected officials" a "great deal." Two months later, a separate poll determined that 75% of Americans believe that "public officials make or change policy decisions as a result of money they receive from major contributors."[28]

Further, in an August 1998 poll of voters in eight states, overwhelming majorities decried actual corruption and expressed desire for systemic reform.[29] A sea change in attitudes has occurred, moreover, as voters now clearly perceive that their own senators are not immune from the corrupting influence of special interest contributions. (Formerly, voters would decry corruption in Congress but disavow the suspicion that their own senators were guilty of ethical lapses.) Between 65% and 75% of voters now believe that campaign contributions affect the votes of their own senators on issues of concern to special interests.

Polling data uniformly demonstrates that the current campaign finance regime has devastated public confidence in government. Contrary to the Court's assurance that "substantial criminal penalties for violating the contribution ceilings" would suffice to "alleviat[e] the corrupting influence of large contributions," the appearance of corruption stemming from public awareness of the opportunities for abuse inherent in the present regime grows apace. A danger the Court identified as a justification for drastic remedial action has been obtained: "confidence in the system of representative government" has been undeniably "eroded to a disastrous extent."[30]

The public's view of the current system, moreover, is not based on imaginary fears. Even officeholders, in their more candid moments, will confirm the stranglehold that money exerts on the political process. U.S. Senator Robert Byrd of West Virginia said in a March 1997 Senate floor speech: "The incessant money chase that permeates every crevice of our political system is like an unending circular marathon. And it is a race that sends a clear message to the people: that it is money, money, money that reigns supreme in American politics."[31] The federal experience teaches that the ingenuity of those who wish to purchase influence in government cannot be squelched by contribution limits alone. Large aggregations of wealth still pour into campaign coffers under practices generally known as bundling. When individuals representing the same corporation, industry or special interest send contributions to a candidate at roughly the same time, they have circumvented the intent of existing contribution limits by bundling together far greater amounts than the law allows. Candidates recognize the actual, unified source of this aggregated largesse and are thus subject to the same "corrupting influence of large contributions" that the Supreme Court reviled.[32]

Typically, a corporation will identify particular candidates and instruct its top brass and employees about where and when to send contributions. Such organized bundling is difficult to monitor because "bundlers" are not required to identify their participation in aggregated donations. By organizing bundles, institutionally related donors evade the important disclosure requirements that apply to PACs, thereby denying the public critical information regarding attempts by special interest groups to affect public policy.

A notable example is MBNA, a Delaware banking and credit card corporation that ranked as the most profligate bundler of individual contributions in the 1994 election cycle and continues to organize substantial bundled donations today. MBNA organized over $868,000 worth of bundled contributions to federal candidates in 1994, with the lion's share, roughly $500,000, going to four senators. Under existing contribution limits, an MBNA PAC would have only been able to donate a total of $30,000 to these four candidates ($5,000 per candidate per primary/election), as only three were contesting a seat. (Alfonse D'Amato was not running for election at the time, but became the chair of the Senate Banking Committee as a result of the Republican shift in 1994.) Through bundling, however, MBNA was able to amplify its message of corporate support by a factor of fifteen.[33]

Sixteen of the top fifty bundlers of contributions to federal candidates in the 1996 election cycle were securities and investment firms. Collectively, the contributions doled out by the employees, officers, and family members connected with these firms totaled over $4,420,000. As a sector, the financial industry remains a dominant source of funding for federal candidates, especially through the evasive technique of bundling.

The authors have received anecdotal accounts of the techniques corporations use to encourage their employees to contribute to the company PAC fund or directly to identified candidates. These techniques include bonuses that reimburse the employee for the contribution or other incentives such as promises to match contributions to the employee's charity of choice. Strong evidence of these kinds of illegal, de facto contributions by corporations can only come from insiders who risk their careers by whistle-blowing.

Conduits are another method of aggregating individual contributions. Individuals, groups, or PACs who collect and deliver contributions as conduits can take credit for (and exert influence by) amassing far more money than the law would allow them to give directly. The Technet PAC collected and delivered to lawmakers at least $180,000 in the 1997–98 elections. An example of their beneficiaries is Senator Spencer Abraham (R-Michigan), sponsor of Technet-backed legislation, for whom $19,500 was collected.

Candidates also effectively solicit bundled contributions by establishing "Leadership PACs"—alter-ego campaign committees that allow donors to double the size of their contributions. Though Leadership PACs may not spend money directly on the sponsoring politician's campaign, they may cover "overhead" and the cost of related political activities (like pollsters and consultants) that contribute indirectly to the sponsor's success. Leadership PACs also collect funds that the sponsor may pass on to support the campaigns of political allies.

The Sixth Circuit majority opinion in *Kruse* asserted that "[t]he problems uncovered on the federal level are explained primarily by the 'soft-money' loophole in contribution restrictions and do not undermine the Supreme Court's conclusion that spending restrictions are not narrowly tailored to addressing the problem of the corrupting nature of money in politics."[34] There was, however, no record evidence supporting the Sixth Circuit's conclusion that the "soft-money" loophole is the only, or even the primary, source of the system's current problems. While soft money contributions have indeed exploded over the last decade, soft money accounted for only 11 percent of the total amount of money spent in the 1996 federal elections.[35] Accordingly, the courts cannot in good faith conclude that the corrupting failures of the present system are attributable to soft money alone and thereby ignore the corrosive effects of bundled contributions.

New Compelling Governmental Interests Justify Campaign Spending Limits

The Court in *Buckley* did not hold that there could never be a new and compelling governmental interest that would justify campaign spending limits. Rather, the Court stated: "No governmental interest *that has been suggested* is sufficient to justify [the congressional campaign spending limits]."[36] The implication is clear. The door remains open to compelling governmental interests that were *not* suggested to the *Buckley* Court. This Court reaffirmed that point in *National Conservative Political Action Committee,* stating that "preventing corruption or the appearance of corruption are the only legitimate and compelling government interests *thus far* identified for restricting campaign finances."[37]

Cincinnati presented two new and compelling governmental interests that justified its campaign spending limits. First, the city has an interest in freeing its elected officials from the pressures of fundraising to ensure that they are able to carry out their representative duties without interference. The increasing amount of time elected officials spend raising money for their campaigns has fueled the erosion of public confidence in the democratic process in Cincinnati. As the city's Campaign Finance Advisory Board found in its final report to the Cincinnati city council, the time candidates spend raising money is directly tied to the rising costs of city council campaigns. Instead of focusing on their responsibilities for governing the city, councilmembers must spend their time chasing the funds they need to compete in an unlimited "arms race" of campaign spending.[38] A regime of unlimited campaign spending has had the same detrimental effect on officeholders' attention to their duties at the federal level.[39] The *Buckley* Court never addressed whether the compelling interest in preserving officeholders' time for carrying out their official duties would justify campaign spending limits, and *Buckley* therefore cannot be read as foreclosing reliance on this interest to support reasonable restrictions on campaign spending.

Cincinnati also presented a new and compelling governmental interest in preventing some city council candidates from blocking other candidates' access to key television advertising time. In Cincinnati, city council candidates with large sums of money early in the election season are able effectively to shut out other candidates from broadcasting their messages on prime-time television in the critical weeks leading to election day—a "blackout" phenomenon. The *Buckley* record did not include this crucial evidence.

As explained in the expert testimony of an advertising executive with twenty-eight years of experience in the creation and production of television advertisements for Cincinnati city council candidates, well-funded candidates engage in media campaigns which "have the effect of preempting the right of other less well-funded candidates from purchasing the most valuable advertising spots." Well-funded candidates in Cincinnati make excessive television advertising purchases at an early point in the campaign so that prime-time advertising is unavailable by the time other candidates have raised sufficient funds to purchase such ads. The city's campaign spending limits provided a means to break up this "effective monopoly on the most valuable advertising time."[40] Under the reasonable spending limits adopted by Cincinnati, candidates would still be able to purchase substantial television advertising time, but would not be able to freeze out similar purchases by other candidates.

The *Buckley* Court did not discuss whether government may act to regulate spending that is strategically designed to *lessen* the amount of information available to voters. State and local governments should be free to protect all candidates' access to the marketplace of ideas by preventing the monopolization of important means of communication. Indeed, in the related First Amendment area of television broadcasting, the Supreme Court recently reaffirmed the governmental interest in promoting the widespread dissemination of information from a multiplicity of sources. In *Turner Broadcasting System, Inc. v. FCC* (1997), the Court upheld the "must carry" provisions of the Cable Television Consumer Protection and Competition Act of 1992, declaring that "Congress has an independent interest in preserving a multiplicity of broadcasters to ensure that all households have access to information and entertainment on an equal footing with those who subscribe to cable." State and local governments surely have at least an equally important interest in preserving candidates' access to a key medium of communication to the voters during a crucial period in the election campaign.[41]

While the Sixth Circuit's majority opinion in *Kruse* rejected the possibility that spending limits could ever be justified by new compelling interests not directly addressed in *Buckley,* Judge Cohn's concurring opinion agreed with the city's contention that *Buckley* did not foreclose that possibility. Judge Cohn wrote: "The Supreme Court's decision in *Buckley* . . . is not a broad pronouncement declaring all campaign expenditure limits unconstitutional. It may be possible to develop a factual record to establish that the interest in freeing officeholders from the pressures of fundraising so they can perform their duties, or the interest in preserving faith in our democracy, is compelling, and that campaign expenditure limits are a narrowly tailored means of serving such an interest."[42] As the first judicial recognition that *Buckley* does not forever foreclose the possibility of placing reasonable limits on campaign spending, Judge Cohn's concurrence represents a substantial development in the legal movement to revisit the question of spending limits.

Avenues for Further Development of Challenges to Buckley

The Supreme Court, by denying Cincinnati's petition for certiorari in November 1998, passed on its first opportunity since *Buckley* to revisit the issue of spending limits. The denial of certiorari in the first case to present the issue, however, does not mean that the door is forever barred, as a number of Supreme Court observers point out.[43] The Court generally moves slowly in revisiting its prior decisions, even those that have received sustained criticism over time. The recent statements of four Supreme Court justices indicating their readiness to revisit the *Buckley* ruling provides ample evidence that the door, in fact, remains open. Reformers must be prepared to sustain a long-term effort to develop favorable cases and to pursue any necessary appeals, so that the Supreme Court will have further opportunities to review the question of spending limits.[44]

In order to maximize the chances of successfully defending spending limits, jurisdictions adopting such limits should pay careful attention to developing the factual record demonstrating why the limits are both reasonable and necessary. It is particularly important that the limits be set at a level that clearly permits candidates to communicate effectively with the electorate and to run viable campaigns, taking into account the costs of media, direct mail, and other campaign costs in the jurisdiction. In Cincinnati, the limit of $140,000 was deemed by the district court to be more than sufficient to run a viable campaign, thus obviating one of the most important potential barriers to the defense of spending limits. While such a finding will not, as *Kruse* demonstrates, necessarily assure final victory in the courts, an unreasonably low limit will almost certainly lead to quick defeat.

The defense of spending limits also requires careful attention to demonstrating that lesser measures, such as contribution limits alone, have been or are likely to be insufficient to curb corruption and the appearance of corruption. If a jurisdiction has had contribution limits in place for a number of years, public opinion polls showing continued pervasive concern about the influence of money on their elected officials will be extremely useful, and perhaps indispensable, in documenting the necessity for more effective measures. Specific instances of influence peddling or evasions of contribution limits, if available, provide additional factual support for spending limits. Careful documentation of the need to preserve officeholders' time from the pressures of fundraising is important, especially in light of Judge Cohn's concurring opinion in *Kruse* finding this interest to be new and compelling. The testimony of candidates, political consultants, and other actors familiar with electoral politics in the jurisdiction is also valuable in documenting why expenditure limits are necessary. Demonstrating that dramatic growth in campaign spending has been accompanied by growing numbers of elections in which no one comes forward to challenge the well-financed incumbent further illustrates the antidemocratic effect of unlimited spending, supporting the need for reform.

Since the conclusion of the *Kruse* case, *Landell v. Sorell* (2000) was decided. The case pertained to the State of Vermont's legislation that enacted campaign spending limits for state elections (which took effect in the 2000 election cycle) and set up a comprehensive system of voluntary public funding for candidates who were running for governor and lieutenant governor. The limits ranged from $300,000 for a challenger in a gubernatorial race to $2,000 for a challenger in a House race. Statewide office incumbents were limited to 85 percent of what challengers may spend, and incumbents in the state legislature were limited to 90 percent of the challenger limits. Vermont's action is significant, because it means that a state legislature placed its weight behind the necessity of spending limits to curb the corrupting influence of money and to assure that elected officials will devote their time to governing rather than fundraising.

Nonetheless in May 1999, the Vermont Right-to-Life Committee challenged Vermont's new reform law, including the provision establishing mandatory spending limits. A second group of plaintiffs represented by the ACLU filed a similar court challenge a few months later. The Vermont Attorney General's Office and a broad coalition of defendant-intervenors represented by the National Voting Rights Institute aggressively defended the new law. Unlike *Buckley* or *Kruse,* in *Landell* the district court reviewed the constitutionality of campaign spending limits with a full factual record developed at trial and upheld most of Vermont's sweeping campaign reform law.[45]

More than two thousand miles away, the City of Albuquerque provides actual history with campaign spending limits. Since 1974, the City of Albuquerque has maintained limits on campaign expenditures for its local elections, making it the only major city in the country with sustained experience with campaign spending limits in operation. In September 1997, a mayoral candidate and three campaign contributors filed suit in state court seeking to strike down the limits on *Buckley* grounds and obtained a preliminary injunction preventing the enforcement of the limits in the October 1997 municipal elections. The city retained the National Voting Rights Institute to defend its limits. In August 1998, the plaintiffs withdrew their complaint, with the unsuccessful mayoral candidate citing his lack of interest in running for local office again. With the limits back in place, the city, with the Institute, is preparing to defend against an anticipated new lawsuit. Albuquerque's unique posture as the only major city with 20 years of real-world experience with spending limits makes it a particularly valuable test case for revisiting *Buckley*. Albuquerque's record shows that spending limits have encouraged electoral competition in city elections, with numerous instances of challengers mounting successful campaigns against incumbents.[46]

RECONSIDERING INTERESTS REJECTED IN *BUCKLEY*

In addition to the new interests presented in *Kruse,* the Court should reconsider certain justifications for campaign spending limits that it summarily dismissed in *Buckley*. Primary among these is the claim that spending limits are necessary to achieve the political equality that is essential to a just democracy and guaranteed to all citizens under the Equal Protection Clause of the Fourteenth Amendment. Two decades of intervening experience since *Buckley,* and parallel developments in political science and philosophy, have clarified the correlation between wealth and disproportionate political power. Though the Court has generally acknowledged "the corrosive and distorting effects of immense aggregations of wealth" as a source of "corruption in the political arena,"[47] it has yet to examine the operation of these effects in detail outside the context of corporate campaign speech. Tenacious researchers have amassed substantial evidence that wealthy interests regularly exert profound influence over legislation and executive policies, often to the detriment of the general public.[48] As noted above, research also indicates that public disaffection with privately financed campaigns grows each year. Advocates of reform should employ this burgeoning data to support renewed legal arguments that spending limits are necessary to protect unwealthy individuals' rights to meaningful political participation in our democracy. Without some guarantee of equal political opportunity, wealth has and will continue to debase our democracy.

Another argument deserving reconsideration is the notion that campaign spending should be viewed as communicative conduct and not as pure speech. When the Court mistook money for speech in *Buckley,* it applied too strict a standard to marginal abridgements of a purported right to spend and mistakenly conferred upon campaign war chests the absolute protection of the First Amendment. Instead, the Court should have analyzed spending limits according to the line of cases that allow partial abridgement of First Amendment rights in the form of time, place, and manner restrictions, or alternatively, as necessary regulation of a scarce communicative resource. In this last vein, advocates should encourage the Court to bring careful scrutiny to the platitudes that suffuse academic and legal discussion of the "free market of ideas." Detailed attention to the actual business of campaigns—the professionalized use of mail targeting, polling, and mass media advertising—will inform a more nuanced understanding of the real market for electoral speech. Competition in this marketplace could then be fruitfully analyzed—and protected—under established principles of antitrust law.

Political Equality

Scholars have criticized many aspects of the Court's muddled analytical framework in *Buckley*. Yet, few phrases in that decision have subdued subsequent prudential and legislative debate more than the Court's famous dictum that "the concept that government may restrict the speech of some elements of our society in order to enhance the relative voice of others is wholly foreign to the First Amendment." A survey of American political philosophy and legal precedent reveal that this claim is overblown, if not, as one scholar observed, "demonstrably incorrect." While the *Buckley* Court chose summarily to subordinate political equality to the First Amendment, many scholars, jurists, and philosophers see political equality as "the cornerstone of American democracy."[49]

Even at a time when the franchise was denied to many citizens, American constitutional thought recognized "establishing a political equality among all" as the primary remedy to political evils.[50] As James Madison famously noted: "Who are to be the electors of the Federal Representatives? Not the rich more than the poor; not the learned more than the ignorant; not the haughty heirs of distinguished names, more than the humble sons of obscure and unpropitious fortune. The electors are to be the great body of the people. . . ."[51]

Modern philosophers place an even higher value on political equality. John Rawls, for instance, recognizes that the "fair opportunity to take part in and to influence the political process" is not merely an aspiration of a just constitutional democracy, but rather a precondition. Noting that "[t]he liberties protected by the principle of participation lose much of their value whenever those who have greater private means are permitted to use their advantages to control the course of public debate," Rawls argues that universal suffrage alone is inadequate to preserve a just system when "the political forum is so constrained by the wishes of the dominant interests that the basic measures needed to establish just constitutional rule are seldom properly presented." A failure to compensate for the disproportionate effects of wealth in politics thus undermines the value of voting.[52]

Recent experience and growing popular sentiment confirm this troubling observation. Indeed, the dominance of wealth in electoral politics diminishes both the practical and the symbolic significance of the franchise. In late 1997, a wealthy international businessman offered staggering and unapologetic testimony to the Senate Governmental Affairs Committee to the effect that he had never registered to vote, preferring instead to purchase executive and legislative support of his agenda through substantial party and candidate donations. His testimony left no doubt that such practices are endemic. Substantial research confirms that the net result of institutionalized influence peddling is special interest legislation that increasingly disfavors whole sectors of society who are unable to make substantial political contributions. As accounts of the actual operation of wealth in politics proliferate, public cynicism about the value of voting grows apace, laying the foundation of a profound constitutional crisis.[53]

The First Amendment cannot protect speech rights to the exclusion of all other values. In numerous contexts, the Court has upheld restrictions on the speech of some elements of society in order to protect other communal interests.[54] The *Buckley* Court's "ritual incantation of the notion of absolute protection" for the quantity as well as the content of political expression cannot be squared with political reality, nor is it supported in theory. Rawls effectively dismisses the Court's First Amendment absolutism by noting that "basic liberties constitute a family, and that it is this family that has priority and not any single liberty itself." "[P]olitical speech," he concludes, "even though it falls under the basic liberty of freedom of thought, must be regulated to insure the fair value of political liberties." Alexander Meiklejohn also recognized that some regulation of political speech in the name of political equality is necessary for the orderly presentation and intelligent deliberation self-government requires. Similarly, Ronald Dworkin deems the *Buckley* dictum rejecting the interest in political equality a "mistake because the most fundamental characterization of democracy—that it provides self-government by the people as a whole—supposes that citizens are equals not only as judges but as participants as well." Dworkin urges that *Buckley* be overruled because its "rigid rule is not just an inconvenience but a serious loss in the quality of the very democracy" that rule supposedly protects. Thus, even as a matter of pure theory, preservation of the conditions under which free speech may take place cannot be wholly foreign to the First Amendment.[55]

This notion is not merely an academic exercise, but has found expression in the courts as well. At the Supreme Court's oral argument in the Missouri campaign contribution limits case in October 1999, Justice Breyer raised the most significant question. He suggested that corruption might be the wrong word and asked why a state cannot say that, in our democracy, "[w]e want to equalize the opportunity. . . ." He discussed this point as "an important constitutional interest on the other side: the constitutional interest in giving everyone in Missouri a more equal chance to participate in this democratic system." Justice Breyer returned to the equality principle in his concurring opinion. "[B]y limiting the size of the largest contributions," he wrote, "such restrictions aim to democratize the influence that money itself may bring to bear upon the electoral process." In support of this statement, Justice Breyer cited *Reynolds v. Sims*, the Court's landmark 1964 ruling articulating, in the context of apportionment, the "one person, one vote" holding. In the *Reynolds* ruling, he reminds us, the Court stated that the Constitution "demands" that each citizen have an "equally effective voice."[56]

Justice Breyer's concurrence in *Nixon v. Shrink* is also significant for its challenge to *Buckley's* famous dictum cited above. "[T]hose words," Justice Breyer wrote, "cannot be taken literally" in that "The Constitution often permits restrictions on the speech of some in order to prevent a few from drowning out the many—in Congress, for example, where constitutionally protected debate, Art. I, §6, is limited to provide every Member an equal opportunity to express his or her views. Or in elections, where the Constitution tolerates numerous restrictions on ballot access, limiting the political rights of some so as to make effective the political rights of the entire electorate."[57]

In his dissent in *First National Bank of Boston v. Bellotti* (1978), Justice Byron White argued that some level of political equalization is in fact *required* by the First Amendment: "The Court's fundamental error is its failure to realize that the state regulatory interests in terms of which the alleged curtailment of First Amendment rights . . . must be evaluated are themselves derived from the First Amendment." In the *First National Bank of Boston v. Bellotti* context—that is, the attempted limitation of corporate spending on ballot initiatives that had no direct effect on the corporation's business—the value of promoting free political debate required the prevention of corporate domination. Justice White recognized that the issue is not whether First Amendment rights may be abridged at all, but instead whether the state has chosen "the best possible balance" between "competing First Amendment interests."[58]

Daniel H. Lowenstein analyzes the issue of political equality by subdividing the issue into two categories: equality of inputs (the idea that each person has an equal right to influence campaign debate—roughly associated with contribution limits); and equality of outputs (the notion that each side of a political debate should have an equal chance to present its case to the public—roughly associated with spending limitations). The former concern primarily values each individual's chance to contribute to debate, while the latter primarily values the electorate's ability to make a fair and intelligent decision. This distinction is useful insofar as it draws separate attention to the rights of the individual and to our collective interest in a functioning democracy. Supreme Court precedents support each of these two interests in a different fashion. *Buckley* and its progeny explicitly condone contribution limits in aid of the equality of inputs. With respect to the latter interest, the more recent campaign finance cases, *FEC v. Massachusetts Citizens for Life (MCFL)* (1986) and *Austin v. Michigan*

State Chamber of Commerce (1990), recognize the potential that large aggrega-tions of wealth may distort the outputs of political process. In other First Amendment contexts, the Court has sought "to secure 'the widest possible dis-semination of information from diverse and antagonistic sources'" and "to as-sure unfettered interchange of ideas for the bringing about of political and so-cial changes desired by the people." Clearly, the Court's First Amendment jurisprudence deems certain speech abridgments instrumental to a functioning democracy.[59]

While the *MCFL* and *Austin* decisions address the speech rights of corpora-tions, the notion that aggregations of wealth can distort the political process implies some baseline of undistorted politics. This would appear to involve the rights of natural persons (as opposed to artificial corporations) to express politi-cal choice through campaign contributions and other activities. If the politics of natural persons can be distorted by aggregations of corporate wealth, how can it not also be distorted by immense aggregations of private wealth? Such distortion would not obtain only if natural persons enjoyed an a priori right to master the public political realm whenever they have means to do so. Taken to the extreme, such an a priori right would obviously destroy democracy. Yet even if the actual operation of wealth in present American politics is less dra-matic than such an extreme scenario, the damage done to the polity is no less troubling. Indeed, as Rawls and Dworkin wonder, how can a democracy long survive political inequality? Such a question need not be answered in the ab-stract when empirical evidence allows us to weigh the damage already done by private wealth against marginal restrictions on speech rights occasioned by re-form.

Indeed, it is crucial to remember that marginal regulation of campaign con-tributions and expenditures does not effect real *equality* in either of the two cat-egories identified by Lowenstein. In the context of contribution limits, one thousand dollars still represents a substantial sum of money. Most working per-sons simply do not have sufficient disposable income to contribute anywhere near the limit, even if they feel tremendous passion about the candidates in question. Accordingly, contribution limits marginally encourage, but do not guarantee, real equality of input in the political system. Similarly, raising the floor through public election financing or capping the ceiling through spend-ing limits will not equalize the output of all political voices. At best, such a regime would prevent certain candidates from monopolizing communications media while giving less wealthy candidates a basic, meaningful opportunity to campaign before the general public.

Creating a ceiling on expenditures does not raise the floor for those whose economic status precludes even the most basic forms of mass political communication. A reform law that employs both spending limits and public financing would more comprehensively serve the interest of political equality. In Vermont, the new spending and public financing regime that is set to take effect in the year 2000 presents just such a test case for the courts, allowing advocates to set forth arguments regarding the factual circumstances and civic interests that justify comprehensive campaign spending limitations. The Vermont legislature specifically found that mandatory spending limits were necessary to protect the viability of the public funding program they had also devised. In contrast, some jurisdictions that provide for elective public funding allow candidates to abandon or supplement the public funding program when an opposition candidate spends beyond certain limits. Such opt-out provisions, of course, may undermine the purpose of public funding statutes by leaving them vulnerable to any nonparticipants who elect to instigate an escalating spending contest. Vermont, by contrast, opted to preempt war chest competition (and its consequent debasement of political discourse) by protecting its public financing statutes with mandatory spending limits. In doing so, Vermont created a regulatory regime that effectively serves the interest of political equality, thereby presenting a test case through which to reevaluate that principle.

The modern Supreme Court's seminal rulings striking down wealth discrimination in the electoral process are rooted in the principle of political equality. In 1966, two years after the Twenty-Fourth Amendment banned poll taxes in federal elections, the Court in *Harper v. Virginia Board of Elections* invalidated a poll tax of $1.50 in Virginia state elections. The Court found that "a State violates the Equal Protection Clause of the Fourteenth Amendment whenever it makes the affluence of the voter or payment of any fee an electoral standard. Voter qualifications have no relation to wealth. . . ."[60]

In *Bullock v. Carter* (1972), the Court again recognized the "real and appreciable impact on the exercise of the franchise" which voters face under a system that excludes them on the basis of their lack of wealth. In *Bullock,* the Court struck down filing fees ranging from $150 to $8,900 that the state of

Texas required primary candidates to pay to their political parties. The Court found that "the very size of the fees imposed under the Texas system [gave] it a patently exclusionary character." The fees violated the equal protection rights of both voters and candidates. Prospective candidates without wealth were precluded from seeking office, and the fees thus limited voters' choices of candidates and burdened less affluent voters more heavily. As the Court noted: "Many potential office seekers lacking both personal wealth and affluent backers are in every practical sense precluded from seeking the nomination of their chosen party, no matter how qualified they might be, and no matter how broad or enthusiastic their popular support."[61] "[W]e would ignore reality," the Court continued, "were we not to recognize that this system falls with unequal weight on voters, as well as candidates, according to their economic status."[62]

In *Lubin v. Panish* (1974) the Court struck down California's $701.60 filing fee for county supervisor elections, ruling that filing fees do not "test the genuineness of a candidacy or the extent of the voter support of an aspirant for public office." "[O]ur tradition," the Court noted, "has been one of hospitality toward all candidates without regard to their economic status."[63]

Many have compared *Buckley* to the notorious pre–New Deal case *Lochner v. New York* (1905), which relied on an idealized notion of the freedom of contract to strike down maximum hour labor laws. As in *Lochner,* the *Buckley* Court relied on idealized notions of a free marketplace of ideas to strike down reasoned attempts to preserve basic democratic values. To persuade the Court that it has erred, advocates must shed light upon the discontinuities between the Court's idealized view of politics and the reality that we have endured over the past twenty years. Defenders of our present plutocratic electoral system elide the substantial relationship between government enforcement of a free market economic regime and the distribution of access to speech in the political arena. Some even resort to a form of latter-day red-baiting by insisting that reformers want government to "enter the business of redistributing both *economic* and *political* power."[64] Aside from such deliberate misrepresentations of the scope and effect of reform proposals, such arguments ignore the fact that economic inequality begets political inequality. Even if one agrees that government should not allocate economic resources in the private realms of property and contract, such a conclusion has no bearing on a government's duty to constitute itself through just electoral procedures, in which each citizen has a meaningful opportunity to participate. Only if one assumes that money is speech does the enforcement of political equality raise *re*-distributive questions. To say that each of us enjoys the right to amass as much wealth as birth, talent, and luck bestow is not to say that we may use that wealth to dominate the process of democratic deliberation.

While spending limits may not necessarily render the voices of all contestants absolutely equal, they nonetheless serve the interest of political equality by making the prospect of political participation more realistic for a greater number of citizens. This compelling rationale alone offers ample justification for their adoption. By broadening access to the marketplace of ideas, spending limits not only ameliorate the present state of political inequality but also enrich the diversity and depth of civic discourse. As set forth below in the following section, such an understanding of spending limits is in concordance with established First Amendment doctrine regarding the protection of key political processes through carefully tailored regulation.

Money and Speech

To one scholar, the Court's analyses of the First Amendment interests at stake in campaign finance cases, taken together, form a "patternless mosaic" of inconsistent, and even contradictory, principles. When viewed through the lens of other First Amendment jurisprudence, the campaign finance cases seem all the more absurd. While the Court has allowed municipalities to absolutely ban political speech in certain public arenas, based entirely on "esthetic" concerns about "visual clutter," it has steadfastly rejected partial limitations on political speech represented by campaign finance reform that are justified by a profound concern for the continued survival of our democracy.[65]

The central obstacle to regulation of campaign spending is the Court's widely criticized equation of money and speech. The objections to this equation are legion, and will not be rehearsed here. It suffices to note that the *Buckley* decision equivocates on this very point. The Court approved contribution limits on the theory that a contribution "serves as a general expression of support for the candidate and his views, but does not communicate the underlying basis for support." Hence, the "quantity of communication does not increase perceptibly with the size of his contribution."[66] If money is, in fact, meaningful speech, this cannot be true: a contribution of one dollar must mean something different from a contribution of a million. Conversely, under the Court's rejection of spending limits, spending ten million dollars to repeat a television ad ten thousand times must mean something significantly different from running that same ad one hundred times—an extremely doubtful proposition. Clearly, the correlation between spending and speech is not absolute. Within certain limits, spending arguably bears a high correlation with meaningful speech (e.g., running an ad enough to achieve a basic saturation, quantifiable as a gross market share rating); but beyond such limits, spending takes on the attributes of conduct, as in Cincinnati, where better-financed candidates purchased all available advertising space well in advance of the election season, effectively preventing opposition candidates from using the medium of television themselves.

Of pressing concern to the reform advocate is the challenge of lending empirical support to the notion that campaign spending cannot be deemed pure speech. Any empirical data tending to rebut the alleged correspondence of spending to ideas will bolster the argument that campaign spending is properly understood as a form of conduct related to speech. Studies analyzing the content (or lack thereof) as well as the effect of repetition in political advertising could prove helpful in this regard. Such data, in turn, will allow advocates to urge courts to apply the more flexible First Amendment analysis applicable to speech-related conduct outlined in *United States v. O'Brien* (1968).[67]

In a related vein, advocates should challenge the *Buckley* Court's decision that spending limitations cannot be sustained as reasonable time, place, and manner regulations which do not discriminate among speakers or ideas. This analysis was rejected by the Court because "expenditure limitations impose direct quantity on political communication and association." The *Buckley* Court assumed that more spending must mean more speech, that is, more substantive contribution to issues of public concern. "A restriction on the amount of money a person or group can spend on political communication during a campaign necessarily reduces the quantity of expression by restricting the number of issues discussed, the depth of their exploration, and the size of the audience reached."[68] This statement, however, does not bear up well when examined under the light of experience. Political campaigns are dominated by thirty- and sixty-second television ads that contain a negligible amount of reliable information and typically involve either oversimplified vitriol concerning the opponent's failings or an anodyne montage associating the candidate with sunrises and smiling babies. More critically, as Ronald Dworkin argues, repetition, the hallmark of television ad campaigns, does not improve collective knowledge on issues of public import. As Judge J. Skelly Wright observed, "[m]oney may register intensities . . . but money by itself communicates no ideas."[69]

More and more scholarship is available assessing the level of content (and accuracy) in political advertising. Studies can be and are conducted measuring the public's substantive understanding of critical issues and the sources of public opinion. Empirical comparisons of the level of political discourse in different jurisdictions could prove very helpful. For instance, empirical studies tracking the experience of Albuquerque, New Mexico, which has operated its municipal elections for the past two decades under a spending limitation regime, and another comparable city operating without such limits would either support or debunk the Court's prognostications about the evils of spending limits. Anecdotal reports from Albuquerque, and the corresponding high rates of voter turnout there, suggest that spending limits both increase voter confidence in the political system and improve the quality of political debate. Reform advocates and legislators need to commission and rely upon such studies when preparing to justify spending limitations in court.

The most forceful analogy in the line of cases dealing with time, place, and manner restrictions is the truck-mounted loudspeaker at issue in *Kovacs v. Cooper* (1949). There, the Court upheld an ordinance prohibiting the use of loud and raucous loudspeakers to broadcast messages on city streets. While the decibel limits in *Kovacs* were upheld on account of the nuisance they created, spending limits serve a far more critical interest. The *Buckley* Court distinguished *Kovacs* and other time, place, and manner restrictions in an unconvincing manner, noting that "expenditure limitations impose direct quantity restrictions on political communication and association." As Judge Skelly Wright observed, this distinction does not bear up well under scrutiny, as the time, place, and manner regulations can also be seen as quantity restrictions on speech. In the *Kovacs* context, muted loudspeakers would reach a far more limited number of citizens.[70]

Finally, limitations on spending, of course, do not limit the amount of campaign speech a candidate may utter. Nothing in a spending limit regime prohibits adherents of a political movement or supporters of a candidate from volunteering their time and energy to engage in more direct, personal forms of political communication. The great traditional means of promoting public discussion, the face-to-face contact by candidates and their activists, is not affected by spending limitations.

Reasonable Regulation of a Limited Resource: The Marketplace of Ideas

Traditional First Amendment discussions often begin by allusion to the inviolable right of citizens to assemble in public parks to speak their minds. But the park analogy does not reflect the reality of political communication in the modern era. Reconciling this inexact analogy with the existing system of unequal access to the dominant media of mass communication would entail certain grim realizations: the "park" is actually owned by (regulated) private companies who charge a fee for those who wish to mount their soapbox. Furthermore, to the extent that the poor may enter the park to speak, they may place their soapboxes only in the marshy swamps where the public rarely strays. Their voices fail to reach those gathered, of necessity, in the well-traveled pathways. The din of wealthy men with bullhorns and amplifiers drowns out all hope of effective communication with the public at large.

With these images in mind, it is incumbent on those who seek reform in the courts to demonstrate empirically that the media used in political speech are in fact limited. For example, in *Kruse*, the City of Cincinnati assembled data to support the argument that television advertising space in city elections is subject to a "blackout effect." It is critical to note in this regard that the limited resource in question is in fact the access to viewers and not to air time. Theoretically, with the advent of digital transmission and cable services, there is an immense capacity for transmitting multiple channels into households. But as every advertising consultant knows, the critical determinant of the value of an advertising spot is the ratings share of the program it accompanies. There are a finite number of households with televisions and the value of a given advertisement spot is determined by the proportional share of total households tuned into a broadcast at a given time. Network sales agents and advertisers rely upon the scientific quantification of viewership provided by independent rating services like the Nielsen Service when negotiating the price of different spots. Free market idealists would deny that there exist meaningful limits to communicative resources on the naive assumption that demand for the public's attention will always engender new supply. This premise, however, is flatly contradicted by the market data used in the real world to assign value to the limited space available for televised political speech.[71]

The Court made clear in *Red Lion Broadcast Co. v. Federal Communications Commission* (1969) that, when a medium of communication is limited, the government cannot help but abridge the speech rights of some to allow effective communication in that medium to take place. In *Red Lion,* the Court unanimously upheld the FCC's fairness doctrine, noting that "[t]he right of free speech of a broadcaster, the user of a sound truck, or any other individual does not embrace a right to snuff out the free speech of others." Drawing on the public's interest in receiving a diversity of viewpoints, the Court held that "[b]ecause of the scarcity of radio frequencies, the Government is permitted to put restraints on licensees in favor of others whose views should be expressed in this unique medium." Clearly, the abridgements of free speech rights approved in *Red Lion* (the denial of broadcast licenses) are more extreme and profound than those incidental to campaign spending limitations. When the state allocates broadcast licenses to a special minority of applicants, "the rest must be barred from the airwaves." "[T]o deny a station license because 'the public interest' requires it 'is not a denial of free speech'." Analogously, the question is not whether the state can properly limit the amount of spending on campaigns, but rather how the state can preserve the rights of all classes in society to participate in self-government. If, as the Court stated in *Red Lion,* "the right of the public to receive suitable access to social, political, esthetic, moral and other ideas . . . may not constitutionally be abridged . . . by Congress," then surely it may not be abridged by a wealthy minority who exercises economic control over the means of mass communication.[72]

In a *Buckley* footnote, the Supreme Court offered a baffling evasion of the necessary abridgment principle set forth in *Red Lion.* The Court acknowledged that *Red Lion* "makes clear that the broadcast media pose unique and special problems not present in the traditional free speech case," but insisted that the question of FECA's validity amounted to nothing but a "traditional free speech case."[73] As noted above, advocates must persuade the Court that, given that broadcast media comprise the dominant, if not exclusive, forum for political speech, spending limits involve the very same principles announced in *Red Lion.* Modern politics is no longer a competition of voices in a public park; rather, it has become a competition of wealthy interests to monopolize the privately owned airwaves of communication.

Antitrust law also recognizes that markets cease to function efficiently when dominated by firms with inordinate market share. Innovation and accountability disappear when the price of entry for new competitors becomes too large. In *Turner Broadcasting System, Inc. v. Federal Communications Commission* (1997), the Court has unequivocally established that "promoting fair competition is a legitimate and substantial Government goal." There, four justices concluded that the must carry provisions of the Cable Act of 1992, which undeniably burdened the First Amendment rights of cable operators, were in part justified by the deleterious effect that an absence of such provisions would have on the economic survival of local broadcast stations. The Supreme Court also reaffirmed the governmental interest of promoting the widespread dissemination of information from a multiplicity of sources. In the area of elections, citizens surely have at least an equally important interest in preserving candidates' access to a key medium of communication to the voters during a crucial period in the election campaign.[74]

As with arguments concerning political equality, advocates must address both the theoretical and empirical errors in the Court's assumptions about access to and competition within the marketplace of ideas. A basic tenet of the moral justification for free markets, as identified by its proponents from Adam Smith through Milton Friedman, is the equality of opportunity (as distinguished from equality of outcomes). When, however, money is mistaken for speech, relative poverty becomes a very real and quantifiable barrier to entry in civic discourse. Once one acknowledges that ideas are the only acceptable specie in the marketplace of ideas, one must accept equality of access to the arena of political debate as the sine qua non of a morally justifiable constitutional system. Advocates must marshal such arguments, armed with empirical data about the actual operation of political speech in specific media, to persuade the Court to abandon its staunch, formalistic opposition to campaign spending limits.

CONCLUSION

As *Nixon v. Shrink Missouri Government PAC* (2000) makes plain, the ground is shifting on the relationship between the Constitution and the power of money politics.[75] With four justices now on record stating that *Buckley* may need to be revisited on the spending limits question and three justices remaining silent on that issue, the Supreme Court's door remains clearly open for a new test case. Advocates of reform should view this movement on the Court as an opportunity to proffer new evidence and analyses that challenge the long-held misconceptions about our political reality.

The law is fond of analogy, not only for its rhetorical heft, but also for its power of elucidation. In *Buckley,* the Supreme Court resorted to analogy to justify its absolute rejection of limits on campaign expenditures, likening such limits to a deprivation of fuel for a car: "Being free to engage in unlimited political expression subject to a ceiling on expenditures is like being free to drive an automobile as far and as often as one desires on a single tank of gasoline."[76] This casual metaphor deserves scrutiny, as it both reveals and obscures crucial aspects of the present unjust system of political participation.

The misconceived car trope rests upon a host of assumptions that are entirely in conflict with political reality. What makes our present electoral system so tragic a violation of the constitution's promise of equal protection is the fact that the vast majority of Americans cannot afford a go-cart, much less a car, nor can they pay the tolls to access the highways of public discourse. And for those who can scrape up enough cash to ride the roads of civic debate, the political highway is already jammed by the thundering semis and sport-utility vehicles of the wealthy. The Court's metaphor perhaps unintentionally concedes the two essential features of the present political landscape: (1) the limited resource of communicative "space"; and (2) the wealth barrier to entry.

The Court has invited proponents of campaign finance reform to prove that change is necessary. In *Bellotti,* the Court noted that if the case for reform "were supported by record or legislative findings that corporate advocacy threatened imminently to undermine democratic processes," it would merit consideration as a compelling interest justifying government regulation of campaign spending.[77] As canvassed above, the evidence is available; indeed, it has become difficult to ignore. Reform advocates must be prepared to support state legislatures and city councils that have the foresight to make the case for reasonable expenditure limits and the political courage to defend such limits in the face of court challenges. Through such efforts, we can hope that *Buckley's* conflation of money with speech will eventually join the constitutional curiosity shop on the shelf next to poll taxes and literacy tests.

CHAPTER 4

Dollars and Sense

In Praise of *Buckley v. Valeo*

Joel M. Gora

FEW SUPREME COURT DECISIONS that protected individual rights have received the kind of mixed reviews given to *Buckley v. Valeo* (1976).[1] Indeed, some academics have put the case on their list of the ten worst decisions of the twentieth century.[2] In my opinion, the academic pundits are dead wrong in rating the *Buckley* decision so poorly. The *Buckley* decision, far from being a derelict ruling or a jurisprudential outcast, was a landmark of political freedom, a ruling which carefully and conscientiously addressed the critical issues of campaign finance controls and free speech rights which still bedevil the nation today. Though not without considerable flaws, the decision stands as a beacon illuminating the view of First Amendment freedoms and political liberty that informed Supreme Court jurisprudence in the second half of the twentieth century. Compared to the limits-driven repressive regime of government command and control of the political process embodied in the Federal Election Campaign Act, the vision of the *Buckley* opinion seeks to put as much control of the funding of the political process as possible into the hands of the people, not the government.

THE CORE OF THE FIRST AMENDMENT

Because of the efforts to demonize the *Buckley* ruling and the repeated rhetoric about how our campaign finance system is corrupting the country and undermining democracy, it is important to remember that campaign finance laws operate in an area of the most fundamental First Amendment concern: they regulate and restrain speech about government and politics. In a ruling in 1995 involving regulation of campaign literature, the Court reminded us of the dangers arising when government attempts to regulate and control political speech, which, "... as we have explained on many prior occasions . . . occupies the core of the protection afforded by the First Amendment. . . ."³ Quoting at length and with approval from *Buckley,* the Court explained why this is so:

Discussion of public issues and debate on the qualifications of candidates are integral to the operation of the system of government established by our Constitution. The First Amendment affords the broadest protection to such political expression in order 'to assure [the] unfettered interchange of ideas for the bringing about of political and social changes desired by the people. . . .' Although First Amendment protections are not confined to 'the exposition of ideas' . . . 'there is practically universal agreement that a major purpose of that Amendment was to protect the free discussion of governmental affairs, . . . of course including discussions of candidates. . . .' This no more than reflects our 'profound national commitment to the principle that debate on public issues should be uninhibited, robust, and wide-open. In a republic where the people are sovereign, the ability of the citizenry to make informed choices among candidates for office is essential, for the identities of those who are elected will inevitably shape the course that we follow as a nation.' '[I]t . . .can hardly be doubted that the constitutional guarantee has its fullest and most urgent application precisely to the conduct of campaigns for political office.'⁴

That is why, the Court concluded, as it had in cases from *Buckley* on, that laws regulating and burdening "core political speech," like a campaign leaflet, or the funding of political speech must be subject to the most "exacting scrutiny."⁵

THE FIRST VICTIMS OF CAMPAIGN FINANCE REFORM

Even before *Buckley,* the civil liberties community and the courts began to encounter the difficulty of reconciling campaign finance controls with First Amendment rights. The first significant case arose when three old-time dissenters came into the offices of the ACLU in the spring of 1972 with what seemed an incredible story. In late May of that year, they had sponsored a two-page ad in the *New York Times* advocating the impeachment of President Richard Nixon for bombing Cambodia and praising the handful of members of Congress who had voted against the bombing. The United States Justice Department hauled the group into federal court, demanded to know how they were organized and who had paid for the ad, threatened the group with injunctions for what they had done and told them they could not engage in further political speech of that nature unless they filed reports and disclosures with the government and otherwise complied with a wide variety of rules and regulations.[6] This was all for sponsoring an issue advertisement publicly criticizing the president of the United States.

Such a consequence seemed particularly paradoxical, because this was at a time when First Amendment case law had developed its most rigorous protection of citizen criticism of government officials and policies.[7] How, in the face of that law, could the government file a lawsuit to suppress that very same citizen criticism of government?

The answer, of course, was campaign finance reform. The government was suing under the brand new Federal Election Campaign Act of 1971.[8] The government's theory was that the two-page ad—even though it spoke solely about issues—mentioned, criticized, or praised people who were candidates for election that year and that this might affect public opinion, which, in turn, might somehow influence the outcome of the federal elections. Accordingly, this rendered this ad hoc group a "political committee," which had to file reports with the government and disclose their contributors and supporters, and, if they failed to do so, they would be enjoined from further political speech until they complied.

In addition, to the extent that the advertisement could be interpreted as "on behalf of" those political figures who were praised and/or "in derogation of" those officials who were criticized, not only did such content render the group a regulatable political committee, but the act and implementing regulations imposed new controls on the placement of such messages in the news media. The rationale of the provision was to enforce a new statutory ceiling on communication media expenditures by federal candidates. But the effect of the rules was that newspapers, magazines, electronic broadcasters, and virtually any other medium of mass communication could not even accept for publication political communication from independent citizens unless proper certifications had been provided by the candidates who benefited from the message, either because they were praised or because their opponents were criticized. For any news medium to run such advertisements without proper certification— which as a practical matter would be impossible to obtain—would constitute a criminal offense by the news medium. A harsher example of a system of prior restraint could hardly be imagined.[9]

In one sense, though, the government was right. Speech like that might influence people's opinions about members of Congress, incumbent politicians, or the president of the United States and influence their vote at the polls and, ultimately, the outcome of the election. And if one is serious about regulating the sources of campaign funding, then issue ads cannot be allowed to slip by. The anti-Nixon impeachment advertisement cost $18,000. Adjusted for inflation, that would be about $50,000 today. That is serious money. So if we are to be serious about controlling political funding and limiting those who do too much of it, or leveling the playing field, or guarding against people using money to buy access and influence, then we had better be prepared to face the prospect of going after people like the ad hoc impeachment group with injunctions and fines and maybe even criminal penalties for pooling their resources and speaking out on the public issues of the day and the public officials involved in those issues.

And if all that has a familiar ring to it, and sounds, in the words of that great modern philosopher, Yogi Berra, "like deja vu all over again," it is because legislative proposals on the front burner today—most notably the McCain-Feingold bill in the United States Senate and the Shays-Meehan bill which passed the House during the summer of 1998—would achieve virtually the same kinds of controls on political speech that were at issue and were rejected twenty-five years ago in the impeachment ad case.[10]

That impeachment advertisement case was a wake-up call to the ferocious First Amendment problems that campaign finance laws could pose. Now, several years later, the issues of money, politics, free speech, and, indeed, democracy itself, remain very much the same.

But that is getting a little bit ahead of the story.

In the 1972 impeachment ad case, the court ruled that campaign finance laws could not be used against nonpartisan, issue-oriented groups engaged in public commentary about the political issues of the day and the public officials involved in those issues. Another prominent court came to a similar conclusion one year later and invalidated the application of the relevant provisions of the Federal Election Campaign Act to groups like the ACLU, whose "major purpose" was the discussion of public issues, not the election of political candidates.[11]

REFORM RUN RIOT

Within a year of the 1972 case, we had Watergate revelations of campaign funding excesses, and even though much of that occurred before effective disclosure went into effect, Congress was stampeded into enacting the sweeping 1974 restrictions on political activity that would give rise to the constitutional challenge in *Buckley v. Valeo*. In an atmosphere filled with the same kind of rhetoric that we hear today about how money is corrupting politics and destroying democracy, Congress passed a law that was the archetype of government control of political funding and therefore of political speech, association and communication. That would result ultimately in government control of democracy itself, because, as the Supreme Court has told us time and again, freedom of political speech is the engine of democracy: ". . . speech concerning public affairs is more than self-expression; it is the essence of self-government."[12]

The Federal Election Campaign Act Amendments of 1974 severely restricted candidates, campaigns, contributors, independent political groups, and even nonpartisan issue groups like the ACLU, which had just been assured by the courts that their advocacy would be free of official restraint. Enforcement of these new restrictions was placed in the hands of a commission completely dominated and controlled by the House and Senate—a cynical breach of traditional separation of powers principles that the *Buckley* Court would soon declare invalid.[13] Specifically:

1. The act severely restricted a candidate's overall campaign expenditures, even if the funding all came from small contributions. Even many *Buckley* critics might concede that the spending limits in the act were unconscionably low and incumbent-protective.[14] The spending limit for House races was $70,000, an extremely low figure even by 1974 standards, and an amount less than the amount that House members spent on average on the free mail frank and constituent services.

2. The act severely limited the amount of money candidates could contribute to their own campaigns, even though candidates could not possibly corrupt themselves. Had they used their money to run for the White House, Ross Perot and Steve Forbes would have wound up in the Big House.

3. Perhaps even worse, independent speakers were all but completely silenced by the new law which placed a ceiling of $1,000 on how much any per-

son could spend on what we now call "independent expenditures." That was about the cost of a one-quarter-page ad in the *New York Times,* criticizing or praising the president of the United States. Spend a dime more on political speech and your free speech would become a felony. This extraordinary and unprecedented restriction was justified as a "loophole-closing device" which would prevent political supporters who could no longer make large contributions directly to candidates from making large independent expenditures instead. Of course, the loophole being closed was essentially the First Amendment itself and its guarantee of no congressional abridgements of the freedom of speech. Only Justice Byron White would have sustained this remarkable provision. Today, $1,000 would barely buy a tombstone ad on the front page of the *New York Times.* Had this provision been sustained and unchanged, it would effectively have eliminated the use of editorial advertisements by citizens to criticize incumbent officials and political candidates.

4. Make the smallest of campaign donations and you would get your name and political affiliation publicly disclosed or kept on file with the government.[15] Even controversial and minor and third parties that the government spent a lot of time and money spying on would have to disclose their most modest contributors, although that might subject such individuals to harassment and retaliation.[16]

5. All the issue-oriented groups that report and comment on the records of incumbents up for reelection would likewise have to file reports with the government disclosing their contributors and supporters. Indeed, the sweeping reforms included one provision specifically targeted on issue advocacy groups that rate and provide "box scores" about how members of Congress vote on issues of concern to the individual groups.[17] Challenged along with the other key provisions of the act, that section was unanimously declared unconstitutional by a D.C. Circuit court which was enthralled by every other significant feature of the law. Only that section drew the complete condemnation of judges spanning the ideological spectrum from David Bazelon and J. Skelly Wright to Edward Tamm and Malcolm Wilkey. The en banc D.C. Circuit unanimously ruled the provision defectively vague and overbroad for seeking to regulate core and vital issue speech unconnected to the specific cause of any candidate.[18] It was an impermissible restriction of citizen and organizational speech about important public issues. The government did not take an appeal

from that ruling and the section was allowed to die, only to see attempts at resurrection in recent years.[19]

But otherwise, the lower court upheld the major features of the new act. How could this sweeping monitoring and control of political speech and activity possibly be called reform? Especially since, as wide-ranging as the law was in terms of the political activity it sought to control, it was no less cynical in what it exempted from those controls. The most outrageous exemption was for the costs of free franked mail, which by itself gave incumbent House members more money to spend on political communication with their constituents than the *whole* amount that a challenger was allowed to spend on his or her entire campaign under the new spending limits. How does that create a level playing field?

To groups like the ACLU, these did not seem to be genuine reforms that would expand political participation and opportunity. Rather, they seemed more to be an unprecedented Incumbent Protection Act. They would suppress the individual and group political advocacy which is at "the core of our electoral process *and* of the First Amendment freedoms"[20] and which is the very engine of democracy. That is why House Minority Leader Dick Gephardt could not have been more wrong when he insisted that "What we have is two important values in direct conflict: freedom of speech and our desire for healthy campaigns in a healthy democracy. You *can't* have both."[21] In fact, and in law, there cannot be one without the other.

REASON REIGNS

That was the statutory scheme that the Court had before it in *Buckley,* which has been severely criticized and even demonized. While certainly not without its flaws, the decision, properly considered, is a landmark of political freedom.[22] The Court correctly recognized that limitations on political funding are limitations on political speech and thereby threaten well-established principles at the core of the First Amendment's protection.

In response to the argument that money is not speech, the Court quite sensibly responded that limitations on how much one could spend to speak were limitations on how much one could speak. Whether the subject is funding for political speech or funding for the arts or funding for abortion counseling or funding for legal services programs, or funding for campaign finance reform advocacy, there is an obvious and inextricable link between restrictions on funding and restrictions on speech, and the *Buckley* Court soundly recognized that "A restriction on the amount of money a person or group can spend on political communication during a campaign necessarily reduces the quantity of expression by restricting the number of issues discussed, the depth of their exploration, and the size of the audience reached."[23] Indeed, in cases both before and after *Buckley,* the Court has consistently understood that efforts to restrain the funding of speech are tantamount to efforts to restrain the speech itself and has applied the *Buckley* principles to invalidate such schemes.[24] Such rulings were particularly appropriate since the restrictions in *Buckley* and similar cases were on the use of private funds and resources to communicate private political messages, not on the use of *public* funds to facilitate those messages.[25]

In response to the claim, relentlessly repeated today, that there is too much campaign spending and that it must be controlled by government, the Court responded that the First Amendment fundamentally denies government the right to make that choice: "The First Amendment denies government the power to determine that spending to promote one's political views is wasteful, excessive, or unwise. In the free society ordained by our Constitution, it is not the government but the people—individually as citizens and candidates and collectively as associations and political committees—who must retain control over the quantity and range of debate on public issues in a political campaign."[26] Who would quarrel with that principle?

In response to the suggestion that the free speech of those with more resources should be restrained in order to enhance the political opportunity of those with less resources—a kind of First Amendment lowest common denominator, a principle for leveling down freedom of speech—the Court responded: "The concept that government may restrict the speech of some elements of our society in order to enhance the relative voice of others is wholly foreign to the First Amendment, which was designed to secure the widest possible dissemination of information from diverse and antagonistic sources *and to assure unfettered exchange of ideas for the bringing about of political and societal changes desired by the people."* That too embodies settled doctrine. *Buckley* critics often stress the first part of this quote, to create the impression that the decision is some kind of royalist ruling, while underplaying the second portion of the quote, which makes it clear that the evil of restricting some speakers is the consequent restraint on public discussion and the instrumental role of freedom of speech and press.

Finally, in answering the claim that issue-oriented speech about incumbent politicians must be regulated because it might influence public opinion and thereby affect the outcome of elections, the Court, with great force, reminded us of the critical relationship between unfettered issue advocacy and healthy democracy. "Discussion of public issues and debate on the qualifications of candidates are integral to the operation of the system of government established by our Constitution." And with equal clarity, the Court observed that in an election season one cannot abstractly discuss issues without discussing the candidates and their stands on those issues. "The distinction between discussion of issues and candidates and advocacy of election or defeat of candidates may often dissolve in practical application. Candidates, especially incumbents, are intimately tied to public issues involving legislative proposals and governmental actions. Not only do candidates campaign on the basis of their positions on various public issues, but campaigns themselves generate issues of public interest." If any reference to a candidate in the context of advocacy on an issue rendered the speaker or the speech subject to campaign finance controls, the consequences for First Amendment rights would be intolerable.

Accordingly, in order to protect First Amendment rights, the Court fashioned the critical "express advocacy" requirement, which holds that only the funding of express advocacy of electoral outcomes may be subject to restraint. All speech which does not in express terms advocate the election or defeat of a clearly identified candidate must remain totally free of any regulation: "So long as persons and groups eschew expenditures that in express terms advocate the election or defeat of a clearly identified candidate, *they are free to spend as much as they want to promote the candidate and his views.*" The Court thus reaffirmed two principles which are critical to today's debate over campaign finance regulation: (1) the area in which campaign finance controls may operate has to be narrowly and carefully and clearly defined; and (2) outside of such area of permissible regulation, no, to repeat, no controls are allowable. These principles, which seem almost self-evident, are nonetheless once again threatened by legislative proposals like McCain-Feingold and Shays-Meehan pending in Washington and in many states.

The *Buckley* Court invoked those principles to strike down congressional ceilings on the amount of campaign expenditures that could be made by candidates, their campaigns, independent groups, and individual citizens. First Amendment rights were vindicated.

COMPROMISE CONTROLS

Those portions of *Buckley* which struck limits on campaign funding vindicated core First Amendment rights in ways that justify praise and certainly do not merit the condemnation that *Buckley* routinely receives. But other parts of the Court's decision bear the hallmark of judicial compromise and have created a regime of partial regulation which has become the epitome of unintended and undesirable consequences.

First, while striking down limits on expenditures by candidates, political committees, or individuals, the Court reversed field and upheld limits on contributions by individuals to political candidates and campaign committees. The Court did so because of its sense that restraints on contributions were less severe than those on expenditures, while more directly implicating concerns with the actual, potential, or apparent corrupting effect of "large" contributions on political candidates who are and/or will become public officials. Though noting that the "Act's contributions and expenditure limitations operate in an area of the most fundamental First Amendment activities," the Court nonetheless concluded that limits on campaign contributions are somehow "lesser" restraints because contributions are one step removed from speech compared to expenditures, the amount of a contribution does not add appreciably to the message of support it embodies and contributors are free to spend unlimited amounts to promote their chosen candidate or cause directly and independently. With respect to corruption, the Court stated that: "It is unnecessary to look beyond the Act's primary purpose—to limit the actuality and appearance of corruption resulting from large individual financial contributions—in order to find a constitutionally sufficient justification for the $1,000 contribution limitation. [T]o the extent that large contributions are given to secure political quid pro quos from current and potential officeholders, the integrity of our system of representative democracy is undermined."[27]

The Court's upholding of contribution limits gave insufficient weight to a number of critical arguments pressed by the challengers. First, a restraint on contributions would become a de facto restraint on expenditures, especially for those candidates who are not well-connected or well-heeled. The primary beneficiaries of the upholding of contribution limits have been personally wealthy candidates who do not need the kindness of strangers and incumbents who have more than enough "friends" or groups of friends, that is PACs, to help fund them. That is one reason why incumbency rates have remained extremely high.

Second, unless adjusted for inflation—which they have not been—those contributions limits make it harder and harder for candidates, especially challengers, to raise funds to get their message out. Indeed, a number of lower courts have recently invalidated "reform" enactments that lowered contributions limits to levels as low as $250 or even $100, reasoning that such draconian restraints made it all but impossible for unwealthy candidates to raise funds for their campaigns.[28] One court even held that a $1,075 contribution limit—the basic amount sustained in *Buckley*—failed to survive strict scrutiny where it was set at such a low level (equivalent today to $320) that it bore no rational relationship to deterring corruption, especially where the limits were put into place in the absence of any record of corruption remotely comparable to that presented in *Buckley*.[29]

Third, the challengers claimed that the tight controls over contributions would cause campaign funding to flow to areas of political communication which were not subject to those restraints, most notably, issue advocacy and political party activity funded by soft money, which is funding precisely not limited to $1,000 from individuals. The Court seemed unmoved by these concerns. But the phenomena of issue advocacy and soft money, and proposals to control both, have dominated campaign finance debate and proposals in recent years.

Finally, the Court gave insufficient attention to the argument that there were less drastic alternatives to deal with the actuality and potential of corruption than the problematic use of contribution limits. The major suggestion was the use of effective disclosure of large contributions to candidates and campaign committees so that the public would have the means to ferret out whatever undue access and influence might possibly be accorded to campaign contributors. But the Court concluded that full disclosure, coupled with laws against bribery and conflict of interest and the activities of a vigorous free press, was an insufficient inoculation or antidote to corruption or the appearance of corruption.[30]

Unfortunately, in the 1999–2000 term the Court reaffirmed *Buckley*'s approach to contribution limits by upholding a $1,075 Missouri contribution cap for statewide races. The case was *Nixon v. Shrink Missouri Government PAC,*[31] and a lower federal court had ruled that limit unconstitutional. The Court reversed, reasoning that the concern with corruption and the appearance of corruption were still important government concerns that were directly addressed by contribution limits. They rejected the arguments that corruption and influence were better addressed through disclosure and that the low contribution limits in Missouri could unduly shift political campaign activity. Thus, the *Shrink Missouri Government PAC* decision leaves the campaign finance landscape looking like it has for the past twenty-five years.

Significantly, the *Buckley* Court also sustained a scheme of public funding for presidential candidates. That, too, has been a mixed blessing. Of course, public funding can be an important antidote to concerns about corruption from private contributions, and the proper kind of public funding can expand the spectrum of political participation and opportunity in a very meaningful way. The Court recognized that potential, but the scheme it upheld contained two serious flaws.

First, the funding arrangement is basically designed to benefit the two major political parties and their candidates, with a premium on past electoral success as a measure of current public benefit. Minor parties and new candidates basically need not apply for preelection funding. The Court sustained this scheme against an equal protection challenge.[32] Second, the funding arrangement requires eligible candidates to limit their overall and state-by-state expenditures in order to get primary matching funds. In order to get general election funds, presidential candidates have to agree not to raise or spend even one dollar of private money for direct campaign activities.

That stipulation, in turn, has had two consequences. First, it has legitimized, without serious consideration, a form of "unconstitutional conditions" whereby candidates must give up all rights to raise and spend private funds in order to receive public campaign funds. This has guaranteed that almost all public funding proposals pressed at the federal level and enacted at the state and local level will have strings attached and, in all likelihood, will benefit incumbents over challengers.[33]

Second, and most notably, the conditioned limits on public funding have led inexorably to the soft money phenomenon and to the rise of soft money and multi-million-dollar party issue campaigns run to skirt those limits.

LESSONS TO LEARN

If there is any lesson we should have learned from twenty-five years of campaign finance controls, it is that limits on campaign funding, apart from constitutional questions, have an equally critical flaw: they just do not work.

Trying to equalize political opportunity and influence through limiting political speech and association is a futile task. Limit the funding of the candidates equally, and the advantage of incumbency or celebrity will disturb the equilibrium, as will the presence of powerful outside voices, independent political groups, labor unions, issue groups, and the news media.[34] Limit wealthy contributors from giving money to candidates, and they will still be able to buy newspapers, fund issue groups and give large amounts of soft money to get their message out in ways that the average person can never hope to equal. The ability of a George Soros or a Rupert Murdoch to use their vast funds to influence the debate on political candidates and public issues—like campaign finance reform, for example—is limitless compared to that of the average citizen. Attempt to limit all those voices and methods of influencing the electorate, on the claim that they are "buying elections" or "drowning out the voice of the people" and you have a First Amendment meltdown.[35]

Far better to deal with such disparities by encouraging average people to band together in groups to support issues and candidates that appeal to them to counter the wealthy few. That is what freedom of speech and association are all about.

The 1974 law limited individual contributions to House and Senate candidates, and we have witnessed a proliferation of PACs, and independent groups and issue advocacy. Challengers have a hard time raising money and incumbents are more insulated against effective challenge. Things are easy only for the well-heeled or the well-connected.

The law sharply limited contributions to presidential candidates, and we have seen the splurge of soft money funding that has gone on for almost twenty years. The highly structured system of public financing of presidential elections, hailed as a model of reform, has become the poster child of the failure of limits-driven public campaign funding controls. Political parties have spent millions of dollars on image ads to influence public opinion in ways favorable to their party or candidate. Make no mistake, the millions of dollars spent by the Democratic Party on such ads effectively decided the outcome of the 1996 presidential campaign in favor of President Clinton, before that campaign had even officially begun.

The Court's split decision in *Buckley* has helped create the campaign finance dilemma we have had ever since. Wealthy candidates can spend unlimited funds on campaigns, while less wealthy candidates are severely limited in trying to raise funds from others to get their message out. Incumbents have built-in fundraising advantages, while unwealthy challengers must scramble for funds. People or organizations who want to give financial support directly to candidates and parties are restrained from doing so, but they are permitted to support issue advocacy or soft money party activity without restraint. Public funding is available, but only primarily to mainstream parties and candidates and only with acceptance of limiting conditions and stipulations.

"REFORM" STRIKES BACK

The "reform" bills pending in Washington and many of the states embody the same kind of limits-based approach that has failed time and again in the past. "Those who cannot remember the past are condemned to repeat it."[36] Two particular features of many of these bills require analysis: the unprecedented controls on issue advocacy and soft money.

Issue Advocacy

The bills' unprecedented regulations of issue advocacy are flatly unconstitutional under settled First Amendment rules. And no amount of pejorative references to "phony" issue ads or "so-called" issue ads or "sham" issue ads can avoid that fact.

The Court fashioned the express advocacy doctrine to safeguard issue advocacy from campaign finance controls, even though such advocacy might influence the outcome of an election. The doctrine provides a clear, objective test that protects political speech by focusing solely on the content of the speaker's words, not the motive in the speaker's mind or the impact on the speaker's audience, or the proximity to an election, or the phase of the moon. The doctrine protects issue discussion and advocacy by allowing citizens to criticize the performance of elected officials at the time that such commentary is most vital in a democracy: during an election season. It may be inconvenient for incumbent politicians when groups of citizens spend money to inform the voters about a politician's public stands on controversial issues like term limits, but it is the essence of free speech and democracy.

The McCain-Feingold bill and the Shays-Meehan bill both abandon the clear and narrow test of express advocacy in favor of an impermissibly expanded definition of that critical term in an unconstitutionally vague and overbroad fashion.[37] Specifically:

1. They impose, in effect, a two-month, sixty-day blackout before any federal election for any radio or television advertisement on any issue if that communication is one that in any way "refers to" any federal candidate. Incumbents love that one. Indeed, such proposals have spawned a public policy phrase, to "deep sixty" a bill, namely, to introduce it within sixty days of an election, thereby disabling and silencing any legislative advocacy groups from commenting on a legislator's views or actions on that bill.

2. The bills would restrain any communication "expressing unmistakable and unambiguous support for or opposition to" any federal candidate. If that had been the law in New York City, for example, and the New York Civil Liberties Union had run an ad during the fall campaign criticizing candidate Mayor Rudolph Giuliani's handling of police brutality issues, that would have been illegal. Police brutality issues have become pervasive in New York City. If McCain-Feingold type laws were in effect, all organized public commentary on Mayor Giuliani's police brutality policies would become ensnared in the web of the Federal Election Campaign Act. So too would an ad run last fall criticizing former Senator Alfonse D'Amato's stand on abortion and praising his Democratic opponent, Congressman, now Senator, Charles Schumer. Indeed, there were many ads during that election claiming that, despite his rhetoric, Senator D'Amato was actively antichoice. Under the proposed legislation, such communications informing the public about vital issues of the day would be run through the meat grinder of the Federal Election Campaign Act.

Indeed, that is the basic purpose of bills like McCain-Feingold, namely, to take issue and party speech which is currently beyond the pale of regulation and bring it within the command and control system of the act. The clear purpose and inevitable effect of such unprecedented restrictions on issue advocacy will be to dampen citizen criticism of incumbent officeholders standing for re-election at the very time when the public's attention is especially focused on such issues.

These bills are in clear violation of First Amendment principles. First, such bills would impose unprecedented federal government controls on critical speech about incumbent politicians at the very time when such commentary is most vital in a democracy: during an election season. The bill would stifle such speech by a radical expansion of the Supreme Court's constitutional definition of what political speech can be subject to campaign finance controls, namely, only speech which "expressly advocates" the election or defeat of political candidates. The result would be to bring under federal election controls all of the individuals and organizations whose speech has been constitutionally immune, that is, free, from any restraint up to now. It would treat such groups as though they were a PAC or partisan organization, and would subject them to all of the restraints applicable to campaign organizations.

These proposals embody the kind of unprecedented restraint on issue advocacy that violates bedrock First Amendment principles, set forth with great clarity in *Buckley* and reaffirmed by numerous Supreme Court and lower court rulings ever since. Indeed, one of the enduring legacies of the *Buckley* decision is its reaffirmation and strengthening of the indispensable First Amendment principle that public discussion of public issues is at the very core of the freedom of speech and of the press.

First, issue advocacy is at the core of democracy. In rejecting the claim that issue-oriented speech about incumbent politicians could be regulated because it might influence public opinion and affect the outcome of elections, the *Buckley* Court reminded us of the critical relationship between unfettered issue advocacy and healthy democracy: "Discussion of public issues and debate on the qualifications of candidates are integral to the operation of the system of government established by our Constitution."[38]

Second, in an election season, citizens and groups cannot effectively discuss issues if they are barred from discussing candidates who take stands on those issues. "For the distinction between discussion of issues and candidates and advocacy of election or defeat of candidates may often dissolve in practical application. Candidates, especially incumbents, are intimately tied to public issues involving legislative proposals and governmental actions. Not only do candidates campaign on the basis of their positions on various public issues, but campaigns themselves generate issues of public interest." If any reference to a candidate in the context of advocacy on an issue rendered the speaker or the speech subject to campaign finance controls, the consequences for First Amendment rights would be intolerable.

Third, to guard against that stifling censorial overbreadth, the Court fashioned the critical "express advocacy" doctrine, which holds that only express advocacy of electoral outcomes may be subject to any form of restraint. Thus, only "communications that in express terms advocate the election or defeat of a clearly identified candidate" can be subject to *any* campaign finance controls.

Finally, and most importantly, all speech which does not in express terms advocate the election or defeat of a clearly identified candidate is totally immune from any regulation; "So long as persons and groups eschew expenditures that in express terms advocate the election or defeat of a clearly identified candidate, *they are free to spend as much as they want to promote the candidate and his views.*"[39]

Nor does it matter whether the issue advocacy is communicated on radio or television, in newspapers or magazines, through direct mail or printed pamphlets. What counts for constitutional purposes is not the medium, but the message. By the same token, it is constitutionally irrelevant whether the message costs $100 or $1,000 or $100,000. It is content, not amount, that marks the constitutional boundary of allowable regulation and frees issue advocacy from any impermissible restraint. The control of issue advocacy is simply beyond the pale of legislative authority.[40]

This unprecedented provision is an impermissible effort to regulate issue speech which contains not a whisper of express advocacy, simply because it "refers to" a federal candidate—who is more often than not a congressional incumbent—during an election season. The First Amendment disables Congress from enacting such a measure regardless of whether the provision includes a monetary threshold, covers only broadcast media, applies only to speech during an election season and employs prohibition or disclosure as its primary regulatory device.

Such a proposal would cast a pall over grassroots lobbying and advocacy communication by nonpartisan issue-oriented groups. It would do so by imposing burdensome, destructive, and unprecedented disclosure and organizational requirements, and barring use of any organizational funding for such communications if any corporations or unions made any donations to the organization. Such proposals would force such groups to choose between abandoning their issue advocacy or dramatically changing their organizational structure and sacrificing their speech and associational rights.

Other severe problems with such bills are the new "coordination" rules, rules which will interfere with the ability of issue organizations to communicate with elected officials on such issues and later communicate to the public in any manner on such on issues. And the greatly expanded activities encompassed within the new category of "express advocacy" would be subject to those greatly expanded coordination restrictions as well. This would be a double deterrent to public discussion: more would be encompassed within the definition of express advocacy, and more discussion with respect to that expanded universe of express advocacy would be ensnared under the coordination rules. In effect, any person or group who talked with a representative about an issue would be subject to the coordination rules and restraints if they publicly commented on the representative's stance on those same issues. And coordinated activity becomes highly controlled activity.

Rules like this could even make tax lawyers jealous.

The net result will be to make it virtually impossible for any issue organization to communicate, directly or indirectly, with any politician on any issue and then communicate on that same issue to the public.

All of this will have an exceptionally chilling effect on organized issue advocacy in America by the hundreds and thousands of groups that enormously enrich political debate. These bills fly in the face of well-settled Supreme Court doctrine which is designed to keep campaign finance regulations from ensnaring and overwhelming all political and public speech. And they will chill issue discussion of the actions of incumbent officeholders standing for reelection at the very time when it is most vital in a democracy: during an election season. It may be inconvenient and annoying for incumbent politicians when groups of citizens spend money to inform the voters about a politician's public stands on controversial issues, like abortion, but it is the essence of free speech and democracy.

Soft Money

The bill would also impose new controls on "soft money" funding of political parties, thus leaving them far less able to use their resources to communicate their message to the voters. Elections are a time when we need more political party speech and activity, not less. "[I]t can hardly be doubted that the Constitutional guarantee [the First Amendment] has its fullest and most urgent application precisely to the conduct of campaigns for political office."[41]

Likewise, the unprecedented and sweeping restraints on soft money funding of issue advocacy and political activity and even a new concept called "federal election activity" by political parties and nonpartisan groups alike also raise severe First Amendment concerns.[42] These activities go beyond express advocacy, and beyond even issue advocacy referring to candidate. The Orwellian concept of regulatable "federal election activity" basically includes things like get-out-the-vote drives and other electoral activities on the theory that the conduct of such praiseworthy democratic activity may somehow be politically motivated or partisan. Will licensing of all "federal election activity" be next? Or with proposals like this is it, in fact, already here?

The same principles that protect unrestrained advocacy by issue groups safeguard issue advocacy and activity by political parties and other organizations. "Soft money" is funding that does not support express advocacy of the election or defeat of federal candidates, even though it may exert an influence on the outcome of federal elections in the broadest sense of that term. As such, it is presumptively protected against government regulation. It supports political activity by parties and nonpartisan organizations such as voter registration, voter education, and get-out-the-vote drives. Because such funding is not used for express advocacy, it can be raised from sources that would be restricted in making federal contributions or expenditures.[43]

To be sure, to the extent that soft money funds issue advocacy and political activities by political parties, it becomes something of a hybrid: it supports protected and unregulatable issue speech and activities, but by party organizations often closely tied to candidates and officeholders. But the kind of sweeping controls on the amount and source of soft money contributions to political parties and disclosure of soft money disbursements by other organizations raise severe constitutional problems. Disclosure, rather than limitation, of large soft money contributions to political parties, but not to other organizations, is the more appropriate and less restrictive alternative.

The proposed legislative labyrinth of restrictions on party funding and political activity can have no other effect but to deter and discourage precisely the kind of political party activity that the First Amendment was designed to protect.

Under the brave new world of the McCain-Feingold and Shays-Meehan bills, every group and individual, PAC or party, who commented on politics and politicians would be subject to federal controls. The only institutions that would remain totally unregulated are the news media. Perhaps that is why so many newspaper editorial boards like those bills. But that is a short-sighted, and increasingly hypocritical stance. The argument that anyone who uses their resources to exert their influence on public opinion during an election season can properly be subject to campaign finance controls is not one easily cabined. Why should those who invoke the First Amendment's Press Clause be any more immune from regulation under that argument than those who invoke the Speech Clause?[44]

A BETTER WAY

We are at a constitutional crossroads on campaign finance reform. Read the *New York Times'* latest editorial and be left with the sense that if the Congress does not pass the McCain-Feingold bill by sundown, democracy, not to mention the Constitution, will be lost forever. Unless the federal government enacts such measures to clamp down immediately on unregulated soft money and issue advocacy and unregistered "federal election activity" and improper "coordination" between citizens and their elected representatives, the Republic is surely doomed. The academic and editorial outcry of support for such an overly broad piece of legislation is almost deafening. There has to be a better way.

Although a bill like McCain-Feingold is unlikely to be passed—let alone to come before the Court—anytime soon, the Court's recent decision in the Missouri contribution limits case indicates that the Court is still deeply divided on these issues. The forces of "reform" which brought us the Federal Election Campaign Act insisted that low and restrictive contribution limits must be maintained as the only democratic line of defense against "corruption" and "undue influence" and the "buying of elections." Unfortunately, the Court sustained extremely low legislatively compelled contribution limits on candidates and their supporters. Reform forces will presumably try to discern a mandate to justify attempts to close every "loophole" in campaign finance controls that can be "plugged" by reference to the authority to limit campaign contributions. They will try to stretch the power to regulate direct campaign contributions to justify an extraordinary expansion of the range of campaign finance controls by making virtually all political party funding, most issue advocacy funding, and some "federal election activity" funding subject to the regime of the FECA, particularly its core restraints on the source and size of political contributions.

For twenty-five years, those of us associated with the ACLU have urged a different approach to the campaign finance dilemma, a triad approach based on three essential principles.

1. Raise or even repeal all limits on campaign contributions or expenditures. They should offend the principles of the First Amendment, they distort First Amendment doctrine, and they simply don't work. Increasingly, there is a growing amount of editorial and political support for at least raising contribution ceilings to the level of inflation, so that the federal ceiling would be $3,000, not $1,000.[45] Except for those extremists who would wish for all political activity to be publicly funded only, with no right of private contribution or expenditure, no one can justify on policy grounds the retention of the $1,000 limit for federal campaigns.

2. Insure timely—indeed, instantaneous—and effective disclosure of large contributions to major political parties and committees, so that the public has immediate access to this information. And make sure that these disclosures come out *before* the election and are widely publicized by the media and watchdog groups like Common Cause so that we will know before the election about the fundraising activities of candidates and their parties. That is the most appropriate and democratic remedy to deal with the concerns over undue access and influence by contributors on elected officials. Let the people decide who's too cozy with the fat cats and the so-called special interests. Let the people know about the "China connection" to presidential fundraising before the election, not after. Let the public know that the president, who agreed only to use public funding for his political campaign in 1996, raised funds for and drafted the copy of Democratic Party campaign advertisements in 1995 that guaranteed his re-election before the official campaign even began.

3. Provide a meaningful and broad-scale package of *serious* public funding and benefits for all qualified political candidates. This is a strategy to provide floors to support and expand political opportunity, not ceilings to restrict political activity. That would be a real investment in democracy.

The most effective and least constitutionally problematic route to genuine campaign finance reform is a system of equitable and adequate public financing. Public financing can expand political opportunity, facilitate political communication, and provide alternate methods of political funding to counter the more traditional sources that may pose problems of undue access and influence.

But proposals for public financing need to avoid certain pitfalls. First, they should not compel candidates and parties to limit their political speech in order to have that speech subsidized by government. Instead, the principle should be one of building floors to support political speech, not ceilings to restrict it. Second, public financing schemes should avoid mechanisms whereby benefits and subsidies to one candidate are triggered by the campaign funding and campaign speech activities of other candidates and even independent groups. Such contingent funding arrangements can confer too much power on government to determine what campaign activities or speech entitles other candidates to increased funds or fundraising opportunities. Third, public financing arrangements should be as inclusive as possible, so that new political voices are enabled, rather than stifled. Finally, public financing should take a mix of different forms so that candidates and parties are not dependent on one single governmental funding source.

If a serious public funding program were coupled with an easing of fundraising restrictions on those candidates who do not opt into the public funding system, the combination might give candidates a real choice about the best way to get their messages out and the voters a real choice about which candidates they prefer.

Here are some of the components of such a campaign finance benefits package.

We could give modest tax credits of up to $100 or even $500 for private political contributions to *any* political party or candidate—Democratic, Republican, or Socialist. That would be the most straightforward and democratic form of public financing of politics—through private choices, publicly amplified. If

50 million voters gave $100 each, you could fund all of federal politics in a year to the tune of about $5,000,000,000 without a penny going through government hands. Now *that's* a good use of the coming federal budget surplus. Likewise, we could give free franked mail privileges to all qualified political candidates, not just Democrats and Republicans, at least during the general election. Incumbents get it free for most of their terms in office, why not let challengers have the same perk during the election season.[46] It would facilitate political communication and reduce the dependence on private funding. That's a serious way to help level the playing field between incumbents and challengers. In addition, we could make serious amounts of public funding or matching funds available to all federal candidates.[47] Finally, afford candidates free air time, with no restrictions or conditions, to get their message across to the voters, although this might pose severe, and perhaps insurmountable, constitutional difficulties.[48]

All of these approaches would have the collateral benefit of allowing candidates to spend less time raising money and more time raising issues. And these strategies have one other thing in common: they expand political opportunity without limiting political speech. They say that if there is to be any leveling principle in the First Amendment, it should be one of level up, not level down. More speech, not silence coerced by law. Time has shown the wisdom of that approach and the folly of an approach based on limits. That should not be surprising because the enduring wisdom of the "more speech" solution is nothing less than the enduring wisdom and very essence of the First Amendment itself:

"Congress shall make no law . . . abridging the freedom of speech, or of the press, or the right of the people peaceably to assemble, and to petition the Government for a redress of grievances."

CHAPTER 5

The Role of Disclosure in
Campaign Finance Reform

Trevor Potter

> Sunlight is said to be the best of disinfectants; electric light the
> most efficient policeman.
>
> —*Buckley v. Valeo* (1976)

> Don't underestimate the common man. People are intelligent
> enough to evaluate the source of an anonymous writing. . . . They
> can evaluate its anonymity along with its message. . . . [O]nce they
> have done so, it is for them to decide what is responsible, what is
> valuable, and what is truth.
>
> —*McIntyre v. Ohio Elections Commission* (1994)

POLITICAL DISCLOSURE LAWS have a mixed constitutional record
in United States Supreme Court First Amendment jurisprudence. Generally, disclosure enjoys a favored position, and is said by the Supreme
Court to advance, rather than restrict, the information available in
the marketplace of ideas. On the other hand, compelled disclosure
has been held in some cases to have a chilling effect on political
speech, and to constitute an impermissible abridgment of free speech.

Disclosure's constitutional status is more relevant than ever. From
a policy standpoint, the importance of the prompt disclosure of campaign finance data and other political information has emerged as
one of the few areas of consensus among those favoring both greater
and lesser regulation of political finance.[1] This consensus dissipates,
however, when the specifics of disclosure proposals are discussed. Is it
constitutionally permissible to require disclosure of the financing of
issue advocacy advertisements when they refer to specific candidates
or elections? The combatants disagree on that issue, with those in fa-

vor of disclosure saying that the Supreme Court would uphold such requirements (citing *Buckley v. Valeo* (1976))[2] and those opposed to issue advocacy disclosure arguing that it is akin to the Ohio disclosure requirement on anonymous leafletters declared unconstitutional by the Court in *McIntyre v. Ohio
Elections Commission* (1994).[3]

The reality is that disclosure's constitutional status is unclear. The Supreme
Court's jurisprudential framework is often unpredictable. Even when the Court
has been consistent in choosing an approach to disclosure laws, it has been inconsistent and unpredictable in applying it. To be sure, this issue takes on particular urgency in light of the importance that both sides in the campaign finance debate attach to disclosure of campaign spending (however differently
defined), and the existence of the Internet as a vehicle for immediate mass dissemination of information required to be reported. Accordingly, by providing
an overview of the Supreme Court's disclosure jurisprudence under the First
Amendment (as it has been applied in several contexts: candidate elections;
candidate-specific issue advocacy; ballot initiative or referenda campaigns; and
broadcast political advertising), this chapter examines disclosure requirements
applicable to lobbyists, foreign agents, government officials, and parties or witnesses in litigation or legislative investigations. It concludes by analyzing what
common strains emerge from these disparate cases, and thus what new approaches are most likely to withstand constitutional review.

BUCKLEY AND DISCLOSURE UNDER
THE U.S. CONSTITUTION

Buckley v. Valeo (1976)[4] established the campaign and political disclosure
framework for campaign finance jurisprudence. In *Buckley,* the Court upheld all
of the disclosure provisions reviewed by the Court, while presaging later decisions which would qualify that holding. More importantly, it established basic
principles which still guide the Court over twenty years later.

The Federal Election Campaign Act (FECA), enacted in 1971 and 1974, laid
out a comprehensive system of federal campaign finance regulation.[5] The disclosure provisions required political committees, political parties, and candidates to register with the Federal Election Commission (FEC) and to disclose
the identity of contributors and the dollar amount of their contributions, as
well as the size and recipients of their expenditures or disbursements. It also

mandated individuals and groups other than political committees or candidates to report independent expenditures over $100 to the FEC.[6]

In reviewing FECA's disclosure provisions, the Supreme Court in *Buckley* had little precedent to guide it. The one previous Supreme Court case reviewing federal election disclosure requirements was *Burroughs and Cannon v. United States* (1934),[7] which reviewed the Federal Corrupt Practices Act of 1925, the first federal campaign finance disclosure law.[8] *Burroughs* included no First Amendment analysis and applied deferential scrutiny, stating that Congress had broad power to regulate federal elections to combat corruption.[9]

Buckley, drawing more on *NAACP v. Alabama* (1958)[10] than *Burroughs,* found that "compelled disclosure, in itself, can seriously infringe on privacy of association and belief guaranteed by the First Amendment." Consequently, the Court applied "exacting scrutiny." Under this intermediate scrutiny standard, the government would have to state an important state interest. Moreover, as the Court said, "we also have insisted that there be a 'relevant correlation' or 'substantial relation' between the government interest and the information required to be disclosed."[11]

Under the disclosure framework it laid out, the Court recognized three state interests justifying disclosure. First, it noted that mandatory disclosure diminishes both actual and apparent corruption. Exposing large contributions to the public discourages contributors and politicians from using money for improper purposes both before and after elections, and also enables voters to detect postelection favors. A second, related interest was detecting violations of the act's contribution limits. Third, the Court recognized that disclosure better enables the public to evaluate candidates and "to place more precisely each candidate along the political spectrum." Additionally, knowledge of a candidate's financial sources permits voters to predict future performance in office by identifying the interests to which a candidate is most likely to be responsive.[12]

Furthermore, in recognizing that government has legitimate interests in requiring disclosure, the appellants in *Buckley* argued that the disclosure provisions should not apply to minor parties on the grounds that disclosure would expose them to harassment and abuse. To address this "speech-chilling" argument, the *Buckley* Court drew on *NAACP v. Alabama* (1958).[13] In that case, Alabama brought suit to bar the NAACP from operating in Alabama due to the organization's failure to comply with the state's Foreign Corporations Registration Act. As part of the litigation, the state sought extensive disclosure of NAACP records, including a complete list of all NAACP members in the state, asserting them as necessary to prove that the NAACP engaged in "intrastate business" activities in Alabama.

The NAACP appealed the court order to comply with the discovery orders, and the Supreme Court unanimously blocked the disclosure, stating that the state interest—proving the NAACP was engaged in business—and its correlation to subpoenaing membership lists were not well demonstrated. By contrast, the Court found the NAACP showed it would sustain substantial injury from disclosure, because its rank-and-file members would suffer reprisal should their membership be revealed. As the Court stated, "[R]evelation of the identity of its rank-and-file members has exposed these members to economic reprisal, loss of employment, threat of physical coercion, and other manifestations of public hostility." The Court also stressed that the NAACP had substantially complied with the state's registration laws and was objecting only to disclosure of "ordinary rank-and-file members."[14] Using the *NAACP* framework, *Buckley,* while upholding the disclosure requirements as applied to minor parties, said that such parties could get an exemption if they could present specific evidence of hostility, threats, harassment, and reprisals against members or the organization itself.[15]

Notably, the Court applied the minor party exemption a few years later in *Brown v. Socialist Workers '74 Campaign Committee* (1982). The Court held that the Socialist Workers Party (SWP) need not make public financial disclosures because it had shown "a reasonable probability that disclosure of the names of contributors and recipients will subject them to threats, harassment, or reprisals from either Government officials or private parties." SWP met the test by showing that members had been subjected to threatening phone calls, hate mail, destruction of their property, police harassment of a candidate, the firing of shots at an SWP office, and the dismissal of several party members from their jobs because of their membership. Similarly, FBI surveillance of the party and its dissemination of information designed to injure the SWP's ability to function constituted government harassment of the type contemplated by *Buckley. Socialist Workers* therefore illustrates *Buckley's* observation that disclosure laws could, in some instances, be unconstitutional as applied to independent and minor parties, but that parties claiming an unconstitutional application face the burden of showing specific and concrete examples of retaliation for their activities. *Socialist Workers* is also significant in that it concluded that *Buckley*'s limits on disclosure requirements should apply to both contributions to as well as expenditures made by a group, because laws requiring the identification of recipients of campaign disbursements can be just as harmful to First Amendment rights as those that require only the disclosure of campaign contributors.[16]

Furthermore, in *Federal Election Commission v. Massachusetts Citizens for Life* (1986), decided a decade after *Buckley,* the Court recognized disclosure's potential for imposing another burden on speech: the administrative cost and burdensome accounting responsibilities imposed by detailed disclosure and reporting laws. This "administrative burden" concern was a direct consideration in *Massachusetts Citizens for Life (MCFL).* There, a pro-life, nonprofit corporation challenged the FECA's absolute ban on corporate political spending. The FEC responded that *MCFL* could form a political action committee (PAC) under the FECA to avoid violating the ban on direct corporate spending. *MCFL* replied by protesting that the strict accounting, disclosure, and reporting requirements imposed on PACs were prohibitive for a small organization.

The Court agreed with *MCFL:* "the administrative costs of complying with such increased responsibilities may create a disincentive for the organization itself to speak." In fact, the Court said that: "Detailed record-keeping and disclosure obligations . . . impose administrative costs that many small entities may be unable to bear. . . . Faced with the need to assume a more sophisticated organization form, to adopt specific accounting procedures, to file periodic detailed reports . . . it would not be surprising if at least some groups decided that the contemplated political activity was simply not worth it."[17] The Court emphasized how burdensome the requirements are when applied to "small entities" and "small groups" whose activities consist predominantly of grassroots activities such as "garage sales, bake sales, and raffles."[18]

Significantly, the Supreme Court identified other grounds for invalidating disclosure: overbreadth and vagueness. For example, in *Buckley* the Court also considered whether the original FECA's dollar thresholds were unconstitutionally low. The 1974 act had two thresholds. Political committees were required to keep records of names and addresses of persons making contributions in excess of $10; and, for persons making aggregate contributions of more than

$100, the committees also were required to disclose their occupation and place of business. While *Buckley* upheld these provisions, it noted that the "thresholds are indeed low," presaging subsequent cases that would find disclosure provisions insufficiently narrowly tailored, and therefore unconstitutionally overbroad.[19]

Buckley articulated other grounds for invalidating disclosure provisions. The Court applied to the FECA the generally applied principle that laws must provide persons with sufficient notice that their actions would be in violation of law in order for that law to be constitutional under the Fifth Amendment's due process clause. Applying this "unconstitutional vagueness" doctrine to the FECA, the Court, in a holding with significant long-term effects on campaign finance law, found the FECA failed the test. The statute as originally drafted and enacted required disclosure of any independent expenditure spent "for the purpose of . . . influencing" an election or nomination. The Court ruled that that statutory language was unconstitutionally vague, and may subject many groups to disclosure requirements even if they were not engaged in partisan campaign activities. As the court said, the definition "could be interpreted to reach groups engaged purely in issue discussion."[20]

The Court, rather than striking the provision altogether, gave the statute a narrow construction, interpreting the disclosure provisions to apply only to "express advocacy" campaign communications. Drawing on similar analysis from an earlier portion of the decision, it restricted the reach of the independent expenditure disclosure provision to "communications that expressly advocate the election or defeat of a clearly identified candidate." Under the Court's construction, the requirements apply only to communications containing language such as "vote for," "elect," "support," "cast your ballot for," "vote against," "defeat," or "reject." Yet, the Court did not address the question whether disclosure requirements that do not suffer from the vagueness problems present in the original FECA could be applied to "issue advocacy" communications, that is, communications that do not use words which expressly advocate the election or defeat of a candidate, but make explicit reference to a candidate.[21]

In summary, *Buckley*'s framework for analyzing the constitutionality of a disclosure regime consists of four steps. First, under the exacting scrutiny test, the provision must advance substantial state interests. Second, the means chosen must have a close relation to that state interest. Third, the nature and extent of the burden or restriction on speech must be analyzed, usually in a very fact-specific way. Fourth, the statute must be analyzed for overbreadth and vagueness. Moreover, *Buckley*, read alone, suggests that, absent compelling facts that disclosure poses a severe restriction on a litigant, the scale tips toward disclosure. Later cases, however, have brought this pro-disclosure leaning into question.

ISSUE ADVOCACY DISCLOSURE AND RELATED ISSUES

Candidate-specific issue advocacy—that is, communications concerning candidates running for elective office, yet which fall short of the express advocacy test—has emerged as one of the most contentious areas of election law in recent years.[22] Yet, since *Buckley* the Supreme Court has never addressed this issue.[23] Lower courts have thus had to confront to what extent *Buckley*'s distinction between express advocacy and issue advocacy should apply to disclosure—and with mixed results. The Court has addressed issue advocacy disclosure in the context of ballot initiative campaigns, also with conflicting outcomes. The Supreme Court has essentially applied the *Buckley* framework in these cases, without consistent results for disclosure statutes. Finally, political broadcast disclosure requirements have been upheld by the lower courts, even in the non-candidate campaign context. This section will examine each of these areas in turn.

Candidate-Specific Issue Advocacy

That the Court has not decided the constitutionality of issue advocacy disclosure is to some extent the result of the parties' litigation strategy in *Buckley*. A notably broad statutory disclosure provision was squarely addressed by the U.S. Court of Appeals for the D.C. Circuit, but that court's decision to strike the provision was not appealed by the government. The provision at issue imposed reporting requirements on any group or individual who engaged in "Any act directed to the public for the purpose of influencing the outcome of an election, or . . . publishes or broadcasts to the public *any material referring to a candidate* . . . setting forth the candidate's position on any public issue, voting record, or other official acts . . . or otherwise designed to influence individuals to cast their votes for or against such candidates or to withhold their votes for such candidate."[24]

The D.C. Circuit in *Buckley* found this language unconstitutional, because it was vague and violated the constitutional rights of groups engaged in protected speech. The circuit court stated:

As we have said, it [section 437a] may undertake to compel disclosure by groups that do no more than discuss issues of public interest on a wholly non-partisan basis. To be sure, any discussion of important public questions can possibly exert some influence on the outcome of an election preceding which they were campaign issues [*sic*] . . . *But unlike contributions and expenditures made solely with a view to influencing the nomination or election of a candidate, issue discussions unwedded to the cause of a particular candidate hardly threaten the purity of the election.* Moreover, and very importantly, such discussions are vital and indispensable to a free society and an informed electorate. Thus the interest group engaging in *nonpartisan discussions* ascends to a high plane, while the governmental interest in disclosure correspondingly diminishes.[25]

This aspect of the court's decision was not appealed by the statute's challengers (it was the only point upon which the challengers prevailed at the Court of Appeals). Nor did the government appeal, apparently believing that the vague language of the provision coupled with the virtually unlimited reach of the disclosure requirement to contributions of ten dollars or more to hundreds of nonpolitical organizations was indefensible. Accordingly, in *Buckley* the Supreme Court was not presented directly with the question whether all campaign speech must contain "express advocacy" to be subject to registration and reporting requirements in disclosure laws, nor when (if ever) issue discussion might be sufficiently "wedded to the cause of a particular candidate" to warrant disclosure.

Moreover, in *North Carolina Right to Life, Inc. v. Bartlett* (1998), a nonprofit corporation challenged the state's registration and reporting requirements of political committees, broadly defined to include "any person, committee . . . the primary or incidental purpose of which is to support or oppose any candidate or political party or to influence or attempt to influence the result of an election . . ." The district court stated that this provision meant that "[g]roups engaging only in issue advocacy are thus subject to spending restrictions and reporting requirements. This violates the First Amendment as construed by the Supreme Court in *Buckley v. Valeo*." The court accordingly found the statute fatally overbroad and unconstitutional.[26]

At issue in *West Virginians for Life, Inc. v. Smith* (1996), concerned the state of

West Virginia's attempt to regulate voter guides by amending into its state law a presumption that any scorecards, voter guides, or other analysis of a candidate's positions or votes, published or distributed within sixty days of an election is presumed to be "for the purpose of advocating or opposing the nomination, election or defeat of a candidate." A right-to-life group challenged this law as a violation of the First Amendment, because it regulated political speech beyond that containing express advocacy.

In granting the group's motion seeking a preliminary injunction, the district court stated that its case was likely to succeed on the merits since the Supreme Court has articulated a bright line standard that separated express advocacy (which could be subject to regulation) from issue advocacy (which could not be regulated). The court specifically criticized the presumption that scorecards or voter guides distributed within sixty days of an election could be regulated as express advocacy. Furthermore, in its decision awarding attorneys' fees and costs, the court justified charging these fees against the state since the statute "attempted to circumvent legal precedent through the transparent device of a presumption" that expenditures made within sixty days of an election are express advocacy."[27]

Other federal lower courts have also extended the legal principle beyond "magic words" express advocacy. For instance, the U.S. Court of Appeals for the Second Circuit in *FEC v. Survival Education Fund, Inc.* (1995) assessed the validity of the provision imposing a disclaimer requirement on any person who makes communications expressly advocating election or defeat or solicits any contribution (i.e., money or thing of value) for the purpose of influencing a federal election. Such communications or solicitations must include a notice in the communication stating who paid for the mailing and whether or not it is authorized by a candidate. The case concerned a July 1984 direct mail fundraising appeal by author and political activist Benjamin Spock on behalf of a pro-nuclear freeze group, which read: "Your special election-year contribution today will help us communicate your views to hundreds of thousands of members of the voting public, letting them know why Ronald Reagan and his anti-people policies must be stopped."[28]

The FEC charged that the solicitation was subject to FECA's contribution solicitation disclosure requirement, even though it did not contain express advocacy. The Second Circuit agreed. The Second Circuit closely reviewed *Buckley* and the legislative history of the FECA, noting that Congress had enacted the solicitation disclosure requirement (which previously had only applied to solicitations containing express advocacy) specifically to cover solicitations whether or not they included express advocacy: "Even if a communication does not itself constitute express advocacy, it may still fall within the reach of sec. 441d(a) if it contains solicitations clearly indicating that the contributions will be targeted to the election or defeat of a clearly identified candidate for federal office. . . . That statement leaves no doubt that the funds contributed would be used to advocate President Reagan's defeat at the polls, not simply to criticize his policies during the election year."[29]

Survival Education Fund held that the disclosure provision was constitutional because *Buckley's* express advocacy test was confined to the definition of independent expenditure; also the disclosure requirement at issue in the case applied only to solicitations that target the election or defeat of a clearly identified candidate. Moreover, it recognized the governmental interest in ensuring that contributors know whether their money is going directly to a candidate or to independent critics of another candidate so they "are not misled into giving money to candidates or causes they do not support."[30]

Notably, too, in 1997 a lower appellate court in Wisconsin in *Elections Board v. Wisconsin Mfrs. and Commerce* went further, explicitly holding that the express advocacy test was not the only possible acceptable constitutional test for permissible disclosure. The state's requirement that groups making contributions and expenditures register as political committees was the basis of an enforcement action against several organizations that sponsored issue advertisements. The advertisements, broadcast in October 1996, discussed a state legislator's vote on specific issues and urged the viewer to call the legislator to protest or express support for the position. For instance, one advertisement asked the viewer to "Call [your state legislator] . . . Tell him not to hike taxes again." The legislators under criticism filed complaints with the Wisconsin Elections Board, and board staff determined that the advertisements were subject to registration and reporting requirements since they were broadcast for "political purposes." The legislators also filed actions for injunctive relief in state court, which were granted during the final days of the 1996 campaign.

In March of 1997, the Elections Board in turn found that the advertisements were express advocacy and thus the sponsors were subject to Wisconsin disclosure laws. When the sponsors still refused to comply on First Amendment grounds, the Elections Board filed suit. The trial court concluded that the state could adopt, although it had not done so, a definition of express advocacy that differed from the one articulated by the Supreme Court in *Buckley* and its progeny, "so long as the definition itself meets constitutional requirements under the First and Fourteenth Amendments." Concluding that the state had failed to provide a clear, advance definition of express advocacy, the court dismissed the state's complaint.[31]

Ballot Initiatives and Referenda

In contrast to candidate-specific issue advocacy disclosure, where the Supreme Court has remained silent, the Court has reviewed another category of issue advocacy disclosure—ballot initiative or referenda disclosure. In that area, the Court has moved from the *Buckley* analysis in two regards that have made ballot initiative disclosure more likely to be found unconstitutional. First, it grants a broader interest in completely anonymous communication. Second, it discounts the issue of quid pro quo corruption in a ballot initiative contest.

First National Bank of Boston v. Bellotti (1978), although not directly concerning disclosure, addressed it in dicta. *Bellotti* asserted that the informational interest first articulated in *Buckley* may justify disclosure in the ballot initiative realm. Citing precedent, the Court suggested that sponsor identification for referenda campaign communications would be constitutional; that is, "Identification of the source of advertising may be required as a means of disclosure so that the people will be able to evaluate the arguments to which they are being subjected." The Court indicated a source disclosure requirement would be justified to further the First Amendment's notion that "the people are entrusted with the responsibility for judging and evaluating the relative merits of conflicting arguments. They may consider in making their judgment, the source and credibility of the advocate."[32]

Citizens Against Rent Control/Coalition for Fair Housing v. City of Berkeley (1981) more directly addressed ballot initiative disclosure. There, the Court considered a Berkeley ordinance which limited contributions to committees formed to support or oppose ballot measures. The ordinance also required disclosure by ballot campaign committees of their contributors. The Court determined that the contribution limits were unconstitutional under the *Bellotti* analysis, since the danger of corruption that justified contribution limits to candidates could not be extended to ballot measure races. While there was no constitutional challenge to the disclosure requirements, the Court wrote favorably of them, indicating that they facilitate public awareness of the sources of support for committees.[33]

Furthermore, in *McIntyre v. Ohio Elections Commission* (1995), the Court addressed a requirement that all ballot initiative literature include disclaimers disclosing the source of the literature. The Ohio Elections Commission fined Margaret McIntyre $100 for distributing unsigned leaflets which omitted an identification disclaimer. Mrs. McIntyre distributed the leaflets, which protested a proposed school tax levy, with the help of her son and a friend. Some of the handbills named her as the author; others were signed merely "Concerned Parents and Taxpayers." The Supreme Court ruled the statute unconstitutional as applied by Ohio to Mrs. McIntyre. Extolling the virtues and historical role of anonymous individual speech, the Court noted that the Ohio statute was a direct regulation of pure speech subject to "exacting scrutiny."[34]

Notably, in *McIntyre,* Ohio asserted the interests analogous to *Buckley:* preventing fraud and libelous statements and providing the electorate with relevant information. Yet, the Court did not find the informational interest persuasive on the facts of the case. The Court stated, "The simple interest in providing voters with additional relevant information does not justify [the disclosure requirement]. Moreover, in the case of a handbill written by a private citizen who is not known to the recipient, [disclosure of the author's name] adds little, if anything, to the reader's ability to evaluate the document's message. Thus Ohio's informational interest is plainly insufficient to support the constitutionality of its disclosure requirement."[35]

Next, the Court addressed the antifraud interest. Although the Court recognized that election-time fraud can have serious adverse consequences for the public at large, it noted that, insofar as it was targeted to combat fraud, the provision in question was duplicative of several more specific prohibitions against making or disseminating false statements during political campaigns in Ohio's Election Code. Therefore the Court found the statute fatally overbroad and not narrowly tailored. The statute applied not only to candidates and their organized supporters but also to individuals acting independently; not only to candidate elections, or to communications made immediately preceding the election, but also ballot issues that present a much smaller risk of libel or the appearance of corruption and to those made weeks in advance. The Court felt that because of the statute's failure to make these distinctions (and its breadth), it was not narrowly tailored to alleviate the dangers of fraud or impropriety. Indeed, the key consideration in the case seems to be the overbreadth issue. In his opinion for the Court, Justice John Paul Stevens said, "A more limited identification requirement" might have been justified.[36]

Also, in *Buckley v. American Constitutional Law Foundation* (1999), the Court reviewed two disclosure provisions of the Colorado statute governing the ballot initiative petition process: (1) A provision requiring disclosure of names and addresses of all persons who served as paid initiative ballot qualification petition circulators, and the total dollar amount paid to each circulator; and (2) a provision requiring all circulators to wear name badges while soliciting signatures for the initiative petitions.[37]

First, the Court unanimously struck the name badge requirement. Justice Ruth Bader Ginsburg, writing for the Court, reasoned that the provision constituted compelled disclosure likely to chill political speech—in this case, the circulation of the petition—without sufficient compelling state interest to justify such a restriction. In her analysis of the name badge provision, Ginsburg focused largely on the chilling effect the badges would have in discouraging persons from serving as circulators. Ginsburg noted testimony from the district court trial that indicated that the name badge requirement exposed circulators to harassment, recrimination, and retaliation, "inhibiting participation in the petitioning process." Colorado attempted to justify the provision by asserting the state's interest in deterring fraud. The Court, however, did not find the interest to be convincing. Specifically, the Court noted Colorado already required circulators to submit an affidavit listing their name and address, thereby enabling law enforcers to investigate fraud without exposing the circulators to harassment. Given these alternative means of affecting the same state interest, the Court dismissed the need for the name badge provision, and struck it down.[38]

Second, Justice Ginsburg then declared unconstitutional certain of the statute's reporting provisions in a section of the Court's opinion joined by only four other justices.[39] Under the Colorado law, petition sponsors were required to file monthly preelection reports and a final postelection report disclosing all paid circulators' names and addresses, and the amount of compensation they received for circulating the petition. No such provision applied to volunteer circulators.

The majority thus upheld the Tenth Circuit's holding that the reporting requirement was unconstitutional, concurring in the lower court's reasoning that the antifraud and informational interests recognized by *Buckley* were already promoted by disclosure of sponsors who made expenditures. Ginsburg wrote, "The added benefit of revealing the names of paid circulators and amounts paid to each circulator, the lower courts fairly determined from the record as a whole is hardly apparent and has not been demonstrated."[40]

Ginsburg concluded her analysis of the reporting requirements by briefly raising other considerations. First, drawing on *Bellotti*, she stated that ballot initiatives do not involve the risk of quid pro quo corruption like candidate elections, thus undermining the anticorruption argument. Second, she said that the risk of fraud or corruption is remote at the petition stage of an initiative. Finally, she disputed and disapproved of the assertion—implicit in the statute and explicitly defended by Colorado—that paid petition circulators are more likely to engage in petition fraud than volunteers. Consequently, she deemed the circulator disclosure portions of the reporting requirements unconstitutional.[41]

Justice Sandra Day O'Connor, joined by Justice Stephen Breyer, wrote a separate opinion, concurring with the majority's holding concerning name badges, but dissenting regarding the disclosure provisions. In a strongly worded opinion, O'Connor termed the majority's opinion a "disturbing" invalidation of "vitally important" disclosure regulations. O'Connor's analysis varied from the majority opinion in several ways. First, unlike the majority, she asserted the reporting requirement needed only to be justified by a low-level scrutiny standard of a legitimate state purpose, not an important or compelling one required by exacting or strict scrutiny. Her analysis of the state interests at issue also differed from the majority. O'Connor said the antifraud and informational interests provide a sufficient basis to uphold the reporting requirement. Regarding the fraud argument, she noted the trial testimony of substantial petition fraud in Colorado by paid petition circulators. O'Connor also forcefully argued for the informational interest by saying that "Colorado's disclosure reports provide facts useful to voters who are weighing the options. Members of the public deciding whether to sign a petition or how to vote on a measure can discover who has proposed it, who has provided funds for its circulation, and to whom these funds have been provided. Knowing the names of paid circulators and the amount paid to them also allows members of the public to evaluate the sincerity or, alternatively, the potential bias of any circulator that approaches them." In concluding, O'Connor said she would uphold the reporting requirement under either exacting scrutiny or a lower standard.[42]

Disclosure of Political Broadcast Advertising (Television and Radio)
—Differing Judicial Perspectives

An issue not addressed by the Supreme Court, and on which courts have taken a variety of approaches, is whether disclosure requirements may be applied to political broadcast (television and radio) issue advertising. Significantly, *McIntyre* explicitly left this an open question, as Justice Stevens's decision for the Court said that that case does not apply to broadcast advertising.[43]

In *Vermont Right to Life Committee, Inc. v. Sorrell* (1998), the federal district court for Vermont addressed a campaign finance reform measure which provided disclosure requirements for "political advertisements and reporting requirements for "mass media activities." Political advertisements were defined in the law as "any communication which *expressly or implicitly* advocates the success or defeat of a candidate." "Mass media activities" included communications that included the name or likeness of a candidate for office. Political advertisements were required to carry the name and address of the person sponsoring it, and designate the candidate, party, or committee on whose behalf it was published. Persons spending $500 or more within thirty days of an election on mass media activities would be required to report the expenditures to the state and to the candidate whose likeness appeared in the spot, within twenty-four hours of making the expenditure. The federal district court held that political advertisements and the expenditures for mass media activities must be narrowly construed to apply only to messages containing express advocacy to save the statutes from unconstitutionality.[44]

In contrast to *Vermont Right to Life Committee, Inc.*, in *KVUE, Inc. v. Moore* (1983), a Texas television station challenged Texas statute broadcast sponsorship regulations, similar to federal regulations discussed below, requiring advertisers to include in advertisements a disclaimer "paid political announcement" and the name and address of the agent who purchased the advertising time. The requirement applied to "any political advertising"—encompassing candidate advertising and issue advertising. The station challenged the statute as an infringement on broadcaster's First Amendment rights, asserting that it "stripped the broadcaster of absolute editorial control" and penalizing speech based on its political content. The U.S. Court of Appeals for the Fifth Circuit summarily dismissed the contention, drawing on *Anderson v. Celebrezze* (1983) and *Storer v. Brown* (1974). The Court stated that the requirements were generally applicable and even protect the integrity and reliability of the electoral process itself, terming this state interest "compelling." The court said the regulations were content-neutral, and that the burden was of "an extremely limited nature."[45]

Federal regulations, similar to the Texas state regulations, have governed political issue advocacy advertisements broadcast by TV and radio stations since passage of the very earliest versions of the Radio and Communications Acts in the 1920s and 30s.[46] FCC regulations promulgated under the Communications Act provide:

(a) When a broadcast station transmits any matter for which money . . . is . . . paid . . . the station at the time of the broadcast shall announce (1) that such matter is sponsored, paid for, or furnished, either in whole or in part, and (2) by whom or on whose behalf such consideration was supplied.

(b) The licensee of each broadcast station shall exercise reasonable diligence to obtain from its employees and from other persons with whom it deals directly information to enable such licensee to make the announcement(s) The announcement required by this section shall . . . fully and fairly disclose the *true identity* of the person or persons, or corporation or other entity by whom or on whose behalf such payment is made. Where the material broadcast is *political matter* or matter involving the discussion of a controversial issue of public importance and a corporation . . . unincorporated group, or other entity is paying for or furnishing the broadcast matter, the station shall . . . [also] require that a list of the chief executive officers or members of the executive committee or of the board of directors . . . shall be made available for public inspection.[47]

The statute and regulation's scope has been substantially unexplored by the courts, and its constitutionality has not been ruled upon yet.[48] However, the scope of the phrase "reasonable diligence" was considered in *Loveday v. FCC*

(1983). In *Loveday*, a group supporting a ballot measure restricting smoking filed a complaint with the FCC asserting that an advertisement against the initiative was sponsored by the tobacco industry, rather than the identified sponsor, Californians Against Regulatory Excess. The group claimed that the law required "the exertion of every effort" by licensees to determine the true sponsors of paid material." Instead, the commission applied, and the court approved, a standard that permitted broadcasters to accept the apparent sponsor's representations that it is the sponsor, when, as here, faced with "undocumented allegations." Requiring broadcasters to investigate would "judicialize the process of being allowed to utter a political statement." The court suggested that such heightened requirements could implicate the First Amendment, and would have the practical effect of discouraging broadcasters to air these advertisements."[49]

While *Loveday* suggested that the identification regulations may have been toothless, recent FCC decisions have demonstrated that the regulations are enforceable and stations do have real responsibilities under them. In 1996, the FCC found that numerous stations broadcasting issue advertisements had violated the sponsorship identification rules by failing to disclose the true sponsor of advertisements opposing an antismoking ballot measure. The advertisements in question identified "Fairness Matters to Oregonians Committee" as the sponsor, even though the Tobacco Institute, a trade association of large tobacco companies, had funded, designed, and implemented the advertisements. In reviewing whether broadcast licensees could be charged with identifying and disclosing such hidden sponsors, the FCC noted preliminarily that broadcast licensees cannot generally be expected to investigate independently whether the persons with whom they deal directly are the true sponsors. The commission held that where a challenge is made to the legitimacy of sponsorship information and where there is strong evidence that both advertisement funding and editorial direction are controlled by someone other than the listed sponsor, however, broadcast licensees are required to exercise "reasonable diligence" in determining who the actual sponsor of the advertisements is and requiring that the proper information be displayed on the advertisement. Here, the commission determined that the stations had not identified the true sponsor, the Tobacco Institute; but it still issued no sanctions against them because they had not had the information necessary to disclose the true sponsor, and it "may have been uncertain how to proceed in the absence of definitive guidance from the Commission."[50]

LOBBYIST DISCLOSURE, FINANCIAL DISCLOSURE, LEGISLATIVE INVESTIGATIONS, AND TRIAL DISCLOSURE

In addition to campaign disclosure, issue advocacy and advertising disclosure, lobbyist disclosure, governmental financial disclosure, and disclosure in the course of court proceedings or legislative investigations all implicate First Amendment interests. These areas are considered in turn.

Constitutionality of Requiring Disclosure of Lobbying Activities

In *United States v. Harriss* (1954), the Supreme Court examined the Federal Regulation of Lobbying Act, which required every person "receiving any contributions or expending any money for the purpose of influencing the passage or defeat of any legislation by Congress" to report contributions (including the name and address of contributors) and expenditures. To avoid the constitutional problem of vagueness, the Court construed the act as applying only to direct communication with members of Congress on pending or proposed federal legislation, including communications directly by lobbyists themselves, their employees, and through letter writing campaigns.

The Court held that the act did not violate the "freedoms guaranteed by the First Amendment—freedom to speak, publish, and petition the government." Although the Court did not state explicitly what level of scrutiny it applied in arriving at this analysis, it balanced possible infringements on First Amendment rights against the government's interests in maintaining the integrity of the governmental process. The statute served Congress's interest in self-protection by enabling it to *evaluate* pressures put upon it, such as who is being hired to lobby, who is paying for lobbying activities, and how much money is being spent. Thus, the "voice of the people" would not be "drowned out by the voice of special interest groups seeking favored treatment while masquerading as proponents of the public weal." The Court held that, under these circumstances, Congress had used its power of self-protection in a "manner restricted to its appropriate end" without offending the First Amendment. The Court reasoned that any burden on First Amendment rights, such as a person remaining silent out of fear of possible prosecution for failing to comply with the act, was too remote and hypothetical to justify striking down the statute.[51]

Several court decisions since *Harriss* have both reaffirmed its holding, which requires disclosure of lobbying expenses as constitutional, and broadened its application.[52] In *Florida League of Professional Lobbyists, Inc. v. Meggs* (1996), for example, the U.S. Court of Appeals for the Eleventh Circuit considered a challenge to Florida's lobbying disclosure law, which required disclosure not only of direct lobbying expenditures but also indirect expenses without direct contact with governmental officials. Although not explicitly stating that strict scrutiny applied, the *Florida League* court appeared to apply that standard. It determined that the state's interest in illuminating the pressures to be evaluated by voters and officials were "compelling." The court further noted that the government's interest in providing a method for evaluating these pressures was even stronger when those pressures were indirect, since they are harder for the public and government to identify without the aid of disclosure.

Like the *Harriss* court, *Florida League* noted that the First Amendment burdens posed by the statute's detractors were too hypothetical to justify invalidating the law. In justifying the above analysis with respect to indirect communications, the court relied on *Harriss*'s construction of "direct communication" as including an "artificially stimulated letter writing campaign." This demonstrates that courts tend to interpret *Harriss* broadly to allow a wide range of disclosure requirements of lobbying activities.[53]

The U.S. Court of Appeals for the Eighth Circuit in *Minnesota State Ethical Practices Board v. National Rifle Association* (1985) extended *Harriss*'s analysis to permit registration and reporting of lobbying where the only activity was correspondence from a national organization to its members in Minnesota, urging their support for specific state legislation. State law required the individual at the national office making the contacts to register as a lobbyist and file regular reports. Applying strict scrutiny, the court concluded that Minnesota's interest in disclosure outweighed any infringement of the group's First Amendment rights. The court observed that the appellants had argued that their situation deserved protection because the activity occurred between members of a voluntary association, but stated that

[W]e do not think this distinction is constitutionally significant. The Act does not focus on the group affiliation of a lobbyist, it focuses on lobbying activity. When persons engage in an extensive letter writing campaign for the purpose of influencing specific legislation, the State's interest is the same whether or not those persons are members of an association. The appellants have articulated no reason why their membership in the NRA should give them any greater constitutional protection with respect to lobbying activity than is enjoyed by other citizens.[54]

The Kentucky Supreme Court upheld that state's lobbyist registration, disclosure, and reporting requirements in *Associated Industries of Kentucky v. Commonwealth* (1995). The court expressly stated that it was applying strict scrutiny to the law to protect the appellant's First Amendment right to petition and freedom of association. The court found the state's law was supported by a compelling interest and was sufficiently narrowly drawn to avoid unnecessary abridgment of association rights. In particular, the Kentucky court found that the Supreme Court's decisions finding compelled disclosure unconstitutional were not universally applicable. The court noted, however, that the law at issue did not compel "disclosure of membership in organizations engaged in advocacy," suggesting that a law requiring the disclosure of membership could be overbroad.[55]

The Foreign Agents Registration Act and United States v. Peace Information Center

The Foreign Agents Registration Act and its disclosure requirements have also withstood constitutional scrutiny. In *United States v. Peace Information Center* (1951), the federal district court held that mandatory disclosure in this area was within the powers of Congress and identified two separate bases for its conclusion: the inherent authority of Congress to legislate on the subject of foreign relations, and the constitutional authority of Congress to legislate concerning national defense. The court did not specify a standard of review, but was deferential to the legislative judgment of constitutionality. Specifically addressing First Amendment concerns, the court observed that the statute "neither limits nor interferes with freedom of speech. It does not regulate expression of ideas. Nor does it preclude the making of any utterances. It merely requires persons carrying on certain activities to identify themselves."[56] The court therefore concluded that foreign agent disclosure is consistent with the First Amendment, not unlike laws requiring a person to register or procure a license before engaging in certain occupations.[57]

Disclosure of Personal Finances by Governmental Officials

Courts have upheld statutes requiring personal financial disclosure against challenges that such statutes violate the individual's right to privacy. In *Plante v. Gonzalez* (1978), for example, the U.S. Court of Appeals for the Fifth Circuit addressed the constitutionality of Florida's financial disclosure requirements for government officials and candidates for state or local office. Several senators challenged the law as abridging their right to privacy under the Fourteenth Amendment. The court distinguished between this claim and claims that compelled disclosure of members in an organization unconstitutionally burdened constitutional rights. As the court stated, "Here, memberships, associations, and beliefs are revealed, if at all, only tangentially. The Amendment calls for disclosure of assets, debts, and sources of income, each to be identified and valued. Although in some particular situations, rigorous application of the Amendment might implicate First Amendment freedoms, when considering the Amendment on its face this threat is too remote to raise the issue."[58] Absent a First Amendment element, the court applied a balancing test, rather than strict scrutiny by weighing "four important state concerns [that] are significantly advanced by the Amendment: the public's "Right to know" an official's interests, deterrence of corruption and conflicting interests, creation of public confidence in Florida's officials, and assistance in detecting and prosecuting officials who have violated the law."[59] Balanced against these interests were the senators' interest in financial confidentiality. The court noted that, as senators, these litigants were legitimately subject to more scrutiny of their affairs than ordinary private citizens (making an analogy to libel law decisions), thereby concluding that the disclosure law did not violate the senators' privacy rights.[60]

In *Igneri v. Moore* (1990), the U.S. Court of Appeals for the Second Circuit sustained provisions of the New York Ethics in Government Act that required annual financial disclosure by a number of government officials as applied to a political party chairman. The court, assessing the disclosure requirement under the intermediate scrutiny, or balancing, analysis applicable to privacy challenges, found a "substantial state interest in exposing and curbing the improper uses" of the influence possessed by party chairman. It stated that "Full disclosure ensures that the financial interests of party chairman—the interests most susceptible to the corrupting force of political power and influence—are available for inspection by state regulators and the concerned citizenry. Financial disclosure functions not merely to subject private persons' finances to public scrutiny but as a means to deter those who might unethically capitalize on their political relationships. Accountability follows publicity."[61]

Similarly, in *Slevin v. City of New York* (1982), the federal district court in New York upheld personal financial disclosure by city officials, candidates for city office, and city employees above a specified salary threshold. Rejecting a privacy challenge to the disclosure requirements, the court stated that the city was "constitutionally free [to require disclosure], so long as in doing so it is seeking to achieve a proper objective through a defensible means. It continued:

[T]he objectives sought by financial disclosure laws are in principle unassailable and theoretically justify a broad scope of inquiry. Honest government is so patently a worthy objective, and the capacity for venality in human behavior is so profound and ingenious, that virtually any disclosure law however intrusive might be rationally justifiable. Financial disclosure laws also derive considerable strength from the benefits widely felt to be derived from openness and from an informed public. . . . The interest in an informed citizenry also supports a legislature's decision to adopt financial disclosure legislation. An informed public is essential to the nation's success, and a fundamental objective of the First Amendment.[62]

In *County of Nevada v. MacMillen* (1974), the California Supreme Court upheld a financial disclosure statute redrafted after a previous version had been declared unconstitutional. In noting the differences between the two statutes, the court stated:

[T]he 1973 act appears to accomplish its legitimate aims in a less intrusive, and considerably more limited, fashion. As noted above, the act's "prohibition" provisions are keyed at enjoining only "substantial" conflicts of interest and relate only to public agency action or decision having an immaterial economic effect upon the official's economic interests. Thus, the act does not forbid an official to participate in agency matters which could have only an insignificant, de minimus economic effect upon his interests. More importantly, the act's "disclosure" provisions are aimed at requiring disclosure only if the official's interests could be "affected materially" by his public service. Moreover, unlike the 1969 act, the 1973 act does not require disclosure of the actual extent of the official's assets and interests, but only whether the value of his investment or real property interest exceeds $10,000 (and whether the aggregate value of income, loans and gifts during the year exceeded $1,000). Finally, the disclosure requirements of the 1973 act apply only to certain specified high-level officials and not to every public official throughout the state. Disclosure of the economic interests of other public officials remains a subject for determination by the local boards and agencies involved.[63]

Finally, the Alaska Supreme Court, in *Falcon v. Alaska Public Offices Commission* (1977), found that state's financial disclosure law was unconstitutional because it would require that official, who also worked as a physician, to identify his patients. The court determined that this violated the physician and patient's privacy rights.[64]

Disclosure Mandated by Courts or Legislative Investigations

As discussed above, in *NAACP v. Alabama* (1958), the Supreme Court found that the NAACP was justified in withholding its membership lists from the State of Alabama. The state had obtained a court order requiring the production of this information as part of an action against the group for failing to qualify before doing business in Alabama. The Court determined that the constitutionally guaranteed rights to free association required that state efforts abridging these rights are subject to strict constitutional scrutiny. Thus, it concluded that the State could request some organizational information, including the identity of officials of the NAACP, but was forbidden by the Constitution from requiring the NAACP to provide a list of rank-and-file members, because the NAACP has demonstrated that "on past occasions revelation of the identity of its rank-and-file members has exposed these members to economic reprisal, loss of employment, threat of physical coercion, and other manifestations of public hostility." The Court observed that such an intrusive request was not justified by the State's specific interest here, which was to establish that the NAACP has been engaged in business in Alabama that required a corporate qualification filing.[65]

Barenblatt v. United States (1959) considered the constitutional concerns of compelled disclosure in the course of a congressional investigation. There, the Court said, "[T]he Congress, in common with all branches of the Government, must exercise its powers subject to the limitations placed by the Constitution on government action," in particular the Bill of Rights. Not only does this abrogate the witnesses' civil rights, but "Congress may only investigate into those areas in which it may potentially legislate." Notably, in cases where witnesses have raised their First Amendment rights as a defense against a charge of contempt for failing to comply with a Congressional subpoena, the Court has applied a strict scrutiny balancing test: "The First Amendment in some circumstances protects an individual from being compelled to disclose his associational relationships. . . . Where First Amendment rights are asserted to bar governmental interrogation, resolution of the issue always involves a balancing test by the courts of the competing private and public interests at stake in the particular circumstances shown."[66]

Gibson v. Florida Legislative Investigation Committee (1963) held that that balancing test requires that the state "convincingly show a substantial relation between the information sought and a subject of overriding and compelling state interest." In other words, "[w]here there is a significant encroachment upon personal liberty, the State may prevail only upon showing a subordinating interest which is compelling." Notably, the Court noted that this burden is more difficult for the government to carry when a witness is being questioned about the activities of others, as opposed to situations where he is asked about his own activities. In *Barenblatt*, for example, the witness could be asked about his activities in the Communist Party, which the Court said "is not an ordinary or legitimate political party." Yet in *Gibson*, the witness could not be queried about whether certain individuals (who were suspected Communists) were NAACP members.

Therefore, these cases show that Congress must demonstrate a compelling state interest in order to overcome the individual's assertion of his First Amendment rights." In *Barenblatt*, the government was able to show a compelling governmental interest in obtaining information about the infiltration of Communists in American higher education due to the Party's avowed goal of overthrowing the United States government, and the long-respected view that the Communist Party could not avail itself of the protections afforded an ordinary political party.[67]

CONCLUSION

The standard of review applied is perhaps the most critical, and least consistent, aspect of the Court's disclosure jurisprudence. The exacting scrutiny standard set forth for disclosure by *Buckley* and *NAACP v. Alabama* usually is specified as the appropriate standard of review, but as a practical matter the Court is inconsistent in its application of the standard. In *McIntyre* and *American Constitutional Law Foundation (ACLF)* the Court, while saying it is applying exacting scrutiny, appears to apply strict scrutiny, requiring statutes to be narrowly tailored—and nonduplicative—to serve compelling state interests.

Also, the anticorruption and antifraud interests enunciated in *Buckley* remain compelling to the Court. But the informational interest is ripe for clarification by the Court. It was dismissed in *McIntyre* and *ACLF*. But, by contrast, the informational interest was found to be sufficiently compelling to enable litigants, a group of voters, to have standing under the FECA in another recent case, *Federal Election Commission v. Akins* (1998).[68]

Moreover, in one of the arguably most consistent standards running throughout the disclosure case law, the Court appears to give substantial weight to the extent to which a disclosure provision severely burdens or restricts speech. First, *Buckley's* analysis, whereby courts analyze the reasonable probability that disclosure exposes persons to hostility, threats, harassment, or reprisal, was clearly articulated in *Brown v. Socialist Workers '74 Campaign Committee*. The "hostility" analysis also is apparent in *McIntyre v. Ohio Elections Committee* and *ACLF*. More generally, the level of scrutiny applied in cases— whether termed exacting or strict scrutiny—appears to directly correlate to the severity of the burden imposed by the disclosure regulation. Thus, where the disclosure provision's burden is perceived as heavy—as was the case in *Socialist Workers '74, McIntyre, Federal Election Commission v. Massachusetts Citizens for Life*—the statutes receive (and generally fail) severe scrutiny. Where the disclosure provision is less burdensome, the standard is more lenient, and the provision is upheld, as in *Buckley v. Valeo, United States v. Harriss,* and *Republican National Committee v. Federal Election Commission* (1997).[69]

To be sure, narrow tailoring of disclosure provisions is a common theme throughout the case law. Specifically, de minimus exceptions, low dollar thresholds, and temporal limitations are often required by the Court. The Court, more specifically, has been especially protective of individuals and small groups. Thus in *McIntyre*, the Court protected Mrs. McIntyre, a lone individual of "modest" means, and in *Massachusetts Citizens for Life*, a "small group" which engages in small "grass roots" activities. In *Socialist Workers '74*, the Court noted the comparatively small budget and electoral success of the party. In *ACLF*, the Court similarly appears concerned about the lack of de minimus exceptions and thresholds of the circulator disclosure, which would expose persons to possible hostility, no matter how limited their involvement, or how small their financial stake in the political activity.

It is noteworthy that all of these cases were brought on behalf of judicially (if not politically) "sympathetic plaintiffs": Mrs. McIntyre; a grassroots local pro-life group; and an unpopular fringe party. By contrast, the Court has yet to strike a political disclosure provision claimed to burden a large or presumably politically powerful organization. Consequently, the exceptions carved out may be more limited in application than they appear.

Perhaps the least clear and most problematic requirement—if it is a requirement—is that disclosure employ the least restrictive alternative. The Court's disapproval of disclosure provisions that are duplicative, which appeared a significant factor in *McIntyre* and *ACLF*, threaten to inject substantial uncertainty on legislatures endeavoring to enact disclosure regimes. The Court needs to clarify this part of their jurisprudence.

The Court's disclosure cases may often be less well explained by any coherent disclosure framework, however, than by the particular facts, and often the collateral legal issues presented, in a given case. For instance, in many of the above cases, the Court has reviewed disclosure statutes as well as other, related statutes. In *Buckley*, the Court's overall approval of the FECA's purposes may explain its tendency to approve even the questionably low thresholds in the original act. In the ballot initiative or issue advocacy cases, the Supreme Court and lower courts' disapproval of disclosure may owe as much to the courts' rejection of contribution or spending limits imposed on issue advocacy. In *ACLF*, the analysis of the disclosure provisions may have been colored by the Court's disapproval of Colorado statutes' generalized disfavoring of professional ballot initiative campaigns. These cases should be viewed in light of the overall statutory scheme reviewed, not merely the disclosure provisions. Other important considerations include whether the disclosure statute is one of general application, as was not the case in *ACLF*, and whether the disclosure provision is content neutral or viewpoint neutral.

It must be said that the status of disclosure of issue advocacy remains as unresolved as the day *Buckley* was announced in 1976. Notwithstanding several lower courts' formalistic application of express advocacy/issue advocacy, the Supreme Court, it should be remembered, did not strike the disclosure provisions, but rather applied narrowing constructions in order to leave intact at least a portion of the FECA disclosure regime. In fact, analysis of disclosure provisions generally must begin with the recognition that the Court has addressed campaign disclosure per se in only four cases since *Buckley: Socialist Workers '74,*

Massachusetts Citizens for Life, McIntyre, and *ACLF,* and of those, *Massachusetts Citizens for Life* and *ACLF* disclosure was only one of several issues.

Further, only in one case—*Socialist Workers '74,* with its exceptional facts—did the Court permit candidate-specific activities to occur without any public disclosure. In *Massachusetts Citizens for Life,* the other case involving candidate-specific speech, the Court held that the organization did not need to register as a political committee because the organization was so small, accepted no corporate funds, and was not principally organized for political purposes. However, the Court still required *Massachusetts Citizens for Life* to file reports with the FEC of all independent expenditures over $200.[70]

Nonetheless, that all four of these cases either disapproved the disclosure provision at issue or imposed an exception or exemption from existing disclosure provisions indicates that the overall trend in disclosure cases has been skepticism towards the pro-disclosure framework enunciated in *Buckley.* And yet, the *Buckley* framework—which was undeniably favorable towards disclosure—still remains the controlling precedent and the gist of constitutional analysis. Like many constitutional questions concerning campaign finance, then, answers are more likely to be announced in the future rather than culled from the past.

Finally, based on the jurisprudential framework in place at this point, it seems clear that the Court will look more favorably on disclosure of candidate-specific activity by larger organizations than on referenda/ballot issue speech by individual local activists like Mrs. McIntyre. Further, the Court will prefer less intrusive forms of disclosure—of only large contributors, with a minimum of administrative burden, and where there is no evidence that serious threats, harassment, or reprisals will result. Within these boundaries, the Court will still look at the substantial state interest, and evidence that the required disclosure advances the legitimate government interests of preventing corruption and fraud, and providing information to voters.

CHAPTER 6

Splitting the Difference

The Supreme Court's Search for the Middle Ground
in Racial Gerrymandering Cases

Barbara Perry

STUDENTS OF CONSTITUTIONAL LAW are familiar with Justice Felix Frankfurter's oft-quoted warning that the U.S. Supreme Court was
entering a "mathematical quagmire" and "a political thicket" when it
tackled reapportionment and redistricting for the first time in the
landmark case of *Baker v. Carr* (1962).[1] Yet perhaps even the perspica-
cious Frankfurter could not have predicted how truly nettlesome the
thicket would become—due in no small measure to the Court's own
convoluted rulings.

Frankfurter's admonition to his brethren almost forty years ago
was, and remains, a truism. How could it be otherwise when the issues surrounding reapportionment and redistricting encompass the
core values of our regime: representation, democracy, and voting
rights? Add to that list the confounding and volatile factor of race,
and the questions over majority-minority districts seem unanswer-
able. Theoretically, representation settles along two separate but potentially related lines. In the *descriptive* or *passive sense,* representatives
"stand for" others "by virtue of a correspondence or connection between them, a resemblance or reflection."[2] Such representatives are
said to mirror societal characteristics of their constituents. *Substantive*
or *active* representatives vigorously pursue the interests of the represented.[3] Either conceptualization can exist separately in a representative, but proponents of majority-minority districts obviously hope
that minority legislators from those districts will be both descriptive
and substantive in their representation.

Nevertheless, questions linger regarding what constitutes representation in a democracy. In a system of single-member districts and winner-take-all results, what happens to the 49 percent of the electorate whose choice is not selected?[4] In majority-minority districts, does a victorious minority candidate represent the so-called filler constituents, that is, Caucasians who were included in the district just to round out the numbers? Are nonvoters truly represented? Some observers argue that what the Supreme Court views as the right to vote in a democracy is no more than the right to participate in a rather meaningless symbolic ritual of casting a ballot, and that what would truly constitute participation in a genuine democracy would be mobilization and collective action around issues that are crucial to the electorate.[5] Majority-minority districts also raise the thorny issue so familiar from affirmative action cases—should society use race to ameliorate the effects of past racial discrimination? If so, what does the Fourteenth Amendment's Equal Protection Clause allow? When the suffrage is involved, what does the Voting Rights Act of 1965, as amended, require?

PRE-*SHAW* HISTORY IN A NUTSHELL

Riding the wave of the civil rights presidency of Lyndon Johnson and the courageous protest movement advocating equal access to the ballot box, the Voting Rights Act (VRA) passed both houses of Congress in 1965 by margins larger than those that had approved the landmark Civil Rights Act one year earlier. The VRA's major provisions banned discriminatory literacy tests for voting, established criminal penalties for individuals who attempted to bar qualified voters from the polls or threatened civil rights workers who were assisting voters, and ordered the United States Justice Department to initiate litigation challenging the use of poll taxes in state and local elections. (The Twenty-fourth Amendment to the U.S. Constitution had outlawed poll taxes in federal elections as of 1964.) Amended both in 1970 and 1982, the Voting Rights Act's Sections 2 and 5 are most pertinent to discussions of majority-minority districts. Section 2 allows private plaintiffs or the Justice Department to bring suit in federal district court challenging a jurisdiction's voting practices that allegedly "result in a denial or abridgment" of the right to vote on the basis of race, color, or language minority status. Section 5 requires states and localities, prior to implementing any changes in voting laws, to submit them either to the attorney general of the United States or the U.S. District Court for the District of Columbia. Only after the attorney general or the district court has "pre-cleared" the change may it be effected.[6]

The implications of the Voting Rights Act of 1965 can be divided into three phases before the 1993 *Shaw v. Reno* case. In the initial phase, the landmark legislation made a swift and demonstrable impact on black voters, officials, and political organizations in the South.[7] In 1960 the percentage of blacks registered to vote ranged from 5.2% in Mississippi to 39.4% in Florida. By the end of 1965 over 50% of blacks were registered to vote in every southern state. In 1965 there were 35 black elected officials in the South. After the 1966 elections 159 blacks held elected office in the same region. Immediately after passage of the VRA, the South also witnessed a proliferation of minority community- and neighborhood-based civic associations and voters' leagues, which labored to elect black candidates.[8]

Through a combination of judicial rulings on legislative amendments to and extension of the Voting Rights Act, the next phase (from the late 1960s through the 1970s) focused on preventing dilution of the impact of minority voters on electoral outcomes. Despite the increase in sheer numbers of black registered voters, the U.S. Congress was still not representative (in the descriptive sense) of minority voters. One could argue, however, that congressional expansion of the VRA offered some proof of substantive representation of minority interests. And in 1977 the Supreme Court upheld race-conscious redistricting to maintain certain percentages of whites and nonwhites in New York districts, although ironically it split a community of Hasidic Jews in Brooklyn who unsuccessfully challenged the districting scheme.[9]

The decade of the 1980s witnessed the third phase of voting rights legislation and litigation. In the 1980 case of *Mobile v. Bolden* the U.S. Supreme Court ruled that to prove a denial of equal protection of voting rights, plaintiffs would have to demonstrate discriminatory purpose or intent on the part of the government, not merely discriminatory result in elections. Congress's 1982 amendments to the VRA modified its Section 2 to adopt, in effect, a result standard, rather than the higher Court-sanctioned intent standard from *Bolden*.[10] The Supreme Court's subsequent interpretation of the amended Section 2 and the result standard, as applicable to claims of minority vote dilution, in the 1986 North Carolina case of *Thornburg v. Gingles,* implicitly required proportional representation. Justice William J. Brennan Jr.'s opinion for a narrowly divided 5:4 Court fashioned a three-part test to determine when states had to redraw districts to accommodate minority voter interests (that is, create majority-minority districts): (1) the minority group is sufficiently numerous and geographically compact to draw such a district; (2) the minority group votes cohesively; and (3) bloc voting among whites tends to result in defeat of candidates preferred by the minority group.[11] Foreshadowing her *Shaw v. Reno* majority opinion for the Court in 1993, Justice Sandra Day O'Connor argued in a concurring opinion in *Gingles* that Congress did not intend to impose on the states proportional representation or safe minority seats.

Nonetheless, with the 1982 VRA amendments on the books, the *Gingles* precedent in control, and an energetic Department of Justice urging creation of majority-minority districts (and refusing to "preclear" districts otherwise under the VRA's Section 5), racial gerrymandering reached its zenith after the 1990 census. Between 1990 and 1993 the number of majority-minority districts for blacks and Hispanics rose from 29 to 52, which resulted in a 50% increase in the number of black members of the U.S. House of Representatives (26 to 39) and a 38% climb in the number of Hispanic representatives (13 to 18).[12]

SHAW V. RENO: A JUDICIAL TURNING POINT

North Carolina, which in the last decade of the twentieth century had no majority-minority congressional districts and had not sent a black Tarheel to Congress since Reconstruction, gained a congressional seat after the 1990 census and created a majority-black district in a plan passed by its legislature in 1991. It submitted the new scheme for preclearance to the Department of Justice, which rejected it for continued dilution of minority voting strength. The Justice Department suggested that North Carolina draw a second black district and even specifically recommended the southeastern part of the state as a likely site for creating it. In response, the state did indeed add a majority-minority district but did so in the central part of the state. The now infamous serpentine Twelfth District ran approximately 170 miles southwest and was sometimes no wider than the I-85 highway corridor it followed from Durham to Greensboro to Charlotte, stringing together black population pockets.[13] The standard joke (also applied to narrow, partisanly gerrymandered districts over the years) was that driving a car with the doors open straight down the district would kill all the constituents![14]

Five white North Carolina voters, two of whom lived in the new Twelfth District, filed suit against federal and state officials, arguing that the two majority-minority districts concentrated black voters arbitrarily without regard to contiguity, compactness, or political subdivisions and with the goal of guaranteeing the election of two black members of Congress. Ruth Shaw, the lead plaintiff in the case, was a Caucasian woman from Durham, who always considered herself a moderate-to-liberal Democrat. In fact, she voted twice in the new Twelfth District for Mel Watt, the first black representative elected to Congress from North Carolina in a century. Moreover, Mrs. Shaw had participated in the 1960s boycotts of businesses that refused to serve blacks. Her consistent desire to achieve a color-blind society led her to join the lawsuit challenging the majority-minority district, which she thought demonstrated a reversion to segregation.[15] A three-judge federal district court dismissed the complaint and ruled that the plaintiffs had failed to make an equal protection claim because favoring minority voters did not constitute invidious discrimination under the Constitution and did not result in the dilution of white voters' electoral strength. The plaintiffs appealed to the U.S. Supreme Court, which accepted the case for its 1992–93 term to determine the procedural question of whether the white North Carolina appellants had stated a cognizable claim in asserting that their state had engaged in unconstitutional racial gerrymandering.

A closely divided Court ruled 5:4, per Justice O'Connor's majority opinion, that the white voters bringing the case could challenge the state's creation of the Twelfth District. Chief Justice William Rehnquist and Justices Antonin Scalia, Anthony Kennedy, and Clarence Thomas joined O'Connor in the ruling. (The majority upheld the district court's dismissal of the claim against the federal government because North Carolina was responsible for fashioning the district.) Although the Court did not determine the merits of the white appellants' case (and remanded it to the district court for a rehearing on the substantive argument), Justice O'Connor's opinion forecast trouble for defending majority-minority districts that were so "extremely irregular" and "bizarre" that they could only be rationally explained as an effort to separate voters on the basis of race. She acknowledged that awareness of race in redistricting is inevitable and not necessarily impermissible; but when racial considerations forced disregard for compactness, contiguity, and political subdivisions, O'Connor called for close scrutiny of state reapportionment that could survive only with a compelling justification. While commentators focused on the Court's criticism of "bizarre" districts, O'Connor had tried to reason that such oddly shaped districts signaled that states had strained to round up minorities with little else in common other than skin color. States then presumed that minorities—no matter how dispersed geographically—would share the same political interests and support the same candidates. O'Connor condemned such racial stereotyping as promoting "political apartheid" and "balkaniz[ation]," which took the country further from, not closer to, the race-neutral goals that she claimed inhered in the Fourteenth and Fifteenth Amendments.

Justice O'Connor's role in forging *Shaw*'s majority opinion was crucial. Two of her colleagues (Scalia and Thomas) believe that under the Fourteenth Amendment race can never be used by the government to remedy past societal racial discrimination, and Rehnquist is not far removed from that posture. Justice Kennedy, a firm believer in race neutrality and often a fence-sitter like Justice O'Connor, joined her opinion. Ironically, she frequently takes a more restraintist view of the Court's role and argues that cases are not justiciable on procedural grounds. She easily could have cast the deciding vote (with the four dissenters, Justices David Souter, Byron White, Harry Blackmun, and John Paul Stevens) to declare the case nonjusticiable on grounds that the white appellants had not proved a direct, concrete, individual injury as required by the doctrine of standing. Instead, she chose to "split the difference" between those who argue that race can never be used to remedy past racial discrimination and those who believe that benign racial classifications do not violate the Constitution. Her majority opinion did not invalidate all racial considerations in gerrymandering, but bizarrely shaped majority-minority districts were now presumptively unconstitutional. Her reasoning implied, however, that compact majority-minority districts might survive even strict scrutiny. This argument could have attracted the four dissenters and gave some hope to proponents of so-called benign race-based districts. O'Connor's position as a swing voter searching for the middle ground is a typical role for her on the Court—one that she has played for most of her nineteen-year tenure on the high bench.[16] If her reasoning in *Shaw v. Reno* seems idiosyncratic, it is because she approaches decisions on a case-by-case basis like her late mentor on the Court, Justice Lewis F. Powell, Jr.

POST-*SHAW* DEVELOPMENTS

Voting rights cases that were not directly linked to the *Shaw* precedent appeared on the Supreme Court's docket during the next term and narrowed the scope of the Voting Rights Act. In *Johnson v. De Grandy* (1994) (a consolidation of three cases) the justices ruled 7:2 in an opinion penned by Justice David Souter that no right of increased minority political representation exists beyond "roughly proportional" numbers. *Holder v. Hall* (1994), a 5:4 decision, determined via Justice Anthony Kennedy's majority opinion that the size of a governmental body (in this case a single commissioner form) cannot be challenged under the VRA as diluting the influence of minority voters because no standard exists for determining what would be a "fair" number of commissioners.[17]

Inevitably, more majority-minority district cases bubbled up to the high court by the 1994–95 term. At the very moment that Timothy McVeigh was violently expressing his views about the U.S. government through the deadly bombing of the Alfred P. Murrah Federal Building in Oklahoma City, the justices of the Supreme Court were ascending the bench in Washington on the morning of April 19, 1995, to hear two new reapportionment cases. Each challenged irregularly shaped majority-black congressional districts, the Eleventh in Georgia and the Fourth in Louisiana. In the latter, Justice O'Connor for a unanimous Court ultimately dismissed the claim by Louisiana voters in *United States v. Hays* (1995) because they did not live in the challenged district and, therefore, lacked standing. They could not show any individualized harm from the formation of the Fourth District in Louisiana.[18]

In the Georgia case of *Miller v. Johnson* (1995), however, the Court ruled on the merits. This time, the Court's other moderately conservative justice and often swing voter, Anthony Kennedy (Justice Powell's successor), wrote the majority opinion in the 5:4 case. Georgia's legislature had created the Eleventh Congressional District after the Justice Department insisted that the state add another majority-black district to the other two already in existence. It was less snakelike in appearance than North Carolina's Twelfth, but it meandered along a 260-mile corridor connecting metropolitan Atlanta's black neighborhoods to the poor black population in the coastal areas of Savannah. Justice Kennedy's majority opinion, joined by the same lineup as in *Shaw* (Justices Rehnquist, Scalia, Thomas, and O'Connor), invalidated the Georgia district because the legislature had unconstitutionally used race as the "predominant factor" in determining its boundaries.

Thus, Kennedy extended *Shaw*'s reach beyond bizarrely shaped districts, which he said offered just one type of circumstantial evidence that race had been the motivating force behind their creation. Plaintiffs could also present more direct evidence of legislative use of race as the overriding factor in redistricting. Kennedy added, "To make this showing, a plaintiff must prove that the legislature subordinated traditional race-neutral districting principles, including but not limited to compactness, contiguity, respect for political subdivisions or communities defined by actual shared interests, to racial considerations."[19] Although such race-based districts were not unconstitutional per se, they could only survive strict scrutiny under the Fourteenth Amendment's Equal Protection Clause by the state's demonstration of a compelling interest in creating them. Kennedy's opinion, however, rejected Georgia's compelling interest claim that the Justice Department required such a district for "preclearance" under Section 5 of the Voting Rights Act; the majority argued that a constitutional reading and application of the VRA did not necessarily require creation of the Eleventh District. Journalists and legal scholars alike were quick to criticize the Court's decision for failure to provide guidance to lower courts on how to determine exactly when race had been the "predominant" factor, among others, in the murky machinations of political gerrymandering.[20]

Typically, Justice O'Connor could not let the opportunity pass without adding a brief word or two to the decision. She contributed a two-paragraph concurrence which tried to refine the majority's properly "demanding" standard by noting that "[t]o invoke strict scrutiny, a plaintiff must show that the state has relied on race in substantial disregard of customary and traditional districting practices."[21] If those state practices included typically drawing boundaries that favored some other ethnic group, majority-minority districts could not be treated less favorably. She concluded with a reassuring note that the Court's standard would not jeopardize most of the country's 435 congressional districts, which she presumed were drawn according to traditional districting principles. She returned, however, to her reasoning in *Shaw*, asserting that its "basic objective" was to make "extreme instances of gerrymandering subject to meaningful judicial review."[22]

The dissenters, Stevens and Souter, from *Shaw*, now joined by the Court's newest appointees, Ruth Bader Ginsburg and Stephen Breyer (both Clinton nominees), worried about the enlarged role the federal judiciary would subsequently have to play in fielding plaintiffs' arguments that race carried more weight in state redistricting decisions than did other factors. Justice Ginsburg, who wrote one of the dissenting opinions, stated ominously from the bench on the day the *Miller* decision was announced that the Court had not uttered the "final word" on the role of race in redistricting.

SHAW REDUX AND BEYOND

Indeed, Justice Ginsburg's prediction was verified by the Court itself when it announced just a few hours after *Miller* came down that it had agreed to hear two more redistricting cases in its next term, 1995–96. "They're *back!*" the tag line from the 1986 movie "Poltergeist II," would indeed apply to the *Shaw* case, which returned to haunt the Court again. In its 1995 incarnation, *Shaw v. Hunt*[23] came back after the Court had remanded *Shaw I* to the lower court for determination of whether North Carolina could refute the racial gerrymandering claim against the First and Twelfth Districts or, if not, could justify the use of race as a compelling state interest. On remand, by a two-to-one vote, the U.S. District Court had upheld North Carolina's 1991 congressional redistricting plan as narrowly tailored to further the state's interests in complying with Sections 2 and 5 of the Voting Rights Act; Shaw and her fellow plaintiffs appealed. The Court dismissed the complaint against District One because the plaintiffs no longer lived there, but in a 5:4 ruling struck down the Twelfth District because it had been created through predominantly racial considerations that could not be justified by any of the "compelling interests" offered by the state to survive strict scrutiny. Chief Justice Rehnquist, writing for Justices O'Connor, Scalia, Thomas, and Kennedy, was particularly unpersuaded by the state's argument that a majority-minority district could be drawn somewhere other than the identifiable region of black voter dilution. The Justice Department had discerned that attenuation of black votes was especially pronounced in the southeastern part of North Carolina and suggested the creation of a majority-minority district there, but the state legislature had insisted on fashioning the second majority-black district in the central part of the state. Moreover, Rehnquist noted that the *Gingles* precedent required a geographically compact minority population to meet the test for forming a majority-minority district.

Mrs. Shaw was pleased that her cause had finally triumphed but was dismayed that charges of racism were hurled at her. She expressed her wish that Representative Mel Watt would be reelected, whatever the ultimate fate of his district, because she believed he was an "excellent" member of Congress. Her counterpart in the Court's second redistricting case of the 1995–96 term, *Bush v. Vera*[24] faced similar criticism for his controversial stand. Al Vera, a Hispanic teacher of government and economics in a Houston high school, at first glance seemed an unlikely candidate to bring a case all the way to the Supreme Court—much less one that would challenge majority-minority districts (both black and Latino) in Texas. Yet his modest, serene, dignified demeanor belied an iron will to fight for equality as he perceived it. His father, a Mexican immigrant to the United States, taught the Vera children that they were Americans and deserving of equal treatment before the law. Al Vera's crusade against districts based on race and ethnicity began as early as 1970 when Texas created a plurality-black congressional district in Harris County (Houston). The late Barbara Jordan was the first in a line of African-Americans elected to the House of Representatives from that district. Unschooled in the ways of litigation, Vera simply wrote a letter of protest to the Justice Department in 1970; he never received a response. After the 1990 round of redistricting created new black and Hispanic congressional districts that were highly irregular in shape and the product of convoluted efforts to protect incumbent seats, he consulted with fellow members of the Republican Party in Texas who shared his political and constitutional views. They contacted the North Carolina attorneys who were challenging the majority-minority districts in the *Shaw* case to obtain names of lawyers in Texas who could assist them pro bono.

Vera and five other Republican voters brought suit in 1994 against Texas's 1991 redistricting plan on the grounds that twenty-four of the state's thirty congressional districts were unconstitutional because they segregated the races and disregarded traditional redistricting principles without a compelling justification. A three-judge federal district court ruled that Districts Eighteen and Thirty (51% and 50% black, respectively) and District Twenty-nine (60% Hispanic) were unconstitutional under the *Shaw v. Reno* precedent. U.S. Court of Appeals Judge Edith Jones (a conservative Reagan appointee to the Fifth Circuit), who served on the three-judge panel, wrote for the U.S. District Court that "minority numbers are virtually all that mattered in the shape of those districts. Those districts consequently bear the odious imprint of racial apartheid, and districts that intermesh with them are necessarily racially tainted."[25]

The new Republican administration of Texas governor George W. Bush, who had defeated Democratic governor Ann Richards, reluctantly appealed the decision to the U.S. Supreme Court. After all, Bush agreed with Vera's cause, but the state's Democratic attorney general, Dan Morales, who remained in office, defended the state's redistricting plan. By the time the Court heard oral argument of the appeal in December 1995, they had handed down *Miller v. Johnson* in the previous term. Now if race could be demonstrated to have been the "predominant factor" in gerrymandering, the state had to meet the high standards of strict scrutiny.

Texas's argument before the high court first tried to avoid triggering strict scrutiny by asserting that the ideal of "one person, one vote" and incumbent protection were the dominant factors in the 1991 redistricting plan. The state argued that creating majority-minority districts was a secondary consideration. The Lone Star State's fallback position was that even if strict scrutiny were applied, Section 2 of the Voting Rights Act provided a compelling state interest to justify the 1991 redistricting plan.

The Supreme Court rejected both arguments, and in another 5:4 decision nullified the trio of Texas majority-minority districts at issue. The Court's line-up to strike down the districts (O'Connor, Kennedy, Rehnquist, Scalia, and Thomas) held firm from the previous racial gerrymandering cases. Yet in *Bush v. Vera* they could not agree on a majority opinion. Justice O'Connor announced the judgment of the Court in a plurality opinion joined by Rehnquist and Kennedy. She argued for her two brethren that Texas had unconstitutionally based its gerrymandering of the Eighteenth, Twenty-ninth, and Thirtieth Districts predominantly on race (using computers to identify minority housing patterns) to the detriment of traditional redistricting principles like compactness. This fact then sabotaged the state's Voting Rights Act argument, which under the *Gingles* precedent requires that a minority group must be geographically compact to warrant creation of a majority-minority district for it. Moreover, Texas had failed to submit compelling proof that it was attempting to counteract the effects of historical racially polarized voting. Justice O'Connor cited the Court's precedents, which, she noted, "acknowledge voters as more than mere racial statistics" and which "play an important role in defining the political identity of the American voter."[26] As she had in *Shaw I*, O'Connor railed against "unjustified racial stereotyping by government actors."[27]

Nevertheless, Justice O'Connor communicated how wedded she was to trying to find the middle ground between race-neutral and race-conscious gerrymandering. She took the unusual step of filing a separate concurrence, despite the fact that she had written the plurality opinion in the decision. Clearly, Rehnquist and Kennedy, who had joined her in the plurality judgment, were not prepared to support the reasoning in her concurrence, which presumably is why she had to include it separately. She wrote that Section 2 of the Voting Rights Act, as interpreted by the Court, is a compelling state interest and that it can coexist with the *Shaw I* precedent and its progeny. Although she acknowledged that this assumption was not determinative in *Shaw II* and *Bush v. Vera,* O'Connor argued that it could provide the framework for achieving the twin goals of combating the "symptoms of racial polarization in politics" while striving "to eliminate unnecessary race-based state action that appears to endorse the disease."[28]

Justice Thomas wrote an opinion, joined by Justice Scalia, also concurring in the judgment. The Court's two most conservative justices wanted to extend the *Miller v. Johnson* standard to trigger strict scrutiny if a state used race to any degree in redistricting.

The now-familiar litany of dissenters (Stevens, Souter, Ginsburg, and Breyer), considered to be the liberals on the Rehnquist Court of the mid–1990s, maintained their position that although "racial classification may risk some stereotyping" it might sometimes be necessary in the context of "the long history of resistance to giving minorities a full voice in the political process."[29] Stevens, who wrote the dissent, called the Court's decision "seriously misguided."[30]

Another fulfillment of Justice Ginsburg's prophesy in *Miller v. Johnson* that the Court had not written the final word on redistricting cases was the return of Georgia's redistricting plan to the Court in the 1996–97 term in *Abrams v. Johnson.*[31] After *Miller* had struck down Georgia's majority-minority Eleventh District because race was the predominant factor in its creation, the case reverted to the Georgia legislature. White Democrats, black Democrats, and Republicans deadlocked over how to redistrict the state and left the matter to a federal district court, which decided that one majority-black district was all that could be fashioned without violating traditional principles of compactness and contiguity. The court drew a majority-minority district around the compact, contiguous black communities of Atlanta. The Justice Department and civil rights groups appealed the district court's plan to the U.S. Supreme Court.

In yet another 5:4 ruling with the exact same voting lineup as the previous four majority-minority cases, the Court affirmed the lower court's scheme for

Georgia. Justice Kennedy's opinion for the Court reasoned that the state need not have more than one majority-minority district and that "[t]he trial court acted well within its discretion in deciding it could not draw two majority-black districts without itself engaging in racial gerrymandering."[32] Kennedy also noted in his opinion, and he emphasized this point by reading it from the bench on the day the decision was announced, that two black members of the House of Representatives from Georgia (Cynthia McKinney and Sanford Bishop, both Democrats) had won reelection in 1996 despite the dismantling of their majority-minority districts after *Miller*. Still, the four dissenters, this time led by Justice Breyer, bemoaned the fact that the Court had tied the hands of legislators who could not use race "even for the most benign or antidiscriminatory purposes."[33]

STUCK IN THE THICKET?

At the turn of the century, which touches off a new round of reapportionment, redistricting, and gerrymandering after the 2000 census, where do we stand on this issue of majority-minority districts? North Carolina's redistricting plan was the only one that had not been resolved as late as the spring before the 1998 congressional elections. After *Shaw v. Hunt* was decided in June 1996, the state got a stay of the order to redraw the problematic Twelfth District and kept its snakelike borders intact for the 1996 election. Congressman Watt was reelected, as he had been in 1994. The North Carolina legislature, split between a Democratic Senate and Republican House, agreed to make the Twelfth more compact. They shortened it to 102 miles long and widened it. A federal three-judge panel approved it unanimously, but one of the original plaintiffs challenged it again. This time, a different trio of federal judges summarily invalidated the district, and it was back to the drawing board for the state legislature. As of the spring of 1998 they had failed to solve their decade-long struggle over the Twelfth District. Expressing the frustration of a candidate who was not sure where to campaign, Representative Watt complained, "I don't want anybody to think I don't have a district."[34] He was reelected in the 1998 election, and in December of that year, as a member of the House Judiciary Committee, he played a visible role in the televised hearings on President Bill Clinton's impeachment.

North Carolina's Twelfth District resurfaced on the Supreme Court's 1998–

99 docket in *Hunt v. Cromartie*,[35] with North Carolina arguing that the district (now with slightly less than a majority of blacks) was really redrawn in 1997 to protect Democratic incumbent Congressman Watt. Counsel representing the voters who challenged the Twelfth District countered that while partisanship may have played a role in the gerrymander, the state attempted to consolidate Democrats who were black.

Conundrums abound in this political and constitutional debate. States are now caught between the Justice Department's edicts to minimize dilution of minority voters under the Voting Rights Act and Supreme Court rulings barring race as the predominant factor in redistricting—unless justified by a compelling state interest, which may or may not include compliance with Justice Department orders. The Court itself has obviously been balkanized by the majority-minority district cases between two evenly divided factions who have diametrically opposite views on the use of race to address past racial discrimination. Justice O'Connor's efforts to "split the difference" between the two factions have drawn criticism from both sides of the debate for producing a murky jurisprudence that often typifies judicial compromise. As studies by political scientists have begun to question the overall efficacy of majority-minority districts, even the civil rights community is less certain about advocating them. They may boost descriptive representation of minorities at the expense of substantive representation. Research indicates that majority-minority districts may create safe seats for minority representatives but dilute minority influence in overwhelmingly white districts that have been "bleached" of constituents of color.[36] These white districts may also lean toward the Republican Party, bolstering the GOP's majority in Congress to the detriment of senior black members of the House of Representatives who could become committee chairs if the Democrats controlled the lower house.[37]

Yet given the complex and multifaceted concepts of representation, democracy, voting rights, race, and partisan politics, which lie at the heart of this dispute, can we expect any more from our constitutional, political, and legal system? Even if we disagree about the outcomes of the system, is it not possible that the Founders' construct of separation of powers, checks and balances, and federalism is operating in all its maddening, frustrating, inefficient glory on the matter of majority-minority districts? The thicket may be uncomfortable, but so is democracy itself.

PART II
Superintending Political Actors

CHAPTER 7

The Right to Party

The United States Supreme Court and
Contemporary Political Parties

John C. Green

I ONCE ASKED AN EXAMINATION QUESTION about the concept of
"responsible" parties and the idea of "party discipline." A desperate
student who obviously had not done the reading answered to this effect:

I believe in responsible parties. As far as I can tell, we Americans are guaranteed the right to party. It is clearly part of the pursuit of happiness and
enshrined by the Founding Fathers in the Bill of Rights. We can get together with friends, let down our hair, and blow off steam. But parties
must be responsible. They must not be too noisy or run too late; they
must discourage drinking and driving, unsafe sex, or general obnoxious-
ness. If we are not responsible, we could lose our right to party. Now as for
discipline, I believe it is a matter of personal preference and thus probably
does not belong at parties.

My student's attempt to bluff his way through the examination
neatly captures an emerging view of political parties in the law. The
United States Supreme Court has created something like the "right to
party" for the formal organizations of the major parties, based on the
associational rights of party members. Advocates of responsible parties and party discipline have been pleased with this development, although the right to party provides legal support for party organizations that are irresponsible from their point of view. In any event, this
line of cases will draw the Supreme Court more deeply into the political thicket, enmeshing it in intraparty disputes and expanding its role
in superintending American democracy.

This chapter describes the origins, development, and consequences of the right to party. After a brief description of the new rights of parties, this jurisprudence is placed in the context of the legal status of the two-party system and its evolution over time. Next, the role of association rights in the "deregulation" of parties at the state level is described, followed by a discussion of the meaning of this change and the right to party.

THE NEW RIGHTS OF PARTIES

Over the last thirty years, the U.S. Supreme Court has reduced the scope of state government regulation of formal organizations of the major political parties, including rules regarding primary and general elections, and the internal arrangements of party committees.[1] These rules were found unconstitutional because they violated the associational rights of party members. The right of association is a legal construct derived from the First Amendment rights of speech, assembly, and petition for redress of grievances. It recognizes that the exercise of such rights by citizens logically extends to their association with one another in political organizations. While not absolute, the right of association limits government regulation of political organizations in order to protect the basic political freedoms of citizens.[2] The Court has now extended such protection to the members of formal party organizations.

Advocates of party responsibility have applauded this jurisprudence because it allows for greater party responsibility and discipline.[3] The concept of party responsibility is the best developed normative view of how parties ought to behave in a democracy.[4] Responsible parties articulate a clear program for public policy before an election, enact the program if they are elected, and defend the program in the subsequent election; likewise, the losing party articulates a clear alternative to the program of its rival in power. This concept requires that the party's candidates and officeholders actively support the party's program, and that party leaders enforce discipline on behalf of the program. Under these circumstances, it is argued, the citizenry can hold parties responsible for government at the ballot box.

From this point of view, American political parties are notoriously irresponsible, frequently failing to articulate clear programs and enforce discipline on their candidates and officeholders. State regulation of political parties, similar to public utility regulation, has allegedly contributed to such irresponsibility by reducing the control parties have over their own activities. Hence, less state regulation would remove an impediment to responsible behavior. However, even advocates of responsible parties admit that this opportunity for greater responsibility may be ignored by party leaders.[5] Other observers are more skeptical, arguing that the new rights of parties are likely to further encourage irresponsibility and a lack of discipline.[6] In terms of the heuristic model presented in chapter 1, the development of the right to party is a good example of the U.S. Supreme Court's micromanagement of political actors.

A potential problem lies precisely with the application of the concept of associational rights to parties: all else being equal, the exercise of individual rights tends to undermine, rather than strengthen, collective responsibility.[7] Indeed, the lack of party discipline arises in large measure from the individual activities of party leaders, candidates, officeholders, activists, and voters. This tendency may be exacerbated by the recent development in party organizations.

THE LEGAL FOUNDATIONS OF AMERICAN POLITICAL PARTIES

Compared to other modern democracies, the American two-party system is a rather odd thing, being both deeply fragmented and nearly comprehensive. On the first count, the major political parties are a diverse collection of organizations, actors, and activities. And on the second count, these fragmented parties have a nearly comprehensive hold on the political system, having the allegiance of most citizens and winning nearly all the elections. Both the fragmentation and comprehensiveness of the major parties have roots in the law.

The basic structure of American government, especially federalism and separation of powers, tends to fragment party organizations. Such fragmentation is further encouraged by the widespread use of single member, plurality elections at all levels of government, a system which advantages the largest local parties over smaller rivals.[8] In addition, the U.S. and state constitutions identify the role of voter and public official, but are silent on parties, the institutions that link the two together. This silence was often deliberate: the Framers of the U.S. Constitution were openly hostile to political parties, which they derided as "factions."

Consequently, many commentators have labeled American government as "antiparty" in its foundations and operation. Certainly it is difficult to create and maintain responsible and disciplined parties under such conditions. However, this argument should not be pushed too far. The very conditions that fragment parties also encourage their formation as a means of coping with divided government. Indeed, political parties formed almost immediately after the antiparty Constitution took effect, led by some of the fiercest critics of factions among the Framers. Each fragment of government—be it geographic, institutional, or role-based—was a potential focal point for organizing parties. Parties formed in states and localities; around the executive and legislative branches; and among voters and officeholders. Once formed, these organizations had strong incentives to coalesce in order to influence enough fragments of the government to actually govern.

Under these conditions, the most stable arrangements were two loose coalitions of party organizations. These "major" parties were extraordinarily successful in political terms, so much so that they changed the way the government operated. For example, the popular election of the president and the creation of congressional districts were both products of the two-party system.[9] Even dissenters from the major coalitions formed their own party organizations as a way to compete. By the late nineteenth century, the golden age of parties, the major party coalitions came to dominate nearly all aspects of political life.

Such parties are sometimes called "control" parties because of their ability to control the personnel of government.[10] This degree of control was sometimes so strong that the parties could behave in a responsible and disciplined fashion. Control parties were especially strong at the local level, weaker at the state level, and weakest at the federal level. The fabled urban "machines" and "bosses" are the best-known examples. Present-day advocates of responsible parties are often nostalgic for control parties, even though such parties often abused their power.

Indeed, the abuses of control parties provoked a spate of state government regulations to prevent vote fraud, excessive patronage, corruption by government officials, and the insulation of party leaders from voters.[11] Among the most important of these regulations was the institution of primary elections for nominations. Along with primaries came legal definitions of party membership and candidate qualifications as well as rules for the internal organization and operation of parties. These changes occurred in the context of stricter state regulation of elections, including ballot access laws, the Australian (secret) bal-

lot and voter registration, and also regulation of patronage and campaign finance. The underlying motive for these regulations was to ensure the integrity
of the elections, prevent corruption, and enhance democratic accountability.

PUBLIC UTILITY PARTIES AND
CANDIDATE-CENTERED POLITICS

Many of these regulations were imposed by antiparty reformers during the
Progressive Era, who were deeply hostile to control parties. However, most of
the elected officials who enacted party regulations were themselves members
of the major parties, and as a consequence, the two-party system was incorpo-
rated into the new regulatory regimes, the parties becoming agents of state
government for the purpose of conducting elections. The major party organizations thus lost a degree of control, but received special privileges not accorded to minor parties or nonpartisan groups. Such parties were like public utilities: private organizations regulated to achieve public purposes.[12] Just as public
utilities were justified by the existence of a "natural monopoly" in certain
goods and services, the major parties were seen as a "natural duopoly." State
government regulated electoral activity in the face of natural concentrations of
power in control parties.

Public utility status moved the two-party system from being dominant to
nearly comprehensive. Although the major party coalitions gained even more
influence over politics and government than in the nineteenth century, formal
party organizations and their leaders, now recognized in law and regulated by
statute, exercised markedly less control over other elements of the party, such
as voters and officeholders. Partly for this reason, local party organizations experienced a long period of party decline in the twentieth century.[13]

Perhaps the best evidence for this decline was the rise of candidate-centered
politics. Primaries gave individual candidates and their supporters freedom to
organize and capture party nominations on their own. Candidates became
largely self-recruited organizers of their own candidacies and campaigns. Such
candidates were thus less beholden to party leaders and were largely au-
tonomous once in office. State regulations often went so far as to prohibit efforts by party leaders to influence candidates in any way, shape, or form, including making endorsements.

What role did the judiciary play in these developments? Both state and federal courts took a hands-off approach. State party regulations were challenged in state court for violating the rights of "voluntary associations," but these cases were overwhelmingly decided in favor of the government's interest in maintaining the integrity of elections "within the bounds of reason and not arbitrarily."[14] The Supreme Court followed a similar pattern, as evidenced in the White Primary Cases.[15] Here state parties were subjected to federal rules based on primaries as state action, but the cases also affirmed the private character of formal party organizations. Parties were still regarded as having many of the rights of private groups, but with less control over their activities: parties had the right to exist and operate within the context of state regulations.[16]

By the mid-twentieth century, advocates of responsible parties found this situation troubling, despite the standards of conduct imposed on parties by state law. Both the American constitutional structure and state laws appeared to limit the ability of the major parties to behave responsibly.[17] From this point of view, the formal organizations of the major parties were supposed to control the government, but in effect, the government controlled them. To some scholars, the height of public utility parties in the 1950s was the "nadir of party freedom."[18] Under the circumstances, greater party responsibility would require the deregulation of the public utility parties at the state level. Arguments in favor of reducing state regulations soon became relevant, albeit from an unexpected source: the rise of a new kind of party organization.

THE RISE OF SERVICE PARTIES

Starting in the late 1960s and gaining momentum in the 1970s and 1980s, the formal party organizations at the national and state levels became stronger and more sophisticated, reversing the traditional distribution of party strength.[19] These shifts resulted from new tasks undertaken by the formal party organizations: the provision of services to candidates.[20]

Unlike the older control parties, service parties made very little effort to determine nominations, opting instead to assist nominated candidates in the general election. Indeed, the rise of service parties is in large measure a response to the advent of candidate-centered politics.[21] In many respects, service parties were a natural extension of public utility parties. After all, public utility parties provided a critical service to candidates and their supporters: publicly regulated forums for organizing candidacies and campaigns—a service not unlike the assistance provided by party caucuses in legislatures.[22]

One kind of assistance to candidates was cash contributions to candidates, but of greater importance was in-kind assistance, such as polling, fundraising, technical training, and political research. A third kind of assistance, independent expenditures on behalf of a candidate or against the opposition, merged cash and in-kind assistance, and may become more important in the near future. The ability of national and state parties to provide these kinds of services to their candidates has made them a major force in national politics, prompting talk of party "renewal" or "revival."[23]

In this context, party organizations could be quite useful to candidates, and thus candidates became interested in taking control of such party organizations. These trends are best illustrated in presidential politics. Beginning in the early 1970s, first the Democrats and then the Republicans reformed their presidential nominating process. These reforms extended primaries to the selection of most national convention delegates and set uniform criteria for the characteristics of delegates.[24] These reforms were motivated by a desire to make the presidential nominations more democratic by giving party voters a direct role. However, the effect of the reforms was to allow candidates to dominate the nominating conventions and thus the national parties.[25] Candidates quickly learned how to file their own slates of delegates in the states and wage elaborate campaigns to elect them to the convention. The net effect has been to make delegates representatives of candidates as opposed to the representatives of state and local party organizations.[26]

Advocates of responsible parties are critical of candidate-centered politics and not especially pleased with the rise of service parties. From this point of view, candidate-centered politics is inherently irresponsible and service parties do little to foster party responsibility or instill discipline. However, some scholars were impressed with the possibilities for greater party responsibility by service parties and this possibility intensified demands for deregulation of parties at the state level.[27]

PARTY DEREGULATION

The rise of service parties put serious strains on state party regulation, independently of scholarly opinion.[28] For the first time, national organizations were the dominant elements of the major party coalitions, and they began to create and set rules for their state and local affiliates. Service parties were also the subjects of more intense battles between contending candidates and among rival interest groups. Inevitably, elements of this conflict appeared in the federal courts, with arguments for deregulating parties advanced by strong parties interested in deregulation.[29] Perhaps it is not a coincidence that the major parties experienced deregulation in a period when other kinds of public utilities, such as telephones and railroads, were deregulated as well.

Beginning in the late 1960s, the Supreme Court developed the concept of associational rights as an argument for removing state party regulations of parties. This concept was first fully presented in a civil rights case, *NAACP v. Alabama* (1958).[30] The state of Alabama required the NAACP to give its membership lists to the state as a condition of registering as a "legal entity," and the NAACP refused on the basis of its members right to privacy in their "associations." The Supreme Court agreed, ruling that First Amendment protection of speech and assembly when combined with the due process clause of the Fourteenth Amendment implied a constitutionally protected right of association. The Court described the right of association as an "indispensable liberty" which the state government could not violate except under unusual circumstances.

Within a decade of this decision, the concept of associational rights was firmly established in the law, mostly to protect organizations representing racial minorities from state laws.[31] During the same period, the Supreme Court was using a similar concept in a parallel line of cases involving another kind of minority, the Communist Party. In these cases, the rights of speech and privacy were advanced to protect the Communist Party from state regulation in a manner similar to the NAACP. For instance, in *Sweezy v. New Hampshire* (1957), the Court stated, "any interference of the right of political association is simultaneously an interference with the freedom of its adherents."[32]

Given these rulings, it was a short step to apply association rights to the major political parties in defense of the freedom of their members. But unlike the regulation of interest groups and minor parties, where the states sought to interfere with political activity, state governments had long regulated the major parties to protect political activity. In a series of cases, the Supreme Court rejected the validity of such justifications for state regulation of parties. These cases arose from intraparty disputes within service parties, where one fragment of a major party claimed that a state government (and in effect, another fragment of the party) was limiting the freedom of its members.[33]

The first set of cases involved disputes between state governments and national party organizations. The first of these cases was *Cousins v. Wigoda* (1974).[34] At issue here was the fate of delegates to the 1968 Democratic National Convention properly elected under Illinois law, but in violation of the new rules of the national Democratic Party. The Democratic National Convention refused to seat the delegates in question and the state of Illinois (then controlled by Democrats and thus a stand-in for the Illinois Democratic Party) sued, arguing that the integrity of the electoral process outweighed the claims of the national party. The Supreme Court ruled in favor of the national Democrats, stating that the state governments had no "constitutionally mandated role" in nominating presidential candidates, and further, state political parties were voluntarily affiliated with the national party by virtue of accepting a call to send delegates to the national convention. If each state had its own rules, the Court reasoned, it would disrupt the nomination process and thus violate the associational rights of the national party members as expressed through the national party's nominating rules.[35]

This line of reasoning was further expanded a decade later in *Democratic Party of U.S. v. LaFollette* (1980).[36] As part of the 1980 presidential race, the Wisconsin Democratic Party chose to incorporate Wisconsin's open primary law into its delegate selection rules. The open primary allowed voters who were not Democrats to vote for the allocation of convention delegates among the various Democratic contenders, in contradiction to national party rules requiring closed primaries, where only Democratic voters could participate. When the Wisconsin plan was rejected by the national Democratic Party, the case eventually came before the Supreme Court, where the Court strongly endorsed the national party's position on the basis of associational rights. The state government's interest in maintaining the integrity of the electoral process did not justify violating the associational rights of national party members to have the delegate selection process of their own choosing.[37]

Other cases extended this argument to disputes between state parties and state governments. A good example is in 1979, the Massachusetts Democratic Party enacted a charter that created a preprimary endorsing convention.[38] To be included in the Democratic primary a candidate for statewide office had to receive at least 15 percent of the votes cast at the convention. The state legislature, controlled by Democrats, refused to amend state election law to allow for the 15 percent rule. The resulting dispute eventually appeared in the state supreme court, which ruled in favor of the party based on associational rights.

Here the state court declared that the party and not the state had an interest in making sure Democratic Party nominees had some minimal support among the party's voters. "Freedom of association," the state supreme court remarked, "would prove an empty guarantee if associations could not limit control over their decision to those who share the interests and persuasions that underlie the association's being."[39] The Supreme Court affirmed the state court's decision.

All these cases involved intraparty disputes between the leaders of formal party organizations and their copartisans in state government. This line of reasoning was extended to cross-party disputes in *Tashjian v. Republican Party of Connecticut* (1986).[40] In 1984, the Connecticut state Republican convention adopted a rule allowing independent voters to participate in statewide (but not local or state legislative) Republican primaries. The Democratic majorities in the state legislature refused to amend state election law to accommodate the state Republican Party's new rules. The Connecticut Republicans then sued and the case was eventually heard by the Supreme Court, which backed the party. In its opinion, the Supreme Court ruled that a party's determination of its membership is "protected by the Constitution." Fifteen states joined Connecticut in its appeal to the Supreme Court arguing that this decision would, in effect, change state election law any time a party were to adopt a rule contrary to state law.[41] This ruling is analogous to *California Democratic Party v. Jones* (2000), where the Supreme Court ruled that the California blanket primary system violated the political parties' associational rights.[42]

Yet another extension of the autonomy of formal party organizations occurred in *Eu v. San Francisco County Democratic Central Committee* (1989),[43] a suit brought to test the constitutionality of California party law by a collection of local party organizations, inspired by academics.[44] Among other things, the case challenged the detailed regulation of internal party organization on the basis of violation of the party members' associational rights. In response, the state of California claimed that internal regulations prevented any one party faction from taking over the party and denying other party members an effective voice in party affairs. The Supreme Court ruled in favor of the plaintiffs, striking down the state regulations. *Eu* advanced the cause of party autonomy by removing regulations aimed at the internal arrangement of the major parties and not directly connected to state election law.[45]

In sum, the Supreme Court substantially removed state regulations of formal party organizations in primaries and other aspects of nominations as well as their internal organization. While these changes did not completely dismantle the public utility parties, the new service parties were granted a great deal of autonomy, while still maintaining their special status in state law. As much as anything, it was this conjunction of autonomy and privilege that pleased advocates of party responsibility and discipline, for now the formal party organizations had the opportunity to behave in a more responsible fashion. However, such an outcome is not guaranteed in an era of service parties.

THE RIGHT TO PARTY

The net effect of this line of cases has been to establish something like the right to party for formal party organizations and their leaders. This right has several interesting features. First, its basis, the associational rights of party members, is not a collection of rights accorded to party organizations as such, but the logical extension of the rights of individual citizens who chose to associate with the party. By this logic, the actions of formal party organization are protected from state regulation only to the extent that they flow directly from the exercise of individual party members' rights. Indeed, the Court has been willing to abridge the associational rights of parties when confronted by the rights of other citizens, as in *Morse v. Republican Party of Virginia* (1996). (Here, the Virginia Republican Party was unable to impose a registration fee on state convention participants because it violated the 1965 Voting Rights Act.)[46] From this perspective, parties are simply instruments for the exercise of the individual rights of party members and not agents of responsibility or sources of discipline—unless the members so desire.[47]

Second, this right to party gives legal sanction for the *activities* of formal party organizations. Parties are not defined by their structure or procedures, but rather by the things they choose to do, which are extensions of things their members choose to do when exercising their fundamental rights. In this context, the term party is a verb, meaning "to engage in certain kinds of acts," instead of a noun, meaning "a regularly constituted organization." Formal party organizations are protected from state regulation when their leaders do things as the result of the exercise of the rights of their members.

Defining parties by their activities is not necessarily undesirable, since freedom to act politically is fundamental to democracy, and the freedom to party is widely regarded as critical to a well-functioning democracy. Neither is it necessarily problematic to allow party leaders to act on behalf of party members. The potential problems are that the Court has to articulate standards for determining who speaks for the parties (thus representing the associational rights of party members), and what the appropriate activities of parties might be (thus setting reasonable and nonarbitrary limits on the activities of party leaders). In both areas, the Court has failed to recognize the fragmentation and comprehensiveness of the American party system, as well as the special features of service parties.[48]

In terms of the first issue, who speaks for the party, it is unclear why the Supreme Court has found that formal party leaders speak for party members instead of the party's officeholders in state government or the party's voters, or why national party leaders are superior in this regard to state or local party leaders. For example, under the *Eu* ruling, could party leaders change the party rules so as to disenfranchise their rivals? While it may be desirable to find ways to create and alter internal party rules, surely there must be some standards for the legitimacy of such rules. What is to keep party leaders from engaging in activities that violate the associational rights of their own party members?

In terms of the second issue, what are the appropriate activities of parties, it is unclear what kinds of party activities are acceptable and which are not. Do associational rights allow members and/or their leaders to impose their will on state or local governments? For example, if the *Tashjian* ruling were taken to its logical extension, party leaders could abolish state primary law by deciding to nominate their candidates in some other fashion. While eliminating primaries might be a good idea, surely it should be done through the normal legislative process and not at the whim of party leaders. What is to prevent a party from violating the rights of the community as a whole?

The rise of service parties has made these questions especially important. It is less clear than ever who speaks for the party and thus whose associational rights are at stake in disputes over party activities. Also, determining the appropriate activities of parties has become even more important, given that service parties can do more things. Candidates and other actors compete for control of party organizations and the services they provide, and once in control, engage in activities that serve their own interests. While intraparty competition is surely desirable, there is a clear need for rules and regulations to govern it. Ironically, it was just this problem that led state governments to regulate control parties in the first place. Indeed, the whole idea behind public utility parties was that electoral institutions should not be open to abuse from powerful private groups.

Interestingly, the right to party appears to set a higher standard for party regulation than other areas of election law, where the Court has tended to defer to state governments. For example, when minor parties, independent candidates, or voters challenge state regulations, the Court has frequently allowed state governments considerable leeway.[49] A good example is *Timmons v. Twin Cities Area New Party* (1996), where the Supreme Court allowed the state of Minnesota to ban fusion ballots (where parties can nominate each other's candidates), but also allowed other states, such as New York, to have them if they so desired.[50] In other aspects of election law, the Court has often attempted to articulate standards to guide state governments.[51] Advocates of responsible parties may want the Court to articulate similar standards for party organizations.

CONCLUSIONS

In sum, the Supreme Court has provided a legal underpinning for the operation of service parties by identifying a "right to party." The winners in intraparty battles control the formal party organizations and have considerable autonomy to deploy their organizations in politics, even to the extent of challenging state election law. Formal party organizations are thus free to "service" the victors in intraparty competition. In effect, the Court has endorsed the dominant trends in formal party organization. One can certainly make a case for such an endorsement, but the Supreme Court should do so by addressing the legitimacy of service parties directly, or leaving such matters to more qualified branches of government.

Under these circumstances, the judiciary will become enmeshed in resolving intraparty disputes. Already a number of significant cases have arisen where losers in intraparty disputes have used the rubric of associational rights to ask the court to intervene on their side.[52] The Supreme Court may find itself supervising the intensely competitive politics of service parties, and thus risks becoming a superintendent in the very heart of the political thicket.

As my student unwittingly suggested, the Supreme Court has guaranteed the "right to party" to American citizens and the major party organizations with which they associate. It is possible that contemporary service parties will use this right responsibly, as advocates of responsible parties hope. They may also choose to do otherwise and make party discipline a matter of personal preference. However, the consequences of such a decision may be serious—for the parties, the Supreme Court, and democracy itself. Even weak students of political parties know that one can lose the right to party if one "partys" irresponsibly.

CHAPTER 8

The United States Supreme Court as an Obstacle to Political Reform

The Weak Constitutional Justification
for the Two-Party System

David K. Ryden

THE MOST DISTINCTIVE and enduring characteristic of the American electoral system has been the political monopoly enjoyed by its two major political parties. The dominance of the two-party system implicates fundamental principles of American politics; it raises important questions involving the role of parties in achieving a representative democracy, and touches on such foundational democratic values as stability, electoral choice, meaningful political participation, governmental responsiveness, and accountability. The two-party system owes its longevity and strength in large part to the vast web of state laws, which present insurmountable barriers to minor and new political parties seeking to challenge the status quo. At the same time, the United States Supreme Court has borne ultimate responsibility for delineating the appropriate constitutional balance between the competing values of open and democratic participation, on the one hand, and the state's interest in stability and ballot control, on the other.

In the recent decision in *Timmons v. Twin Cities Area New Party* (1997),[1] however, the Court appears to have abandoned its role as institutional guardian of representative values. It disregarded bedrock democratic values of representativeness, openness, and choice in deference to the state's articulated interest in a stable two-party system. As a result, the major political parties that dominate those state legislatures are thoroughly entrenched as the architects of those rules which preserve the status quo, and which inure and redound to their benefit. With the Court's complicity, the incumbent officeholders and parties have free rein to perpetuate their power at the expense of developing or new parties. Yet *Timmons* comes at a time when, and in a political environment where, the electorate is less engaged in politics and less bound to the major parties; on the contrary, alternative partisan voices are increasing in number and frequency, and the public is ever more friendly to the presence of new parties.

It is the premise of this chapter that the Court's shortsightedness has potentially disastrous consequences for American politics. The basic goal of "fair and effective representation" has been subordinated to legitimate, but lower rank, values of political stability and ballot control. The by-product is a politics characterized by two increasingly polarized, ossified, unresponsive major parties, less able or likely to provide meaningful representation for the host of interests present in society. The state of the parties and their tenuous standing with the public compel a revisiting of the assumptions underlying the two-party system. Moreover, the active engagement of the Supreme Court is imperative to the careful consideration of questions that have for too long eluded serious examination. The adjudicatory principle of deference to politically elected state officials, embraced by a majority of the Court, may as a general matter be acceptable. But when the matter at hand pertains directly to the power and position of those officials, instincts of self-preservation and protraction of power render them untrustworthy caretakers of representative government.

PARTIES, POLITICS, AND BALLOT ACCESS LAW

Parties are "more the products of their environment than architects of it."[2] Their activities are molded by overarching contextual forces, which both constrain and create opportunities for successful performance of party functions. One of the most important of these is the legal environment. Parties operate within a constitutional framework that divides power among various branches of government, disperses power among differing levels of government, and overlays upon them a system of checks and balances and other structural constraints. Statutory curbs further complicate things as a maze of state laws (along with an occasional federal law) define parties' nominating powers, fundraising capabilities, organizational autonomy, and other attributes.

This inhospitable legal environment has made it extremely difficult for minor parties to translate public misgivings with the major parties into sustained electoral success. The oppressive constitutional construct merges with a network of state and federal election laws which are overtly hostile to minor parties. Single-member districts and winner-take-all, first-past-the-post electoral arrangements create enormously high hurdles for minor and new parties. Large-scale grassroots organization building, a seeming prerequisite for a serious third-party movement, seems beyond the reach of minor parties. Voters are deeply conditioned to the two-party system; they are disinclined to waste votes on unelectable candidates. Minor and new parties are severely disadvantaged in garnering access to the ballot, qualifying for public financing, securing candidate placement position on the ballot, and in the structuring of primary laws. This amalgamation of constitutional, political, and legal biases has produced an impenetrable set of barriers to the formation and maintenance of a three- or multiple-party system.

The Supreme Court has had a major role in defining the limits of the legal bias in favor of the major parties. Minor parties have preferred litigation and the judicial appeals process to legislative reform, given that remedies are unlikely to come from state legislatures that are captive to, and admittedly well served by, the two-party system. Legal challenges aimed at loosening the major parties' electoral stranglehold have raised questions of whether they are deserving of their privileged legal status. Consequently, the Court has been influential in determining to what extent the values promoted by the two-party system are enshrined in the Constitution, and alternatively how friendly the Constitution should be to third-party challenges.

The Court's efforts to clarify minor parties' legal status and to locate them within the constitutional framework have focused primarily on state restrictions on access to the ballot. Since George Wallace's independent presidential bid in 1968, the Court has periodically examined the statutory criteria for allowing minor parties or independents a slot on the ballot, with decidedly mixed results.[3] Commentators have noted the inconsistent nature of the Court's ballot access law, as it has vacillated between outcomes reflecting differing emphases on the manifold values at stake.[4]

Wallace's independent candidacy was at the center of the first ballot access case, *Williams v. Rhodes* (1968).[5] His American Independent Party had failed to meet the petition qualifications for third-party candidacy in Ohio on time and had been denied a place on the ballot. The Court rejected the state statute in question as unfairly advantaging established major parties and unconstitutionally violating "the right of individuals to associate for the advancement of political beliefs" and "to cast their votes effectively."

The Court's decision in *Jenness v. Fortson* (1971),[6] just three years later, was difficult to reconcile with *Williams*. *Jenness*, like *Williams*, centered around a petition requirement for third-party ballot access in Georgia; the requirement exempted only parties who had received 20 percent support in the previous election. This time, however, the Court upheld the requirement, despite its clear restriction of individual voting rights. Instead it favored the state interest in reasonable ballot access restrictions and the importance of major parties in avoiding confusion of the democratic process.

In *Lubin v. Panish* (1974),[7] the Court returned to its support of expanded voting rights in *Williams*, rejecting a California statute used to bar an indigent who could not afford a filing fee from running for city office. While the Court continued to uphold the state's legitimate interest in reasonably sized ballots, "California's failure to provide alternative means of qualifying for the ballot violated the plaintiff's freedom of association."[8] *Lubin* made no distinction between major and minor parties, requiring only that "ballot access . . . be genuinely open to all, subject to reasonable requirements." Individual access to the ballot was ruled as important as the major parties' role in organizing electoral majorities.

In the same year, however, the Court upheld a different California ballot access statute in *Storer v. Brown* (1974).[9] This statute denied access to independent candidates who had been affiliated with a major party within a year of the primary. In upholding the law, the Court cited a legitimate state interest in avoiding splintered parties and giving the public a clearly defined choice on the ballot. "The Court implicitly accepted the elementary importance of a two-party system in achieving these goals"[10]—a sharp contrast to *Lubin*, in which the two major parties were taken to have no special priorities or greater rights.

The Court continued to waver in its next ballot access case, *Anderson v. Celebrezze* (1983).[11] *Anderson* revolved around John Anderson's independent presidential bid in 1980. As with George Wallace in *Williams*, Anderson declared his candidacy too late to satisfy the time limit for Ohio's petition requirement, and was thus denied a place on the ballot. As in *Williams*, the Court struck down Ohio's statute as violating the associational rights of Anderson's supporters.

"The Court portrayed the independent candidate as a rallying point for like-minded citizens. The denial of Anderson's position on the ballot consequently hampered those citizens' freedom to associate."[12] While extending the associational rights of voters declared in *Williams, Anderson* stood in sharp contrast to the *Storer* case, in which the Court expressed a state interest in *avoiding* splintered parties.

In those cases striking down state ballot restrictions *(Williams v. Rhodes, Lubin v. Panish, Anderson v. Celebrezze)*, the Court came down on the side of democratized ballot laws permitting greater numbers of candidates, enhanced political participation, and increased voter choices. When it upheld the state's regulatory power *(Jenness v. Fortson, Storer v. Brown)*, it relied upon a constitutional preference for a stable two-party system, the avoidance of splintered parties and factionalism, and limited electoral choices. But in none of these cases did the Court make a case for the two-party system. Doffing its hat to the two-party system in *Williams v. Rhodes,* the Court cited the need for a greater modicum of support for a party to get on the ballot, but never elaborated on the benefits of strong established parties. "It merely recognized the goals of avoiding confusion, deception, and frustration of the democratic process, leaving unexplained how the major parties accomplished those goals."[13]

The Court's inability to articulate a constitutional basis for the two-party system was on display in its 1992 *Burdick v. Takushi*[14] decision upholding a Hawaii state ban on write-in voting. It cited the interest in promoting strong, stable parties as means of channeling and organizing expressive activity at the polls. Otherwise it wholly ignored the functional attributes of parties or how ballot access rules might relate to them. It left the state-recognized, judicially sanctioned duopoly solidly in place, but without adequate justification as to its primacy.[15]

The implicit rationale for the two-party system not articulated by the Court is one of controlling the ballot to maximize the significance and meaning behind elections. Elections require institutionalized means of focusing public opinion and implementing majority preferences if they are to serve as representative guides to governance. Limits on who can run for office are intended to shape and sharpen ballot choices. Narrowing the numbers of candidates in general elections, and the labels under which they run, channels public opinion and gives meaning to the votes cast. These objectives are not without cost, but come at the expense of competing values of expanded choice. A demarcated ballot between competing party programs and candidates runs counter to unhampered, unfettered individual electoral participation and greater ballot access.[16]

TIMMONS V. TWIN CITIES AREA NEW PARTY

For those hoping for a more thoughtful and nuanced explication of major- and minor-party rights and interests, *Timmons v. Twin Cities Area New Party* (1997)[17] was a sore disappointment. The case technically was not a ballot access case; rather it addressed *who* parties could place on the ballot once they had earned the legal right to a line on the ballot. It involved a direct constitutional confrontation between minor party interests and the maintenance of a strong two-party system. The case grew out of the Minnesota New Party's decision to nominate as its candidate for a state house seat a Democratic incumbent running unopposed in the Minnesota Democratic-Farmer-Labor (DFL) primary. This practice of multiple parties nominating the same candidate is known as fusion balloting, and has often been an effective tactic to advance the views of third and minor parties. Neither the candidate nor the DFL objected to the New Party's decision. Minnesota law, however, prohibits an individual from appearing on the ballot as the candidate of more than one party, and state election officials refused the New Party's nominating petition. (Fusion balloting is similarly prohibited by some forty other states in the country.) While neutral on its face, the fusion prohibition burdens minor parties, since any candidate twice nominated is sure to opt for the major-party nomination if forced to choose. The New Party challenged the law as a breach of its First Amendment associational rights.

In a decision rife with crosscutting ramifications for partisan organizations, the Court upheld the fusion ban. The six-member majority emphasized the authority of the state to enact reasonable regulations of parties, elections, and ballots to reduce election- and campaign-related disorder. It acknowledged the state's "strong interest in the stability of their political system" and explicitly found that the U.S. Constitution allows states to protect "political stability . . . through a healthy two-party system."[18] States were not required constitutionally to lower or remove the many hurdles facing third parties in the American political arena. The "correspondingly weighty valid state interests in ballot integrity and political stability" justified the two-party bias. The opinion marked a victory for the major parties, but constitutes the nadir of the Court's jurisprudence on political representation and parties.

PARTIES, THE COURT, AND THE CONSTITUTION

Timmons presented difficult questions regarding the constitutional status of political parties and the party system, the relative standing of major and minor parties, and the role of the Court in entertaining questions directly impacting the elected branches of government. Such questions have always been problematic, given parties' lack of historical grounding in the Constitution. The relationship between parties, party systems, and the Court is one historically marked by ambivalence and ambiguity. Denigrated by the Framers and absent from the Constitution and Bill of Rights, parties sprang up out of necessity rather than predesign. The American party system and the tradition of party government developed outside the constitutional framework, "an anomaly engrafted onto a constitutional system that did not plan for them,"[19] and arguably was hostile to them. On the one hand, party values and objectives are in opposition to fundamental principles underlying the Constitution. The constitutional design was intended to produce a government that could perform without the need for parties; indeed, it was structured to preclude their rise, or at least to control their influence. The constitutional pillars of federalism and the separation of powers were the structural guarantors of limited government, dividing and dispersing power, and making it more difficult for the newly constituted national government to achieve tangible results. Parties were and are a means of overcoming those constitutional barriers to governmental action. For those hoping to reform the Framers' plan for limited government into a more programmatic, activist, and energetic state, parties are a necessity.[20] In this sense, parties and the Constitution are by their nature fundamentally at odds, and pull in opposite theoretical directions.[21]

On the other hand, the Constitution contains provisions that have proven critical to the formation and maintenance of parties. The First Amendment rights of expression, assembly, and association made it possible for parties to originate and perpetuate. Moreover, pro-party scholars and theorists have long contended that parties are essential to the realization of other fundamental principles and values bound up in the Constitution; they assert that parties, while existing and operating outside of the Constitution, are instrumental in the accomplishment of foundational constitutional values such as democratic responsiveness, consent, equality, public choice, and accountability. Parties are indispensable means of building consensus across branches and levels of government within a system of separated powers and in an era when citizens look to the federal government to provide a raft of services. Without party structures, effective governance is inconceivable.[22] Hence the argument for a constitutional order which incorporates political parties and party systems, notwithstanding their absence from the constitutional text.[23]

This lack of clarity in the parties' position relative to the Constitution has presented a dilemma for the Court. Given the historical prominence of parties in electoral politics, the Court has inevitably been asked to consider the constitutional status of parties. It has encountered parties frequently and in a variety of contexts, from patronage practices and partisan primaries to parties' role in the drawing of district lines, the funding of campaigns, and ballot access. In weighing the constitutional rights and restraints applicable to parties, the Court has been a determinative force in shaping the legal environment in which they must operate. While molding the practical operation of the political system generally and parties specifically, the Court has had a substantial effect on how well or poorly parties fulfill their functions as channels of representative government.

The parties' extraconstitutional nature complicates jurisprudential decision making and interpretation. Of what value are originalist modes of interpretation? On what basis can and should the Court decide such cases? How should it balance the Framers' disdain for parties with the reality of their integral place in contemporary politics? In short, the means required to treat parties in a doctrinally consistent or theoretically sound manner seem beyond the reach of the Court. Parties' hazy constitutional standing means that "the party institution is unlikely to conform very neatly to lawyerly doctrinal categories."[24]

The Court's task is further complicated by ongoing disagreement over the value of parties and the optimal form of party politics. In addition to the Framers' antipathy toward parties and the absence of textual guidance, the Court lacks a clearly accepted, normative understanding of parties and their role and functions. Little consensus exists within the legal and political science communities for a constitutionally grounded responsible party government that might inform the Court's consideration of parties. And the larger political culture is inhabited by a public increasingly hostile to parties and partisan organizational control of elections and government.

The consequence has been a modern era of Supreme Court jurisprudence marred by a basic indifference toward parties as institutional safeguards of representative democratic politics. In ballot and voter access issues, the Court has blurred obvious distinctions between independent candidacies and party organizations. It has actually subordinated parties to other groups in carving out a group right to representation in gerrymandering disputes. In campaign finance, parties were excluded altogether from the discussion until recently. In severely circumscribing patronage, the Court has refused even to acknowledge the possibility that such practices might solidify the institutional foundations of partisan organizations or enhance their effectiveness as governing agents.

These judicial shortcomings have had practical ramifications for the effectiveness of modern parties. Certainly a host of independent factors have contributed to the decline of political parties. But the Court has reinforced a legal environment that is largely unfriendly to parties. It has upheld states' power to regulate parties. It has confirmed (with minor exceptions) progressive reforms that badly weakened parties in their electoral, organizational, and governing capacities. It has been complicit in undermining party influence in favor of an individualistic, unmediated, participatory form of politics. In sum, the constitutional environment erected by the Court has as a rule made more difficult the parties' task of reversing their fortunes.

The theoretical deficiencies in the Court's parties/politics jurisprudence are well illustrated by the *Timmons* decision. For instance, the Court's easy embrace of the state interest in promoting a stable, strong two-party system certainly demands more justification than what the Court offered, given the absence of constitutional footing for parties. How does the Court square the constitutional acknowledgment of a two-party system (or any party system) in light of the Framers' disavowal of parties, and their desire to restrain them?[25] The Founders would have contested the notion that the state should work to preserve and stabilize a two-party system. Yet the Court explicitly recognizes that as a legitimate, constitutionally protected state interest.

Moreover, if the Framers had conceded the need for a party system, a multiparty system would appear to be more consistent with their intentions than a two-party system. James Madison's exposition in "Federalist No. 10" revealed the Framers' deep-seated fear of factions (that is, parties), and how best to control them.[26] For Madison and his colleagues, the greatest threat to liberty was the disproportionate influence of a single sect or faction that might dominate the interests of other groups or the general welfare of the public. The structural response to that threat was to broaden and enlarge the republic, incorporating as many voices as possible, thereby making it more difficult for any particular group or interest to dominate. The diffusion of power by maximizing the interests participating in the political sphere would mitigate against any single voice wielding undue power or control. The partisan lock that the two major parties hold today hardly fits the Madisonian vision. It enables the two dominant factions to muffle alternative minor-party voices while reinforcing their own standing. The Framers likely would be more disturbed by this scenario than by power fragmented among a host of partisan organizations.

THE COURT AS CARETAKER OF REPRESENTATIVE GOVERNMENT

In *Timmons*, the Court forewent serious efforts to confront these theoretical challenges by acquiescing to the popularly elected branches of government. The conservative philosophical inclinations of the majority frequently lead them to defer to Congress and state legislatures, especially in those situations when the constitutional text or Framers' intentions are not definitive. This jurisprudential mode of decision making was at the heart of Rehnquist's opinion in *Timmons*.

[The] Constitution permits the Minnesota Legislature to decide that political stability is best served through a healthy two-party system. . . . In deciding that Minnesota's fusion ban does not unconstitutionally burden the New Party's First and Fourteenth Amendment rights, we express no views on the New Party's policy-based arguments concerning the wisdom of fusion. It may well be that, as support for new political parties increases, these arguments will carry the day in some State legislatures. But the Constitution does not require Minnesota, and the approximately 40 other States that do not permit fusion, to allow it.[27]

For Rehnquist, the constitutional silence as to party systems permits state legislatures to bolster that system by banning practices that might be destructive to it. It would be inappropriate for the Court to second-guess that policy choice in the absence of clear constitutional authority.

Putting aside the general merits of the judicial philosophy of deference to elected bodies, I posit that such a philosophy is inappropriate, in this case and in that special catalogue of cases that are instrumental in shaping the workings of the political system, because it is potentially devastating for representative politics. While the Constitution may not furnish precise solutions to difficult political questions, democratic theory argues in favor of a more assertive Court. The conservative impulse to yield to legislative edict is potentially lethal within the context of that class of cases that involve directly the power and position of the legislators themselves. These include disputes over term limits, redistricting and gerrymandering, and campaign finance reform. In *Timmons* and other cases implicating the two-party system, the two dominant parties control the political system and have an inherent conflict of interest. Their instinctive tendency will be to take whatever measures are needed to perpetuate continuation in office, to solidify their hold on power at the expense of minor developing parties. The outcome will be to aid and abet the major parties and their incumbent officeholders in maintaining the status quo. Hence, the Court is justified in acting more aggressively in those situations where popularly elected policy makers are likely to promote their own interests before those of the greater good or sound public policy.[28] Otherwise, the Court is consigned to the role of accomplice in legislative entrenchment; in short, it becomes a major obstacle to legitimate political reform.

TOWARD A JUDICIAL DOCTRINE OF PARTIES

The myopia of the Court's capitulation to state legislatures is attributable to a lack of understanding of party theory. The Court has long struggled with two competing notions of parties; one is of the party as a private entity and hence insulated from the regulation of the state; the other is of the party as the functional equivalent of the state, standing in for it in certain contexts in which it then becomes subject to the regulation by the state. In ballot access and other cases in which the Court has reinforced the two-party system, it has ignored the morphing of parties into the state. It has blindly acknowledged the "state's interest" in stability through the two-party system, even where the parties and the state are functionally equivalent.

A modest understanding of party theory would protect the Court from this mistake. Party scholars have trichotimized parties for purposes of analysis and scholarship. Parties in their *organizational dimension* participate in a host of grassroots campaign and electoral activity; recruiting candidates, raising money, writing platforms, registering, and so on. In the process, they hope to maximize the *electoral dimension,* the identity between voter and party reflected in the voting behavior of the electorate in the selection of their leaders. The ultimate objective is to produce parties in their *governing dimension,* in which they comprise the structures for organizing and carrying out the tasks of policy making and governance. Unfortunately, the Court has demonstrated "an almost studied ignorance of the interdependence of the organizational, electoral, and governmental functions" of parties.[29] An elementary understanding of these theoretical and functional facets of partisan entities is essential to appropriate constitutional treatment of them. For example, the parties' governing function points to the merging of the parties' identity with that of the state, an overlap that has powerful implications for the operation of representative government. The major parties in their governing and electoral modes converge to stifle representation. The dominant parties in government, motivated by mutual self-interest, work in tandem to produce laws (such as the fusion ban), that favor them in their electoral form (by undermining the electoral performance of minor parties).

The blurring of the lines between the governing parties and the government belies the Court's easy reliance upon the articulated "state interest" behind the fusion ban. The "state's interest" is less at stake than are the interests of the two dominant parties that control it. Regulations are imposed, not for the sake of good government, but toward the end of safeguarding power by those holding it. The "state's interest" becomes a cover for the interests of the beneficiaries of the regulation, the two parties responsible for its passage. What suffers is the basic fairness and equity of the system. How can the state impartially regulate parties when it is comprised of the two major parties? How can the "state interest" control when it is tantamount to the interests of the two dominant parties? As Justice John Paul Stevens noted in his dissent in *Timmons:* "In most States, perhaps in all, there are two and only two major political parties. It is not surprising, therefore, that most States have enacted election laws that impose burdens on the development and growth of third parties. The law at issue in this case is undeniably such a law. The fact that the law was both intended to disadvantage minor parties and has had that effect is a matter that should weigh against, rather than in favor of, its constitutionality."[30]

The most significant flaw with *Timmons,* then, is the Court's perception of its role. When the major parties exploit their preferred positions within government to generate self-serving regulations, a more assertive judiciary is necessary to overcome the inherent conflict of interest. These circumstances compel a more stringent mode of review, one in which the Court strictly scrutinizes purported legislative objectives for merit.[31] The Court should require more than a perfunctory showing. States should make a specific showing of actual harm justifying state action before imposing restrictive regulatory powers in the purported interests of political stability. The states (that is, the major parties) should not be permitted to implement regulations that further depress minor parties in the name of a purely hypothetical or speculative threat or danger. There must be a showing, either empirical, historical, or otherwise, that the harms that are anticipated have actually occurred.

A MATTER OF POLITICAL REPRESENTATION

But is the judiciary competent to decide these issues? In order to check the actions of parties within government acting as the state, the Court must articulate a jurisprudential doctrine to serve as a decision-making tool in these contexts. This requires a basic understanding of political representation and its realization. The Court has lacked a coherent theory of parties and politics generally to guide its decision making. In ballot access issues, the Court defers to state legislative will rather than substantive consideration of political representation; it does not appreciate how representation is accomplished, nor does it comprehend the role played by major and minor parties within the party system. Invoking principles of ballot integrity and stability of the legislative process, the Court never explains the significance of those values in a representative government or how the practice of fusion undermines or otherwise relates to them. Yet the propriety of fusion, like ballot access and other issues relating to the electoral process, is primarily a question of *representation*. Party systems are an integral component of a political system that is presumed to be representative in nature. When the representatives themselves have a conflict of interest that precludes their taking measures to adequately safeguard the well-being of the representative process, the Court must intervene to ensure the integrity of the representative system. This requires some grasp of the multitude of concepts, activities, and actors that contribute to the realization of political representation.

This is admittedly no easy task. Representation is not reducible to simple definition or easy categorization. It occurs through a maze of activity (legislative roll call voting, ballot behavior by the electorate, campaigning, constituent service, campaign donations, lobbying); it is performed by a multitude of political actors (political parties, interest groups, individuals, legislatures, legislators, the government); and it is designed to produce a variety of results (sound policy outcomes, a responsive government, accountable public servants, political fairness and equity, the voicing of opinions and interests, the selection of representatives).[32] Given the complexity of political representation, it is unrealistic to expect from the Court a coherent or integrated jurisprudential theory of representative democratic governance. Democratic political theorists and experts on representation cannot agree on it—what can one expect from judges with little or no training in it?

Nevertheless, the Court can infuse its decision making with a consideration of the elements of representation theory, unlike what it did in *Timmons*. In this instance, it compels that the Court consider carefully the function and operation of party systems and their relation to representational goals. The Court is capable of identifying those dimensions of representation theory that best fit a given situation. But any conceptual framework for analyzing constitutional notions of representation must acknowledge the richness, complexity, and variety of its faces, forms, and manifestations. We should expect the Court to choose the doctrinal path that best comports with the complex reality of political representation, that unclogs the channels of representation so that the multiplicity of modes and actors constituting the labyrinth of representation are free to operate.

FUSION BALLOTING—THE MINOR PARTIES' LAST CHANCE?

The *Timmons* Court's approval of fusion bans was hardly an inconsequential victory for the two-party system and its beneficiaries. Supporters and detractors of fusion agree that the practical ramifications for major and minor parties are considerable. The ban foreclosed a rare avenue for tangible minor-party inroads into the two-party hierarchy, bolstering the hand of the two dominant parties while further diminishing the likelihood of measurable success for minor or new parties.[33] It deprives minor parties of tangible opportunities to alter, influence, and affect the politics of elections and governance. First, fusion might increase the emphasis by the candidate on the issues, policies, and positions of the minor party. A twice-nominated candidate has an incentive to woo the new party's voters, since a second place on the ballot will aid his performance. That candidate is likely to take seriously the agenda of the minor party, giving greater attention to its issues to hold its support. Second, the minor party might actually influence the selection of the nominee of the major party, possibly to the point of being able to insist on a minor-party member as the fusion nominee. Third, a strong third-party showing aided by fusion balloting could allow the party to claim credit for the electoral victory, thereby meriting the loyalty of the successful fusion candidate. This might translate into patronage, a cabinet position, or some other voice or presence in the new administration. Fourth, there is likely to be enhanced media exposure for the minor party and its platform via the fusion candidate. This stems from the fact that elections are more than simply about picking officeholders, but have an *expressive* function as well, generating ideas, causes, issues, and interests, and attracting attention to them. This is especially important if the two-party system that selects the officeholders is to fulfill its representative function. For example, the New Party strategy has been built much more around influencing the Democratic Party and pulling it in a leftward direction than in actually winning office.

Fusion also is likely to improve minor parties' long-range electoral performance, in the form of greater public support for and participation in the party's activities and organization. Historical and contemporary examples illustrate the capacity of minor parties to use fusion to effectively alter the dynamics of electoral politics. The practice was widely used with great success by the Greenbackers and Populist parties and others during the heyday of party politics at the turn of the century, an era when issue-oriented third parties also flourished. More recently, the Liberal and Conservative parties have used fusion to gain an unusually prominent role in the New York state politics, New York being one of the few states to permit fusion.[34] A fifth benefit of fusion is the greater capacity of minor parties to run a full slate of candidates. Fusion enables them to attract higher-caliber candidates for all offices by nominating for lower-level offices major-party candidates who have the chance to win. Finally, benefits should accrue over time to the minor party in terms of grassroots organization, participation, and enthusiasm. Fusion enables a new party to maximize its support by attracting independents or those Democrats and Republicans who would otherwise not waste a vote on an unelectable third-party candidate. This greater electoral strength should in turn generate incentive and enthusiasm for a minor party to organize and recruit members.

FUSION, PARTY SYSTEMS, AND POLITICAL REPRESENTATION

By foreclosing these benefits, *Timmons* artificially insulates major parties from minor-party challenges during a time when the public mood otherwise might be far more sympathetic to such challenges. The decision further solidifies the two-party duopoly at the expense of serious minor-party challenges that might otherwise disturb the status quo. But do the conflicting values of representation, stability, and ballot integrity warrant reinforcing the two-party system? Ultimately the question is one of representation, and whether or not the two-party system as it currently operates is capable of generating fair and effective representation. Has the Court successfully "reconnect[ed] questions of party rights to the process of representation?"[35] A careful reading of *Timmons* reveals that it has not. The word "representation" is never used in the majority opinion, nor is the concept ever discussed by the majority. A strong case can be made that the electoral rules have been so skewed in favor of the two-party system that the realization of a fair, equitable, and responsive system of representation has been seriously jeopardized. Unfortunately, the Court never joins the issues, failing to consider or engage such arguments.

Fusion and the benefits redounding to minor parties enhance representation in many ways. First, the fusion candidate represents a greater number of voters who electorally supported her. She will be more inclined to "act for" those who had a part in electing her once in office, including members of the minor party that helped elect her. In contrast, a minor party with little or no electoral clout will go unheeded. Second, the possibility of patronage or a physical presence in government may positively impact governance, cultivating policy outcomes acceptable to a greater segment of the public. Third, a greater range of issues will get a hearing during the campaign, since fusion amplifies the issues and ideas of the minor party (via the exposure and coverage the fusion candidate is likely to receive). Fourth, these factors should combine to produce more responsive public officials, who cannot ignore significant alternative voices and interests that otherwise could be dismissed due to the legal biases of the two-party system. Fifth, the minor party and its adherents are symbolically represented through the affiliation of their party label with the winner of the election. Finally, the most significant contribution is likely to come from the enhanced competition between parties that in the long run will produce a more representative system. Interparty competition is critical to the relationship between party performance and the fulfillment of representative values. The level of interparty competition is a direct function of how open the system is to minor-party challenges. That is, "Generally, the quality of a party's performance of . . . representative functions depends on the degree of both intraparty and interparty democracy. . . . Interparty democracy concerns the kind of partisan competition that exists at the various levels of the electoral system; it focuses on whether electoral choice is confined to one or two partisan alternatives, or whether third-party and independent challengers are relatively competitive."[36]

Fusion practices and the fortified minor-party challenges should produce sharper, more focused, better attuned (i.e., more representative) major parties. Major parties that must be cognizant of credible minor parties and their voters' desires and issues will be more responsive and more accountable (i.e., more representative). In contrast, the legal entrenchment of the two major parties that insulates them from any real third-party challenges has created ossified entities that often fail the test of representativeness. Stronger minor-party challenges would compel the Democratic and Republican parties, if they are to maintain their dominant positions, to address the concerns of the electorate clearly and directly. The presence of stronger third-party challenges should eventually secure the representation of significant voices within the electorate that do not fit neatly into the major-party coalitions. "Multiple party nomination may promote, rather than jeopardize, the integrity of the election system and the stability of the political process by fostering greater competition, greater participation, and greater representation in American politics."[37] Ultimately, this is a question of the representative integrity of the system in the face of little or no competition or choice and major parties that are artificially enhanced through the score of two-party system biases.

THE COURT, PARTIES, AND PUBLIC OPINION

Electoral representation, as a function of party systems, also entails public opinion. Nancy Maveety describes it as "a linkage between public opinion, partisan affiliation, and electoral behavior. . . . electoral representation is a process whose outcome is the allocation of political power, or control over political decision making. From this perspective, representation rights concern the value of votes (or participatory actions generally) in terms of the power that they exert."[38] Electoral laws that distort the linkage between public opinion and party performance at the polls result in a less representative system. This is precisely what the ossified two-party system does, muffling, even ignoring, public opinion by nullifying the meaningful input of third-party adherents into political decision making. It minimizes the representative value of their votes in terms of the power it generates. The goal of stability evolves into a hardened, inflexible party system. A legally encased two-party system does not give the two major parties sufficient incentive to reflect and respond to a wide array of interests in society. Stability must be counterbalanced by the need for competition and accountability.

The two-party legal bias undermines the likelihood of reform from within that might accomplish this. Major parties perform best when they fear minor-party challenges. By highlighting important issues the major parties would rather not face, minor-party competition produces more responsive and intellectually honed parties. The more diffused the competition, the more dulled, conservative, and averse to risk the major parties become. In a party system that is receptive to minor-party activity, the party that wants to win elections must respond to the concerns of significant independent or third-party movements. Note the intense competition between Republicans and Democrats over the Perot constituency and the budgetary and fiscal issues he raised in 1992. Legal barriers that obfuscate sizable third-party support only calcify the major parties, rendering them less responsive to concerns of voters and widening the breach between parties and an alienated electorate.

There has been much debate over the continuing strength and viability of American parties. But the most important measure of a strong party is that it maintains broad electoral appeal and the loyalty of the citizenry.[39] Ultimately, the state of the parties rests on their standing with, and relevance to, the people. The most energized organizations or cohesive governing parties are of little use if people dismiss them as insignificant or corrupt, and consequently withdraw from the political process. All the talk of better organized or more clearly defined policy-oriented parties is wasted breath without an attuned, informed electorate. Parties that have been jettisoned by much of the public as ineffectual and unnecessary cannot satisfy the constitutional goals of accountability, public choice, and the legitimization of democratic government.[40] By this measure, today's major parties are at risk.

Democrats and Republicans are perceived as not adequately reflecting the preferences and interests of voters. They have failed to cultivate voter loyalty to them or the political system. Yet manufactured legal props distort the level of public support and make significant voter shifts to third parties unlikely. *Timmons* strengthens an already oppressive legal regime, the cumulative effect of which is to discourage fresh interests or new voices from seeking power through new parties or existing minor parties.[41] As Justice Stevens noted in his dissent: "It demeans the strength of the two-party system to assume that the major parties need to rely on laws that discriminate against independent voters and minor parties in order to preserve their positions of power. Indeed, it is a central theme of our jurisprudence that the entire electorate, which necessarily includes the members of the major parties, will benefit from robust competition in ideas and governmental policies."[42]

The failure of debilitated, enervated parties to serve as necessary conduits for republican values warrants, even compels, their constitutional status. Too often, Court decisions have eviscerated parties' capacity to serve constitutional ends. But it is not for the courts to artificially prop up the major parties through legal means. The influence of political parties has been circumscribed by a historical tradition of weak parties, constitutional indifference, and public hostility. The Court can do little about the latter, nor should it. The laws and courts ought not to attempt what parties are unable to do for themselves, which is to merit the loyalty of the electorate. The Court can remedy its constitutional indifference and create a permissive constitutional environment within which parties can flourish; it remains up to the parties themselves to rise to meet that challenge. Moreover, what is at first glance a resounding endorsement of the two-party system may in fact be an illusory victory which carries the seeds of further party decline. Further dampening of minor-party activity will not necessarily translate into enhanced well-being of the two major parties. Further muffling of legitimate minor-party outlets may well only amplify the frustration and disgust with the major parties and the system as a whole. The legal favoritism the Court has helped bestow upon the major parties will not stem the decline of partisanship among the electorate or quell the public's lack of confidence in partisan institutions. The major parties themselves must clearly demonstrate their continued relevance to a highly skeptical public. To show that they are worthy of the constitutional protections they enjoy, the major parties must sharpen their traditional and unique democratic functions. Ironically, they might be better able to do this in the face of stiffer minor-party challenges. It is for the Court to scrutinize laws such as ballot access criteria under the bright light of the realities of the political process, with an eye toward their impact on parties, voters, and representation.[43]

PLURALISM, GROUP POLITICS, AND THE PARTISAN RIGHT OF ASSOCIATION

So how is the Court to rectify its party-poor decision making? One cannot expect the Court to have a full-fledged or consistent theory of representation. But it should be able to articulate some mediating principles as it weighs the implications of its decisions. While the Court's reticence to intervene more aggressively in these cases is understandable, given the lack of consensus in other corners, it is potentially fatal. A healthy dose of representation theory is needed.

With respect to the Court's treatment of parties and party systems, the theoretical key to the riddle lies in group/pluralist accounts of politics. The pluralist descriptive ideal of representative government and policy decision making is one of competition and interaction between as many collective interests as possible.[44] At the heart of pluralism is a realization of the politics of group conflict,[45] and the central importance of collective political involvement to individual political existence. Group affiliation is essential to individuals who hope to have some meaningful say in a large-scale democracy. Moreover, it is the give-and-take between groups, in a system that seeks to include as many group voices as possible, which produces the soundest policy outcomes for the greatest number of citizens.

Group theory implies the need for legal structures that maximize outlets for the expression of group political behavior, and that also generate, accommodate, and arbitrate group interests and conflicts. Laws responsible for political representation must acknowledge the importance of groups, starting with political parties. One means by which the Court has accomplished this recognition in the past is through the First Amendment right of association as a means of achieving "fair and effective representation."

In the 1980s, that right appeared to be firmly established. One scholar concluded that the legacy of the Court under Chief Justice Warren Burger was a doctrinal shift in emphasis "from individual participation to the political access of group interests . . . a broader constitutional discussion of the functions of representation." The Burger Court was responsible for infusing representation policy with group politics, "validat[ing] group-based representation claims across a range of political institutions [to] bring constitutional doctrine into harmony with pluralist politics." It did so by "systematically apply[ing] the First Amendment freedom of association to protect the rights of party members as a group." In the context of ballot access, this meant acknowledging "the importance of group association for effective political action, . . . view[ing] collective association as instrumental to some, as yet inchoate, conception of group representation."[46]

Timmons suggests a major step backward by the Rehnquist Court with respect to the associational rights of partisan organizations, in particular those of minor parties. *Timmons* hinged on a minimalist view of associational rights, as the Court subordinated minor-party associational rights to the state's interest in stability and ballot integrity. Though the fusion ban denied parties the right to nominate the same candidate, the Court cavalierly denied that the ban involved any core associational activities or burdened associational rights. In other words, "Whether the Party still wants to endorse a candidate who, because of the fusion ban, will not appear on the ballot as the Party's candidate, is up to the Party. . . . In sum, Minnesota's laws do not restrict the ability of the New Party and its members to endorse, support, or vote for anyone they like."[47] The Stevens dissent (joined by Justices Ruth Bader Ginsburg and David Souter) skewered this logic, noting that "[t]he fact that the Party may nominate its second choice surely does not diminish the significance of a restriction that denies it the right to have the name of its first choice appear on the ballot. . . . The ban leaves the Party free to nominate any eligible candidate except the particular 'standard bearer who best represents the party's ideologies and preferences.'"[48]

The majority's narrow construction given to the partisan right of association was decidedly antiparty. What activity goes more to the heart of party association than deciding who shall be its designated nominee on the ballot? That task is at the very center of carrying out those basic purposes for which parties exist—to advance a message by identifying a candidate who represents that message, nominating her, and working to elect her to office. The fusion ban interferes with the most basic right of a party to select that person who best reflects and embodies its collective identity. In the end, the Court's dismissive treatment of partisan association may ultimately be destructive of all party rights, and cannot bode well for parties generally. These decisions frequently come down to the weighing of the rights of association against the state's regulatory interest. The long-term effect may be to weaken party autonomy in avoiding a state regulatory machinery which is usually invoked in an environment hostile to parties.

The *Timmons* majority found it significant that the minor party and its members can still vote for the candidate they like, just not under their party label. This argument is premised upon a crabbed, individualistic understanding of association. It defines associational rights only in terms of the individuals who belong to the party, with no regard for the organization itself. According to this view, association is an incidental by-product of the vote for the person. One associates only to the extent one expresses the same electoral support for a candidate as do other voters. But this is association in the most ephemeral sense. It neglects the representative benefits achieved through formal party affiliation, and the amplification of one's political voice through like-minded partisan organizational behavior.[49]

Therein lies the theoretical misconception which has plagued the Court's doctrinal elucidation of associational rights. Political association suggests a cognizance of the organizational models of collective political action. The Court's individualistic explication of that right obscured the organizational character of collective political activity. It neglected the intertwining of the participatory rights of individuals and the associational rights of the groups to which they belong, especially parties. If collective representation is essential to meaningful individual political existence, as pluralist group theory suggests, then partisan associational rights and "fair and effective representation" are inextricably linked. Instead, the Court has treated association as "but the medium through which its individual members seek to make more effective the expression of their own views."[50]

This richer understanding of association would not free the Court of the difficult determination of what partisan activities rise to the level of constitutional protection. But the right of association for minor parties and their members must at the very least include the right to select the "standard bearer who best represents the party's ideologies and preferences."[51] The right means little if the party is denied the ability to promote candidates "at the crucial juncture at which the appeal to common principles may be translated into concerted action, and hence to political power in the community."[52] In the end, the Court seems to have little conscious awareness of the uniqueness of party functions, especially in the context of minor parties. "The treatment of and effect on parties is virtually incidental to a broader devotion to individualistic rights of association."[53]

The realization of fair and effective representation of all groups requires a more fully textured definition of rights of association, one which is extended to all partisan organizations, both major and minor. Associational freedoms cannot be discussed apart from the relationship between the performance of party functions and the realization of political representation. The achievement of "fair and effective representation" has become a hopeless pipe dream, thanks to the thorough corruption of the pluralist ideal. The pluralist account has been badly distorted by group disparities in resources that have heavily skewed the system in favor of certain groups to the detriment, marginalization, or outright exclusion of others. Representation is further undermined by a two-party system that serves "interest-group liberalism" and the campaign contributors, rather than the host of voices and interests existing out in the world. These forces in turn permit the more ideologically driven party activists to shape the major parties, to the exclusion of minor parties and more centrist voices.

CONCLUSION

The U.S. Supreme Court cannot avoid its primary responsibility for those structures and institutions that yield representative democracy. Formal legal arrangements are determinative of the practical workings of representative government. The guardian of those systems must be the Court, since the vested interests of the legislators render them incapable of so doing. But is the Court capable of carrying out that daunting responsibility? Can it carve out constitutional principles that address issues of representation both in a thoughtful and realistic manner?

To date, the Court has largely sidestepped this role. The rejuvenation of our representative system compels that it do better. This places a heavy onus on political science and legal communities alike to assist the judiciary in this considerable task. Political scientists and theorists must make the case for parties cogently and understandably. The legal community and political scientists must work together in interdisciplinary fashion to present cases with some coherent doctrinal basis.

But primarily it requires the Court to elucidate a set of mediating principles, a conceptual approach to representation that will enlighten judges and justices as to the possible repercussions a particular issue might have for the functioning of the system. I have suggested elsewhere that one such principle might be the generation of "conflicts of interests" through party/group channels of politics. In a nutshell, it recognizes that the multifaceted demands of representation are best met through the cultivation of conflicts of interest—that is, by maximizing the conflicting interests which a legislator must acknowledge and to which she must respond (i.e., consistent with Madison's "Federalist No. 10"). Strong, healthy, energized party systems are the key to simultaneously maximizing and controlling those conflicts.

For example, a duopolistic party system fails to optimize the interests bearing on the legislator and legislature, since credible third-party voices cannot break through the legally oppressive electoral machinery. Permitting fusion balloting, by comparison, would enhance representation by increasing the interests to which the legislator must be attuned. She cannot dismiss or ignore the voice of the minor party (if she is a fusion candidate), that helped to elect her. Similarly, on a collective level, fusion forces the major party to be more aware of and responsive to the minor-party agenda, heightening the conflicts of interest brought to bear on the party and making it more representative.

In the end, I am not ready to wholeheartedly embrace a multiparty system. But an analysis of party systems from a functional perspective within the context of representation objectives will furnish the Court with a badly needed framework for addressing important questions. It might enable the Court to better locate minor and new parties on the constitutional/legal spectrum. Only by an increased focus on the goal of fair and effective representation will the Court realize that minor and major parties alike constitute important and legitimate means of satisfying democratic functions.

CHAPTER 9

Ironies Abound in the United States Supreme Court's Rulings Limiting Political Patronage

David M. O'Brien

IRONIES ABOUND ALONG THE INROADS MADE into political patronage by the U.S. Supreme Court, especially from *Elrod v. Burns*[1] in
1976 and *Branti v. Finkel*[2] in 1980, to *Rutan v. Republican Party of Illinois*[3] in 1990 and *O'Hare Truck Service, Inc. v. City of Northlake*[4] in 1996.
Those rulings have been highly controversial inside and outside of
the Court, because they extended First Amendment protection to
"nonpolicymaking" state and local employees in holding that their
political affiliation may not be the basis for their being hired, promoted, or fired.

Notably, in lamenting and foreboding opinions dissenting Justices
Lewis F. Powell, Jr., and Antonin Scalia denounced the rulings for (1)
stripping political parties of an importance resource, and (2) consequently contributing to the erosion of a competitive two-party political system, while (3) failing to appreciate how the practice of political
patronage helped to uplift ethnic and racial minorities, and (4) for
opening the floodgates for litigation.[5] In doing so, they echoed the
views of some political scientists concerned with the demise of a competitive two-party system and the judiciary's interference with the political process.[6]

However, first, consider a 1997 decision, *Jenkins v. Medford,*[7] handed
down by the U.S. Court of Appeals for the Fourth Circuit. That case
began when Bobby Lee Medford won election as sheriff in Buncombe
County, North Carolina, in November 1994. He fought a good fight
against the incumbent, promising supporters either jobs or promo-

tions in the sheriff's department. Once in office, Medford promptly fired Steven Jenkins and several other deputy sheriffs who had in their off hours campaigned against him. They in turn sued on the ground that their First and Fourteenth Amendment rights were violated. In short, a typical instance of political patronage: "To the victor go the spoils." Indeed, the facts are almost identical to those in *Elrod*; both cases involved the practice of political patronage and the dismissal of deputy sheriffs.

Prior to *Elrod,* such dismissed and disgruntled public employees could not have sued. Their only recourse was the polls, the next election, and not the courts. And for much of the nineteenth and first half of the twentieth century, machine-style patronage politics dominated major cities, particularly in Chicago, New York, and Philadelphia.[8] In recognizing the First Amendment free speech and association rights of public employees, *Elrod* and other rulings contributed to changing that.

Still, in *Jenkins* the Fourth Circuit held (8-5), in what the dissenters deemed an "ironic decision,"[9] that the dismissed deputies had no constitutional claims and Medford was within his authority to fire them. When that decision was appealed in 1998, moreover, the Supreme Court denied review, leaving the appellate court's decision undisturbed.

Before turning to the Fourth Circuit's opinion in *Jenkins,* it is helpful to review briefly how the Supreme Court came to enter the "political thicket" of state and local political patronage and to arrive at the crossroads that it did in balancing the First Amendment claims of public employees against the tradition of patronage and democratic politics.

THE COURT AND THE "POLITICAL THICKET"
OF POLITICAL PATRONAGE

From at least one perspective—namely, that of federal employees—the Court's defense of the First Amendment rights of state and local employees appears ironic. Historically, the Court has not been sympathetic to federal employees' free speech claims.[10] Throughout much of the nineteenth century, the federal government, like state and local governments, was governed by a political spoils system.[11] With the passage of the Pendleton Act in 1883 Congress moved toward creating a merit-based system of federal employment. Subsequently, in 1907 President Theodore Roosevelt amended civil service rules to provide that employees covered by the rules could take no "active part" in political campaigns. Three decades later, amid the expansion of the government under President Franklin D. Roosevelt's New Deal and growing concerns about politicians' manipulation of public employees, Congress revisited the issue.[12] In 1939, Senator Carl Hatch (D-New Mexico) succeeded in pushing through Congress the first of several so-called Hatch Acts, or, as officially titled, "An Act to Prevent Pernicious Political Activities." One of the most controversial provisions of the Hatch Act provides that "no officer or employee in the executive branch of the Federal Government, or any agency or department thereof, shall take part in political management or political campaigns. All such persons shall retain the right to vote as they may choose and to express their opinions on all political subjects." This and other provisions of the Hatch Act were extended in 1940 to state and local employees whose programs receive federal funding. Public employees were hence barred from holding office in political parties, soliciting funds for candidates, and managing political campaigns, among many other political activities.[13]

Twice the Court ruled on First Amendment challenges to the Hatch Act and both times upheld its restrictions. In 1947, in *United Public Workers of America v. Mitchell,*[14] with two justices not participating, the Court split four to three in rebuffing federal employees' First Amendment claims. Although conceding that the law infringed on their First Amendment freedoms, Justice Stanley Reed's opinion for the Court applied a balancing test, weighing those freedoms against a "congressional enactment to protect a democratic society against the supposed evil of political partisanship by classified employees of Government." A quarter of a century later, writing for the majority in *United States Civil Service Commission v. National Association of Letter Carriers* (1973),[15] Justice Byron White remained unwilling to second-guess Congress and, again, simply deferred to Congress on the matter.

Without judicial intervention and a Court apparently unsympathetic to the First Amendment claims of public employees, the Hatch Act and other civil service reform legislation curbed political spoils systems not only in the federal government, but also in state and local government. In the 1950s and 1960s, often under pressure from the federal government,[16] states and localities gradually adopted "Little Hatch Acts," enforcing merit principles and restricting state and local employees' political activities.[17] Thus, political patronage in federal, state, and local government was greatly diminished, though by no means completely eliminated.[18] As political scientist Larry Sabato observed, political patronage gradually became "a mere shadow of its former self."[19] Indeed, in 1998 only about 8,000 of the federal government's 2.6 million employees were political appointees, occupying patronage positions.[20]

Although upholding the Hatch Act's restrictions on federal employees' political expression and activities in 1947, and again in 1973, the Court nevertheless moved toward giving greater protection to state and local employees' claims of free speech in the 1960s. Until then, the Court maintained the classical view that constitutional rights could be suspended as a condition of public employment.[21] As Justice Oliver Wendell Holmes, writing for the Supreme Court of Massachusetts, put it: a public employee "may have a constitutional right to talk politics, but he has no constitutional right to be a policeman."[22]

In the 1960s, though, the Court gradually took a less deferential position on the exercise of judicial review and the operation of the political process. And the *Elrod* line of cases, arguably, grew out of the ground broken in the 1960s by the "reapportionment revolution,"[23] on the one hand, and the Court's chipping away at the "right-privilege"[24] distinction for public employees, on the other.

Once the Warren Court (1953–69) abandoned the view championed by Justice Felix Frankfurter in *Colegrove v. Green* (1946)[25] that reapportionment was a "political question" for Congress and state legislatures (not the judiciary) to decide, further inroads on political patronage were, perhaps, inevitable. In abandoning *Colegrove's* position in 1962 and inaugurating the reapportionment revolution, Justice William J. Brennan, Jr., writing for the Court in *Baker v. Carr* (1962),[26] laid the basis for imposing the principle of "one person, one vote"[27] and eventually extending it to virtually all state and local elected offices.[28] In doing so, the Warren Court struck a severe and highly controversial blow at political patronage. For malapportioned electoral districts were the supreme achievement of political patronage; they preserved incumbents' seats and the leverage that certain (rural) voters had over other (urban) voters in controlling political spoils.

The significance of *Baker v. Carr's* watershed ruling is hard to minimize. In recognizing litigants' standing to raise and the justiciability of reapportionment controversies, the Warren Court opened a window of opportunity for First and Fourteenth Amendment challenges to a range of other election laws and practices. Subsequent decisions underscored the Court's newfound commitment to ensuring fair and open political competition in elections based on the enforcement of the First and Fourteenth Amendments, which in turn made further judicial inroads on political parties' control over elections and patronage.[29]

At the same time, the Warren Court whittled away at the right-privilege distinction. It did so initially by striking down loyalty oath requirements as too vague or overly broad, thereby extending First Amendment protection to public employees.[30] Again writing for the Court in *Keyishian v. Board of Regents* (1967),[31] and overturning precedents to the contrary,[32] Justice Brennan held that public employers may neither deny persons employment because of the exercise of their First Amendment rights, nor condition their employment on the sacrifice of those freedoms.

Once the Court effectively undermined the right-privilege distinction, especially after the ruling *Keyishian*, the Court faced the problem of how to accommodate the government's interest, as an employer, in providing effective public services with public employees' free speech claims. As a result, the following year the Court crafted a new "balancing test" in *Pickering v. Board of Education of Township High School District* (1968).[33] *Pickering's* balancing test requires the weighing of the interests of public employees, as citizens, in commenting on "matters of public concern" against the government employer's interest in "promoting the efficiency of the delivery of public services it performs through its employees."[34] That test is applied on a case-by-case basis, taking into consideration the content and context of the employee's speech and the effect on the employer, among other factors.

The Burger Court (1969–86) and Rehnquist Court (1986—) stood by *Pickering*.[35] But *Pickering's* test only applies when employees are terminated because of their private political *expression*. When employees are terminated for their speech as public employees, not as citizens, the Burger Court applied a different test. That test, set forth in *Connick v. Myers* (1983),[36] draws a slightly different balance between public employees' First Amendment claims and governmental interests. There, the Court ruled that public employees' work-related speech is covered by the First Amendment but only if it embraces "a matter of public concern" and does not disrupt the workplace.[37]

In suing Bobby Medford, Jenkins's attorney raised both the *Pickering* and *Connick* First Amendment claims. But the Fourth Circuit's majority in *Jenkins* dismissed them with dispatch and little analysis, drawing an angry protest from the dissenters.[38] Instead, the Fourth Circuit devoted its opinion almost entirely to analyzing the alternative claim and test established in *Elrod v. Burns* for the termination of public employees because of their political affiliation, not their political expression.

THE FIRST AMENDMENT AND PATRONAGE DISMISSALS

The Court both built on its developing doctrine under *Pickering* of the First Amendment's protection for public employees' political expression and broke new ground in *Elrod v. Burns* (1976). By the late 1960s and early 1970s the practice of political patronage in Chicago and surrounding Cook County, Illinois, as well as elsewhere, was under attack in the lower federal courts on a number of fronts, from candidates running for office and employees fired because of their political affiliation. The Court let some suits challenging Cook County's patronage system play out for years, leaving them for the lower courts to ultimately resolve,[39] but not so with *Elrod v. Burns*.

At issue in *Elrod v. Burns* was the permissibility of the dismissal of all non–civil service employees, who also all happened to be Republicans, in the Cook County sheriff's office by the newly elected sheriff, Richard Elrod, a Democrat. John Burns, a chief deputy, and several other employees responded by raising First and Fourteenth Amendment objections to their dismissals. With Justice John Paul Stevens not participating, the Court split five to three in holding that Elrod violated Burns's constitutional rights by firing him solely because he had not supported or been affiliated with the Democratic Party. Moreover, Justice William Brennan's opinion for the Court was joined only by Justices Byron White and Thurgood Marshall.

Although the holding in *Elrod* commanded wide attention and engendered considerable controversy, concurring Justices Potter Stewart and Harry Blackmun underscored the narrowness of the majority's ruling. They emphasized that the Court had not addressed "the broad contours of the so-called patronage system." The decision, as they underscored, resolved the single question of "whether a nonpolicymaking, nonconfidential government employee can be discharged or threatened with discharge from a job that he is satisfactorily performing upon the sole ground of his political beliefs."[40] And only on that narrow issue did they join the plurality.

Their concurrence, nevertheless, failed to mollify the dissenters (Chief Justice Warren Burger and Justices Lewis Powell and William Rehnquist). In particular, Justice Powell staunchly defended patronage hiring and firing practices as part of the American political tradition; a matter for the political process, not the courts, to determine; and as "a tolerable intrusion on the First Amendment interests of employees . . ."[41]

Elrod's holding was, therefore, precarious and limited. Notably, Justice Brennan was forced to concede a large exception: employee terminations due to their party affiliation remained permissible if they "further some vital government end by a means that is least restrictive of freedom of belief and association,"[42] or the employees are deemed to be "policymakers."[43]

Four years later in *Branti v. Finkel* (1980),[44] with the Court splitting six to three and Justices Stewart, Powell, and Rehnquist dissenting, the Court held that the First Amendment protects district attorneys from being discharged solely for their political views and associations. Here, a newly appointed public defender, Peter Branti, who belonged to the Democratic Party, discharged several assistant public defenders because they did not have the support of the Democratic Party. As in *Elrod,* in *Branti* the Court ruled that the First Amendment forbids government officials from discharging or threatening to discharge public employees simply because of their party affiliation, unless it is demonstrated that "party affiliation is an appropriate requirement for the effective performance of the public office involved."[45]

The controversy and struggle within the Court over the permissibility of political patronage continued in *Rutan v. Republican Party of Illinois* (1990).[46] There, Justice Brennan managed to pull together just a bare majority for extending *Elrod* and *Branti* and further limiting political patronage in the hiring, promoting, and transferring of public employees in state and local government. Almost a decade earlier in 1980, Illinois's Republican governor James Thompson issued an executive order freezing all hiring of state employees and placing virtually all of the state's 62,000 civil service positions under the jurisdiction of his personnel office. Cynthia Rutan and several other public employees who had never supported the Republican Party were subsequently denied promotions. Rutan sued on the ground that her promotion was denied for purely partisan reasons, thereby violating her First Amendment freedoms.

Writing for *Rutan*'s bare majority, but nonetheless a "firm five" as he would say, Justice Brennan proclaimed:

Employees who do not compromise their beliefs stand to lose the considerable increases in pay and job satisfaction attendant to promotions, the hours and maintenance expenses that are consumed by long daily commutes, and even their jobs if they are not rehired after a "temporary" layoff. These are significant penalties and are imposed for the exercise of rights guaranteed by the First Amendment. Unless these patronage practices are narrowly tailored to further vital governmental interests, we must conclude that they impermissibly encroach on First Amendment freedoms.[47]

Justice Brennan's extension of *Elrod* and *Branti* in *Rutan* sharply divided the Court. In a long and bitter dissent, joined by Chief Justice Rehnquist and Justices Sandra Day O'Connor and Anthony Kennedy, Justice Antonin Scalia countered:

The merit principle for government employment is probably the most favored in modern America, having been widely adopted by civil-service legislation at both the state and federal levels. But there is another point of view. . . . [P]atronage stabilizes political parties and prevents excessive political fragmentation—both of which are results in which States have a strong governmental interest. Party strength requires the efforts of the rank-and-file, especially in "the dull periods between elections," to perform such tasks as organizing precincts, registering new voters, and providing constituent services.[48]

Lamenting the decline of a strong two-party system since the end of World War II, Justice Scalia concluded that political patronage was not "a significant impairment of free speech or free association," and that "the desirability of patronage is a policy question to be decided by the people's representatives."[49]

The four dissenters not merely blasted Justice Brennan's bare majority; they called for the overturning of *Rutan,* along with *Elrod* and *Branti.* When Justice Brennan retired at the end of the term, speculation immediately mounted that *Rutan* might well be overruled by the increasingly conservative Rehnquist Court. That speculation escalated when, shortly before announcing his own retirement at the end of the following term, Justice Marshall in his last opinion delivered from the bench, dissenting in *Payne v. Tennessee* (1991),[50] warned that *Rutan* and other precedents decided by bare majorities were in jeopardy.

Ironically and surprisingly, the Rehnquist Court subsequently not only declined to reverse the *Elrod-Branti-Rutan* line of rulings but, instead, extended them. Five years after *Rutan*, the departures of Justices Brennan and Marshall as well as Justices White and Blackmun left only one justice (Justice Stevens) who had voted with *Rutan*'s majority on the high bench. Nevertheless, the Court further extended the First Amendment's protection for public employees to independent contractors for the government in two 1996 decisions, *Board of County Commissioners, Wabaunsee County, Kansas v. Umbehr*,[51] and *O'Hare Truck Service, Inc. v. City of Northlake*.[52] Moreover, it did so with just two dissenters, Justices Scalia and Clarence Thomas.

Umbehr stemmed from a dispute between the Wabaunsee County governing board and one of its independent trash haulers, who was also one of the board's most outspoken critics. When the board terminated Keen Umbehr's contract (so that it would not be automatically renewed), he sued, charging that the county's retaliation for his criticisms violated the First Amendment. The Court agreed, reaffirming *Pickering* and *Connick*, in holding that the First Amendment protects independent contractors, no less than government employees. Writing for the Court, Justice Sandra Day O'Connor explained the application of the balancing process set forth in *Pickering* and *Connick* as follows:

Umbehr must show that the termination of his contract was motivated by his speech on a matter of public concern, an initial showing that requires him to prove more than the mere fact that he criticized the Board members before they terminated him. If he can make that showing, the Board will have a valid defense if it can show, by a preponderance of the evidence, that, in light of their knowledge, perceptions and policies at the time of the termination, the Board members would have terminated the contact regardless of his speech. The Board will also prevail if it can persuade the District Court that the County's legitimate interests as contractor, deferentially viewed, outweigh the free speech interests at stake.[53]

In *O'Hare Truck Service, Inc.*, the Court extended the First Amendment's protection accorded to government employees in *Elrod, Branti*, and *Rutan* to independent contractors or regular providers of services to the government. There, the owner of O'Hare Truck Service, Inc., refused to contribute to the mayor's reelection campaign and supported his opponent instead. After the mayor's reelection, his contract was terminated and he sued. This time writing for the Court, Justice Stephen Breyer held that independent contractors, like public employees, may not be discharged for refusing to support a political party or its candidates, unless they hold "policymaking" positions.

Given the bare majority ruling in *Rutan* and the subsequent changes in the

Rehnquist Court's composition, the lopsided seven-to-two lineup in *Umbehr* and *O'Hare Truck Service* appears ironic, if not paradoxical. Yet, a number of factors undoubtedly came into play and explain the ruling. First, the Court's changing composition in the late 1980s and early 1990s pushed Justices Kennedy and O'Connor into centrist positions.[54] Both are also firmly committed to enforcing the First Amendment against viewpoint discrimination, and have become even more so since joining Justice Scalia's dissent in *Rutan*.[55] In particular, the First and Fourteenth Amendments have become so tightly interwoven in Justice Kennedy's jurisprudence that he has emerged as a strong opponent of balancing and a staunch defender of equal liberty for all with respect to free speech.[56] Justice David Souter also takes a rather uncompromising position on the First Amendment.[57] Justice Stevens voted with the majority in *Rutan*, of course, and while Justices Ruth Bader Ginsburg and Stephen Breyer joined the Court after that decision, they are generally supportive of First Amendment claims as well. Together, these justices constitute a solid majority in favor of adhering to *Elrod* and *Rutan*. And that helps explain why Chief Justice Rehnquist did not dissent, again, in *O'Hare:* the fight over whether to overrule *Elrod* and *Rutan* was over. Justice Scalia's dissension in *Rutan* no longer proved persuasive and his dissents in *Umbehr* and *O'Hare* were joined only by Justice Clarence Thomas.

Second, after the agonizing battle over whether to overrule *Roe v. Wade*[58] in *Planned Parenthood of Southeastern Pennsylvania v. Casey*,[59] the Rehnquist Court became more circumspect about overturning precedents, and has done so less frequently since that 1992 decision.[60] Third, since the issue of overruling *Elrod* and *Rutan* no longer bitterly divided the justices in *O'Hare*, its limited extension of those rulings was comparatively noncontroversial, as indicated by the justices' lineup. In other words, *O'Hare* was a small step compared to those made in *Elrod* and *Rutan*, and it was in lockstep with the Court's contemporary reading of the First and Fourteenth Amendments guarantees for free speech and equality.

Fourth, and perhaps most importantly, particularly for Justices Kennedy and O'Connor, who were not on the bench when *Elrod* was decided but who dissented in *Rutan*, more than two decades after coming down *Elrod* appears less controversial than when announced and its limitations are, perhaps, more fully appreciated. In *Elrod*, Justice Brennan was forced to strike a crucial balance between policymaking and nonpolicymaking employees when acknowledging a substantial exception for those in policymaking positions. That balance and malleable exception to *Elrod*'s holding is one that a majority of the Rehnquist Court can now live with. It is an exception, if read and applied broadly, that could dwarf *Elrod*'s protection against patronage dismissals, or so some judges and commentators warn.[61] Yet, that may also have contributed to the lopsided vote in *O'Hare* and partly explain the Court's declining to review the Fourth Circuit's decision in *Jenkins v. Medford.*

AT THE INTERSECTION OF LAW AND POLITICS

The majority's decision in *Jenkins v. Medford,* according to its dissenters, was "indeed ironic."[62] Not only did the appellate court's decision appear to run contrary to *Elrod, Branti, Rutan,* and *O'Hare,* it overruled one of its own precedents, set in 1984 in *Jones v. Dodson.*[63] In that earlier decision, the Fourth Circuit reached precisely the opposite conclusion from *Jenkins,* holding that deputy sheriffs were not policymakers and, hence, were protected from patronage dismissals. In a strongly worded dissent in *Jenkins,* Judge Diana Motz pointed out that in overturning *Jones v. Dodson* and holding instead that deputy sheriffs are policymakers, and therefore exempt from protection accorded in *Elrod,* the majority "relie[d] on broad, and often misleading, generalizations"[64] about the position of deputy sheriffs, which had not changed since the circuit's earlier ruling contrariwise.

Yet, there isn't a great deal of irony in the Fourth Circuit's decision in *Jenkins,* nor much difficulty in explaining it. While the underlying factual basis for the circuit's analysis had not changed, the composition of the circuit had. As a result, a majority of the Fourth Circuit now viewed political patronage more favorably. And at long last we arrive at the biggest irony in the Court's rulings and judicial intervention into the practice of political patronage: namely, that the federal judiciary curbed patronage in the first place, since federal judgeships are prime patronage appointments. To be sure, presidents differ in the weight that they give to (1) rewarding party faithful, (2) advancing their own legal policy goals, and (3) candidates' professional qualifications, in their judicial selection processes.[65] President Ronald Reagan, for instance, put into place one of the most ambitious and rigorous selection processes because of his administration's position that federal judgeships were crucial to achieving its legal policy goals.[66] Other presidents, however, such as Democratic presidents Jimmy Carter and Bill Clinton, have been neither so inclined nor in a position to have had the same kind of impact on the federal bench.[67]

Most federal judges make it to the bench because of their compatibility with the appointing president's philosophy of judicial selection and some degree of political patronage. They in turn reflect, to some extent, their presidential and/or senatorial benefactors' political and judicial philosophies. Hence, judges appointed by presidents (Johnson, Nixon, Reagan, and Bush) who emphasized political patronage and their own legal policy goals in judicial recruitment would be expected to be more deferential to the practice of patronage than federal judges appointed by presidents (Eisenhower, Ford, Carter, and Clinton) who gave greater weight to the professional qualifications of judicial candidates than to patronage politics or to achieving their legal policy goals through judicial appointments.

In light of that hypothesis, the lineup in *Jenkins v. Medford* remains revealing, though not particularly surprising. The majority's opinion was delivered by Judge Donald Stuart Russell. He had extensive personal experience with political patronage, having served as South Carolina's governor and U.S. senator prior to President Lyndon B. Johnson's naming him to a district court and his elevation to the appellate bench by President Richard M. Nixon. His opinion was joined by another Nixon appointee (Judge H. Emory Widener) and six others who were named by Presidents Ronald Reagan and George Bush.[68] Of them, Judges J. Harvie Wilkinson and L. Michael Luttig had also clerked, respectively, for Justice Powell and Judge Scalia as well as Chief Justice Burger; both had also worked in the Reagan administration's Department of Justice. By contrast, the five dissenters included one appointed by President Gerald Ford[69] and two each named by Presidents Jimmy Carter and Bill Clinton.[70]

Leaving aside the politics of the judiciary, let's return to the dissenters' complaint that the majority in *Jenkins v. Medford* "swallow[s] the rule"[71] established in *Elrod* in order to embrace the tradition of political patronage: the fact remains that the *Elrod* line of cases left a large exception for the patronage dismissals of employees engaged in policymaking. It is an exception that other lower federal courts are exploiting,[72] no less than the Fourth Circuit. And it is an exception that not only Justice Brennan's plurality in *Elrod* was forced to concede but one that the Rehnquist Court appears comfortable with, or more than willing to maintain, especially in light of its denial of review of *Jenkins v. Medford*.[73]

CONCLUSION

In conclusion, it bears emphasizing that the controversy over the inroads made on political patronage by the *Elrod* line of cases appears overblown and to underestimate the influence of politics on law as well as how constitutional principles constrain democratic politics. To return to the criticisms raised by dissenting Justices Powell and Scalia, among others, that *Elrod* and subsequent rulings strip political parties of an important resource and contribute to the decline of a competitive two-party political system: The simple fact remains that *Elrod* was limited and preserved room for the continued practice of patronage politics. Moreover, other factors certainly played a much larger role than the *Elrod* line of rulings in the "decomposition" of the political parties.[74]

Furthermore, as a number of studies demonstrate,[75] the reform of old-style patronage politics in federal and state and local governments began long before *Elrod*. In historical and political perspective, the Court's rulings appear to support University of Virginia Law School professor Michael J. Klarman's provocative thesis that the Court is generally behind the times and tends to follow the dominant national political coalition.[76] That is certainly the case with the demise of political patronage.

In addition, Justice Scalia and other critics of the Court's rulings are not entirely accurate or candid in lamenting the decline of political patronage because it ostensibly helped to uplift ethnic and racial minorities. There is another side to that story and ample studies show that political patronage historically did not promote widespread upward mobility for minorities.[77] Finally, contrary to Justice Scalia's charge that *Elrod* and *Rutan* would invite a flood of litigation, the number of patronage dismissal cases filed in federal courts does not appear to have substantially affected by the Court's rulings, and the number in appellate courts has actually declined in the 1990s.[78]

In sum, the Court did not kill political patronage, but only tried to assert constitutional principles in the face of democratic politics. Moreover, political patronage was diminishing for a long time before *Elrod* and still remains alive.[79] The Court's rulings on patronage dismissals were "behind the times" and lagged behind the movement to reform the spoils system of democratic politics. They were also significantly limited—limited both in their scope and in their impact, at least when compared to the major inroads on political patronage made by other political institutions. In terms of the ongoing political controversy over "judicial activism" and the judiciary's intervention into the political process, the *Elrod* line of rulings does not stand up to the Warren Court's "reapportionment revolution" or the Rehnquist Court's rebuff of the political process and the creation of majority-minority voting districts.[80] Furthermore, they left plenty of room for the lower federal courts to maintain and reinforce the practice of political patronage, as *Jenkins v. Medford* underscores.

CHAPTER 10

Whitewater, Iran-Contra, and the Limits of the Law

Katy J. Harriger

IN THE WAKE OF THE WATERGATE SCANDAL, Congress passed a number of new laws designed to respond to the perceived institutional failures revealed by the crisis. Among these was the provision for appointment of special prosecutors in the Ethics in Government Act of 1978.[1] Hoping to avoid another constitutional crisis like the one provoked by President Richard Nixon when he had Archibald Cox fired in the infamous "Saturday Night Massacre," Congress provided for judicial appointment of an independent special prosecutor when the attorney general determined that there was sufficient cause to investigate or prosecute political appointees in the executive branch for violations of federal criminal law.

Several significant assumptions about the political system underlay the special prosecutor provisions. The first was that there was an inherent conflict of interest when the attorney general was called upon to investigate allegations of criminal wrongdoing against executive branch colleagues. Even if there was no actual conflict, there was still presumed to be a significant appearance of conflict that undermined public confidence in any such investigation.[2] Second, and of central importance in this chapter, supporters of the arrangement believed it would elevate the "rule of law" over "politics." Archibald Cox had framed the issue with his simple but dramatic statement on the night of his firing, arguing that the outcome of the case would demonstrate whether this was a government of laws or of men.[3] The U.S. Supreme Court further embraced the notion, finding that the president was not above the law in its decision that ultimately forced Nixon's resignation.[4] Congressional supporters of the independent prosecutor arrangement took up the "rule of law" argument as well, insisting that judicial appointment of a prosecutor was necessary in order to remove politics from the administration of justice and insure that executive branch officials received equal treatment under the law.[5] Federal appellate court judges were presumed to be sufficiently removed from politics to be able to make appointments of independent counsel that would be perceived as impartial.

Since Watergate, only two cases among the twenty pursued under the independent counsel statute have implicated the president directly and have, consequently, received sufficient media attention to create widespread public awareness of the investigations. In both Iran-Contra and Whitewater,[6] the independent counsels and the statute under which their appointments were authorized have been the target of extensive criticism. In response to that criticism, the rule of law argument has been used to justify the investigations. The special congressional committee that investigated Iran-Contra concluded that the scandal demonstrated that the executive had not respected "the rule of law."[7] In his memoir about the investigation, Independent Counsel Lawrence Walsh makes the same argument, characterizing the case as a "conflict between the rule of law, as administered by the courts and prosecutors, and the system of political checks and balances, as exercised by the president and the Congress."[8] More recently, and in the face of the most intense criticism leveled at an Ethics Act prosecutor, Kenneth Starr insisted that his investigation of President Clinton is necessary to uphold the rule of law and defend the "temple of justice."[9]

In this chapter, I explore this notion of independent counsel investigations as representing the upholding of law over politics. I argue that it is not coincidental that in the two cases for which the independent counsel arrangement was most clearly designed, the investigations have been the most controversial and the independent counsel has been the most criticized. What has been most clearly revealed in these cases is not the triumph of law over politics but instead the limits of the law in addressing cases of profound political importance. Federal court judges have played significant roles in superintending the independent counsel process through endorsing its constitutionality,[10] supervising grand juries and trials that arise in investigations,[11] and in ruling on other legal challenges related to the cases.[12] But their presence in the process has not depoliticized the process as the authors of the statute had hoped.

"THE LIMITS OF THE LAW": AN EXPLANATION

In this chapter, "the limits of the law" has two meanings and it is important to lay those out here for the reader. On the one hand, "limits" is used in a negative sense, referring to inadequacies, or what the law can not accomplish. On the other hand, "limits" can be understood in a different light, as constraints placed on those who exercise public power, a value enshrined in the U.S. Constitution. Similarly, law should be understood as existing on more than one level and in this chapter I move among these levels. First, there is the criminal law being interpreted and applied to the particular allegations of each case. Second, there is the law that authorizes the independent counsel to investigate these criminal law allegations. And finally, there is the more general and fundamental law of the Constitution, within which all of the public actors in these legal dramas operate. Courts play a significant but different role depending upon what level of law we are discussing. At the level of enforcement and interpretation of the criminal law they are critical actors with central roles in the process. In the independent counsel process they are central in the appointment process and are the most important institutional check on the independent counsels' power. But at the level of the fundamental constitutional law, their impact is restricted by the competing exercise of power by the legislative and executive branches.

In considering the limits of the law in the context of the Iran-Contra and Whitewater cases then, there are two different approaches that I will take. I will argue that these two cases reveal the inadequacies of the criminal law and the independent counsel statute to address allegations of misconduct against the president. But I will also argue that in the realm of constitutional law, the cases reveal the way in which the limits on power embodied in the separation of powers are at work, both limiting the power of the independent counsel and providing for alternative ways of addressing official misconduct allegations. Whether or not we conclude that the "rule of law" is in conflict with "politics" in cases of this sort depends upon which level of analysis we adopt.

THE LAW OF INDEPENDENT COUNSELS

The practice of appointing independent investigators for national political scandals is long-standing in American politics. In the twentieth century the ad hoc appointment of independent prosecutors occurred in the Teapot Dome scandal of the 1920s, the Truman Tax Scandals of the 1950s, and the Watergate scandal of the 1970s. In each of these cases the president and/or the attorney general played some role in the appointment of the investigators.[13] It was the Watergate scandal, and more specifically the firing of Watergate Special Prosecutor Archibald Cox in the infamous Saturday Night Massacre, that ultimately led to the creation of a statutorily required arrangement for independent investigation and prosecution of executive branch misdeeds. Congress believed that insulating a prosecutor from executive control by providing for judicial appointment would guarantee independence and reassure the public that executive branch misconduct would be impartially investigated.[14]

In 1978 Congress passed the Ethics in Government Act. Among other things, the statute provided for the temporary appointment of independent counsels when there were allegations of criminal misconduct against top-level executive branch officers, including the president and vice president. The actual arrangement that made this appointment possible reflected the five-year debate in Congress over how to create an independent prosecutor that could withstand constitutional scrutiny.[15] Since the law enforcement power was viewed traditionally as part of the executive branch, was it constitutional to remove that power from that branch? In the end, Congress compromised on this issue, leaving the power to conduct a preliminary investigation into the allegations with the attorney general, and giving her the power to trigger an independent appointment if she concluded that there was the need for further investigation or prosecution.[16] The power to appoint an independent counsel was placed with a special judicial panel made up of three senior U.S. Court of Appeals judges who were themselves appointed to the panel by the chief justice of the U.S. Supreme Court.[17] The ability to remove an independent counsel for "good cause" rested with the attorney general, but such a decision was reviewable by a federal district court.[18]

Despite this compromise, the statute was subjected to constitutional challenge in a number of cases filed by targets of independent investigations. The case that ultimately reached the U.S. Supreme Court arose from one of the more obscure cases involving allegations that Department of Justice staff member Theodore Olson lied to congressional investigators during an investigation involving the Environmental Protection Agency (EPA) in the early 1980s. Olson filed suit against independent counsel Alexia Morrison, claiming that the provisions under which she operated unconstitutionally violated the separation of powers arrangement by placing law enforcement powers in the hands of an officer not under the control of the executive and by giving the power to appoint that officer to judges. In *Morrison v. Olson* (1988) the U.S. Supreme Court upheld the independent counsel provisions in a seven-one decision.[19]

Writing for the Court, Chief Justice William Rehnquist found that the appointments clause of Article II of the U.S. Constitution authorized Congress to place appointment of independent counsel with a court of law. The fact that the independent counsel was subject to removal by the attorney general and had limited tenure and duties made her an "inferior officer" for constitutional purposes.[20] In addition, Rehnquist argued, there was no Article III violation because the duties given the special court panel were largely ministerial in nature or incident to the appointment power granted in Article II.[21] Finally, the Court rejected the claim that the arrangement violated the separation of powers principle, taken as a whole, because it impermissibly interfered with executive power. Here the Court relied upon its precedent involving independent regulatory agencies, holding that the provisions were not "of such a nature that they impede the President's ability to perform his constitutional duty." Rehnquist noted that Congress had not given itself any powers to control the executive. While it was "undeniable that the Act reduces the amount of control and supervision," the attorney general was given ways to supervise and control the prosecutorial power exercised by the independent counsel, the most important being the removal power.[22]

In a scathing dissent, Justice Antonin Scalia challenged the majority's complacency with the statute. Noting that the Olson case arose out of an inter-branch conflict over executive privilege claims in a congressional investigation, Scalia argued that the independent counsel statute allowed for political disputes of this nature to be turned into criminal investigations. "Nothing is so politically effective," he wrote, "as the ability to charge that one's opponent and his associates are not merely wrongheaded, naïve, ineffective, but, in all probability, 'crooks.'" He contended that the attorney general had no real discretion in triggering the appointment of an independent counsel and that the "context of this statute is acrid with the smell of threatened impeachment." Rejecting the majority's notion that Congress may carve out some small part of executive power under certain circumstances, Scalia argued that Article II gives "all of the executive power" to the president, including the power over law enforcement. He dismissed the idea that the attorney general maintains some control over the independent counsel, noting that this is "somewhat like referring to shackles as an effective means of locomotion." Scalia concluded his dissent by noting the political popularity of the Ethics Act and the difficulty of getting rid of it. He feared that by upholding the statute and failing to see its danger, the Court had "permanently encumbered the Republic with an institution that will do it great harm."[23]

The effect of the *Morrison* decision was two-fold. First, having answered the constitutional questions raised by the statute, it altered the policy debate about it. Prior to the decision, the statute's opponents focused on the constitutional issues. After the decision, it was more difficult to do this and the debate shifted to questions of cost, length of investigation, and the actions of individual independent counsels. Second, it limited the legislation options available to Congress should it reconsider the arrangement in the future. By emphasizing the "inferior" nature of the office, the controls available to the attorney general, and the limited nature of the court panel's authority, the Court seemed to warn against any efforts to make the independent counsel more independent from the executive by removing the attorney general from the process or expanding the role of the court panel. Finally, while he was seriously outnumbered on the constitutional analysis, Scalia's dissent did raise important questions about the potential abuse of power by an independent counsel. While it was difficult to see Alexia Morrison as the dangerous usurper of power he warned of in the dissent, his words seemed prophetic to many when the target of investigation became the White House instead of unknown subordinates. The Iran-Contra and Whitewater cases bring into sharper focus the questions raised by Scalia about the unchecked power of independent counsel.

IRAN-CONTRA AND THE LIMITS OF THE LAW

When the Iran-Contra scandal broke near the end of 1986 it seemed tailormade for an independent counsel appointment. The allegations implicated the president and the attorney general, as well as a number of other high-ranking executive officials. The charges that the government had traded arms for hostages with Iran, and that the money gained from the arms sale had been diverted to fund a war in Nicaragua that had little public support, were of the kind that posed a real threat to public confidence. The fact that the White

House moved so quickly in announcing its intent to seek an independent counsel appointment and that the Department of Justice offered a parallel appointment to the independent counsel when the constitutionality of the provisions was challenged demonstrates the widespread belief that such an appointment was necessary.

In retrospect, however, the outcome of the Iran-Contra investigations suggests the inadequacies rather than the benefits of resorting to criminal investigation and prosecution by an independent counsel. Consider, for example, the outcomes of the cases brought by Lawrence Walsh. Of the fourteen people against whom criminal indictments were brought under the Iran-Contra investigation, only five had their convictions stand. All five were minor players in the case, private citizens involved in either the arms sales, the diversion of funds, or the subsequent attempt to coverup these events. Of the public officials involved, six of those indicted were pardoned by President George Bush in December of 1992, two had their convictions overturned on appeal, and one had his case dismissed by a judge because of the inability to use the classified documents needed to successfully prosecute him (see table 10.1).[24]

The competing institutional and political forces at work in Iran-Contra can explain these outcomes. These forces included the congressional interest in public investigation and exposure, the congressional power to immunize witnesses in exchange for their public testimony, the executive power to pardon and to control access to classified documents, the judicial power to review lower court cases and overturn convictions based on the application of principles of law, the power of the media to cover these events and shape public opinion, and the partisan interests in protecting a popular president from impeachment.

The competing institutional interests of Congress and the independent counsel in the Iran-Contra case provide a prime example of the way in which dispersed power can hamper investigation. In fact, in his final report, Walsh noted that "The Iran/contra prosecutions illustrate in an especially stark fashion the tension between political oversight and enforcement of existing law."[25] The special prosecutor may not answer to Congress but neither does the Congress answer to the special prosecutor. In its desire to pursue the political issues that were raised by Iran-Contra, Congress chose to publicize its hearings and immunize key witnesses in a manner that had a profoundly negative impact on the ability of Lawrence Walsh to pursue his criminal cases. Walsh was forced

Table 10.1. Outcomes of Iran-Contra Indictments

Pardoned	Overturned	Dismissed	Convicted
Elliot Abrams, Asst. Secretary of State (withholding information from Congress)	Oliver North, National Security Council (sixteen felony counts including obstruction, taking gratuities, destroying documents)	Joseph F. Fernandez, CIA Station Chief, Costa Rica (conspiracy to defraud government, obstruction)	Carl R. Channel, fund-raiser (conspiracy to defraud government)
Duane Clarridge, Chief of Latin American Division, CIA (perjury)	John Poindexter, National Security Advisor (conspiracy, false statements, destruction of documents, obstruction)		Thomas Clines, retired CIA agent (income tax violations for concealing funds earned by helping supply contras)
Alan D. Fiers, Jr., CIA Central American Task Force (withholding information from Congress)			Albert Hakim, businessman (supplanting government official's salary, theft of government property)
Clair E. George, Deputy Director of Operations, CIA (false statements and perjury before Congress)			Richard Miller, private fund-raiser (conspiracy to defraud government)
Robert McFarlane, National Security Adviser (withholding information from Congress)			Richard Secord, retired Air Force, businessman (false statements to Congress)
Caspar Weinberger, Secretary of Defense (obstruction, perjury, false statements)			

to speed up his investigation in order to develop his case prior to the grants of immunity. Because Congress, the administration, and the defendants were anxious to get the scandal over with as quickly as possible, the needs of the prosecution took a back seat to the needs of these other actors. The press also pressured Congress for prompt public hearings. In early 1987 the *New York Times* urged Walsh and the congressional committees to compromise but concluded that "if many more weeks pass, Congress will have to choose between informing itself and the public, and preserving Mr. Walsh's prosecution options. At that point, having already given him four months or more, it will have to choose the informing function of open hearings."[26]

Attorneys for the defendants saw advantages to their clients in having both a congressional investigation and a criminal investigation simultaneously. One attorney told a *Washington Post* reporter; "With parallel proceedings you have an opportunity to confuse things. You can take advantage of the different interests, the obvious conflict between the independent counsel not wanting immunity and the Hill wanting to hear from these guys now."[27] In fact, it has been suggested that Oliver North's initial suit challenging the constitutionality of the independent counsel statute was designed to take advantage of this situation. The further delays that would result might "give that wavering congressman or senator a push."[28]

The decision by Congress to grant immunity to Oliver North and John Poindexter affected Walsh's work not just initially but throughout the trials as well. It caused substantial delays in getting to trial, disruptions during the conduct of the trial,[29] and ultimately called into question the whole point of the lengthy and expensive criminal investigation. The decisions by the U.S. Court of Appeals for the D.C. Circuit to overturn the convictions of North[30] and Poindexter[31] required Walsh to demonstrate that there was no use of immunized testimony at all, even with witnesses whose memories might have been refreshed in watching the televised hearings. This proved to be an impossible standard to meet[32] and the convictions fell.

In addition to their impact on the Iran-Contra cases, the D.C. Circuit opinions will have a significant effect on the future ability of prosecutors, whether independent or regular, to pursue some kinds of official misconduct cases. As Walsh warned in his final report, the decisions "will make almost impossible the prosecution of any case involving public immunized statements that requires testimony by persons sympathetic to the accused, such as co-conspirators or other associates." He argued that "the cases most sharply affected . . . will, by definition, be prosecutions involving conduct that has far flung implications for national policy—those where Congress has determined that the national interest requires an immediate public examination of the activity at issue."[33]

Walsh was also engaged in a battle with the executive branch over classified documents. Throughout 1988 and 1989 the trial of Oliver North was delayed by the complicated legal wrangling between the attorney general, the independent counsel, the defense, and the district court over the best way to handle the myriad classified documents the defense claimed were relevant to the case.[34] The procedures for deciding on the admissibility and availability of classified information in criminal trials are provided for in the Classified Information Procedures Act of 1980 (CIPA).[35] The statute was designed to try to avoid "graymail" by criminal defendants whose job or alleged crime might make classified information relevant to their defense, thus forcing the government to drop a prosecution because of the danger to national security of the threatened exposure of the classified information. The CIPA attempted to balance the right of the defendants to a fair trial with the need of the government to protect classified information through pretrial discovery and trial procedures governing the use of information. The act requires defendants to give advance notice of their intent to use classified information in their defense and to describe the information and its relevance to their case. Then the trial court must hold in camera hearings as to the use, relevance, and admissibility of the information. If it decides that the defendant needs the information, the government may offer a substitute. If the court rejects that substitute, the government must ultimately decide whether the information can be used at trial. The attorney general may submit an affidavit certifying that release of the information would do damage to the national security. Then the judge must decide whether the case can go forward without the information. If not, the court may dismiss the indictment.

The CIPA procedures were designed to ease the "friction" that occurs between the Justice Department and intelligence agencies when prosecutions arise involving classified information.[36] Certainly no one anticipated that a CIPA case might pit an independent counsel against the attorney general and the intelligence agencies combined.[37] The attorney general and the intelligence agencies worked in tandem, sometimes as Walsh's adversaries in the proceedings before the court regarding CIPA decisions. In the seven months before the trial, the CIPA process worked fairly smoothly. Walsh challenged none of the twenty CIPA orders issued by Judge Gerhard A. Gesell. But final authority over what information could be disclosed remained with the attorney general, which allowed the executive branch "to impose broad de facto limits on Walsh's freedom to prosecute, even though the independent counsel law barred them from controlling his prosecution directly."[38]

Only significant compromises by the independent counsel allowed the

North case to go forward at all. In November of 1988 Judge Gesell announced that he would begin North's trial in January of the next year and that he intended to give North "wide latitude" to use documents to challenge the credibility of government witnesses. Gesell indicated that he did not intend to dismiss the case unilaterally and that if the trial were to be stopped, it would have to occur through the exercise of the presidential pardon or the filing of CIPA affidavits by the attorney general.[39] On December 1, President Ronald Reagan announced that he did not intend to pardon North prior to the trial but that he would have to move to prevent the disclosure of some of the secrets North claimed were essential to his defense.[40] After intense negotiations between Walsh and Attorney General Richard Thornburgh, during which Thornburgh made it clear that the government would not permit the disclosure of some of the information Gesell had found to be essential to North's defense, Walsh announced on January 5, 1989, that he would seek dismissal of the central conspiracy charges against North. Gesell agreed to dismiss the charges only after the attorney general certified that the interests of national security required the documents to be kept secret. Thornburgh submitted a sworn affidavit to that effect on January 13, and the charges were dropped. "There is no way known to the court," Gesell said, "or found in any of the cases, to force the attorney general to prosecute a case the attorney general doesn't want to prosecute."[41] During the next year Walsh was forced to drop the same conspiracy counts in the other cases.

The impact on the independent counsel's case was profound in the sense that it allowed Walsh to focus only on the narrower charges involving North's personal behavior (lying to Congress, destroying documents, accepting an illegal gratuity) and not on the central issue of the scandal, the conduct of a foreign policy in contradiction with the laws of the United States: "The guts of the original indictment lay in its first two counts, which examined the full sweep of the defendant's covert plan to sell arms to Iran and to direct the profits to the Nicaraguan contras. . . . In contrast to these two core charges, the rest of the original twenty-three count indictment focused on epiphenomenona, not the heart of the affair."[42]

At the broadest level, the Iran-Contra scandal was an institutional dispute about the relative importance of the Congress and the president in the conduct of foreign affairs. This also complicated the task set before independent counsel Walsh. The ambiguity of the extent of constitutional powers creates further problems for the investigation and prosecution of official misconduct cases. Without accepting the argument that the scandal was "merely" an interbranch constitutional struggle,[43] it is nonetheless important to recognize that there was such a struggle at the root of this case. The significance of this political debate about foreign affairs powers explains Congress's willingness to jeopardize the criminal prosecution of key witnesses in order to have them testify in public hearings and the independent counsel's decision to drop a number of the charges of which these witnesses were initially accused.[44]

The incompatibility of political disputes with criminal investigations is also revealed in the difficulty of defining behavior as criminal in order to apply the criminal law. The independent counsel was forced to frame narrowly the charges against North and Poindexter in order to maximize the likelihood of conviction. The problem with focusing on the charges of misleading Congress was that, while serious, "it is only a small part of the larger story." About the 1990 trial of John Poindexter, Theodore Draper argues that the independent counsel's criminal investigation was set in motion in an attempt to "stave off a potential threat of impeachment and appease public dismay. Once launched, the legal process took on a life of its own and became excessively 'legal' in order to get convictions on any grounds that could stand up in court." The consequence, argues Draper, was that the "main offenses against responsible constitutional government" were subordinated to peripheral allegations more easily prosecuted.[45] The use of the criminal law thus diverted our attention from the constitutionally important questions that underlie these cases but that are not easily accessible through the formal processes of the criminal law.

If ambiguities about the legitimate exercise of power by these higher-ups precluded their prosecution and the immunity grants to North and Poindexter precluded theirs, then no one could be held legally accountable for the events of Iran-Contra. In fact, Walsh points to the troublesome consequence of this outcome in his final report. He argues that the actions taken by Congress and the executive that thwarted the criminal investigation impose "costs on society that far transcend the failure to convict a few lawbreakers. There is significant inequity when . . . the more peripheral players are convicted while the central figures in the criminal enterprise escape punishment. And perhaps more fundamentally, the failure to punish governmental law breakers feeds the perception that public officials are not wholly accountable for their actions."[46]

Finally, the Iran-Contra experience points out the limits of the independent counsel statute itself in terms of its ability to accomplish the goals of impartial and independent investigation of alleged criminal misconduct by executive branch officials. In cases like Iran-Contra, where the survival of the presidency appears to be in question, and thus, where the political stakes in the outcome are quite high, it is naive to think that "politics" can be removed from the case by introducing an "independent" investigator. As Lawrence Walsh pointed out in his final report, the independent counsel has no established institutional support upon which to rest his fight in this high-stakes game. "He is told to create an office and to confront the Government without any expectation of real cooperation, and, indeed, with the expectation of hostility, however veiled. That hostility will manifest itself in the failure to declassify information, in the suppression of documents, and in all of the evasive techniques of highly skilled and large, complex organizations."[47] In fact, Walsh challenges the notion that one can even have an "independent" prosecutor. "Time and again," he found himself "at the mercy of political decisions of the Congress and the Executive branch."[48]

WHITEWATER AND THE LIMITS OF THE LAW

At this writing the Whitewater investigation has yet to be concluded but there is enough evidence on the public record to see its similarities with Iran-Contra. The underlying facts of the cases have little in common except for the allegations of cover-up and attempt to obstruct investigation of the initial allegations. The most significant differences are that the case led to impeachment proceedings and that none of the various allegations that Kenneth Starr investigated have at their core a constitutional dispute about the exercise of power. What the two cases have in common, however, is that each implicated the president in misconduct that could be considered criminal and each resulted in significant media coverage of the case and substantial criticism of the independent counsel himself. This level of public attention makes these two cases more alike than they are with any of the previous and relatively obscure cases investigated under the act.[49]

Both Robert Fiske, the first Whitewater investigator appointed by Janet Reno, and Kenneth Starr encountered the problem of simultaneous congressional investigation and the possibility that immunity might be given to key witnesses in the hearings. Each met with congressional investigators to try to persuade them to avoid using immunity grants that might threaten their prosecutions. In the wake of the Iran-Contra experience, congressional investigators were more solicitous of the independent counsel concerns.[50]

But the independent counsels were concerned not just about immunity grants but about the general effect of congressional investigation on their ability to discover evidence needed for the criminal investigation. Robert Fiske wrote to the Senate and House Banking Committees that their interviews with Whitewater witnesses "could jeopardize our investigation in several respects, including the dangers of Congressional immunity, the premature disclosures of the contents of documents or of witnesses' testimony to other witnesses on the same subject (creating the risk of tailored testimony) and of premature public disclosure of matters at the core of the criminal investigation."[51]

While Congress's willingness to delay the hearings might be attributed to its desire to avoid undermining the independent counsel's work, there are partisan explanations that better explain this deference. Delaying the hearings meant they would more likely be held closer to the 1996 presidential season, when they might do more damage to the president than they would have in 1994. It was also the case that the brief preliminary hearings had generated very little public interest despite extensive press coverage of the allegations.[52] Had the scandal generated more heat, the incentives to hold public hearings and to immunize witnesses surely would have been greater and would have created the same dynamic encountered by Walsh.

Kenneth Starr also had to deal with aggressive partisan criticism of his investigation, and even more so than in the Iran-Contra investigation, that criticism has resonated with the public and undermined his credibility as an impartial investigator of the president. While the president's popularity rose after the allegations involving Monica Lewinsky surfaced, support for Starr and his investigation plummeted. A spring 1998 national poll showed an approval rating of only 18%.[53] After Judge Susan Wright threw out the Paula Jones case, 57% of the public believed that Starr should end his investigation into the allegations that Clinton committed perjury in his deposition in the Jones case.[54]

The release of the Starr report to Congress in September of 1998 "created at least as much controversy as consensus."[55] As the public focus moved from the independent counsel to the Congress in the fall of 1998, similar disparities in public approval persisted. The Republicans lost seats in the House of Representatives and failed to gain any in the Senate during the November election. Even after the House impeached him, Clinton remained popular while the public continued to be critical of congressional Republicans and the Starr investigation.[56] An early 1999 Gallup poll showed that 53% of respondents believed that Clinton "was a victim of an unfair investigation into his personal life."[57]

It seems inevitable that such counterattack would come when a presidency is threatened. The president has at his disposal the institutional resources to challenge an independent counsel that are not available to his executive branch colleagues. In addition to a substantial public relations operation that has ready access to the media, he has access to outstanding and aggressive legal counsel (and the ability to raise funds to pay for that counsel) and institutional prerogatives like executive privilege that hamper the ability of the independent counsel to promptly and thoroughly investigate the case before him. Litigation over attorney-client privilege[58] and the protective function of the Secret Service[59] contributed both to delay in investigating the Whitewater and Lewinsky matters and to the mounting criticism of Starr.[60]

The temporary status of the independent counsel probably invites the use of delay tactics by targets of the investigations, although it is important to note that this is a not uncommon white-collar criminal defense tactic.[61] But the issue of time, and how much is spent by an independent counsel in investigating Ethics Act cases, has become a central part of the criticism of the statutory arrangement. Thus defendants can simultaneously use delay tactics to slow the pace of an independent counsel investigation while publicly questioning the amount of time the independent counsel is taking. Both Lawrence Walsh and Kenneth Starr had this problem and received little public or congressional sympathy for the delays they encountered.

The tactics adopted that cause delay are not necessarily illegitimate ones. Particularly when delaying tactics implicate the presidency, there is some public value to be attained by claiming and defending such notions as executive privilege, attorney-client privilege, the relationship between the president and the Secret Service, and the access to classified documents. Independent counsels involved in investigating the president will inevitably encounter these concerns, and in choosing to litigate them, as Kenneth Starr did, they will inevitably have their investigation delayed. It is significant in this regard that the House of Representatives rejected the article of impeachment that accused President Clinton of abuse of power for making such claims.[62]

With the failure of the Senate to convict Clinton, it appears that politics triumphed over the rule of law, in the narrow sense of that term. Certainly the House managers in their case to the Senate emphasized that this was the negative consequence if the Senate failed to convict. But at the level of the fundamental law, one could alternatively interpret this outcome as the upholding of the law. The Constitution's Framers imagined that removing the president would be, and should be, a difficult task. By placing that power in the hands of the two elected legislative bodies, they made it a fundamentally political process. By requiring extraordinary majorities, they also recognized that partisan dislike alone should not be enough to remove the one national officer elected by all of the people. A relatively weak criminal case[63] was rejected when subjected to the constitutional processes designed to address such situations.

POLITICS, LAW, AND INDEPENDENT COUNSELS

The rhetoric of post-Watergate reform placed a high premium on the rule of law and legal solutions to the governmental problems revealed in the scandal. Having survived a constitutional crisis in which a president resigned rather than being impeached for his role in a criminal conspiracy to obstruct justice, congressional reformers sought to avoid another such crisis with the creation of an independent investigative body to handle such cases. The independent counsel statute was one part of a larger "anti-corruption project" that followed Watergate, advanced by "moral entrepreneurs" both inside and outside of government.[64] Frank Anechiarico and James B. Jacob chronicle the increasing tendency to place our faith in "comprehensive legal strategies" to deal with public corruption. The consequence of this faith in legalism is that when corruption continues, "failure is attributed to poor drafting and not enough law; typically the solution is 'smarter' legal interventions. Some reformers have an extraordinary belief in the efficacy of legal threats to deter corrupt behavior; others cynically recognize that the best way to deal with scandals is to paper them over with ineffective laws that are not meant to be enforced."[65] In the two cases that are most like Watergate that have arisen under the Ethics in Government Act, we can see the limits of this approach. In each case, despite the full and thorough pursuit of allegations against the president, criminal investigative and prosecution efforts were limited or thwarted by the actions of political actors in the system. Some of these actors had much to gain personally by the exercise of their institutional prerogatives. Others simply followed competing institutional interests. But in either case, such interactions reveal the naivete of believing that politics could be removed from the administration of the law in these areas.

Given the limited usefulness of the criminal sanction in cases of this sort, should we simply conclude that law must always give way to politics when presidential wrongdoing is alleged? If we mean by law the application of the criminal law, then this seems to be true. But the other evidence in these stories suggests that what may instead be necessary is a reconsideration of what we mean by "the rule of law." What law are we talking about? If we move to the level of constitutional law—the powers allocated by the Constitution to public officials elected by the people—then there seems no obvious conflict between law and politics. In fact, there seems ample ability within the system as it exists to address official misconduct and to hold public officials accountable for that conduct. To accept that, we have to set aside the notion that criminalization is the only way to address abuses of the public trust. We have to place more faith in constitutional structures and democratic politics and less in criminal law strategies. We should recognize the very real danger that the availability of the independent counsel mechanism can invite institutional irresponsibility on the part of Congress, encouraging it to avoid the difficult political choices associated with alternative accountability mechanisms such as investigative hearings[66] and impeachment[67] by insisting that the case be handled by an independent counsel. Finally, we need to find some sense of proportion in the weighing of the benefits to be gained by criminal investigation and prosecution and the costs to be absorbed in the body politic of having the president vulnerable to criminal investigation for reasons other than clear and egregious violations of the criminal law.

Thinking about the independent counsel in the context of the larger constitutional structure helps to explain the problems encountered by independent counsels in their investigations. It challenges the claims made by Justice Scalia that the independent counsel operates without checks on his power. It reveals the way in which structural and definitional barriers can limit the effectiveness of criminal investigation and prosecution as a means to handle politically charged misconduct cases. Finally, it encourages us to expand our notion of what we mean by "the rule of law" and to consider whether the structural arrangements in the constitutional system provide adequate or alternative means for addressing official misconduct.

CHAPTER 11

The Influence of the NAACP
Legal Defense Fund on the United States
Supreme Court's Decision Making in
Minority Voting Rights Law

Steven C. Tauber

> The right to vote is crucial not just as a symbol of democratic participation
> but because it is preservative of all other rights.
>
> —Lani Guinier

AS LANI GUINIER'S QUOTE ILLUSTRATES, voting rights have been a vital
component of racial minorities' struggle for political equality. By supervising
the electoral process, the U.S. Supreme Court has contributed immensely to
expanding racial minority suffrage. However, as a reactive institution, the
Supreme Court can govern only when cases are brought to it. Public interest
groups are often responsible for initiating cases in the federal judiciary, and the
National Association for the Advancement of Colored People Legal Defense
and Education Fund (NAACP-LDF) has been a principal group litigating on behalf of minority voting rights. By providing the intellectual and financial support for some of the most important landmark voting rights cases, the LDF has
shaped minority voting rights policy, although its influence in this area has
been limited by external factors. This chapter focuses in detail on extent of the
NAACP-LDF's contributions to minority voting rights law.

INTEREST GROUPS AND THE FEDERAL JUDICIARY

In order to appreciate fully the NAACP-LDF's influence on voting rights, the
theoretical underpinnings of interest group litigation must first be explored.
When David Truman wrote that "the activities of judicial officers of the United
States are not exempt from the processes of group politics," he recognized that
despite its supposedly countermajoritarian nature, the federal judiciary, like
the popularly accountable branches, is subject to group pressure. When

219

Clement Vose detailed the NAACP's campaign to end racially restrictive housing covenants, he demonstrated thoroughly that interest groups are able to influence legal policy by sponsoring litigation. Since regional African-American groups were clearly outmatched in local arenas, the NAACP, a national civil rights organization, fought the restrictive covenants in the federal judiciary, which would respond only to legal arguments and not political pressure. Vose illustrated how the NAACP's carefully planned legal strategy was more successful than the neighborhood associations' legal strategy, ultimately resulting in the U.S. Supreme Court's ruling that restrictive contracts were unenforceable.[1]

Furthermore, Vose placed the NAACP's litigation campaign within a broader theoretical framework. He suggested that groups unable to influence policy in the majoritarian institutions have recourse in the federal judiciary. For politically weak African Americans seeking housing equality, the NAACP's skillful legal argument was the major component to victory. Vose's approach to studying interest group litigation centered on the notion that a disadvantaged group's legal strategy leads to success in a landmark case, which, in turn, transforms legal policy in favor of the disadvantaged group. Vose's work spawned a number of similar studies of other interest groups' attempts to impact judicial policy making through a strategy of sponsoring landmark cases in order to achieve a desired political outcome.[2]

More recently, scholars have recognized that interest group influence over judicial policy extends beyond landmark cases. The Supreme Court makes policy not only through landmark cases, but also through a gradual evolution of decisions over time. Research focusing on a single case provides only a snapshot of how a group manages to win (or lose) at a particular point in time. Current interest group litigation research has taught us that interest groups also influence policy by filing amicus curiae (friend of the court) briefs and sponsoring routine cases at all levels of the judiciary. Furthermore, this more recent research has shown that a group's legal argument and strategy, while important, is not the only explanation of success (or failures) in the judicial arena. Extralegal factors, such as the ideology of the judges deciding cases and the role of the U.S. Department of Justice, influence judicial decision making[3] and, thus, may affect the extent that an interest group is able to impact case outcomes. When the extralegal environment coincides with the policy objectives of a particular group, then that group is more likely to succeed in its efforts; and conversely, if the extralegal environment conflicts with a group's goals, then influencing legal policy becomes a more onerous task.[4]

In this chapter, I adopt both the traditional and contemporary approaches to the analysis of the NAACP-LDF's influence on voting rights policy. By sponsoring landmark cases, the NAACP-LDF contributed to important developments in minority voting rights law. However, when considering the totality of voting rights litigation, it becomes clear that extralegal factors have influenced the organization's effectiveness. The influx of conservative justices appointed by Presidents Richard Nixon, Ronald Reagan, and George Bush and the participation of the United States Justice Department have shaped the NAACP-LDF's ability to win cases.

THE BIRTH OF THE NAACP AND THE FIGHT FOR SUFFRAGE

The Civil Rights Act of 1870 furnished the U.S. government with the tools to enforce the Fifteenth Amendment's ban on racial discrimination in voting, and promised universal black male suffrage. However, the U.S. Supreme Court's interpretation of the federal government's power to enforce voting rights allowed southern whites to resist black registration. In holding that Congress held no authority over the actions of state officials, the Court in 1876 allowed individual voting registrars to escape federal prosecution for refusing to register blacks.[5] That same year the U.S. Supreme Court, reasoning that the federal government had no authority to regulate local elections, overturned the federal conviction of whites who massacred blacks, who themselves had been meeting to discuss a local election campaign.[6] By the onset of the twentieth century, the Supreme Court had completely eviscerated Reconstruction's voting rights laws, with Justice Oliver Wendell Holmes proclaiming that federal courts lacked the requisite jurisdiction to decide black suffrage cases.[7]

In response to the federal government's failure to address racial discrimination, black leaders began to form groups to combat discrimination, and changing suffrage laws was primary among their goals. In 1905, the black scholar W. E. B. Dubois invited to Niagara Falls, New York, twenty-nine intellectuals who shared his desire to pressure the federal government to provide for equal rights. The delegates to this meeting created the Niagara Movement, which issued a number of demands designed to foster political equality, equal education and employment opportunities, the abolition of Jim Crow laws, and universal male suffrage. Despite its initial expansion, the Niagara Movement was forced to disband as a result of factional squabbling over the best strategy for achieving civil rights. But after a mass lynching in Springfield, Illinois, Dubois, white industrialist John Milholland, and other civil rights leaders formed the National Association for the Advancement of Colored People (NAACP). The NAACP shared the same goals as the Niagara Movement, except that the inclusion of white elites provided the biracial NAACP with greater resources to conduct its crusade. From the outset, NAACP leaders resolved that litigation would be one of its chief weapons in its battle to attain civil rights.[8]

Like the Niagara Movement, the NAACP placed a high premium on eliminating barriers to suffrage, but the Supreme Court's previous rulings on this issue made this goal appear quite imposing. Consequently, the NAACP team of attorneys developed a two-pronged, long-term strategy designed to maximize their chances of changing the Court's interpretation of minority voting rights. First, the NAACP imposed central order on local civil rights organizations fighting suffrage discrimination. It also pursued a "chipping away" strategy in which it would litigate the easy cases first, and then build up to the harder yet more significant ones. The NAACP inaugurated its battle against voting discrimination by filing an amicus curiae brief in support of the U.S. Justice Department's fight against the discriminatory grandfather clause.[9]

Shortly after helping to defeat the grandfather clause, NAACP attorneys embarked upon attacking a larger, more significant problem when it launched its own voting rights litigation campaign. Absent any leadership from the Justice Department, the NAACP decided to assail directly a particularly virulent form of voting discrimination: the white primary, an election where a political party could exclude blacks from participating in primary elections. More specifically, the Democratic Party contended that as a private organization it was not covered under the Fifteenth Amendment and was free to exclude blacks from participating in its primaries. In Houston, Texas, C. N. Love, who was denied a ballot for the Democratic primary on account of race, challenged the constitutionality of the white primary. Love's attorney, R. D. Evans of Waco, was a small-town lawyer who tried to litigate this case without the help of the NAACP or any other national organization. Evans's brief to the U.S. Supreme

Court not only did not contain sufficient discussion of precedent, it was poorly composed and did not address how the Court should remedy the violation. After the U.S. Supreme Court refused to decide the issue on grounds that it could not fashion a remedy, the NAACP resolved that it should litigate this issue and eliminate this form of discrimination.[10]

The NAACP was presented with the opportunity to do so in 1923 when the Texas State Legislature banned blacks from participating in Democratic Party primaries statewide. Dr. L. A. Nixon, an El Paso dentist, challenged this law as state-sponsored voting discrimination in violation of the Fifteenth Amendment, and this time the NAACP entered the fray. In order to minimize tensions between its national policy goals and the concerns of local Texas NAACP branches, the central organization worked with local attorneys. However, the NAACP still maintained control from its New York City headquarters. Although the NAACP initially allowed local El Paso attorney Fred C. Knollenberg to manage the litigation on behalf of Dr. Nixon, the organization quickly grew dissatisfied with his lackluster performance. Consequently, the NAACP's Louis Marshall, who had established a reputation in New York City as a clever and skillful advocate, took control of the case. He, not Knollenberg, decided each tactical move and developed the long-term strategy. This action marked the first time that a civil rights interest group sponsored litigation to influence voting rights policy.

Marshall's brief to the U.S. Supreme Court, like the renowned Brandeis Brief, relied more upon empirical data from the political science literature than upon legal doctrine. He offered census information and election returns as evidence that the deep South was a one-party (Democratic) region where blacks comprised a significant portion but not a majority of the population. If blacks voted as a bloc, they could impact the outcome of a primary election, which in a one-party region translates into significant power in determining the ultimate winner. To exclude blacks from the primary was in effect to disenfranchise them and violate the Fifteenth Amendment. This strategy proved to be partially successful when a unanimous Supreme Court found Texas's law to be unconstitutional. However, the Court's reasoning differed slightly from the NAACP's position since it held that the statute was a violation of the Fourteenth Amendment Equal Protection Clause and did not consider the Fifteenth Amendment argument that Louis Marshall had proffered.[11] Nevertheless, the NAACP had accomplished a great deal by bringing the white primary case to the Court and establishing a record of the discriminatory effects of the white primary.[12]

After its loss in the Supreme Court, the Texas legislature cleverly drafted a new statute that would give state party committees the authority to impose voting qualifications. Accordingly, the Democratic State Executive Committee of Texas proscribed blacks from voting in Democratic primaries throughout the state. When Dr. Nixon was refused a ballot in the 1928 Democratic primary, a second generation of NAACP legal minds, led by Nathan Margold, Louis Marshall's son James, and Charles Houston, challenged this exclusion as a violation of the Fifteenth Amendment and Fourteenth Amendment Equal Protection Clause. After losing in the lower courts, the NAACP appealed its case to the Supreme Court, arguing that this white primary stemmed from state action as much as the one that the Court had previously invalidated. In 1932 the Supreme Court struck down the white primary because the party's discrimination still emanated from state authority and thus was subject to the Fifteenth Amendment.[13]

While the NAACP was able to secure victories against the white primary, independent lawyers were not as successful. After the Supreme Court forbade state involvement in establishing white primaries, the Texas Democratic Party, without prompting from the state government, prohibited black participation in primaries. Two non-NAACP-affiliated Houston lawyers—J. Altson Atkins and Carter Wesley—challenged this practice as a violation of the Fifteenth Amendment. While the NAACP offered informal advice (in fact Atkins and Wesley were former law partners of NAACP attorney James Nabrit), it recognized that the case was not winnable since the discrimination did not emanate from state authority. The NAACP was not prepared to waste precious resources on a losing cause. The U.S. Supreme Court in 1935 unanimously ruled that even though nomination by the Texas Democratic Party is tantamount to winning the election, the party's actions are still private and not covered under the Fifteenth Amendment.[14]

Soon after the Court upheld the Democratic Party's white primary, the NAACP encountered organizational difficulties. There was consensus among the staff attorneys to expand litigation activities, but the national organization lacked the requisite funds. Moreover, since the NAACP was primarily a lobbying organization, donors could not deduct their contributions from their taxes. In fact, at a board meeting, NAACP leader Walter White pointed out that John D. Rockefeller, Jr., declined to renew his $750 contribution because it was not tax deductible. White proposed establishing an entirely separate organization to conduct the NAACP's litigation activities. On March 30, 1940, the NAACP thus created the NAACP Legal Defense and Education Fund as a purely litigating organization. Since contributions to litigating groups are tax deductible, the LDF quickly obtained the resources necessary not only to assume the NAACP's litigation burden, but also to expand upon it.[15]

Flush with new money, the LDF resumed its interest in the white primary. Moreover, the LDF attorneys recognized that the legal climate had changed in their favor. The U.S. Supreme Court had recently held that the United States government could prosecute individuals who committed voting fraud in primary elections, since primaries were integral to the electoral process.[16] Despite the risk of rankling clients and supporters, LDF attorneys Thurgood Marshall and William Hastie capitalized upon this doctrinal shift and applied this new conception of primaries to the issue of the constitutionality of the white primary. Marshall chose to attack primary elections for the U.S. House of Representatives and Senate because those positions were directly covered under the Constitution. Using legal precedent and empirical evidence, the LDF argued that in the one-party South, the candidate who wins the Democratic Party primary is the candidate that ultimately serves in office. The white primary, therefore, excludes blacks from the only meaningful election to determine their representatives in the U.S. House and Senate. He argued further, that since the State of Texas recognized the Democratic Party as the official nominating instrument, the exclusion of blacks amounted to state action. In an 8:1 ruling, the U.S. Supreme Court adopted the LDF's arguments and overturned the white primary as a violation of the Fifteenth and Fourteenth Amendments.[17] After almost twenty years, the NAACP and the LDF's efforts had resulted in the eradication of the discriminatory white primary.[18]

THE LEGAL DEFENSE FUND AND MINORITY VOTE DILUTION

Ending the white primary, however, did not eliminate voting discrimination. Localities could still employ literacy tests and poll taxes that were presumably race neutral, but were implemented unequally to the disadvantage of blacks.[19] At the behest of President Lyndon Johnson, Congress passed the Voting Rights Act of 1965. The permanent sections of the act prohibited voting discrimination, allowed the U.S. attorney general to sue to eliminate literacy tests, and authorized federal officials to supervise voting registration. Of particular importance were the act's temporary sections (four and five), which employed complex formulas to identify states and localities with a history of voting discrimination. In those regions, the Voting Rights Act disallowed literacy tests and required that any alteration of a voting procedure must be precleared with the U.S. Department of Justice. The Voting Rights Act of 1965 not only prohibited most forms of voting discrimination, but it also expanded the opportunity to litigate on behalf of minority voting rights.

While the Voting Rights Act had ensured equal access to the ballot, it did not address equal effectiveness of the vote. The LDF, in particular, was concerned with minority vote dilution, which Chandler Davidson defines as "a process whereby electoral laws or practices, either singly or in concert, combine with systematic bloc voting among an identifiable group to diminish the voting strength of at least one other group."[20] In other words, a districting plan dilutes minority votes if it systematically prevents a sizable enough racial minority group from electing candidates of its choice. While minority vote dilution is easy to define, it is difficult to determine the extent that the Voting Rights Act prevents minority vote dilution, and this subject has been a source of great controversy. In 1980, the LDF entered this battle by challenging the at-large election of the three-member city commission in the City of Mobile, Alabama, because it diluted black votes in violation of the U.S. Constitution and Section Two of the Voting Rights Act of 1965. Since blacks were concentrated in certain areas of the city, they would be able to elect members in a district-based system, but they were sufficiently outnumbered in the city to prevent them from electing any candidates in the at-large system. The Supreme Court, however, declined to overturn the electoral scheme, arguing that in order to prove a violation of Section Two of the Voting Rights Act, plaintiffs must show that the vote dilution resulted from an intent to discriminate. Merely establishing that a system results in an electoral disadvantage for racial minorities was not sufficient to meet the standard of discrimination embodied in the Voting Rights Act.[21]

LDF attorneys realized that in order to fight against minority vote dilution, the language of the Voting Rights Act needed to be altered to include a "results test" to prove illegal minority vote dilution. If Section Two specifically pro-scribed systems that resulted in minority vote dilution, then the Supreme Court would be compelled to invalidate them. Fortunately for the LDF, Con-gress planned to amend the Voting Rights Act in 1982, and the LDF attorneys seized this opportunity to change the language of Section Two. While the LDF's tax-exempt status prevents it from lobbying, it is still free to offer advice to those drafting statutory language. However, the group had to overcome daunting obstacles. In the Republican-controlled Senate, the LDF encountered opposition from the chair of the Judiciary Subcommittee on the Constitution, Orrin Hatch (R-Utah), who opposed any modification to Section Two. Hatch argued that inserting a results test would mandate proportional representation for racial minorities, leading to minority redistricting quotas. LDF attorneys urged senators that such a change would not amount to proportional represen-tation, and Senator Robert Dole (R-Kansas) settled this dispute by offering a compromise bill to amend Section Two. Whereas the amended version of Sec-tion Two prohibits practices where the "totality of circumstances" prevents a racial minority group from electing candidates of its choice, Section Two stipu-lates that the law should not be interpreted to require that a group be elected in a proportion equal to its proportion of the population. Consequently, the LDF helped to insert a "results test" into the Voting Rights Act and increased its ability to end practices that diluted the votes of racial minorities.[22]

THE LEGAL DEFENSE FUND AND THE SUPREME COURT'S INTERPRETATION OF THE RESULTS TEST

The next phase in the battle over minority vote dilution took place in the U.S. Supreme Court, which was charged with the responsibility of interpreting the results test. Blacks living in multimember districts for the North Carolina State House of Representatives and Senate protested that the multimember dis-tricts diluted their vote in violation of the amended Section Two of the Voting Rights Act. The state of North Carolina, assisted by the Reagan Justice Depart-ment, insisted that blacks had been able to elect at least a few candidates; therefore, the redistricting plan did not result in minority vote dilution. The LDF offered the Court a much different interpretation of the results test as it applied to the North Carolina case. It argued that even if blacks had been elected on occasion, the "totality of circumstances" demonstrate a pattern of whites voting en bloc sufficient to prevent blacks from electing their desired candidates. In 1986, the Supreme Court adopted the LDF's conception of the results test and invalidated North Carolina's redistricting plan.[23]

Consequently, in a span of six years, the LDF was able to reverse an earlier defeat by encouraging Congress to redraft the Voting Rights Act and providing the Supreme Court with an interpretation of the amended language that would invalidate districts that diluted minority votes. In order to remedy minority vote dilution, states had drawn districts in which a majority of the residents are nonwhite. These districts are known as *majority-minority* districts, and they contributed extensively to increasing minority representation in elected bodies. In the first election after the 1990 census (1992), thirteen new black members of Congress were elected, and all of them came from majority-minority districts in the South. Additionally, record numbers of racial minorities were elected to state legislative positions in the early 1990s, largely as a result of majority-minority districts.[24] Moreover, the LDF expanded on its initial success by sponsoring litigation which resulted in the Supreme Court applying the Section Two "results test" to districts for state judicial elections.[25] In short, the LDF's campaign against minority vote dilution has served to increase minority representation at all levels of government.

MINORITY VOTE DILUTION: EPILOGUE

These LDF-sponsored advances in minority representation, however, sparked a backlash against majority-minority districts, and the U.S. Supreme Court began to rule against the position of racial minorities on race and redistricting cases. The Twelfth Congressional District of North Carolina was a majority-minority district that was irregularly shaped, and a group of white residents complained that it was a racial gerrymander in violation of the Fourteenth Amendment Equal Protection Clause. In 1993, the Supreme Court in *Shaw v. Reno* ruled that race-based districts, even those drawn to remedy prior minority vote dilution, were subject to Equal Protection Clause challenges and would be held to a strict scrutiny standard.[26] While the Court did not invalidate the district (nor did it hold that majority-minority districts were unconstitutional per se) this ruling marked the beginning of the reversal of the

Court's policy on race and redistricting.[27] Two years later, the Supreme Court overturned the Justice Department's Section Five preclearance policy requiring states to create majority-minority districts wherever possible, and in the process, the Court invalidated Georgia's Eleventh Congressional District, even though it was not bizarrely shaped like North Carolina's Twelfth District.[28] In subsequent cases the Supreme Court struck down North Carolina's Twelfth Congressional District,[29] and Texas's Eighteenth, Twenty-ninth, and Thirtieth Congressional Districts.[30]

Thus far this chapter has established that by litigating landmark cases, the NAACP-LDF has been a vital actor in the struggle to achieve minority voting rights. Since voting rights law is comprised of more than landmark cases, it is important to examine the extent that the group has been able to register a significant impact on the totality of voting rights cases. When considering the totality of cases, the extralegal environment emerges as a force that could potentially limit the·LDF's influence over the U.S. Supreme Court's minority voting rights decision making. This section discusses how two extralegal elements of judicial decision making—the Department of Justice and the changing ideology of the Supreme Court—constrain the LDF's ability to impact the U.S. Supreme Court's minority voting rights decisions.

THE DEPARTMENT OF JUSTICE

Research has demonstrated that the U.S. Department of Justice, and the U.S. Solicitor General in particular, has been quite successful in winning cases before the U.S. Supreme Court.[31] Moreover, the U.S. Department of Justice has actively litigated on behalf of racial minority voters. The Voting Rights Act presented a new opportunity for the Department of Justice to participate in voting rights cases. In addition to Section Five (which compels Justice Department action), Section Two confers upon the Justice Department the discretion to litigate to force the creation of majority-minority districts. Immediately after the Voting Rights Act was passed, the Justice Department announced it would litigate vigorously to enforce the Voting Rights Act.[32] Consequently, the LDF and Justice Department litigated together on many cases. In these cases, the LDF enjoyed the benefits of the Justice Department's resources. In short, the work of the U.S. Justice Department has enhanced the LDF's effectiveness in minority voting rights cases.

However, on certain occasions the LDF prevailed when the Justice Department declined to participate. For example, the Justice Department abstained from participating in the white primary cases. Justice Department attorney Herbert Wechsler feared that in retaliation for his participation, the Senate Judiciary Committee, which was dominated by opponents to civil rights, would drastically reduce the Justice Department and federal judiciary's jurisdiction in civil rights issues. Moreover, during the Reagan administration, the Justice Department acted primarily against the interest of minority voters, especially in major cases. With the Justice Department's massive resources and success in federal court marshaled against the LDF's interests, the LDF faced increased difficulties when litigating minority voting rights cases.[33]

In the 1990s, the Justice Department resumed its support of minority voting rights. Even the conservative Bush Justice Department moderated the Reagan Justice Department's position on voting rights, often siding with racial minorities. John Dunne, the Bush administration's assistant attorney general for civil rights, publicly expressed support for helping minorities increase representation.[34] The Clinton Justice Department has consistently supported racial minorities in minority voting rights claims as well. Despite the fact that Justice Departments in the 1990s have been more favorable to positions of racial minorities in voting rights cases, the Supreme Court during the same time frame has more often ruled against the LDF and racial minorities. Nevertheless, the Justice Department's litigation in support of minority voting rights has clearly affected the LDF's success in minority voting rights cases.

THE CHANGING IDEOLOGY OF THE SUPREME COURT

In addition to the Department of Justice, the changing ideology on the Court has impacted the LDF's influence on minority voting rights law.[35] Moreover, since presidents tend to appoint to the Supreme Court ideologically compatible justices, presidential appointment strongly influences the Court's decisions. For example, many of Franklin D. Roosevelt's appointments believed that the Supreme Court was the institution where politically disadvantaged groups, like racial minorities, could offset their disadvantage. In 1935, when the Supreme Court upheld white primaries as constitutional, conservative justices like Willis Van Devanter, George Sutherland, Pierce Butler, and James C. McReynolds dominated the bench. However, by 1944, when the Court disallowed white primaries, Roosevelt had replaced those justices with the far more liberal Hugo Black, Stanley Reed, Frank Murphy, and Wiley Rutledge, respectively.[36]

As more liberal justices assumed the bench during the 1950s and 1960s (e.g., Earl Warren, William Brennan, Abe Fortas, and Thurgood Marshall), the Supreme Court issued a number of revolutionary rulings that expanded civil liberties, protected the rights of the criminally accused, and limited racial discrimination. These decisions, emanating from an unelected, unaccountable branch of government, angered many Americans. In 1968, presidential candidate Richard Nixon capitalized on this emotion by promising to appoint to the Court conservative, strict constructionists, who would not thwart the will of the majority on behalf of the politically disadvantaged. Nixon fulfilled his promise by appointing four conservative justices: Chief Justice Warren Burger, Harry Blackmun, Lewis Powell, and William Rehnquist. This trend continued with Presidents Reagan and Bush, who packed the Court with conservatives, such as Sandra Day' O'Connor, Anthony Kennedy, Antonin Scalia, and Clarence Thomas.[37] By 1992, strict constructionists dominated the Supreme Court, which accordingly began to issue more conservative decisions. This conservative transformation of the U.S. Supreme Court from 1969 has presented a tremendous obstacle for the LDF. A more conservative judiciary is less receptive to the LDF's liberal arguments; consequently rendering the organization's task in securing minority voting rights victories a more difficult one. In the late 1980s, the president of the LDF, Robert Prieskel, and the director-counsel, Julius Chambers, commented on this changing ideological environment: "Unfortunately, the highest court in the land is contributing to the adversity that confronts us. In one ruling after another last term, the Supreme Court eroded vital legal protection to Blacks, women, and other minorities."[38] In fact, the increase of conservative justices presents a reasonable explanation for the Supreme Court's rulings in the 1990s overturning majority-minority districts.

Although it is clear that the LDF has contributed substantially to minority voting rights law by sponsoring landmark cases, the preceding section has shown that extralegal factors may limit the group's influence over the U.S. Supreme Court's decision making for the totality of voting rights cases. In order to examine fully the LDF's impact on voting rights law, it is necessary to determine systematically the extent of the LDF's influence over minority voting rights cases and to account for legal and extralegal influences on these decisions. Accordingly, I examined the sixty-one minority voting rights cases that the U.S. Supreme Court decided from 1924,[39] specifically assessing the LDF's influence and testing the extent that extralegal factors have constrained its influence.

Of the 61 voting rights cases, 39 (63.9%) were decided in favor of the racial minority group, and the LDF sponsored or submitted an amicus curiae brief in 25 of the 61 cases (41.0%). The LDF has undoubtedly been an active participant in the Supreme Court's development of minority voting rights policy. Furthermore, the fact that 68.0% of the cases in which the LDF participated were decided in favor of the racial minority side evidences further the LDF's effectiveness in litigating minority voting rights cases. However, it is important to emphasize that 61.1% of the cases in which the LDF did not participate were also decided in favor of the racial minority group. In other words, although the LDF won a majority of its voting rights cases, it did not fare significantly better than other parties litigating minority voting rights cases (see table 11.1).[40]

A more complex examination of the LDF's influence considers the way in which the extralegal environment influences the LDF's success. I suggested above that the Department of Justice participation on behalf of racial minorities should enhance the LDF's effectiveness. In fact, 84.6% of the cases in which both the LDF and Justice Department participated were decided in favor of the racial minority, yet only one-third of the cases in which the Justice Department participated without the LDF was decided in favor of the racial minority. In short, of those cases in which the Justice Department participated, the LDF's presence exerts a tremendous impact in the likelihood of a decision

Table 11.1. The Presence of the NAACP Legal Defense Fund and the Outcome of Minority Voting Rights Cases, 1924–97

	Presence of the LDF		
Outcome of the Case	Not Present	Present	Total
Anti–Racial Minority	14 (38.9%)	8 (32.0%)	22 (36.1%)
Pro–Racial Minority	22 (61.1%)	17 (68.0%)	39 (63.9%)
TOTAL	36 (100%)	25 (100%)	61 (100%)

Note: N = 61; column percentages in parentheses.
  Chi-square of 0.304 is not statistically significant at the .1 level.

Table 11.2. The Presence of the NAACP Legal Defense Fund and the Outcome of Minority Voting Rights Cases, Controlling for Department of Justice Participation, 1924–97

With Justice Department Pro–Minority Participation

	Presence of the LDF		
Outcome of the Case	Not Present	Present	Total
Anti–Racial Minority	6 (66.7%)	2 (15.4%)	8 (36.4%)
Pro–Racial Minority	3 (33.3%)	11 (84.6%)	14 (63.6%)
TOTAL	9 (100%)	13 (100%)	22 (100%)

Chi-square of 6.044 is statistically significant at the .05 level.

Without Justice Department Pro–Minority Participation

	Presence of the LDF		
Outcome of the Case	Not Present	Present	Total
Anti–Racial Minority	8 (29.6%)	6 (50.0%)	14 (35.9%)
Pro–Racial Minority	19 (70.4%)	6 (50.0%)	25 (64.1%)
TOTAL	27 (100%)	12 (100%)	39 (100%)

Note: N = 61; column percentages in parentheses.
Chi-square of 1.489 is not statistically significant at the .1 level.

favoring the racial minority.[41] The fact that the LDF is more likely to make a difference in cases in which the Justice Department participated suggests a synergistic relationship between the LDF and Justice Department. It also bears noting that the LDF is clearly not influential in the cases where the Justice Department did not participate. A total of 70.4% of the cases with neither LDF or Justice Department participation were decided in favor of the racial minority group, yet only half of the cases in which the LDF participated but the Justice Department did not were decided in favor of the racial minority (see table 11.2).

In addition to the Justice Department's participation, the ideology of the Supreme Court justice constrains the extent that the LDF influences minority voting rights decisions. More specifically, the Burger Court in 1969 and Rehnquist Court in 1986 both represented a conservative shift in judicial ideology.

As a result, the LDF should be less effective after 1969. In fact, during the pre–Burger Court years, every case the LDF litigated was decided in favor of the racial minority, yet only two-thirds of the cases in which the LDF did not participate were decided in favor of the racial minority. The LDF clearly had achieved a record superior to other parties litigating minority voting rights claims. However, during the Burger and Rehnquist Courts the LDF has not presented an advantage compared to other litigants. In this more conservative period, 60.0% of LDF cases were decided in favor of the racial minority group, and 59.3% of non-LDF cases were decided in favor of the racial minority group.[42] In short, the LDF enjoyed a greater relative advantage during the pre–Burger Court years (see table 11.3).

The U.S. Supreme Court has played a major role in securing voting rights for racial minorities, and the NAACP-LDF has been a key actor in the Supreme Court's decision making process. This chapter has focused on the LDF's substantial contribution to the minority voting rights struggle. The organization was the primary force behind some of the most important landmark voting rights cases of the twentieth century. These cases ended discrimination and allowed racial minorities to elect candidates of their choice to state courts, city councils, county commissions, mayorships, governorships, state legislatures, and the U.S. Congress. Undoubtedly, the LDF's work in the field of minority voting rights has been instrumental to the cause of civil rights. Nevertheless, the LDF's effectiveness has been constrained by the extralegal environment. Specifically, the more conservative Supreme Court resulting from Nixon, Reagan, and Bush appointments has been far more hostile to the claims of minority voting rights, and has clearly limited the LDF's effectiveness.

In the 1990s, this conservative majority prevailed in voting rights issues as the Court began to rethink its earlier position requiring states to draw majority-minority districts whenever possible. By the 1990s, the Court began to invalidate legislative districts that were drawn predominately to elect racial minorities.[43] This development clearly altered the legal climate contrary to the LDF's policy goals, and consequently, the organization has begun to stress some alternatives to litigation. Nevertheless, the organization has continued to participate in minority voting rights litigation.

The LDF still considers voting rights litigation to be an important part of its civil rights mission, as it states in its official literature.[44] Additionally, LDF attor-

Table 11.3. The Presence of the NAACP Legal Defense Fund and the Outcome of Minority Voting Rights Cases, Controlling for Burger-Rehnquist Court, 1924–97

Pre-Burger Court (1924–68)

	Presence of the LDF		
Outcome of the Case	Not Present	Present	Total
Anti–Racial Minority	3 (33.3%)	0 (00.0%)	3 (21.4%)
Pro–Racial Minority	6 (66.7%)	5 (100.0%)	11 (78.6%)
TOTAL	9 (100%)	5 (100%)	14 (100%)

Chi-square of 2.121 is not statistically significant at the .1 level.

Burger/Rehnquist Courts (1969–97)

	Presence of the LDF		
Outcome of the Case	Not Present	Present	Total
Anti–Racial Minority	11 (40.7%)	8 (40.0%)	19 (40.4%)
Pro–Racial Minority	16 (59.3%)	12 (60.0%)	28 (59.6%)
TOTAL	27 (100%)	20 (100%)	47 (100%)

Note: N=61; column percentages in parentheses.
Chi-square of 0.003 is not statistically significant at the .1 level.

neys publicly credit the increased number of minority elected officials to the creation of majority-minority districts.[45] In fact, even after the Supreme Court began to strike down majority-minority districts, the LDF still participated in voting rights litigation.[46] As the year 2000 census will probably suggest, race and redistricting will undoubtedly reemerge as a salient issue and the LDF is likely to be an active participant in the electoral battle. The organization will continue to challenge those districts that do not contain a sufficient number of racial minorities; and it will assist in protecting the existence of majority-minority districts that face challenges in the Supreme Court.

Conversely, the LDF has and will continue to react to the changing legal and political climate by diversifying its approach to enhancing minority voting rights and representation. As Roderick Bohanan said when assuming the leadership of the Indianapolis chapter of the NAACP, "Voting rights in Indianapolis isn't an issue anymore, but how effectively people use their voting rights is."[47] I would expect the LDF to work with other groups to increase minority voter registration and turnout. Furthermore, the LDF will most likely advise congressional leaders who draft legislation affecting minority voting rights. Just as Elaine Jones and Lani Guinier convinced Congress in 1982 to leave intact Section Five of the Voting Rights Act,[48] LDF attorneys will consult with lawmakers to ensure that the federal government still protects minority voting rights when the act is slated to be renewed in 2007. In sum, despite recent events, the LDF will be active in the struggle to preserve minority voting rights, as it has been in the past.

CHAPTER 12

"A December Storm over the U.S. Supreme Court"

Bush v. Gore and Superintending Democracy

Christopher P. Banks

Courts, in my judgment, should not generally supervise or oversee the election process. Nor, I think, should courts be afforded wide latitude to decide election disputes or, in fact, to be the ultimate judges of who won the election.

> —George Terwilliger, attorney and advisor for George W. Bush

Forget it. Five Republicans. We're going right into the tank.

> —William Daley, Gore's campaign chairman, telling the vice president of his prospects before the U.S. Supreme Court

Article II . . . authorizes federal superintendence over the relationship between state courts and state legislatures.

> —Justice Ruth Bader Ginsburg commenting on Chief Justice William Rehnquist's interpretation of Article II of the U.S. Constitution, in her dissent in *Bush v. Gore* (2000).

ON DECEMBER 12, 2000, in *Bush v. Gore* (2000) the Supreme Court of the United States reversed the Florida Supreme Court's order to recount by hand approximately 170,000 undervotes cast in Florida as part of Vice President Al Gore's legal challenge to claim the American presidency. In a per curiam (unsigned) opinion issued about two hours before expiration of the "safe harbor" deadline that required the states to deliver their electoral votes in accordance with federal law, the Court divided 5:4 along ideological lines to stop the recount. The effect of this decision was to give Texas Governor George W. Bush the White House. In so ruling, the Rehnquist Court held that the state election code's "intent of the voter" standard was too nebulous to conduct a fair recount under the equal protection guarantee of the Fourteenth Amendment, and that there was no time left to complete the recount anyway because of the lapsing safe harbor deadline. The four liberal-leaning brethren bitterly disagreed, with one, Justice Stephen Breyer, stating that the selection of the president is an important political, and not legal question. Another jurist, Justice John Paul Stevens, asserted that the only loser in the whole debacle is the "Nation's confidence in the judge as an impartial guardian of the rule of law." Given the strident disagreement on the Court, it is little wonder that the unprecedented ruling, along with all the electoral turmoil that preceded it, has been referred to as a "December storm over the U.S. Supreme Court" by Associate Justice Ruth Bader Ginsburg.[1]

The Court's controversial ruling ended a long, protracted litigation process that tested the nation's resolve and brought into sharp relief the wisdom of having the federal judiciary resolve a disputed presidential election. From one perspective the Supreme Court's involvement in the electoral contest helped *elect* a president in accordance with the rule of law and democratic principles, namely, equality and due process of law. But from another perspective, the high court *selected* the executive by judicial fiat, or an arbitrary exercise of raw power that contravened law and undermined popular sovereignty. The stark difference between these viewpoints is partially explained by what Alexander Bickel called the "counter-majoritarian difficulty," or the problem of having nonelected, life-tenured judges using their discretion to question majority rule through judicial review. As an academic construct the concept is vexing enough, but when applied to the electoral context and the vagaries of judicial philosophy, it is even more troublesome. Voters, as participants in the political process, begin to realize the consequences of having the Supreme Court superintend democracy, a role that typically requires applying general, abstract legal standards to the practical reality of applied politics. The electorate then sees, for the first time, that the Court's decision making in campaign and elections jurisprudence is profound, especially when politically motivated judges assume the task of interpreting the U.S. Constitution.[2]

This book aptly illustrates the uneasy relationship between law and politics, as well as the success and failure of the Supreme Court's management of the political arena through law. Collectively, the analyses inform us of the inherent tension between reconciling individual liberty and public rights in cases dealing with the regulation of political affairs. They also raise the possibility that court intervention may be illegitimate, or at least perceived as such, because the judiciary is either too activist or too restrained in resolving political cases. As *Bush v. Gore* (2000) especially reveals, they also tell us that the Court is a policymaking institution and that its decisions in the political thicket often have an impact on governance that extends well beyond the specific needs or desires of the litigants in cases.[3] In many ways, then, *Bush v. Gore* epitomizes much of what this book is about: exploring the legal and political consequences of exercising the judicial choice to intervene in a political process that is built upon principles of liberty, representation, and popular sovereignty. It is thus worthwhile to study that choice, along with its legal and political ramifications, and significantly, whether it had to be made at all.

THE RULES OF THE POLITICAL WORLD

One day after the Supreme Court of the United States decided *Bush v. Gore* (2000), Justice Clarence Thomas informed some high school students that the Court's decision making was not politically motivated. Since he could not recall any partisan discussions among the Court's membership during his tenure, Thomas said that one should not "try to apply the rules of the political world" to the Supreme Court.[4] Yet, as Campaign 2000 unfolded, and with more than fifty lawsuits filed in the thirty-six-day presidential contest, it became obvious that the nation's highest court would play a key role, if not a decisive one, in discovering who would occupy the White House. By December 12, the U.S. Supreme Court's superintendence of this process settled the outcome.[5]

The election consisted of two distinct periods that invoked state and federal judicial power. The first was the protest phase, which lasted from election day, November 7, to November 26, the extended deadline for ballot certification that the Florida Supreme Court set in its November 21 ruling in *Palm Beach County Canvassing Board v. Harris* (2000). The second, the contest phase, occurred between November 27, the day Al Gore challenged Florida's decision to award its twenty-five electoral votes to George W. Bush, and December 12, the date of the final U.S. Supreme Court ruling in *Bush v. Gore*. As Table 12.1 shows, even though there were a number of lawsuits filed in state and federal court, during both phases three significant decisions by the federal courts determined the final result: (1) the U.S. Court of Appeals for the Eleventh Circuit's ruling in *Siegel v. LePore* (2000) denying Bush's application for a preliminary injunction to stop hand recounts; (2) the U.S. Supreme Court's decision to vacate and re-

Table 12.1. Chronology of Key Litigation Events in Federal Courts during 2000 Presidential Campaign

		Court		
Date	Eleventh Circuit, in *Siegel v. LePore*	U.S. Supreme Court, in *Bush v. Palm Beach County Canvassing Board*	U.S. Supreme Court, in *Bush v. Gore*	
Nov 7	Election Day			
Nov 13	Dist. Ct., S. Fla. refuses to block hand recounts (J. Middlebrooks)			
Nov 14		Fla. Leon Cty. Ct. (J. Lewis) upholds 7-day recount deadline		
Nov 21		Fla. Sup. Ct. allows hand recounts to continue; extends certification deadline to Nov. 26		
Nov 26	Protest period ends			
Nov 27			Gore files contest lawsuit in Leon Cty. Ct. (J. Sauls)	
Dec 4		U.S. Sup. Ct. vacates Fla. Sup. Ct. ruling, stopping hand recounts	Leon Cty. Ct. (J. Sauls) rules against Gore, stops recounts	
Dec 6	11th Cir. denies preliminary injunction to stop hand recounts			
Dec 8			Fla. Sup.Ct. orders hand count of undervotes to start	
Dec 9			U.S. Sup. Ct. issues stay, stopping hand recounts	
Dec 12	Election contest ends		U.S. Sup. Ct. stops hand recount of undervotes	

mand the Florida Supreme Court's decision to continue the hand recounts in *Bush v. Palm Beach County Canvassing Board* (2000) and (3) the U.S. Supreme Court's rulings in *Bush v. Gore*, first issuing a stay and then stopping the recount and ending the election.

On November 13, in *Siegel v. LePore* (2000) (J. Donald Middlebrooks), the U.S. District Court of South Florida ruled against candidate Bush's petition for a preliminary injunction to stop the manual recount of disputed ballots. Two days later, on November 15, Bush appealed Judge Middlebrooks's order to the Eleventh Circuit and asked for a reversal, claiming that the lower court erred in not stopping the recount on the grounds that it violates the Fourteenth Amendment's due process and equal protection clauses, along with the free speech provision of the First Amendment.[6]

Although the Eleventh Circuit, sitting en banc, did not issue a judgment in *Siegel v. Lepore* until twenty-one days later on December 6, its 8:4 ruling affirming the district court revealed it chose not to enter the political fray when it had an opportunity to do so. After noting the "limited role of the federal courts in assessing a state's electoral process" and its general reluctance to decide unnecessary constitutional issues on the merits, the per curiam opinion explained that the plaintiffs did not establish a substantial likelihood of irreparable harm, a requirement that had to be satisfied before the court could grant an injunction. Given the paucity of evidence on the record, the court could not say that continuing the recount would cause immediate harm. Not only had Bush been certified as the winner of the state's twenty-five electoral votes, it was speculative to claim that his lead would vanish later if the recount proceeded. Significantly, too, the full court dismissed the argument that a violation of constitutional rights—in this case equal protection, due process, or voting rights—always establishes irreparable injury.[7]

Chief Judge R. Lanier Anderson III, an appointee of President Jimmy Carter, agreed but went even further in a separate concurring opinion. After surveying the circuit's precedents that showed "comparable deference to state regulation of elections," Anderson stated that "federal court intervention is not appropriate in 'garden variety' disputes over election irregularities, but that redress of alleged constitutional injuries is warranted if 'the election process itself reaches the point of patent and fundamental unfairness.'" Under these principles, an equal protection violation was not present when every ballot was being treated unequally in a postelection recount; and Florida election law had sufficient standards that cabined the canvassing board's discretion in discovering voter intention and also corrected vote tabulations affecting the election's outcome. The due process claim, Anderson argued, was also weak because there was little credible proof to suggest that the board deviated from performing a good-faith effort under the election statutes to ascertain the voter's intent in the recount. While the "preliminary injunction posture of th[e] case cautions against federal court intervention," the chief judge said, the plaintiffs "have not made a clear showing that an injunction before trial is definitely demanded by the Constitution if there is scant evidence of a likelihood of success or irreparable injury."[8]

Siegel's four dissenters, Judges Joel F. Dubina, Stanley F. Birch, Jr., Gerald B. Tjoflat, and Edward E. Carnes (who were appointed by Presidents Ronald Reagan, George Bush, Richard Nixon, and George Bush, respectively), separately but uniformly expressed little hesitation in saying that the circuit court ought to decide the case. Whereas Judge Dubina's brief dissent thought that the majority was wrong in not reaching the merits, Judge Birch's more extensive comments centered on the Florida legislature's "abdicat[ion] [of] its responsibility to prescribe meaningful guidelines for ensuring that [the] manual recounts would be conducted fairly, accurately, and uniformly." For Birch, the Florida statutes on manual recounts violated equal protection and due process by giving the county canvassing boards "an unfunded mandate [to] discern the voter's intent without any objective statutory instructions to accomplish that laudable goal." This legislative failure, Birch wrote, precluded any "meaningful judicial review . . . by a Florida court." Moreover, he suggested, it jeopardized the right to vote and helped foster the cynical, but false, perception that courts could not discharge their duty in an apolitical fashion. Specifically, he stated:

Just as the electorate was divided in their good faith effort to cast their votes for our nation's chief executive, the members of this court have discharged their duty to interpret the law in the context of this case in an unbiased and sincere effort. Inevitably the pundits will opine that a judge's decision is somehow linked to the political affiliation of the President that appointed the judge. While we at all levels of the judiciary have come to expect this observation we continue to regret that some "think" that is so. It may be true that a judge's judicial philosophy may reflect, to some degree, the philosophy of the appointing President—not a surprising circumstance—but to assume some sort of blind, mindless, knee-jerk response based on the politics of the judge's appointer does us and the rule of law a grave injustice. More importantly it is just wrong.[9]

While the two other dissenters, Judges Tjoflat and Carnes, echoed Birch's remarks, the latter jurist emphatically rejected the suggestion that the court should stay out of the "political thickets" when basic constitutional rights are threatened.[10]

By the time the Eleventh Circuit delivered its December 6 opinion, the political and judicial landscape had changed rapidly. Two interventions, one by the Florida Supreme Court on November 21 and the second on December 4 by the U.S. Supreme Court, moved the election into the contest phase and signaled that each court was moving in politically disparate directions (despite some agreement about the fundamental principles of law at stake). In *Palm Beach County Canvassing Board v. Harris* (2000) the Florida Supreme Court—a bench entirely composed of Democratic appointees—unanimously authorized the canvassing boards to conduct manual recounts where voting machine failure was not the only cause for errors in the vote tabulation. Since "our society has not yet gone so far as to place blind faith in machines," the court reasoned that "Florida law provides a human check on both the malfunction of tabulation equipment and error in failing to accurately count the ballots." By employing traditional principles of statutory construction and acknowledging the high value that the Florida Constitution put on preserving the right to vote, the court extended the deadline for certifying the votes until November 26. This narrow construction of the election laws, the court intimated, prevents it from "substantially rewriting the Code," a task best left to "the sound discretion of the body best equipped to address it—the Legislature." To do otherwise would wrongly permit "technical statutory requirements" to trump "the substance of [voting] right[s]," since having "an accurate vote count is one of the essential foundations of our democracy."[11]

The right-to-vote issue, however, was not part of the U.S. Supreme Court's rationale when it granted certiorari on November 24. Moreover, even though the petition for review stated that the Florida State Supreme Court ruling "poses a clear and present danger to that right," it is not a central feature of the Court's December 4 opinion vacating the state court's decision. If explicit vindication of a fundamental constitutional right was not the direct or controlling impetus for federal court intervention, why did the U.S. Supreme Court enter the political controversy? This is a key question, because, as some in the Bush camp worried, there were good reasons to believe that some of the Court's conservative justices would be disinclined to take the case. High-level strategists in the Bush camp, among them George Terwilliger and Benjamin Ginsberg, feared the Court conservatives would not want to intercede because of: (1) Justice Antonin Scalia's narrow view of the standing doctrine; (2) Justice Sandra Day O'Connor's political experience as a state legislator, which would mitigate against federal court intervention; and (3) Chief Justice William Rehnquist's Tenth Amendment jurisprudence favoring states' rights. Clearly it was reasonable to suspect (as Gore's legal team probably did) that the Rehnquist Court's federalism jurisprudence—with its strong preference for empowering the states—would dictate that the national court defer to the Florida court, particularly in an election case.[12]

The legal arguments asking for, and contesting, certiorari at this critical stage provide some insight as to why the Court granted review and, perhaps, why it ultimately held in the Texas governor's favor in *Bush v. Gore* on December 12. Significantly, both sides covered the same ground in their rendition of the relevant constitutional landscape: the need to respect principles of federalism and states' rights while dutifully performing the judicial role of preserving institutional legitimacy. Needless to say, each legal team applied these concepts quite differently to fit their litigation objectives, here and in subsequent filings with the Court. Accordingly, the principles form a conspicuous part of the final result that decided the presidency.

The certiorari petition characterized the Florida Supreme Court as an activist court, "embark[ing] on an *ad hoc,* standardless, and lawless exercise of judicial power" that usurped declarations of the political branches and threatened majority will. Extending the certification deadline and authorizing a selective manual recount under nebulous criteria of voter intent contravened several federal provisions, including the Fourteenth Amendment (due process and equal protection), the First Amendment (free speech and association), Article II, Section 1 (regarding the appointment of electors), and Volume 3 United States Code Section 5 (the "safe harbor" statute giving "conclusive" effect to the selection of electors by December 12). Appointing electors was hence a basic federal concern that superceded state election law under the Supremacy Clause (Article VI) of the U.S. Constitution, for what is "[a]t stake is the lawful resolution of a national election for the office of President of the United States." Accordingly, the petition maintained, "[t]his is precisely the type of question that the Nation justifiably expects [the Supreme] Court to decide" because, "absent a decision by [the Supreme] Court, the election results from Florida could lack finality and legitimacy," which could result in "the ascension of a President of questionable legitimacy, or a constitutional crisis."[13]

The brief opposing the writ painted a different picture. After decrying the "intemperate and insupportable mischaracterizations of [the Florida Supreme Court's] decision as usurping the role of the state legislature," the brief identified "profound reasons of institutional legitimacy that counsel against a grant of certiorari." One was adhering to the values underlying federalism, which mandate that the states carry out their delegated authority to pick electors pursuant to Article II, Section 1, the safe harbor statute, and the Tenth Amendment. Another was displacing the role of the lower court, which faithfully discharged its duty to construe the state election statutes in a manner consistent with discerning voter intent. A third was recognizing that judicial superintendence would create *less* legitimacy in the election by spiraling "the election process in untoward and unprecedented directions." Indeed, "[i]ntervention . . . would cause irreparable delay at a critical moment and would work a significant intrusion into a matter—the selection of electors—that is both fundamental to state sovereignty and constitutionally reserved to the States." The petition therefore was a "bald attempt to federalize a state law dispute" of "the garden-variety [kind] that federal courts routinely decline to consider," especially when the "Court's obligation is at its peak to preserve the principles of federalism that it has articulated and enforced" elsewhere.[14]

On November 24 the U.S. Supreme Court granted certiorari in *Bush v. Palm Beach County Canvassing Board* on two of the three legal questions presented in Bush's petition, both of them relating to whether the state court's ruling violated Article II, Section 1, the safe harbor statute, or due process. Significantly the Court ignored the third issue—whether the selective manual recounts violated equal protection—and in lieu thereof asked the parties to brief another issue: ascertaining the legal consequences of violating the safe harbor statute. This new issue ironically gave the Florida legislature, which authored a "friend of the court" (amicus curiae) brief after the grant order was issued, the chance to argue that the case was nonjusticiable under the political question doctrine, a rationale that the Gore team could have exploited—but did not—in arguing that federal court intervention was not warranted. Specifically, the amicus brief asserted two alternative but conflicting legal claims. The first was that the case involved a political question because the safe harbor statute intended that the state legislature, and not the state supreme court, pick its electors. Conversely, if the case was deemed fit for judicial determination, then the national tribunal, and not the state one, ought to decide it since substantial issues of federal law were implicated.

In the end, the U.S. Supreme Court decided *Bush v. Palm Beach County Canvassing Board* on December 4 by avoiding the substantive issues raised by the litigants, preferring instead to vacate the case and remand it for the purpose of clarifying whether the lower court used federal or state law as a basis for its judgment. Knowing if the judgment rests on federal or state grounds is key, because generally a federal court does not have the power to hear issues of state law; but, as in this case, there might be an exception if the Florida Supreme Court was asserting that the Florida Constitution superseded election statutes enacted by the Florida legislature. Under that interpretation—where the Florida judiciary was possibly violating Article II or the safe harbor statute—the federal court has the power to intercede and disrupt the state court's ruling. This latter issue, in fact, became the focal point of the case, since Chief Justice Rehnquist expressed concern during oral arguments that the state supreme court's actions undercut *McPherson v. Blacker* (1892), a precedent establishing that Article II grants the state legislature, and not the courts, the exclusive power to appoint electors. Construing *McPherson* in this fashion would doom the vice president's chances to win in two ways. Article II would first limit judicial authority by preventing the state court from ordering a recount, because doing so usurps the legislature's power to select electors. More subtly (and although it was not described in these terms), adhering to this view of *McPherson* is also consistent with returning power back to the states, a hallmark of Rehnquist Court federalist jurisprudence.[15]

Furthermore, the outcome in *Bush v. Palm Beach County Canvassing Board* overlapped with a number of events that affected the fight for Florida's electoral votes. Although the Florida Supreme Court's ruling gave Al Gore the chance to pick up more votes by extending the certification deadline, *Palm Beach County Canvassing Board* was one of a number of significant legal and political victories for Governor Bush. On the day after the Florida Supreme Court made its ruling, the Miami-Dade County Canvassing Board stopped its recount efforts due to the improbability that it could complete the task. Extending the certification deadline to November 26 had already shortened the time for Gore to contest the election under Florida law; and by the time the U.S. Supreme Court reached its decision, George W. Bush had already been certified as the official victor. Moreover, the Florida legislature was threatening to convene a special session for the purpose of selecting a new slate of pro-Bush electors in the event Gore secured a victory at the high court. The decision from the U.S. Supreme Court vacating the Florida Supreme Court's ruling to keep the recount going now made it extremely difficult, if not impossible, for the state and federal courts to sanction another recount that would be completed by December 12, the safe harbor deadline that was only eight days away.

Even so, the U.S. Supreme Court's opinion coincided with another judicial event in Florida that created another chance for the vice president to win in the courts. On December 4, Leon County Circuit Court Judge N. Sanders Sauls ruled against Gore in the lawsuit he filed on November 27 contesting the election, on the grounds that he failed to establish a "reasonable probability" that the outcome would have changed but for the difficulties associated with counting ballots. That defeat prompted an appeal, which the Florida Supreme Court heard on December 7. The next day, in another stunning 4:3 decision in *Gore v. Harris* (2000), the supreme court reversed the trial court in part and ordered that a manual recount be conducted for all legally cast votes across the state where there was an undervote (i.e., votes that were cast but not recorded by the machine in punch ballot counties). In noting that "[w]e are dealing with the essence of the structure of our democratic society," the majority reasoned that the election code gives the state legislature, and therefore the people, the authority to select presidential electors under the authority of the U.S. Constitution. Since the choice of who serves as electors is an expression of the people's will, discerning the voters' intent with respect to uncounted but legally cast votes is a critical issue that the judiciary must resolve, especially in a disputed election where time is running out.[16]

But Chief Justice Charles T. Wells, along with two other colleagues (Judges Major B. Harding and Leander J. Shaw, in separate dissents), vehemently disagreed. In a lengthy opinion that foreshadowed many of the arguments in the

U.S. Supreme Court's *Bush* decision, Wells expressed his "deep and abiding concern that the prolonging of judicial process in this counting contest propels this country and this state into an unprecedented and unnecessary constitutional crisis," something that "will do substantial damage to our country, our state, and to this Court as an institution." He argued that the Court should have used judicial restraint because "[e]lections involve the other branches of government." "[A] hovering judicial involvement" over elections is not justified simply because, he wrote, a "judicial majority subjectively concludes . . . [that] it is 'the right thing to do.'" Moreover, Wells's dissent identified an equal protection problem with authorizing a selective manual recount that, in the end, would not be tolerated at the U.S. Supreme Court or Congress (as did Bush's legal team in its original certiorari petition to the U.S. Supreme Court). Not only was it unrealistic to think that there was enough time to do a recount (and provide for subsequent judicial review in the courts), excluding some ballots from counting would "plainly be changing the rules after the election and . . . [be] unfairly discriminatory against votes in the precincts in which there was no manual recount." The press of time and the lack of a consistent, objective standard for identifying voter intent, moreover, seriously threatened to disenfranchise the voters because there was a real risk that the recount would not be finished by December 12, the safe harbor deadline.[17]

The passage of time would disclose how prescient the state supreme court chief justice was in predicting the reaction of the majority of the U.S. Supreme Court when it heard the case under appeal. In declaring that "this contest simply must end" in dissent, Wells was echoing the sentiments of a frustrated electorate who still did not know who its president was after nearly a month of fighting in the courts. As Wells saw it, the combatants were desperately holding onto their political lives while falling into a bottomless electoral abyss akin to a constitutional crisis. This was bad enough; but it was made infinitely worse since they were taking the reputation, and perhaps the legitimacy, of the judiciary with them. The rules of the political world, Wells seemed to be saying, were infecting the rationality of the bench. And, as the nation was about to discover too, they illustrate that the Supreme Court of the United States rules when it superintends democracy.[18]

THE U.S. SUPREME COURT RULES

Vice President Al Gore's unexpected victory in the Florida Supreme Court impelled Governor George W. Bush to scramble and try to regain the political momentum he once had but lost because of the vagaries of the legal system. In order to neutralize the defeat he ironically, but predictably, sought further relief in the federal court on Front Street across from the nation's capital. In his December 8 application to stay enforcement of the lower court order he made all the arguments Chief Justice Wells raised that would, in fact, prove to be decisive—that ordering a selective manual recount caused irreparable harm and violates Article II, the federal safe harbor statute and, under the Fourteenth Amendment, equal protection and due process. Paradoxically, a unifying theme of Bush's legal claims centered on circumscribing judicial power, but only in the sense that the state, but not the federal, supreme court lacked authority to act. Not surprisingly, Gore's legal team inverted Bush's claims, arguing that the state supreme court justifiably interceded by engaging in routine statutory construction and preserving the right to vote through a lawful exercise of judicial review. From this perspective the national court had to show restraint by deferring to the lower state court ruling. For Gore, then, federal judicial interference would wrongfully emasculate state court power and threaten "basic principles of democracy," especially if the Court amazingly fashioned a rule holding that a candidate for public office is irreparably harmed by having all the votes counted.[19]

On December 9 the U.S. Supreme Court ruled 5:4 in Bush's favor by issuing the stay and, while treating the emergency petition as a writ of certiorari, agreeing to review the merits of the case immediately. The Court's action, again, had a devastating impact on Gore's chances of winning for two reasons. First, for a stay to be issued there had to be a "reasonable probability" that four justices thought that review was necessary because there was a "significant possibility" that the Court would reverse on the merits. In that four justices from the Court's more liberal bloc dissented (Justices John Paul Stevens, David Souter, Ruth Bader Ginsburg, and Stephen Breyer), it meant that five, and not just four, conservative justices (Justices Antonin Scalia, William Rehnquist, Clarence Thomas, Anthony Kennedy, and Sandra Day O'Connor) had serious doubts about the validity of Gore's legal claims. Second, Justice Antonin Scalia took the unusual step of writing a separate concurrence supporting the stay order, a conspicuous signal to the litigants (and country) that there was a firm bloc of justices poised to decide the election in Bush's favor.[20]

Notably, whereas Justice Scalia's concurrence was written alone, Justices Souter, Ginsburg, and Breyer signed on to Justice John Paul Stevens's dissent. Justice Scalia's view of the matter—along with the Court's role in deciding it—stood in stark contrast to the dissent's view. After noting that issuing the stay indicates that Bush has a "substantial probability of success," Scalia said a key issue was ascertaining if the votes to be recounted were, under Florida law, "legally cast votes." Counting ballots of dubious validity might cause "irreparable harm [to Bush] and to the country, by casting a cloud upon what he claims to be the legitimacy of the election." "Count first," Scalia continued, "and rule upon legality afterwards, is not a recipe for producing election results that have the public acceptance democratic stability requires." Moreover, Scalia also was incredulous that the standard created by the lower court to determine the voter's intent was constitutional.[21]

Stevens, in rebuttal, responded that the Court's superintendence violated at least "three venerable rules of judicial restraint," including the maxim that courts act "cautiously" in deciding "questions whose resolution is committed at least in large measure to another branch of the Federal Government." For Stevens, the other two rules compelled that the Court defer to the Florida Supreme Court's interpretation of its own law, and that it ought not to decide "federal constitutional questions that were not fairly presented to the court whose judgment is being reviewed." Bush, also, did not meet his "heavy burden" of demonstrating irreparable harm. If anything, suggested Stevens, "there is a danger that a stay may cause irreparable harm to [Gore]—and, more importantly, the public at large." This is because "[p]reventing the recount from being completed will inevitably cast a cloud on the legitimacy of the election" and violate "the basic principle, inherent in our Constitution, and our democracy, that every legal vote should be counted."[22]

Issuing the stay, of course, foreshadowed the outcome of *Bush v. Gore* (2000), the final chapter of the unprecedented 2000 presidential (litigation) contest. While seven justices "agree[d] that there [were] constitutional problems with the recount ordered by the Florida Supreme Court that demand[ed] a remedy," the Court split 5:4 on what that remedy should be. Two justices, David Souter and Stephen Breyer, joined the more conservative bloc (Chief Jus-

tice Rehnquist and Justices O'Connor, Scalia, Kennedy, and Thomas) in a per curiam opinion holding that the manual recount authorized by the Florida Supreme Court lacked sufficient minimal standards and violated equal protection under the Fourteenth Amendment. Even though it was a central argument of the contestants, the majority significantly avoided deciding whether the state court had authority under Florida election law to determine a voter's intent and, likewise, if the court had the power to compel a manual recount under that definition. Sidestepping this question had two advantages. The Court first did not have to decide how to apply the *McPherson* precedent, that is, whether it barred the state court from exercising its delegated authority under the state constitution (i.e. judicial review) to construe the election statutes in a way that possibly violated Article II of the U.S. Constitution. More importantly, it also allowed the Court to use the factual record to make a plausible case that equal protection is violated with a selective and standardless recount.

In reversing the lower court ruling, the *Bush* majority zeroed in on the problem of discovering, and then implementing, voter intent during a manual recount. Voting intent, the Court wrote, "is unobjectionable as an abstract proposition and a starting principle." But, the Court continued, "[t]he problem inheres in the absence of specific standards to ensure its equal application." The lack of uniform standards, in other words, leads to unequal treatment of all the legally cast votes, since, as the record revealed, county canvassing boards used different standards for counting votes. By "ratifying" this unequal treatment through its ruling, for example, the lower court wrongfully permitted undervotes, but not overvotes (i.e., ballots having more than one vote that were not recorded by the machine) to possibly be counted during a hand recount. Lacking a uniform standard of when to count a vote also, in the Court's view, led to a number of practical and procedural difficulties that compromised the individual right to vote and, in effect, made fashioning a judicial remedy impossible, especially since the safe harbor deadline was about to lapse. Given these problems, the order authorizing the recount was reversed and the case was remanded for further proceedings, thus ending, for all intents and purposes, the election contest.[23]

Simply relying upon equal protection as the basis for reversal was not enough for three of the five justices in the *Bush* majority. Chief Justice Rehnquist, in a concurrence joined by Justices Scalia and Thomas, saw the case differently since this was not "an ordinary election," but rather one involving the presidency of the United States. Even in spite of the usual deference federal courts give state court decisions under principles of comity and federalism, this was one of the "few exceptional cases in which the Constitution imposes a duty or confers a power on a particular branch of a State's government." Under *McPherson*, the chief justice wrote, the power under Article II, Section 1 to select electors rests exclusively with the state legislatures; and how that power is exercised is informed by the federal safe harbor statute. As a result, any deviation from the statutory regime for appointing electors is constitutionally suspect.

The concurring justices asserted that the Florida Supreme Court ruling was such a departure, several times over. Not only did it take away the canvassing boards' discretion to recount the ballots past the certification deadline, it also set new deadlines as to when late ballots would be counted and, in the process, frustrated the legal ability of the secretary of state to disregard them if she wanted to under her interpretation of the election laws. The state court's decision, moreover, wrongly required the counting of improperly marked ballots, or undervotes, even though the election scheme had several procedures in place to tally votes that were legally cast and reject those that were not. By substituting its own judgment for the one expressed by the state legislature in its election laws, the state supreme court frustrated Florida's desire to use the safe harbor statute and protect its choice of electors from challenge after December 12. The Court's decision, therefore, as well as its "inquiry [into the validity of the state supreme court's interpretation of the election laws] does not imply a disrespect for state courts," Rehnquist maintained, "but rather a respect for the constitutionally prescribed role of state legislatures."[24]

THE QUINTESSENTIAL CASE OF POLITICAL ILLEGITIMACY?

While the conservative bloc controlled the outcome in *Bush v. Gore* (2000), the dissenting liberal coalition stood united in stating that the Court's superintendence of the presidential election was misguided and, to varying degrees and for different reasons, that it posed a real or potential threat to the Court's institutional legitimacy. For Justice Stevens, the Court's *Bush* opinion was anything but an illustration of respect for the role of state legislatures. Instead, it was much ado about nothing, creating an equal protection violation where none existed. The lower court, argued the oldest member of the Court, merely "did what courts do," which in this context meant engaging in statutory construction. Unlike Rehnquist, he believed the state constitution, which constrained state legislative power, also vested in the state court the power of judicial review over election laws pursuant to Article V of the state constitution and, more broadly, Article II of the U.S. Constitution and the safe harbor statute. As a result, the federal court should defer to the state supreme court since "[n]either [the safe harbor statute or Article II] grants federal judges any special authority to substitute their views for those of the state judiciary on matters of state law."

For Stevens, moreover, the state court's reliance on the voting intent standard was not judicial innovation, but rather a reasonable interpretation of the law; despite its problematic application, a constitutional violation did not result, especially if all disputed votes across the state were evaluated by the final determination of a judge. Even if there was a violation, the proper remedy was a remand, not a reversal, so a single uniform standard could be developed. At least if that path was taken, Stevens asserted, Florida voters would not be disenfranchised because all questionable legal votes would be counted. Federal interference with local election laws, he objected, could only be explained as "[a]n unstated lack of confidence in the impartiality and capacity of the state judges who would make the critical decisions if the vote count were to proceed." "Otherwise," he continued in a lament that paradoxically sounded like what circuit Judge Stanley Birch said in his dissent arguing *for* federal court intervention, "[the petitioners'] position is wholly without merit. The endorsement of that position by the majority of this Court can only lend credence to the most cynical appraisal of the work of judges throughout the land. It is confidence in the men and women who administer the judicial system that is the true backbone of the rule of law. Time will one day heal the wound to that confidence that will be inflicted by today's decision. One thing, however, is certain. Although we may never know with complete certainly the identify of the winner of this year's Presidential election, the identity of the loser is perfectly clear. It is the Nation's confidence in the judge as an impartial guardian of the rule of law."[25]

Justices Souter, Ginsburg, and Breyer, in separate discourses, delivered similar messages in their dissents. Souter's opinion, for example, characterized the Court's meddling as the latest mistake in a series of missteps that only impeded the political system from "work[ing] itself out" and deciding the presidency without the Court's help. Like Stevens, Justice Souter contended that the safe harbor statute outlined a permissive, and not mandatory, deadline; and he found little merit in the argument that the state supreme court was overreaching when it simply evaluated its own election law. While he conceded that the manner in which dubious ballots were interpreted presented a constitutional question and "a meritorious argument for relief," Souter reiterated that "[i]t is an issue that might well have been dealt with adequately by the Florida courts if the state proceeding had not been interrupted." Or, he continued, "if [it was] not disposed of at the state level it could have been considered by the Congress in any electoral vote dispute." Although he thought time was running out, he still believed that the Court should make the best of a bad situation (it created) by issuing a remand, a solution that was feasible and, as a constitutional matter, wise.[26]

Ruth Bader Ginsburg also argued against the outcome, although she was more direct in accusing the majority of letting its political preferences drive it. Even if there was an equal protection problem, she said the safe harbor statute deadline was not compulsive; and "the Court's reluctance to let the recount go forward . . . ultimately turns on its own judgment about the practical realities of implementing a recount, not the judgment of those much closer to the process." Ginsburg found it extraordinary to argue, as the chief justice did, "that Florida's Supreme Court has veered so far from the ordinary practice of judicial review that what it did cannot properly be called judging." As the Court's own inability to agree on the outcome illustrates, reasonable minds disagree on how to best interpret Florida election law. But, she continued, "[m]y disagreement with the Florida court's interpretation of its own State's law does not warrant the conclusion that the justices of that court have legislated." Accordingly, she dissented because she fundamentally objected to the chief justice's assertion that "Article II . . . authorizes federal superintendence over the relationship between state courts and state legislatures." Quite simply, she retorted, an "ordinary principle" that "reflects the core of federalism" should have been used to decide the case: that "Federal courts defer to state high courts' interpretations of their own state law."[27]

Whereas his dissenting colleagues were inspired to rely upon principles of statutory construction, judicial deference, and federalism to make their case, Justice Breyer looked to the history of the 1876 presidential election to imply that the Court is wrong in "repeating it" in deciding the 2000 presidential contest. While Breyer avoided answering the equal protection question raised by the lack of uniform standards, he may have done so because it had the "quintessential" characteristics of a political question that is best resolved in Congress. After noting that remanding the case was a better remedy than stopping the recount, Breyer criticized the concurring justices for stating that Article II of the U.S. Constitution was violated because the state court's ruling "distorted" Florida's election statutes. Like the other dissenters, he could not find any distortion; instead, all he discovered was an interpretation of the law concerning voter intent by the state supreme court that was entitled to deferential effect. In this light he thus saw that this case did not concern a legal issue that the U.S. Supreme Court had to settle. "Of course," he explained, "[t]he selection of the President is of fundamental national importance. But that importance is political, not legal. And this Court should resist the temptation unnecessarily to resolve tangential legal disputes, where doing so threatens to determine the outcome of the election."[28]

In other words, the high stakes of the contest counseled against federal superintendence, not for it. From Breyer's perspective, Governor George W. Bush was not asking the Court to protect a "basic human right," but only for procedural fairness implicating "the constitutional allocation of power." On that basis the Court's intrusion in a state political matter was unnecessary, especially given the myriad of federal law (i.e., the safe harbor statute, the Twelfth Amendment, and the Electoral Count Act, as amended) that vests power in states' courts and the U.S. Congress to reconcile disputes involving electors. Moreover, he argued, little is to be gained and much might be lost if the federal courts intercede, as evidenced by the Court's participation in determining the victor of the Hayes/Tilden election of 1876. There, Breyer recounted, three states each sent a slate of electors to the Capitol, whereupon Congress created an electoral commission of representatives from the Senate, the House, and the U.S. Supreme Court. The commission was evenly divided by party lines but, unexpectedly, Justice Joseph P. Bradley replaced Justice David Davis, an independent who was supposed to cast the deciding vote. The political uproar that followed after Bradley's decision to accept the vote from the electors supporting Hayes was predictable. But the lesson to be learned, suggested Breyer, was that the decision, which was inherently political, dwarfed the significance of the legal question that was involved, which was minimal to nonexistent. Consequently, the Court's intervention did nothing to "lend [the] process legitimacy." Since, he said, "the Court is not acting to vindicate a fundamental constitutional principle . . . [n]o other strong reason to act is present. Congressional statutes obviate the need. And, above all, in this highly politicized matter, the appearance of a split decision runs the risk of undermining the public's confidence in the Court itself." For these reasons, "[w]hat the Court does today," Justice Breyer concluded, "the Court should have left undone."[29]

WAS THE 2000 CAMPAIGN A "POLITICAL QUESTION?"

At the end of its opinion in *Bush v. Gore* (2000), the majority spoke at length about its reluctance to discharge its duty in such a politically volatile case. After explaining why the Florida Supreme Court's December 8 decision ordering the recount to proceed was a constitutional violation of the equal protection clause, the Court made this comment, in dicta: "None are more conscious of the vital limits on judicial authority than are the members of this Court, and none stand more in admiration of the Constitution's design to leave the selection of the President to the people, through their legislatures, and to the political sphere. When contending parties invoke the process of the courts, however, it becomes our unsought responsibility to resolve the federal and constitutional issues the judicial system has been forced to confront."[30] This observation, when juxtaposed against Justice Stephen Breyer's claim that avoiding the dispute would best conserve the Court's institutional legitimacy, calls into question how much compulsion was really brought to bear on the Supreme Court to decide the case. Since it is true that courts are not self-starters, it is correct to say that judicial decision making is the culmination of an "unsought responsibility." But it is misleading to infer that the Court did not have multiple chances to avoid the case initially or after it put the case on the docket. Clearly the decision to enter the political thicket was an act of volition, both in initially taking *Bush v. Palm Beach County Canvassing Board* and *Bush v. Gore*, and then in deciding them on the merits after oral argument. It was also an act of policy-making, with the presidency on the line. When seen in this light, the wisdom of the judiciary micromanaging election law comes into sharper focus, and it becomes imperative to see if there are any legal arguments that Gore (or anyone else) could have made to convince the Court to abstain from deciding the case.

One possibility, as directly raised by the Florida legislature in its amicus brief in *Bush v. Palm Beach County Canvassing Board*, and more indirectly by the dissenters in *Bush v. Gore*, is the political question doctrine. Under the doctrine, disputes involving the selection of presidential electors are inherently political and best resolved by the political branches of government, and not the unelected judiciary. The basis for understanding it is found in *Marbury v. Madison* (1803), where Chief Justice John Marshall said that "[t]he province of the court is, solely, to decide on the rights of individuals, not to inquire how the executive, or executive officers, perform duties in which they have a discretion. Questions in their nature political, or which are, by the constitution and the laws, submitted to the executive, can never be made in this court."[31] Paradoxically, and perhaps fittingly, these words *limit* judicial authority in a landmark ruling that *grants* the Supreme Court the power of judicial review, a court-created prerogative to review majoritarian preferences (i.e., legislative statutes or executive regulations) when individual rights are compromised.

Nevertheless, as a constraint it still means that "[i]f cases arising under a constitutional provision are deemed to be a political question, then that provision is effectively left to the political branches and majoritarian decision-making."[32] Scholars considering the scope of the doctrine downplay its significance by asserting that the Court has restricted its use to a very narrow category of constitutional law cases and, since there is no clear line between law and politics, wondering aloud if it even exists.[33] As Marshall's comments imply, however, the doctrine is, at its core a judicial choice that assumes there are good reasons for courts to avoid some disputes (i.e., where they are self-interested in the outcome). It also constitutes a belief that constitutional violations are remediable by the political branch to which the matter is entrusted.[34]

The real issue, then, is not whether the political question doctrine exists, because it surely does; rather, the more pressing question is identifying when it should apply.[35] Before 1962, the Supreme Court drew a discernible line by holding that it barred federal courts from entering the politics of apportionment controversies. For the Court to decide such questions, held Justice Felix Frankfurter in *Colegrove v. Green* (1946), is to do "what is beyond its competence to grant." In so holding, Frankfurter expressed his fear that the judiciary, as a branch of government that could only negate unconstitutional violations, could not act like a legislature in redrawing political districts. For this reason the Court would not be able to fashion an adequate constitutional remedy, thereby frustrating the actualization or vindication of rights, its overriding judicial function. Moreover, he stated, "[i]t is hostile to a democratic system to involve the judiciary in the politics of the people"; and, "it is not less pernicious if such judicial intervention in an essentially political contest be dressed up in the abstract phrases of the law." This is true, he wrote, even if the people's representatives on the state level fail to act. In that case, the true remedy is found elsewhere, in a place other than in the courts. For Frankfurter, under the

Constitution the "duties in our governmental scheme [often] depend on the fi-
delity of the executive and legislative action and, ultimately, on the vigilance
of the people in exercising their political rights." Accordingly, "[c]ourts ought
not to enter this political thicket."[36]

All of this changed as the Warren Court (1954–69) due process revolution
took hold. In *Baker v. Carr* (1962), a case that is factually indistinguishable from
Colegrove, the Supreme Court reversed course and determined that the federal
judiciary was fit to hear redistricting cases. Justice William Brennan, Jr., the author of the Court's 6:2 ruling, outlined the criteria for identifying a political
question:

Prominent on the surface of any case held to involve a political question is found a
textually demonstrable constitutional commitment of the issue to a coordinate political department; or a lack of judicially discoverable and manageable standards for
resolving it; or the impossibility of deciding without an initial policy determination
of a kind clearly for non-judicial discretion; or the impossibility of a court's under-
taking independent resolution without expressing lack of the respect due coordinate branches of government; or an unusual need for unquestioning adherence to a
political decision already made; or the potentiality of embarrassment from multifarious pronouncements by various departments on one question.[37]

Subsequent rulings from the Court, as in *Williams v. Rhodes* (1968) (concerning the selection of presidential electors in Ohio), indicate that very few cases
are nonjusticiable under this doctrine. In *Williams,* Justice Hugo Black quickly
dismissed the possibility of its use by citing several precedents and concluding
that "[the] claim that the political-question doctrine precludes judicial consideration of these cases requires very little discussion."[38] One could reasonably
conclude, too, that the verbal gymnastics of the *Baker* definition makes it too
ambiguous, or much too complicated, to apply to actual cases, as some critics
maintain.[39] Still, *Baker's* criteria may fit snugly into the context of the 2000
presidential election.

First, Article II, Section 2 of the U.S. Constitution is a "textually demonstrable commitment" to let Congress select the winner after the states pick their
slate of electors; or, put differently, it is a command that the state legislatures
appoint their electors for Congress to ratify. Second, the Court's inability to
agree on the proper remedy after hearing the case indicates that there was a
"lack of judicially discoverable and manageable standards for resolving" the
due process or equal protection issues, or more generally, the voting intent is-

sue. Third, selecting the president without judicial interference is ultimately a "policy determination" by Congress in the event it must pick a president after the states have discharged their own duties in casting electoral votes in a close or disputed election. Fourth, it was "impossible" for the Court to "undertake independent resolution" of the case since doing so usurps Congress's role in deciding the election if it had been required to under the U.S. Constitution. Fifth, the "unusual" circumstances of the election presents a "need" for the Court to "unquestioning[ly] adhere" to the political decisions that were already made by the state of Florida regarding the outcome of the election, especially, one could surmise, if the Florida legislature formed another slate of Bush electors in the event the recount continued and the vice president won the "first" set of electoral votes. Finally, and perhaps needless to say in light of the political turmoil that characterized the 2000 race, since various political institutions on the state and federal level, namely the Florida secretary of state, the Florida judiciary, the Florida legislature, and the lower federal courts, all played an integral part of the election dispute up until the point in time the Supreme Court decided to intervene, it was evident that there was a "potentiality of embarrassment from multifarious pronouncements by various departments on one question."

Significantly, too, at least one interested party in the 2000 campaign tried to convince the Court to stay out of the dispute on political question grounds. The Florida legislature specifically made this argument in its amicus brief after certiorari was granted in *Bush v. Palm Beach County Canvassing Board,* a moment in time that not coincidentally was the first opportunity for the Court to opt out of the election drama. As the state legislature framed it, the issue of failing to make a timely selection of presidential electors under federal law is not an issue for the Court to resolve under the *Baker* precedent. Rather,

Such questions should be determined by the State Legislature or, if it fails to act by December 18 when the Electors cast their votes, by Congress when it counts those electoral votes on January 6, 2000 [*sic*]. Such a ruling that these are non-justiciable questions to be resolved by the political branches would recognize that the Constitution vests the State Legislatures with the power to appoint Electors, and Congress with the power to count their votes. It also makes the most sense of the United States Code governing how Congress exercises its counting powers. The alternative would put this Court in the uncomfortable position of seeking to enjoin how Congress exercises its constitutional counting authority and how the State Legislatures exercise their constitutional appointment authority. . . . A ruling of nonjusticiability would avoid involving [the U.S. Supreme Court] in a political dispute best resolved by the political process. . . . What is at stake here is after all a political determination of who shall be the next President. The issue to be determined is uniquely political. Nor is it likely to recur. Thus, in this rare circumstance, it is entirely appropriate to have it resolved by the branches of government that are most responsive to the will of the people.[40]

As the brief suggests, the Florida legislature was asking the Court to abstain from deciding the issue because it was prudent to do so. Indeed, a number of prudential considerations help structure the decision to stay out of the political thicket. Some of these considerations have been identified by Alexander Bickel, a constitutional law scholar who was cited by Justice Breyer in his *Bush* dissent. The "foundation, in both intellect and instinct," Bickel writes, "of the political question doctrine [is] the Court's sense of lack of capacity, compounded in unequal parts of (a) the strangeness of the issue and its intractability to principled resolution; (b) the sheer momentousness of it, which tends to unbalance judicial judgment; (c) the anxiety, not so much that the judicial judgments will be ignored, as that perhaps it should but will not be; (d) finally ("in a mature democracy"), the inner vulnerability, the self-doubt of an institution which is electorally irresponsible and has no earth to draw strength from."[41] Justice Breyer perceived the 2000 campaign as implicating these factors, and it is easy to see why. The unusual events surrounding the election and the uncertainty of determining the victor under our constitutional design points up the "strangeness of the issue and its intractability to principled resolution." The political implications of having the nation's highest court decide the presidency underscores the "momentousness" of the occasion, which plausibly could "unbalance judicial judgment" and lead to an "anxious" uneasiness that it "should be" ignored, but ultimately will not be. And, as the 5:4 decisions in issuing the stay and deciding the merits in *Bush v. Gore* suggest, there is sufficient reason to suspect the Court had qualms about whether it was doing the right thing in becoming involved.

WHO WILL RUE THE DAY?

If the political question doctrine is considered as an abstract theory or principle of constitutional law, perhaps the legal scholars are correct in saying that it does not exist. But when it is seen as a matter of constitutional prudence, there is a good possibility they are wrong. The unique circumstances of the campaign, as influenced by the reality that the final outcome was likely to rest upon a choice made either by the national legislature, which directly represents the people, or the national court, an unelected body once removed from the people, make the 2000 presidential election the kind of political question that should have been avoided through an exercise of prudential discretion, which really is no more than a carefully balanced judgment of political statecraft. As Bickel tells us, "some questions are held to be political pursuant to a decision that there ought to be discretion free of principled rules." By asserting its will on the electorate, the Supreme Court directly affected the people's choice of president when it clearly did not have to do so.[42]

Yet, as a matter of applied politics, it might be too much to believe that the Court would have been receptive of any assertion of nonjusticiability. Even assuming that it is a viable legal principle, with the notable exceptions of the Florida legislature and, perhaps, Al Gore, the principal litigants of the case saw no reason to use it. It was certainly not in Bush's interest to do so, *if* one assumes that the conservative Court would be favorably predisposed to his position on policy grounds. It is easy to make that assumption, however, since the initial fear that the Bush legal team had about the Rehnquist Court's pro–states' rights, federalism jurisprudence was apparently unfounded. Moreover, as its amicus brief reveals, the Florida legislature was ambivalent on whether the doctrine, as applied, could really help since it raised both the possibility of its use and the improbability that the Court would accept that argument. Gore, on the other hand, must have faced an intractable dilemma in pondering its use. If he asserted the claim, the Court might agree that it bars hearing the case on the merits, a circumstance that would have in turn forced the Florida representatives to act, with uncertain consequences for the country or Gore's political life. By not raising it, though, he ran the risk of affirmative federal court intervention that would virtually invite the conservative Court to hold in Bush's favor. By not making the justiciability argument, this might show that he hedged his bets, in effect gambling that it was better to avoid it altogether and hope that the Supreme Court would put aside its partisanship and decide the case under neutral principles of law once it went into the political thicket.[43]

As commentators from both sides of the aisle have criticized the Court's decision because it was flimsy in law or logic and principally driven by results, it appears the vice president guessed incorrectly. If so, then what the Court did is either legally or institutionally unsound, particularly since it could have chosen to let the political process run its course by staying out of the campaign. The opportunity to abstain surely existed because the Florida legislature squarely presented the issue to the Court in its amicus brief (or it could have applied it *sua sponte,* even if the argument was not made). Although the results can be interpreted differently, polling data from the Gallup organization implies that the citizenry believes that ideological considerations influenced the outcome in *Bush v. Gore* (2000). The public opinion polls make it plausible to think that the country is asking itself whether it was worth it for the Court to interfere in the electoral process.[44]

In the end, since the Court chose to enter the political thicket, its intervention in *Bush v. Gore* (2000) must be judged by two assumptions that bind the act of interpreting constitutional law with the reality of applied politics in our American democracy: (1) a principled exercise of the power of judicial review; and, (2) consent of the governed.[45] In this light an assessment about what the Court did in deciding the election is not judged by the outcome, because it is irrelevant whether George W. Bush or Al Gore won the presidency. The more important question, by far, is whether the people believed that the Court had the authority to decide the issue in the first place. In other words, the principled use of judicial power, even if it is correctly described as being "countermajoritarian" (or political) in scope, is only legitimized by the people's consent or approval of what the judiciary is doing in establishing the rule of law. As Alexander Bickel suggests, a "coherent, stable—and *morally supportable*—government is possible only on the basis of consent, and . . . the secret of consent is the sense of common venture fostered by institutions that reflect and represent [the citizenry] and that [they] can call to account."[46]

Therefore, although the Court's historic role as protector of individual rights must be respected as a virtuous ideal, the value of preserving the Court's institutional standing is of equal significance. The two ideas are interdependent: the judicial capacity to act as a faithful guardian of political rights depends on whether the people support the rule of law and, in final analysis, the judiciary as a coequal, political institution. Justice Breyer recognized this principle of statesmanship when he argued that the Court should not have addressed the equal protection issue that was raised in *Bush v. Gore*, since, in his view, vindicating a basic constitutional right was not part of Bush's request to obtain procedural fairness in the election recount. Hence Breyer suggested that noninterference best preserved judicial legitimacy, a constitutional value that is too precious to ignore or trivialize when the nation is looking for political leadership from its government. Judicial restraint would have been closer to what Marshall had in mind in generating the political question standard: "that the province of the Court, *solely*, is to decide on the rights of the individuals."[47]

As the *Bush* dissenters and the extrajudicial commentary made by the justices after the election poignantly reveal, certainly the justices were very cognizant of the implications, legal or otherwise, of deciding which candidate became the nation's chief executive.[48] Regardless of who won the prize of the presidency, perhaps the enduring lesson of *Bush v. Gore*—as well as of this book—can only be measured by what the Court and country loses by superintending democracy. As the Supreme Court reminds us in *Nixon v. Shrink Missouri Government PAC* (2000), a campaign finance case, "Democracy works 'only if the people have faith in those who govern, and that faith is bound to be shattered when high officials and their appointees engage in activities which arouse suspicions of malfeasance and corruption.'" If a stain of illegitimacy remains with the Court and it diminishes the people's faith in government, then Justice Steven's lament will turn into a regrettable prophesy that can only harm the American republic. But only time will tell if the Court's foray into Campaign 2000 is judged this harshly and if the Court will rue the day it decided the 2000 presidential election.[49]

Appendix. Summaries of Key Cases

Buckley v. Valeo, 424 U.S. 1 (1976)

PER CURIAM

These appeals present constitutional challenges to the key provisions of the Federal Election Campaign Act of 1971 (Act), and related provisions of the Internal Revenue Code of 1954, all as amended in 1974.

These statutes at issue . . . contain the following provisions: (a) individual political contributions are limited to $1,000 to any single candidate per election, with an overall annual limitation of $25,000 by any contributor; independent expenditures by individuals and groups "relative to a clearly identified candidate" are limited to $1,000 a year; campaign spending by candidates for various federal offices and spending for national conventions by political parties are subject to prescribed limits; (b) contributions and expenditures above certain threshold levels must be reported and publicly disclosed; (c) a system for public funding of Presidential campaign activities is established by Subtitle H of the Internal Revenue Code; and (d) a Federal Election Commission is established to administer and enforce the legislation.

I. CONTRIBUTION AND EXPENDITURE LIMITATIONS

The major contribution and expenditure limitations in the Act prohibit individuals from contributing more than $25,000 in a single year or more than $1,000 to any single candidate for an election campaign and from spending more than $1,000 a year "relative to a clearly identified candidate." Other provisions restrict a candidate's use of personal and family resources in his campaign and limit the overall amount that can be spent by a candidate in campaigning for federal office.

The critical constitutional questions presented here go to whether the specific legislation that Congress has enacted interferes with First Amendment freedoms or invidiously discriminates against nonincumbent candidates and minor parties in contravention of the Fifth Amendment.

A. General Principles

The Act's contribution and expenditure limitations operate in an area of the most fundamental First Amendment activities. Discussion of public issues and debate on the qualifications of candidates are integral to the operation of the system of government established by our Constitution. . . . A restriction on the amount of money a person or group can spend on political communication during a campaign necessarily reduces the quantity of expression by restricting the number of issues discussed, the depth of their exploration, and the size of the audience reached. This is because virtually every means of communicating ideas in today's mass society requires the expenditure of money. The distribution of the humblest handbill or leaflet entails printing, paper, and circulation costs. Speeches and rallies generally necessitate hiring a hall and publicizing the event. The electorate's increasing dependence on television, radio, and other mass media for news and information has made these expensive modes of communication indispensable instruments of effective political speech.

The expenditure limitations contained in the Act represent substantial rather than merely theoretical restraints on the quantity and diversity of political speech. The $1,000 ceiling on spending "relative to a clearly identified candidate" would appear to exclude all citizens and groups except candidates, political parties, and the institutional press from any significant use of the most effective modes of communication. Although the Act's limitations on expenditures by campaign organizations and political parties provide substantially greater room for discussion and debate, they would have required restrictions in the scope of a number of past congressional and Presidential campaigns and would operate to constrain campaigning by candidates who raise sums in excess of the spending ceiling.

By contrast with a limitation upon expenditures for political expression, a limitation upon the amount that any one person or group may contribute to a candidate or political committee entails only a marginal restriction upon the contributor's ability to engage in free communication. A contribution serves as a general expression of support for the candidate and his views, but does not communicate the underlying basis for the support. The quantity of communication by the contributor does not increase perceptibly with the size of his contribution, since the expression rests solely on the undifferentiated, symbolic act of contributing. At most, the size of the contribution provides a very rough index of the intensity of the contributor's support for the candidate. A limitation on the amount of money a person may give to a candidate or campaign organization thus involves little direct restraint on his political communication, for it permits the symbolic expression of support evidenced by a contribution but does not in any way infringe the contributor's freedom to discuss candidates and issues.

Given the important role of contributions in financing political campaigns, contribution restrictions could have a severe impact on political dialogue if the limitations prevented candidates and political committees from amassing the resources necessary for effective advocacy. There is no indication, however, that the contribution limitations imposed by the Act would have any dramatic adverse effect on the funding of campaigns and political associations. The overall effect of the Act's contribution ceilings is merely to require candidates and political committees to raise funds from a greater number of persons and to compel people who would otherwise contribute amounts greater than the statutory limits to expend such funds on direct political expression, rather than to reduce the total amount of money potentially available to promote political expression.

The Act's contribution and expenditure limitations also impinge on protected associational freedoms. Making a contribution, like joining a political party serves to affiliate a person with a candidate . . . (and) enables like-minded persons to pool their resources in furtherance of common political goals. The Act's contribution ceilings thus limit one important means of associating with a candidate or committee, but leave the contributor free to become a member of any political association and to assist personally in the association's efforts on behalf of the candidates. . . . By contrast, the Act's $1,000 limitation on independent expenditures "relative to a clearly identified candidate" precludes most associations from effectively amplifying the voice of their adherents, the original basis for the recognition of First Amendment protection of the freedom of association.

In sum, although the Act's contribution and expenditure limitations both implicate fundamental First Amendment interests, its expenditure ceilings impose significantly more severe restrictions on protected freedoms of political expression and association than do its limitations on financial contributions.

B. Contribution Limitations

1. The $1,000 Limitation on Contributions by Individuals and Groups to Candidates and Authorized Campaign Committees

Section 608(b) provides, with certain limited exceptions, that "no person shall make contributions to any candidate with respect to an election for Federal office, which, in the aggregate, exceed $1,000.". . . It is unnecessary to look beyond the Act's primary purpose—to limit the actuality and appearance of corruption resulting from large individual financial contributions—in order to find a constitutionally sufficient justification for the $1,000 contribution limitation. Under a system of private financing of elections, a candidate lacking immense personal or family wealth must depend on financial contributions from others to provide the resources necessary to conduct a successful campaign. The increasing importance of the communications media and sophisticated mass-mailing and polling operations to effective campaigning make the raising of large sums of money an ever more essential ingredient of an effective candidacy. To the extent that large contributions are given to secure a political quid pro quo from current and potential office holders, the integrity of our system of representative democracy is undermined.

Of almost equal concern as the danger of actual quid pro quo arrangement is the best impact of the appearance of corruptions stemming from public awareness of the opportunities for abuse inherent in a regime of large individual financial contributions. In *CSC v. Letter Carriers* (1973), the Court found that the danger to "fair and effective government" posed by partisan political conduct on the part of federal employees charged with administering the law was a sufficiently important concern to justify broad restrictions on the employees' right of partisan political association. Here, as there, Congress could legitimately conclude that the avoidance of the appearance of improper influence "is also critical . . . if confidence in the system of representative Government is not to be eroded to a disastrous extent."

The Act's $1,000 contribution limitation focuses precisely on the problem of large campaign contributions—the narrow aspect of political association where the actuality and potential for corruption have been identified—while leaving persons free to engage in independent political expression, to associate actively through volunteering their services, and to assist to a limited but nonetheless substantial extent in supporting candidates and committees with financial resources. Significantly, the Act's contribution limitations in themselves do not undermine to any material degree the potential for robust and effective discussion of candidates and campaign issues by individual citizens, associations, the institutional press, candidates, and political parties.

We find that, under the rigorous standard of review established by our prior decisions, the weighty interests served by restricting the size of financial contributions to political candidates are sufficient to justify the limited effect upon First Amendment freedoms caused by the $1,000 contribution ceiling.

Appellants argue that the contribution limitations work such an invidious discrimination between incumbents and challengers that the statutory provisions must be declared unconstitutional on their face. . . . There is no such evidence to support the claim that the contribution limitations in themselves discriminate against major-party challengers to incumbents. While the limitations may have a significant effect on particular challengers or incumbents . . . the record provides no basis for predicting that such adventitious factors will invariably and invidiously benefit incumbents as a class. Since the danger of corruption and the appearance of corruption apply with equal force to challengers and to incumbents, Congress had ample justification for imposing the same fundraising constraints upon both.

The charge of discrimination against minor-party and independent candidates is more troubling, but the record provides no basis for concluding that the Act invidiously disadvantages such candidates. As noted above, the Act on its face treats all candidates equally with regard to contribution limitations. Although there is some force to appellants' response that minor-party candidates are primarily concerned with their ability to amass the resources necessary to reach the electorate rather than with their funding position relative to their major-party opponents, the record is virtually devoid of support for the claim that the $1,000 contribution limitation will have a serious effect on the initiation and scope of minor-party and independent candidacies. Moreover, any attempt to exclude minor parties and independents en masse from the Act's contribution limitations overlooks the fact that minor-party candidates may win elective office or have a substantial impact on the outcome of an election.

In view of these considerations, we conclude that the impact of the Act's $1,000 contribution limitation on major-party challengers and on minor-party candidates does not render the provision unconstitutional on its face.

C. Expenditure Limitations

The Act's expenditure ceilings impose direct and substantial restraints on the quantity of political speech. The restrictions, while neutral as to the ideas expressed, limit political expression "at the core of our electoral process and of the First Amendment freedoms." *Williams v. Rhodes* (1968).

1. The $1,000 Limitation on Expenditures "Relative to a Clearly Identified Candidate"

Section 608(e)(1) provides that "(n)o person may make any expenditure . . . relative to a clearly identified candidate during a calendar year which, when added to all other expenditures made by such person during the year advocating the election or defeat of such candidate, exceeds $1,000."

We turn then to the basic First Amendment question—whether Section 608(e)(1), even as thus narrowly and explicitly construed, impermissibly burdens the constitutional right of free expression. The Court of Appeals summarily held the provision constitutionally valid on ground that "section 608(e) is a loophole-closing provision only" that is necessary to prevent circumvention of the contribution limitations. We cannot agree.

We find that the governmental interest in preventing corruption and the appearance of corruption is inadequate to justify Section 608(e)(1)'s ceiling on independent expenditures. First . . . unlike the contribution limitations' total ban on the giving of large amounts of money to candidates, Section 608(e)(1) prevents only some large expenditures. So long as persons and groups eschew expenditures that in express terms advocate the election or defeat of a clearly identified candidate, they are free to spend as much as they want to promote the candidate and his views.

Second . . . the independent advocacy restricted by the provision does not presently appear to pose dangers of real or apparent corruption comparable to those identified with large campaign contributions. The parties defending Section 608(e)(1) contend that it is necessary to prevent would-be contributors from avoiding the contribution limitations by the simple expedient of paying directly for media advertisements or for other portions of the candidate's campaign activities. Yet such controlled or coordinated expenditures are treated as contributions rather than expenditures under the Act. Section 608(e)(1) limits expenditures for express advocacy of candidates made totally independently of the candidate and his campaign. Unlike contributions, such independent expenditures may well provide little assistance to the candidate's campaign and indeed may prove counterproductive. The absence of prearrangement and coordination of an expenditure with the candidate or his agent not only undermines the value of the expenditure to the candidate, but also alleviates the danger that expenditures will be given as a quid pro quo for improper commitments from the candidate. Rather than preventing circumvention of the contribution limitations, Section 608(e)(1) severely restricts all independent advocacy despite its substantially diminished potential for abuse.

While the independent expenditure ceiling thus fails to serve any substantial governmental interest in stemming the reality or appearance of corruption in the electoral process, it heavily burdens core First Amendment expression. Advocacy of the election or defeat of candidates for federal office is no less entitled to protection under the First Amendment than the discussion of political policy generally or advocacy of the passage or defeat of legislation.

It is argued, however, that the ancillary governmental interest in equalizing the relative ability of individuals and groups to influence the outcome of elections serves to justify the limitation on express advocacy of the election or defeat of candidates imposed by Section 608(e)(1)'s expenditure ceiling. But the concept that government may restrict the speech of some elements of our society in order to enhance the relative voice of others is wholly foreign to the First Amendment, which was designed "to secure 'the widest possible dissemination of information from diverse and antagonistic sources,'" and " 'to assure unfettered interchange of ideas for the bringing about of political and social changes desired by the people.'" *New York Times Co. v. Sullivan* (1964). The First Amendment's protection against governmental abridgement of free expression cannot properly be made to depend on a person's financial ability to engage in public discussion.

The Court's decisions in *Mills v. Alabama* (1966) and *Miami Herald Publishing Co. v. Tornillo* (1974), held that legislative restrictions on advocacy of the election or defeat of political candidates are wholly at odds with the guarantees of the First Amendment. In *Mills*, the Court addressed the question whether "a State, consistently with the United States Constitution, can make it a crime for the editor of a daily newspaper to write and publish an editorial on Election Day urging people to vote a certain way on issues submitted to them." We held that "no test of reasonableness can save (such) a state law from invalidation as a violation of the First Amendment." Yet the prohibition of Election Day editorials invalidated in *Mills* is clearly a lesser intrusion on constitutional freedom than a $1,000 limitation on the amount of money any person or association can spend during an entire election year in advocating the election or defeat of a candidate for public office. More recently in *Tornillo*, the Court held that Florida could not constitutionally require a newspaper to make space available for a political candidate to reply to its criticism. Yet under the Florida statute, every newspaper was free to criticize any candidate as much as it pleased so long as it undertook the modest burden of printing his reply. The legislative restraint involved in *Tornillo* thus also pales in comparison to the limitation imposed by Section 608(e)(1).

For the reasons stated, we conclude that Section 608(e)(1)'s independent expenditure limitation is unconstitutional under the First Amendment.

2. Limitation on Expenditures by Candidates from Personal or Family Resources

The Act also sets limits on expenditures by a candidate "from his personal funds, or the personal funds of his immediate family, in connection with his campaigns during any calendar year. Section 608(a)(1).

The ceiling on personal expenditures by candidates on their own behalf, like the limitations on independent expenditures contained in Section 608(e)(1), imposes a substantial restraint on the ability of persons to engage in protected First Amendment expression. The candidate, no less than any other person, has a First Amendment right to engage in the discussion of public issues and vigorously and tirelessly to advocate his own election and the election of other candidates. Indeed, it is of particular importance that candidates have the unfettered opportunity to make their views known so that the electorate may intelligently evaluate the candidates' personal qualities and their positions on vital public issues before choosing among them on Election Day. Section 608(a)'s ceiling on personal expenditures by a candidate in furtherance of his own candidacy thus clearly and directly interferes with constitutionally protected freedoms.

The primary governmental interest served by the Act—the prevention of actual and apparent corruption of the political process—does not support the limitation on the candidate's expenditure of his own personal funds. . . . Indeed, the use of personal funds reduces the candidate's dependence on outside contributions and thereby counteracts the coercive pressures and attendant risks of abuse to which the Act's contribution limitations are directed.

The ancillary interest in equalizing the relative financial resources of candidates competing for elective office, therefore, provides the sole relevant rationale for Section 608(a)'s expenditure ceiling. That interest is clearly not sufficient to justify the provision's infringement of fundamental First Amendment rights. First, the limitation may fail to promote financial equality among candidates. A candidate who spends less of his personal resources on his campaign may nonetheless outspend his rival as a result of more successful fundraising efforts. Indeed, a candidate's personal wealth may impede his efforts to persuade others that he needs their financial contributions or volunteer efforts to conduct an effective campaign. Second, and more fundamentally, the First Amendment simply cannot tolerate Section 608(a)'s restriction upon the freedom of a candidate to speak without legislative limit on behalf of his own candidacy. We therefore hold that Section 608(a)'s restriction on a candidate's personal expenditures is unconstitutional.

3. Limitations on Campaign Expenditures

Section 608(c) places limitations on overall campaign expenditures by candidates seeking nomination for election and election to federal office. Presidential candidates may spend $10,000,000 in seeking nomination for office and an additional $20,000,000 in the general election campaign.

No governmental interest that has been suggested is sufficient to justify the restriction on the quantity of political expression imposed by Section 608(c)'s campaign expenditure limitations. The major evil associated with rapidly increasing campaign expenditures is the danger of candidate dependence on large contributions. The interest in alleviating the corrupting influence of large contributions is served by the Act's contribution limitations and disclosure provisions rather than by Section 608(c)'s campaign expenditure ceilings.

The interest in equalizing the financial resources of candidates competing for federal office is no more convincing a justification for restricting the scope of federal election campaigns. Given the limitation on the size of outside contributions, the financial resources available to a candidate's campaign, like the number of volunteers recruited, will normally vary with the size and intensity of the candidate's support. There is nothing invidious, improper, or unhealthy in permitting such funds to be spent to carry the candidate's message to the electorate. Moreover, the equalization of permissible campaign expenditures might serve not to equalize the opportunities of all candidates, but to handicap a candidate who lacked substantial name recognition or exposure of his views before the start of the campaign.

The campaign expenditure ceilings appear to be designed primarily to serve the governmental interests in reducing the allegedly skyrocketing costs of political campaigns. Appellees and the Court of Appeals stressed statistics indicating that spending for federal election campaigns increased almost 300% between 1952 and 1972 in comparison with a 57.6% rise in the consumer price index during the same period. The mere growth in the cost of federal election campaigns in and of itself provides no basis for governmental restrictions on the quantity of campaign spending and the resulting limitation on the scope of federal campaigns. The First Amendment denies government the power to determine that spending to promote one's political views is wasteful, excessive, or unwise. In the free society ordained by our Constitution it is not the government, but the people—individually as citizens and candidates and collectively as associations and political committees—who must retain control over the quantity and range of debate on public issues in a political campaign.

For these reasons we hold that Section 608(c) is constitutionally invalid.

II. REPORTING AND DISCLOSURE REQUIREMENTS

Unlike the limitations on contributions and expenditures imposed by 18 U.S.C. Section 608, the disclosure requirements of the Act, 2 U.S.C Section 431et seq., are not challenged by appellants as per se unconstitutional restrictions on the exercise of First Amendment freedoms of speech and association. Indeed, appellants argue that "narrowly drawn disclosure requirements are the proper solution to virtually all of the evils Congress sought to remedy." The particular requirements embodied in the Act are attacked as overbroad—both in their application to minor-party and independent candidates and in their extension to contributions as small as $11 or $101. Appellants also challenge the provision for disclosure by those who make the independent contributions and expenditures, Section 434(e). The Court of Appeals found no constitutional infirmities in the provision challenged here. We affirm the determination on over breadth and hold that Section 434(e), if narrowly construed, also is within constitutional bounds.

Unlike the overall limitations on contributions and expenditures, the disclosure requirements impose no ceilings on campaign-related activities. But we have repeatedly found that compelled disclosure, in itself, can seriously infringe on privacy of association and belief guaranteed by the First Amendment. The strict test established by *NAACP v. Alabama* (1958) is necessary because compelled disclosure has the potential for substantially infringing the exercise of First Amendment rights. But we have acknowledged that there are governmental interests sufficiently important to outweigh the possibility of infringement, particularly when the "free functioning of our national institutions" is involved.

The governmental interests sought to be vindicated by the disclosure requirements are of this magnitude. They fall into three categories. First, disclosure provides the electorate with information "as to where political campaign money comes from and how it is spent by the candidate" in order to aid the voters in evaluating those who seek federal office. It allows voters to place each candidate in the political spectrum more precisely than is often possible solely on the basis of party labels and campaign speeches. The sources of a candidate's financial support also alert the voter to the interests to which a candidate is most likely to be responsive and thus facilitate predictions of future performance in office.

Second, disclosure requirements deter actual corruption and avoid the appearance of corruption by exposing large contributions and expenditures to the light of publicity. This exposure may discourage those who would use money for improper purposes either before or after the election. A public armed with information about a candidate's most generous supporters is better able to detect any post-election special favors that may be given in return. And, as we recognized in *Burroughs and Cannon v. United States* (1934), Congress could reasonably conclude that full disclosure during an election campaign tends "to prevent the corrupt use of money to affect elections." . . .

Third, and not least significant, record keeping, reporting, and disclosure requirements are an essential means of gathering the data necessary to detect violations of the contribution limitations described above.

The disclosure requirements, as a general matter, directly serve substantial governmental interests. In determining whether these interests are sufficient to justify the requirements we must look to the extent of the burden that they place on individual rights.

It is undoubtedly true that public disclosure of contributions to candidates and political parties will deter some individuals who otherwise might contribute. In some instances, disclosure may even expose contributors to harassment or retaliation. These are not insignificant burdens on individual rights, and they must be weighed carefully against the interests which Congress has sought to promote by this legislation. In this process, we note and agree with appellants' concession that disclosure requirements—certainly in most applications—appear to be the least restrictive means of curbing the evils of campaign ignorance and corruption that Congress found to exist. . . .

In summary, we find no constitutional infirmities in the record keeping, reporting, and disclosure provisions of the Act.

III. PUBLIC FINANCING OF PRESIDENTIAL ELECTION CAMPAIGNS

Public financing of Presidential election campaigns produced the scheme now found in Section 6096 and Subtitle H of the Internal Revenue Code of 1954. Both the District Court and the Court of Appeals sustained Subtitle H against a constitutional attack. Appellants renew their challenge here, contending that the legislation violates the First and Fifth Amendments. We find no merit in their claims and affirm.

Appellants argue that Subtitle H is invalid (1) as "contrary to the 'general welfare,'" Art. I, Section 8, (2) because any scheme of public financing of election campaigns is inconsistent with the First Amendment, and (3) because Subtitle H invidiously discriminates against certain interests in violation of the Due Process Clause of the Fifth Amendment. We find no merit in these contentions.

Although "Congress shall make no law . . . abridging the freedom of speech, or of the press," Subtitle H is a congressional effort, not to abridge, restrict, or censor speech, but rather to use public money to facilitate and enlarge public discussion and participation in the electoral process, goals vital to a self-governing people. Thus, Subtitle H furthers, not abridges, pertinent First Amendment values. Appellants argue, however, that as constructed public financing invidiously discriminates in violation of the Fifth Amendment.

Equal protection analysis in the Fifth Amendment area is the same as that under the Fourteenth Amendment . . . In several situations concerning the electoral process, the principle has been developed that restrictions on access to the electoral process must survive exacting scrutiny. The restriction can be sustained only if it furthers a "vital" governmental interest, *American Party of Texas v. White* (1974), that is "achieved by a means that does not unfairly or unnecessarily burden either a minority party's or an individual candidate's equally important interest in the continued availability of political opportunity." *Lubin v. Panish* (1974). Subtitle H does not prevent any candidate from getting on the ballot or any voter from casting a vote for the candidate of his choice; the inability, if any, of minor-party candidates to wage effective campaigns will derive not from lack of public funding but from their inability to raise private contributions. Any disadvantage suffered by operation of the eligibility formulae under Subtitle H is thus limited to the claimed denial of the enhancement of opportunity to communicate with the electorate that the formulae afford eligible candidates. But eligible candidates suffer a countervailing denial. As we more fully develop later, acceptance of public financing entails voluntary acceptance of an expenditure ceiling. Non-eligible candidates are not subject to that limitation. Accordingly, we conclude that public financing is generally less restrictive of access to the electoral process than the ballot-access regulations dealt with in prior cases. In any event, Congress enacted Subtitle H in furtherance of sufficiently important governmental interests and has not unfairly or unnecessarily burdened the political opportunity of any party or candidate.

CONCLUSION

In summary, we sustain the individual contribution limits, the disclosure and reporting provisions, and the public financing scheme. We conclude, however, that the limitations on campaign expenditures, on independent expenditures by individuals and groups, and on expenditures by a candidate from his personal funds are constitutionally infirm. Finally, we hold that most of the powers conferred by the Act upon the Federal Election Commission can be exercised only by "Officers of the United States," appointed in conformity with Art. II, Section 2, clause 2, of the Constitution, and therefore cannot be exercised by the Commission as presently constituted.

Mr. Justice Stevens took no part in the consideration or decision of these cases.

Timmons v. Twin Cities Area New Party,
520 U.S. 351 (1997)

Chief Justice REHNQUIST delivered the opinion for the Court.

Most States prohibit multiple-party, or "fusion," candidacies for elected office. The Minnesota laws challenged in this case prohibit a candidate from appearing on the ballot as the candidate of more than one party. Minn. Stat. Section 204B.06, subd. 1(b) and 204B.04, subd. 2 (1994). We hold that such a prohibition does not violate the First and Fourteenth Amendments to the United States Constitution.

Respondent is a chartered chapter of the national New Party. Petitioners are Minnesota election officials. In April 1994, Minnesota State Representative Andy Dawkins was running unopposed in the Minnesota Democratic Farmer-Labor Party's (DFL) primary. That same month, New Party members chose Dawkins as their candidate for the same office in the November 1994 general election. Neither Dawkins nor the DFL objected, and Dawkins signed the required affidavit of candidacy for the New Party. Minn. Stat. Section 204B.06 (1994). Minnesota, however, prohibits fusion candidates. Because Dawkins had already filed as a candidate for the DFL's nomination, local election officials refused to accept the New Party's nominating petition.

Fusion was a regular feature of Gilded Age American politics. Particularly in the West and Midwest, candidates of issue-oriented parties like the Grangers, Independents, Greenbackers, and Populists often succeeded through fusion with the Democrats, and vice versa. Republicans for their part, sometimes arranged fusion candidacies in the South, as part of a general strategy of encouraging and exploiting divisions within the dominant Democratic Party. See generally Argersinger, "A Place at the Table": Fusion Politics and Antifusion Laws, 85 Amer. Hist. Rev. 287, 288–290 (1980).

Fusion was common in part because political parties, rather than local or state governments, printed and distributed their own ballots. These ballots contained only the names of a particular party's ticket in the ballot box without even knowing that his party's candidates were supported by other parties as well. But after the 1888 presidential election, which was widely regarded as having been plagued by fraud, many States moved to the "Australian ballot system." Under that system, an official ballot, containing the names of all the candidates legally nominated by all the parties, was printed at public expense and distributed by public officials at polling places. By 1896, use of the Australian ballot was widespread. During the same period, many States enacted other election-related reforms, including bans on fusion candidacies. Minnesota banned fusion in 1901. This trend has continued and, in this century, fusion has become the exception, not the rule. Today, multiple-party candidacies are permitted in just a few States, and fusion plays a significant role only in New York.

The First Amendment protects the right of citizens to associate and to form political parties for the advancement of common political goals and ideas. As a result, political parties' government, structure, and activities enjoy constitutional protection.

On the other hand, it is also clear that States may, and inevitably must, enact reasonable regulations of parties, elections, and ballots to reduce election- and campaign-related disorder.

When deciding whether a state election law violates First and Fourteenth Amendment associational rights, we weigh the "character and magnitude" of the burden the State's rule imposes on those rights against the interests the State contends justify that burden, and consider the extent to which the State's concerns make the burden necessary. Regulations imposing severe burdens on plaintiffs' rights must be narrowly tailored and advance a compelling state interest. Lesser burdens, however, trigger less exacting review, and a State's "'important regulatory interests'" will usually be enough to justify "'reasonable, nondiscriminatory restrictions.'" No bright line separates permissible election-related regulation from unconstitutional infringements on First Amendment freedoms.

The New Party's claim that it has a right to select its own candidate is uncontroversial, so far as it goes. That is, the New Party, and not someone else, has the right to select the New Party's "standard bearer." It does not follow, though, that a party is absolutely entitled to have its nominee appear on the ballot as that party's candidate. A particular candidate might be ineligible for office, unwilling to serve, or, as here, another party's candidate. That a particular individual may not appear on the ballot as a particular party's candidate does not severely burden that party's association rights.

The New Party relies on *Eu v. San Francisco County Democratic Central Committee* (1989) and *Tashjian v. Republican Party of Connecticut* (1986). In *Eu*, we struck down that California election provisions that prohibited political parties from endorsing candidates in party primaries and regulated parties' internal affairs and structure. And in *Tashjian*, we held that Connecticut's closed-primary statute, which required voters in a party primary to be registered party members, interfered with a party's associational rights by limiting "the group of registered voters whom the Party may invite to participate in the basic function of selecting the Party's candidates." But while *Tashjian* and *Eu* involved regulation of political parties' internal affairs and core associational activities, Minnesota's fusion ban does not. The ban, which applies to major and minor parties alike, simply precludes one party's candidate from appearing on the ballot, as that party's candidate, if already nominated by another party. Respondent is free to try to convince Representative Dawkins to be the New Party's, not the DFL's, candidate. Whether the Party still wants to endorse a candidate who, because of the fusion ban, will not appear on the ballot as the Party's candidate, is up to the Party.

The Court of Appeals also held that Minnesota's laws "keep the New Party from developing consensual political alliances and thus broadening the base of public participation in and support for its activities." The burden on the Party was, the court held, severe because "(h)istory shows that minor parties have played a significant role in the electoral system where multiple party nomination is legal, but have no meaningful influence where multiple party nomination is banned." In the view of the Court of Appeals, Minnesota's fusion ban forces members of the new party to make a "no-win choice" between voting for "candidates with no realistic chance of winning, defect(ing) from their party and vot(ing) for a major party candidate who does, or declin(ing) to vote at all."

But Minnesota has not directly precluded minor political parties from developing and organizing. Nor has Minnesota excluded a particular group of citizens, or a political party, from participation in the election process. The New Party remains free to endorse whom it likes, to ally itself with others, to nominate candidates for office, and to spread its message to all who will listen.

The Court of Appeals emphasized its belief that, without fusion-based alliances, minor parties cannot thrive. This is a predictive judgment which is by no means self-evident. But, more importantly, the supposed benefits of fusion to minor parties do not require that Minnesota permit it. Many features of our political system— e.g., single-member districts, "first past the post" elections, and the high costs of campaigning—make it difficult for third parties to succeed in American politics. But the Constitution does not require States to permit fusion any more than it requires them to move to proportional-representation election or public financing of campaigns.

The New Party contends that the fusion ban burdens its "right . . . to communicate its choice of nominees on the ballot on terms equal to those offered other parties, and the right of the party's supporters and other voters to receive that information," and insists that communication on the ballot of a party's candidate choice is a "critical source of information for the great majority of voters . . . who . . . rely upon party 'labels' as a voting guide."

It is true that Minnesota's fusion ban prevents the New Party from using the ballot to communicate to the public that it supports a particular candidate who is already another party's candidate. In addition, the ban shuts off one possible avenue a party might use to send a message to its preferred candidate because, with fusion, a candidate who wins an election on the basis of two parties' votes will likely know more—if the parties' votes are counted separately—about the particular wishes and ideals of his constituency. We are unpersuaded, however, by the Party's contention that it has a right to use the ballot itself to send a particularized message, to its candidate and to the voters, about the nature of its support for the candidate. Ballots serve primarily to elect candidates, not as a fora of political expression. Like all parties in Minnesota, the New Party is able to use the ballot to communicate information about itself and its candidate to the voters, so long as that candidate is not already someone else's candidate. The Party retains great latitude in its ability to communicate ideas to voters and candidates through its participation in the campaign, and Party members may campaign for, endorse, and vote for their preferred candidate even if he is listed on the ballot as another party's candidate.

In sum, Minnesota's laws do not restrict the ability of the New Party and its members to endorse, support, or vote for anyone they like. The laws do not directly limit the Party's access to the ballot. They are silent on parties' internal structure, governance, and policy making. Instead, these provisions reduce the universe of potential candidates who may appear on the ballot as the Party's nominee only by ruling out those few individuals who both have already agreed to be another party's candidate and also, if forced to choose, themselves prefer that other party. They also limit, slightly, the Party's ability to send a message to the voters and to its preferred candidates. We conclude that the burdens Minnesota imposes on the Party's First and Fourteenth Amendment associational rights—though not trivial—are not severe.

The Court of Appeals determined that Minnesota's fusion ban imposed "severe" burdens on the New Party's associational rights, and so it required the State to show that the ban was narrowly tailored to serve the compelling state interests. We disagree; given the burdens imposed, the bar is not so high. Instead, the State's asserted regulatory interests need only be "sufficiently weighty to justify the limitation" imposed on the Party's rights. Nor do we require elaborate, empirical verification of the weightiness of the State's asserted justifications.

The Court of Appeals acknowledged Minnesota's interests in avoiding voter confusion and overcrowded ballots, preventing party-splintering and disruptions of the two-party system, and being able to clearly identify the election winner. Minnesota argues here that its fusion ban is justified by its interests in avoiding voter confusion, promoting candidate competition (by reserving limited ballot space for opposing candidates), preventing electoral distortions and ballot manipulations, and discouraging party splintering and "unrestrained factionalism."

States certainly have an interest in protecting the integrity, fairness, and efficiency of their ballots and election processes as a means for electing public officials. Petitioners contend that a candidate or party could easily exploit fusion as a way of associating his or its name with popular slogans and catchphrases. For example, members of a major party could decide that a powerful way of "sending a message" via the ballot would be for various factions of that party to nominate the major party's candidate as the candidate for the newly formed "No New Taxes," "Conserve Our Environment," and "Stop Crime Now" parties. In response, an opposing major party would likely instruct its factions to nominate that party's candidate as the "Fiscal Responsibility," "Healthy Planet," and "Safe Streets" parties' candidate.

Whether or not the putative "fusion" candidates' names appeared on one or four ballot lines, such maneuvering would undermine the ballot's purpose by transforming it from a means of choosing candidates to a billboard for political advertising. The New Party responds to this concern, ironically enough, by insisting that the State could avoid such manipulation by adopting more demanding ballot-access standards rather than prohibiting multiple-party nomination. However, as we stated above, because the burdens the fusion ban imposes on the Party's associational rights are not severe, the State need not narrowly tailor the means it chooses to promote ballot integrity. The Constitution does not require that Minnesota compromise the policy choices embodied in its ballot-access requirements to accommodate the New Party's fusion strategy. See Minn. Stat. Section 204B.08, subd. 3 (1994) (signature requirements for nominating petitions). Relatedly, petitioners urge that permitting fusion would undercut Minnesota's ballot-access regime by allowing minor parties to capitalize on the popularity of another party's candidate, rather than on their own appeal to the voters, in order to secure access to the ballot. That is, voters who might not sign a minor party's nominating petition based on the party's own views and candidates might do so if they viewed the minor party as just another way of nominating the same person nominated by one of the major parties. Thus, Minnesota fears that fusion would enable minor parties, by nominating a major party's candidate, to bootstrap their way to major-party status in the next election and circumvent the State's nominating-petition requirement for minor parties. See Minn. Stat. Section 200.02, subd. 7 (defining "major party") and 204D.13 (describing ballot order for major and other parties). The State surely has a valid interest in making sure that minor and third parties who are granted access to the ballot are bona fide and actually supported, on their own merits, by those who have provided the statutorily required petition or ballot support.

States also have a strong interest in the stability of their political systems. This interest does not permit a State to completely insulate the two-party system from minor parties' or independent candidates' competition and influence . . . nor is it a paternalistic license for States to protect political parties from the consequences of their own internal disagreements. That said, the States' interest permits them to enact reasonable election regulations that may, in practice, favor the traditional two-party system . . . and that temper the destabilizing effects of party splintering and excessive factionalism. The Constitution permits the Minnesota Legislature to decide that political stability is best served through a healthy two-party system. And while an interest in securing the perceived benefits of a stable two-party system will not justify unreasonably exclusionary restrictions . . . States need not remove all of the many hurdles third parties face in the American political arena today.

In *Storer* we upheld a California statute that denied ballot positions to independent candidates who had voted in the immediately preceding primary elections or had a registered party affiliation at any time during the year before the same primary elections. After surveying the relevant caselaw, we "ha(d) no hesitation in sustaining" the party-disaffiliation provisions. We recognized that the provisions were part of a "general state policy aimed at maintaining the integrity of . . . the ballot," and noted that the provision did not discriminate against independent candidates. We concluded that while a "State need not take the course California has . . . California apparently believes with the Founding Fathers that splintered parties and unrestrained factionalism may do significant damage to the fabric of government. See "The Federalist, No. 10" (Madison). It appears obvious to us that the one-year disaffiliation provision furthers the State's interest in the stability of its political system."

Our decision in *Burdick v. Takushi* (1992) is also relevant. There, we upheld Hawaii's ban on write-in voting against a claim that the ban unreasonably infringed on citizens' First and Fourteenth Amendment rights. In so holding, we rejected the petitioner's argument that the ban "deprive(d) him of the opportunity to cast a meaningful ballot," emphasizing that the function of elections is to elect candidates and that "we have repeatedly upheld reasonable, politically neutral regulations that have the effect of channeling expressive activit(ies) at the polls."

Minnesota's fusion ban is far less burdensome than the disaffiliation rule upheld in *Storer*, and is justified by similarly weighty state interests. By reading *Storer v. Brown* (1974) as dealing only with "sore-loser candidates," the dissent, in our view, fails to appreciate the case's teaching. Under the California disaffiliation statue at issue in *Storer*, any person affiliated with a party at any time during the year leading up to the primary election was absolutely precluded from appearing on the ballot as an independent or as the candidate of another party. Minnesota's fusion ban is not nearly so restrictive; the challenged provisions say nothing about the previous party affiliation of would-be candidates but only require that, in order to appear on the ballot, a candidate not be the nominee of more than one party. California's disaffiliation rule limited the field of candidates by thousands; Minnesota's precludes only a handful who freely choose to be so limited. It is also worth noting that while California's disaffiliation statute absolutely banned many candidacies, Minnesota's fusion ban only prohibits a candidate from being named twice.

We conclude that the burdens Minnesota's fusion ban imposes on the New Party's associational rights are justified by "correspondingly weighty" valid state interests in ballot integrity and political stability. In deciding Minnesota's fusion ban does not unconstitutionally burden the New Party's First and Fourteenth Amendment rights, we express no views on the New Party's policy-based arguments concerning the wisdom of fusion. It may well be that, as support for new political parties increases, these arguments will carry the day in some States' legislatures. But the Constitution does not require Minnesota, and the approximately 40 other States that do not permit fusion, to allow it. The judgment of the Court of Appeals is reversed.

It is so ordered.

Elrod v. Burns, 427 U.S. 347 (1976)

Justice BRENNAN announced the judgment of the Court, in which Justice WHITE and Justice MARSHALL joined.

This case presents the question whether public employees who allege that they were discharged or threatened with discharge solely because of their partisan political affiliation or nonaffiliation state a claim for deprivation of constitutional rights secured by the First and Fourteenth Amendments.

Petitioners, Richard J. Elrod, Richard J. Daley, the Democratic Organization of Cook County, and the Democratic County Central Committee of Cook County . . . alleged that they were discharged or threatened with discharge solely for the reason that they were not affiliated with or sponsored by the Democratic Party. They sought declaratory, injunctive, and other relief for violations of the First and Fourteenth Amendments. . . . The District Court denied their motion for a preliminary injunction and . . . dismissed their complaint. . . . The Seventh Circuit . . . reversed and remanded. We affirm.

The Cook County Sheriff's practice of dismissing employees on a partisan basis is but one form of the general practice of political patronage. . . .

Patronage practice is not new to American politics. It has existed at the federal level at least since the Presidency of Thomas Jefferson, although its popularization and legitimation primarily occurred later, in the Presidency of Andrew Jackson. The practice is not unique to American politics. It has been used in many European countries, and in darker times, it played a significant role in the Nazi rise to power in Germany and other totalitarian states. More recent times have witnessed a strong decline in its use, particularly with respect to public employment. Indeed, only a few decades after Andrew Jackson's administration, strong discontent with the corruption and inefficiency of the patronage system of public employment eventuated in the Pendleton Act, the foundation of modern civil service. And on the state and local levels, merit systems have increasingly displaced the practice. . . .

The decline of patronage employment is not . . . relevant to the question of its constitutionality. It is the practice itself, not the magnitude of its occurrence, the constitutionality of which must be determined. . . . Rather, inquiry must commence with identification of the constitutional limitations implicated by a challenged governmental practice.

The cost of the practice of patronage is the restraint it places on freedoms of belief and association. In order to maintain their jobs, respondents were required to pledge their political allegiance to the Democratic Party, work for the election of other candidates of the Democratic Party, contribute a portion of their wages to the Party, or obtain the sponsorship of a member of the Party, usually at the price of one of the first three alternatives. Regardless of the incumbent party's identity, Democratic or otherwise, the consequences for association and belief are the same. An individual who is a member of the out-party maintains affiliation with his own party at the risk of losing his job. He works for the election of his party's candidates and espouses its policies at the same risk. The financial and campaign assistance that he is induced to provide to another party furthers the advancement of that party's policies to the detriment of his party's views and ultimately his own beliefs, and any assessment of his salary is tantamount to coerced belief. . . .

It is not only belief and association which are restricted where political patronage is the practice. The free functioning of the electoral process also suffers. Conditioning public employment on partisan support prevents support of competing political interests. Existing employees are deterred from such support, as well as the multitude seeking jobs. As government employment, state or federal, becomes more pervasive, the greater the dependence on it becomes, and therefore the greater becomes the power to starve political opposition by commanding partisan support, financial and otherwise. Patronage thus tips the electoral process in favor of the incumbent party, and where the practice's scope is substantial relative to the size of the electorate, the impact on the process can be significant.

Patronage, therefore, to the extent it compels or restrains belief and association, is inimical to the process which undergirds our system of government and is "at war with the deeper traditions of democracy embodied in the First Amendment." As such, the practice unavoidably confronts decisions by this Court either invalidating or recognizing as invalid government action that inhibits belief and association through the conditioning of public employment on political faith.

Particularly pertinent to the constitutionality of the practice of patronage dismissals are *Keyishian v. Board of Regents* (1967) and *Perry v. Sindermann* (1972). In *Keyishian,* the Court invalidated New York statutes barring employment merely on the basis of membership in "subversive" organizations. *Keyishian* squarely held that political association alone could not, consistently with the First Amendment, constitute an adequate ground for denying public employment. In *Perry,* the Court broadly rejected the validity of limitations on First Amendment rights as a condition to the receipt of a governmental benefit, stating that the government "may not deny a benefit to a person on a basis that infringes his constitutionally protected interests—especially, his interest in freedom of speech. For if the government could deny a benefit to a person because of his constitutionally protected speech or associations, his exercise of those freedoms would in effect be penalized and inhibited. . . ."

Patronage practice falls squarely within the prohibitions of *Keyishian* and *Perry.* Under that practice, public employees hold their jobs on the condition that they provide, in some acceptable manner, support for the favored political party. The threat of dismissal for failure to provide that support unquestionably inhibits protected belief and association, and dismissal for failure to provide support only penalizes its exercise. The belief and association which government may not ordain directly are achieved by indirection. And regardless of how evenhandedly these restraints may operate in the long run, after political office has changed hands several times, protected interests are still infringed and thus the violation remains.

One interest which has been offered in justification of patronage is the need to insure effective government and the efficiency of public employees. It is argued that employees of political persuasions not the same as that of the party in control of public office will not have the incentive to work effectively and may even be motivated to subvert the incumbent administration's efforts to govern effectively. We are not persuaded. The inefficiency resulting from the wholesale replacement of large numbers of public employees every time political office changes hands belies this justification. And the prospect of dismissal after an election in which the incumbent party has lost is only a disincentive to good work. Further, it is not clear that dismissal in order to make room for a patronage appointment will result in replacement by a person more qualified to do the job since appointment often occurs in exchange for the delivery of votes, or other party service, not job capability. More fundamentally, however, the argument does not succeed because it is doubtful that the mere difference of political persuasion motivates poor performance; nor do we think it legitimately may be used as a basis for imputing such behavior. The Court has consistently recognized that mere political association is an inadequate basis for imputing disposition to ill-willed conducts. . . .

Even if the first argument that patronage serves effectiveness and efficiency be rejected, it still may be argued that patronage serves those interests by giving the employees of an incumbent party the incentive to perform well in order to insure their party's incumbency and thereby their jobs. Patronage, according to the argument, thus makes employees highly accountable to the public. But the ability of officials more directly accountable to the electorate to discharge employees for cause and the availability of merit systems, growth in the use of which has been quite significant, convince us that means less intrusive than patronage still exist for achieving accountability in the public work force and, thereby, effective and efficient government. The greater effectiveness of patronage over these less drastic means, if any, is at best marginal, a gain outweighed by the absence of intrusion on protected interests under the alternatives. . . .

A second interest advanced in support of patronage is the need for political loyalty of employees, not to the end that effectiveness and efficiency be insured, but to the end that representative government not be undercut by tactics obstructing the implementation of policies of the new administration, policies presumably sanctioned by the electorate. The justification is not without force, but is nevertheless inadequate to validate patronage wholesale. Limiting patronage dismissals to policymaking positions is sufficient to achieve this governmental end. Nonpolicymaking individuals usually have only limited responsibility and are therefore not in a position to thwart the goals of the in-party.

No clear line can be drawn between policymaking and nonpolicymaking positions. While nonpolicymaking individuals usually have limited responsibility, that is not to say that one with a number of responsibilities is necessarily in a policy-making position. The nature of the responsibilities is critical. Employee supervisors, for example, may have many responsibilities, but those responsibilities may have only limited and well-defined objectives. An employee with responsibilities that are not well defined or are of broad scope are more likely functions in a policymaking position. In determining whether an employee occupies a policymaking position, consideration should also be given to whether the employee acts as an adviser or formulates plans for the implementation of broad goals. . . .

It is argued that a third interest supporting patronage dismissals is the preservation of the democratic process. According to petitioners, "'we have contrived no system for the support of party that does not place considerable reliance on patronage. The party organization makes a democratic government work and charges a price for its services.'" The argument is thus premised on the centrality of partisan politics to the democratic process.

Preservation of the democratic process is certainly an interest protection of which may in some instances justify limitations on First Amendment freedoms. . . . But however important preservation of the two-party system or any system involving a fixed number of parties may or may not be, we are not persuaded that the elimination of patronage practice or, as is specifically involved here, the interdiction of patronage dismissals, will bring about the demise of party politics. Political parties existed in the absence of active patronage practice prior to the administration of Andrew Jackson, and they have survived substantial reduction in their patronage power through the establishment of merit systems.

Patronage dismissals thus are not the least restrictive alternative to achieving the contribution they may make to the democratic process. The process functions as well without the practice, perhaps even better, for patronage dismissals clearly also retard that process. Patronage can result in the entrenchment of one or a few parties to the exclusion of others. And most indisputably, as we recognized at the outset, patronage is a very effective impediment to the associational and speech freedoms which are essential to a meaningful system of democratic government. Thus, if patronage contributes at all to the elective process, that contribution is diminished by the practice's impairment of the same. . . .

Today, we hold that subordination of other First Amendment activity, that is, patronage dismissals, not only is permissible, but also is mandated by the First Amendment. . . .

In summary, patronage dismissals severely restrict political belief and association. Though there is a vital need for government efficiency and effectiveness, such dismissals are on balance not the least restrictive means for fostering that end. There is also a need to insure that policies which the electorate has sanctioned are effectively implemented. That interest can be fully satisfied by limiting patronage dismissals to policymaking positions. Finally, patronage dismissals cannot be justified by their contribution to the proper functioning of our democratic process through their assistance to partisan politics since political parties are nurtured by other, less intrusive and equally effective methods. More fundamentally, however, any contribution of patronage dismissals to the democratic process does not suffice to override their severe encroachment on First Amendment freedoms. We hold, therefore, that the practice of patronage dismissals is unconstitutional under the First and Fourteenth Amendments. . . .

Shaw v. Reno, 509 U. S. 630 (1993)

Justice O'CONNOR delivered the opinion of the Court.

This case involves two of the most complex and sensitive issues this Court has faced in recent years: the meaning of the constitutional "right" to vote, and the propriety of race-based state legislation designed to benefit members of historically disadvantaged racial minority groups. As a result of the 1990 census, North Carolina became entitled to a twelfth seat in the United States House of Representatives. The General Assembly enacted a reapportionment plan that included one majority-black congressional district. After the Attorney General of the United States objected to the plan pursuant to section 5 of the Voting Rights Act of 1965, the General Assembly passed new legislation creating a second majority-black district. Appellants allege that the revised plan, which contains district boundary lines of dramatically irregular shape constitutes an unconstitutional racial gerrymander.

The voting age population of North Carolina is approximately 78% white, 20% black, and 1% Native American; the remaining 1% is predominantly Asian. The black population is relatively dispersed; blacks constitute a majority of the general population in only 5 of the State's 100 counties. Geographically, the State divides into three regions: the eastern Coastal Plain, the central Piedmont Plateau, and the western mountains. The largest concentrations of black citizens live in the Coastal Plain, primarily in the northern part. The General Assembly's first redistricting plan contained one majority-black district centered in that area of the State.

Forty of North Carolina's one hundred counties are covered by section 5 of the Voting Rights Act of 1965, which prohibits a jurisdiction subject to its provisions from implementing changes in a "standard, practice, or procedure with respect to voting" without federal authorization. The jurisdiction must obtain either a judgment from the United States District Court for the District of Columbia declaring that the proposed change "does not have the purpose and will not have the effect of denying or abridging the right to vote on account of race or color" or administrative preclearance from the Attorney General. Because the General's Assembly's reapportionment plan affected the covered counties, the parties agree that section 5 applied. The State chose to submit its plan to the Attorney General for preclearance. The Attorney General, acting through the Assistant Attorney General for the Civil Rights Division, interposed a formal objection to the General Assembly's plan. The Attorney General specifically objected to the configuration of boundary lines drawn in the south-central to southeastern region of the State. In the Attorney General's view, the General Assembly could have created a second majority-minority district "to give effect to black and Native American voting strength in this area" by using boundary lines "no more irregular than (those) found elsewhere in the proposed plan," but failed to do so for "pretextual reasons."

Under section 5, the State remained free to seek a declaratory judgment from the District Court for the District of Columbia notwithstanding the Attorney General's objection. It did not do so. Instead, the General Assembly enacted a revised redistricting plan, that included a second majority-black district. The General Assembly located the second district not in the south-central to southeastern part of the State, but in the north-central region along Interstate 85.

The first of the two majority-black districts contained in the revised plan, District 1, is somewhat hook shaped. Centered in the northeast portion of the State, it moves southward until it tapers to a narrow band; then, with finger-like extensions, it reaches far into the southernmost part of the State near the South Carolina border. District 1 has been compared to a "Rorschach ink-blot test," and a "bug splattered on a windshield."

The second majority-black district, District 12, is even more unusually shaped. It is approximately 160 miles long and, for much of its length, no wider than the I-85 corridor. It winds in snakelike fashion through tobacco country, financial centers, and manufacturing areas "until it gobbles in enough enclaves of black neighborhoods." Northbound and southbound drivers on I-85 sometimes find themselves in separate districts in one county, only to "trade" districts when they enter the next county. Of the 10 counties through which District 12 passes, 5 are cut into 3 different districts; even towns are divided. At one point the district remains contiguous only because it intersects at a single point with two other districts before crossing over them. One state legislator has remarked that "'(i)f you drove down the interstate with both car doors open, you'd kill most of the people in the district.'"

The Attorney General did not object to the General Assembly's revised plan. But numerous North Carolinians did. The North Carolina Republican Party and individual voters brought suit, alleging that the plan constituted an unconstitutional political gerrymander.

"The right to vote freely for the candidate of one's choice is of the essence of a democratic society" *Reynolds v. Sims* (1964). For much of our Nation's history, that right sadly has been denied to many because of race. The Fifteenth Amendment, ratified in 1870 after a bloody Civil War, promised unequivocally that "(t)he right of citizens of the United States to vote" no longer would be "denied or abridged . . . by any State on account of race, color, or previous condition of servitude." U. S. Const., Amdt. 15, section 1.

But "(a) number of states . . . refused to take no for an answer and continued to circumvent the fifteenth amendment's prohibition through the use of both subtle and blunt instruments, perpetuating ugly patterns of pervasive racial discrimination." Ostensibly race-neutral devices such as literacy tests with "grandfather" clauses and "good character" provisos were devised to deprive black voters of the franchise. Another of the weapons in the States' arsenal was the racial gerrymander—"the deliberate and arbitrary distortion of district boundaries . . . for (racial) purposes." In the 1870s, for example, opponents of Reconstruction in Mississippi "concentrated the bulk of the black population in a 'shoestring' Congressional district running the length of the Mississippi River, leaving five others with white majorities." Some 90 years later, Alabama redefined the boundaries of the city of Tuskegee "from a square to an uncouth twenty-eight-sided figure" in a manner that was alleged to exclude black voters, and only black voters, from the city limits. *Gomillion v. Lightfoot* (1960).

Alabama's exercise in geometry was but one example of the racial discrimination in voting that persisted in parts of this country nearly a century after ratification of the Fifteenth Amendment. In some States, registration of eligible black voters ran 50% behind that of whites. Congress enacted the Voting Rights Act of 1965 as a dramatic and severe response to the situation. The Act proved immediately successful in ensuring racial minorities access to the voting booth; by the early 1970s, the spread between black and white registration in several of the targeted Southern States had fallen to well below 10%.

But it soon became apparent that guaranteeing equal access to the polls would not suffice to root out other racially discriminatory voting practices. Drawing on the "one person, one vote" principle, this Court recognized that "(t)he right to vote can be affected by a *dilution* of voting power as well as by an absolute prohibition on casting a ballot." *Allen v. State Bd. Of Elections* (1969). Where members of a racial minority group vote as a cohesive unit, practices such as multimember or at-large electoral systems can reduce or nullify minority voters' ability, as a group, "to elect the candidate of their choice." Accordingly, the Court held that such schemes violate the Fourteenth Amendment when they are adopted with a discriminatory purpose and have the effect of diluting minority voting strength. Congress, too, responded to the problem of vote dilution. In 1982, it amended section 2 of the Voting Rights Act to prohibit legislation that *results* in the dilution of a minority group's voting strength, regardless of the legislature's intent. 42 U. S. C. section 1973; see *Thornburg v. Gingles* (1986); *Voinovich v. Quilter* (1993).

It is against this background that we confront the questions presented here. In our view, the District Court properly dismissed appellants' claims against the federal appellees. Our focus is on appellants' claim that the State engaged in unconstitutional racial gerrymandering. That argument strikes a powerful historical chord: It is unsettling how closely the North Carolina plan resembles the most egregious racial gerrymanders of the past.

An understanding of the nature of appellants' claim is critical to our resolution of the case. In their complaint, appellants did not claim that the General Assembly's reapportionment plan unconstitutionally "diluted" white voting strength. They did not even claim to be white. Rather, appellants' complaint alleged that the deliberate segregation of voters into separate districts on the basis of race violated their constitutional right to participate in a "color-blind" electoral process.

Despite their invocation of the ideal of a "color-blind" Constitution, see *Plessy v. Ferguson* (1896) (Harlan, J., dissenting), appellants appear to concede that race-conscious redistricting is not always unconstitutional. That concession is wise: This Court never has held that race-conscious state decision-making is impermissible in *all* circumstances. What appellants object to is redistricting legislation that is so extremely irregular on its face that it rationally can be viewed only as an effort to segregate the races for purposes of voting, without regard for traditional districting principles and without sufficiently compelling justification. For the reasons that follow, we conclude that appellants have stated a claim upon which relief can be granted under the Equal Protection Clause.

The Equal Protection Clause provides that "(n)o State Shall . . . deny to any person within its jurisdiction the equal protection of the laws." U. S. Const., Amdt. 14, section 1. Its central purpose is to prevent the States from purposefully discriminating between individuals on the basis of race. *Washington v. Davis* (1976). Laws that explicitly distinguish between individuals on racial grounds fall within the core of that prohibition.

No inquiry into legislative purpose is necessary when the racial classification appears on the face of the statute. See *Personnel Administrator of Mass. v. Feeney* (1979). Express racial classification are immediately suspect because, "(a)bsent searching judicial inquiry . . . there is simply no way of determining what classifications are 'benign' or 'remedial' and what classifications are in fact motivated by illegitimate notions of racial inferiority or simple racial politics." *Richmond v. J. A. Croson Co.* (1989).

Classifications of citizens solely on the basis of race "are by their very nature odious to a free people whose institutions are founded upon the doctrine of equality." *Hirabayashi v. United States* (1943). They threaten to stigmatize individuals by reason of their membership in a racial group and to incite racial hostility. Accordingly, we have held that the Fourteenth Amendment requires state legislation that expressly distinguishes among citizens because of their race to be narrowly tailored to further a compelling governmental interest.

These principles apply not only to legislation that contains explicit racial distinctions, but also to those "rare" statutes that, although race neutral, are, on their face, "unexplainable on grounds other than race." As we explained in *Feeney:*

"A racial classification, regardless of purported motivation, is presumptively invalid and can be upheld only upon an extraordinary justification. This rule applies as well to a classification that is ostensibly neutral but is an obvious pretext for racial discrimination."

Appellants contend that redistricting legislation that is so bizarre on its face that it is "unexplainable on grounds other than race," demands the same close scrutiny that we give other state laws that classify citizens by race. Our voting rights precedents support that conclusion.

In *Guinn v. United States* (1915), the Court invalidated under the Fifteenth

Amendment a statute that imposed a literacy requirement on voters but contained a "grandfather clause" applicable to individuals and their lineal descendants entitled to vote "on (or prior to) January 1, 1866." In other words, the statute was invalid because, on its face, it could not be explained on grounds other than race.

The Court applied the same reasoning to the "uncouth twenty-eight-sided" municipal boundary line at issue in *Gomillion*. Although the statute that redrew the city limits of Tuskegee was race neutral on its face, plaintiffs alleged that its effect was impermissibly to remove from the city virtually all black voters and no white voters.

The majority resolved the case under the Fifteenth Amendment. Justice Whittaker, however, concluded that the "unlawful segregation of races of citizens" into different voting districts was cognizable under the Equal Protection Clause. The Court's subsequent reliance on *Gomillion* in other Fourteenth Amendment cases suggests the correctness of Justice Whittaker's view. *Gomillion* thus supports appellants' contention that district lines obviously drawn for the purpose of separating voters by race require careful scrutiny under the Equal Protection Clause regardless of the motivations underlying their adoption.

The Court extended the reasoning of *Gomillion* to congressional districting in *Wright v. Rockefeller* (1964). At issue in *Wright* were four districts contained in a New York apportionment statute. The plaintiffs alleged that the statute excluded nonwhites from one district and concentrated them in the other three. Every Member of the Court assumed that the plaintiffs' allegation that the statute "segregated eligible voters by race and place of origin" stated a constitutional claim. The majority accepted the District Court's finding that the plaintiffs had failed to establish that the districts were in fact drawn on racial lines. Although the boundary lines were somewhat irregular, the majority reasoned, they were not so bizarre as to permit of no other conclusion. Indeed, because most of the nonwhite voters lived together in one area, it would have been difficult to construct voting districts without concentrations of nonwhite voters.

Wright illustrates the difficulty of determining from the face of a single-member districting plan that it purposefully distinguishes between voters on the basis of race. A reapportionment statute typically does not classify persons at all; it classifies tracts of land, or addresses. Moreover, redistricting differs from other kinds of state decision-making in that the legislature always is aware of race when it draws district lines, just as it is aware of age, economic status, religious and political persuasion, and a variety of other demographic factors. That sort of race consciousness does not lead inevitably to impermissible race discrimination. As *Wright* demonstrates, when members of a racial group live together in one community, a reapportionment plan that concentrates members of the group in one district and excludes them from others may reflect wholly legitimate purposes. The district lines may be drawn, for example, to provide for compact districts of contiguous territory, or to maintain the integrity of political subdivisions.

The difficulty of proof, of course, does not mean that a racial gerrymander, once established, should receive less scrutiny under the Equal Protection Clause than other state legislation classifying citizens by race. Moreover, it seems clear to us that proof sometimes will not be difficult at all. In some exceptional cases, a reapportionment plan may be so highly irregular that, on its face, it rationally cannot be understood as anything other than an effort to "segregate . . . voters" on the basis of race. *Gomillion,* in which a tortured municipal boundary line was drawn to exclude black voters, was such a case. So, too, would be a case in which a State concentrated a dispersed minority population in a single district by disregarding traditional districting principles such as compactness, contiguity, and respect for political subdivisions. We emphasize that these criteria are important not because they are constitutionally required—they are not—but because they are objective factors that may serve to defeat a claim that a district has been gerrymandered on racial lines.

Put differently, we believe that reapportionment is one area in which appearances do matter. A reapportionment plan that includes in one district individuals who belong to the same race, but who are otherwise widely separated by geographical and political boundaries, and who may have little in common with one another but the color of their skin, bears an uncomfortable resemblance to political apartheid. It reinforces the perception that members of the same racial group—regardless of their age, education, economic status, or the community in which they live—think alike, share the same political interests, and will prefer the same candidates at the polls. We have rejected such perceptions elsewhere as impermissible racial stereotypes. By perpetuating such notions, a racial gerrymander may exacerbate the very patterns of racial bloc voting that majority-minority districting is sometimes said to counteract.

The message that such districting sends to elected representatives is equally pernicious. When a district obviously is created solely to effectuate the perceived common interests of one racial group, elected officials are more likely to believe that their primary obligation is to represent only the members of that group, rather than their constituency as a whole. This is altogether antithetical to our system of representative democracy.

For these reasons, we conclude that a plaintiff challenging a reapportionment statute under the Equal Protection Clause may state a claim by alleging that the legislation, though race neutral on its face, rationally cannot be understood as anything other than an effort to separate voters into different districts on the basis of race, and that the separation lacks sufficient justification. It is unnecessary for us to decide whether or how a reapportionment plan that, on its face can be explained in nonracial terms successfully could be challenged. Thus, we express no view as to whether, "the intentional creation of majority-minority districts, without more," always gives rise to an equal protection claim. We hold only that, on the facts of this case, appellants have stated a claim sufficient to defeat the state appellees' motion to dismiss.

Racial classifications of any sort pose the risk of lasting harm to our society. They reinforce the belief, held by too many for too much of our history, that individuals should be judged by the color of their skin. Racial classifications with respect to voting carry particular dangers. Racial gerrymandering, even for remedial purposes, may balkanize us into competing racial factions; it threatens to carry us further from the goal of a political system in which race no longer matters—a goal that the Fourteenth and Fifteenth Amendments embody, and to which the Nation continues to aspire. It is for these reasons that race-based districting by our state legislatures demands close judicial scrutiny.

In this case, the Attorney General suggested that North Carolina could have created a reasonably compact second majority-minority district in the south-central to southeastern part of the State. We express no view as to whether appellants successfully could have challenged such a district under the Fourteenth Amendment. We also do not decide whether appellants' complaint stated a claim under constitutional provisions other than the Fourteenth Amendment. Today we hold only that appellants have stated a claim under the Equal Protection Clause by alleging that the North Carolina General Assembly adopted a reapportionment scheme so irrational on its face that it can be understood only as an effort to segregate voters into separate voting districts because of their race, and that the separation lacks sufficient justification. If the allegation of racial gerrymandering remains uncontradicted, the District Court further must determine whether the North Carolina plan is narrowly tailored to further a compelling government interest. Accordingly, we reverse the judgment of the District Court and remand the case for further proceedings consistent with this opinion.

Bush v. Gore, 531 U.S. 98 (2000).

PER CURIAM.

I

On December 8, 2000, the Supreme Court of Florida ordered that the Circuit Court of Leon County tabulate by hand 9,000 ballots in Miami-Dade County. It also ordered the inclusion in the certified vote totals of 215 votes identified in Palm Beach County and 168 votes identified in Miami-Dade County for Vice President Albert Gore, Jr., and Senator Joseph Lieberman, Democratic Candidates for President and Vice President. The Supreme Court noted that petitioner, Governor George W. Bush asserted that the net gain for Vice President Gore in Palm Beach County was 176 votes, and directed the Circuit Court to resolve that dispute on remand. The court further held that relief would require manual recounts in all Florida counties where so-called "undervotes" had not been subject to manual tabulation. The court ordered all manual recounts to begin at once. Governor Bush and Richard Cheney, Republican Candidates for the Presidency and Vice Presidency, filed an emergency application for a stay of this mandate. On December 9, we granted the application, treated the application as a petition for a writ of certiorari, and granted certiorari.

The proceedings leading to the present controversy are discussed in some detail in our opinion in *Bush v. Palm Beach County Canvassing Bd. (Bush I)*. On November 8, 2000, the day following the Presidential election, the Florida Division of Elections reported that petitioner, Governor Bush, had received 2,909,135 votes, and respondent, Vice President Gore, had received 2,907,351 votes, a margin of 1,784 for Governor Bush. Because Governor Bush's margin of victory was less than "one-half of a percent . . . of the votes cast," an automatic machine recount was conducted under § 102.141(4) of the election code, the results of which showed Governor Bush still winning the race but by a diminished margin. Vice President Gore then sought manual recounts in Volusia, Palm Beach, Broward, and Miami-Dade Counties, pursuant to Florida's election protest provisions. Fla. Stat. § 102.166 (2000). A dispute arose concerning the deadline for local county canvassing boards to submit their returns to the Secretary of State (Secretary). The Secretary declined to waive the November 14 deadline imposed by statute. §§ 102.111, 102.112. The Florida Supreme Court, however, set the deadline at November 26. We granted certiorari and vacated the Florida Supreme Court's decision, finding considerable uncertainty as to the grounds on which it was based. *Bush I.* On December 11, the Florida Supreme Court issued a decision on remand reinstating that date.

On November 26, the Florida Elections Canvassing Commission certified the results of the election and declared Governor Bush the winner of Florida's 25 electoral votes. On November 27, Vice President Gore, pursuant to Florida's contest provisions, filed a complaint in Leon County Circuit Court contesting the certification. Fla. Stat. § 102.168 (2000). He sought relief pursuant to § 102.168(3)(c), which provides that "receipt of a number of illegal votes or rejection of a number of legal votes sufficient to change or place in doubt the result of the election" shall be grounds for a contest. The Circuit Court denied relief, stating that Vice President Gore failed to meet his burden of proof. He appealed to the First District Court of Appeal, which certified the matter to the Florida Supreme Court.

Accepting jurisdiction, the Florida Supreme Court affirmed in part and reversed in part. *Gore v. Harris* (2000). The court held that the Circuit Court had been correct to reject Vice President Gore's challenge to the results certified in Nassau County and his challenge to the Palm Beach County Canvassing Board's determination that 3,300 ballots cast in that county were not, in the statutory phrase, "legal votes."

The Supreme Court held that Vice President Gore had satisfied his burden of proof under § 102.168(3)(c) with respect to his challenge to Miami-Dade County's failure to tabulate, by manual count, 9,000 ballots on which the machines had failed to detect a vote for President ("undervotes"). Noting the closeness of the election, the Court explained that "on this record, there can be no question that there are legal votes within the 9,000 uncounted votes sufficient to place the results of this election in doubt." A "legal vote," as determined by the Supreme Court, is "one in which there is a 'clear indication of the intent of the voter.'" The court therefore ordered a hand recount of the 9,000 ballots in Miami-Dade County. Observing that the contest provisions vest broad discretion in the circuit judge to "provide any relief appropriate under such circumstances," Fla. Stat. § 102.168(8) (2000), the Supreme Court further held that the Circuit Court could order "the Supervisor of Elections and the Canvassing Boards, as well as the necessary public officials, in all counties that have not conducted a manual recount or tabulation of the undervotes . . . to do so forthwith, said tabulation to take place in the individual counties where the ballots are located."

The Supreme Court also determined that both Palm Beach County and Miami-Dade County, in their earlier manual recounts, had identified a net gain of 215 and 168 legal votes for Vice President Gore. Rejecting the Circuit Court's conclusion that Palm Beach County lacked the authority to include the 215 net votes submitted past the November 26 deadline, the Supreme Court explained that the deadline was not intended to exclude votes identified after that date through ongoing manual recounts. As to Miami-Dade County, the Court concluded that although the 168 votes identified were the result of a partial recount, they were "legal votes [that] could change the outcome of the election." The Supreme Court therefore directed the Circuit Court to include those totals in the certified results, subject to resolution of the actual vote total from the Miami-Dade partial recount.

The petition presents the following questions: whether the Florida Supreme Court established new standards for resolving Presidential election contests, thereby violating Art. II, § 1, cl. 2, of the United States Constitution and failing to comply with 3 U.S.C. § 5, and whether the use of standardless manual recounts violates the Equal Protection and Due Process Clauses. With respect to the equal protection question, we find a violation of the Equal Protection Clause.

II

A

The closeness of this election, and the multitude of legal challenges which have followed in its wake, have brought into sharp focus a common, if heretofore unnoticed, phenomenon. Nationwide statistics reveal that an estimated 2% of ballots cast do not register a vote for President for whatever reason, including deliberately choosing no candidate at all or some voter error, such as voting for two candidates or insufficiently marking a ballot. In certifying election results, the votes eligible for inclusion in the certification are the votes meeting the properly established legal requirements. This case has shown that punch card balloting machines can produce an unfortunate number of ballots which are not punched in a clean, complete way by the voter. After the current counting, it is likely legislative bodies nationwide will examine ways to improve the mechanisms and machinery for voting.

B

The individual citizen has no federal constitutional right to vote for electors for the President of the United States unless and until the state legislature chooses a statewide election as the means to implement its power to appoint members of the Electoral College. U.S. Const., Art. II, § 1. This is the source for the statement in *McPherson v. Blacker* (1892), that the State legislature's power to select the manner for appointing electors is plenary; it may, if it so chooses, select the electors itself, which indeed was the manner used by State legislatures in several States for many years after the Framing of our Constitution. History has now favored the voter, and in each of the several States the citizens themselves vote for Presidential electors. When the state legislature vests the right to vote for President in its people, the right to vote as the legislature has prescribed is fundamental; and one source of its fundamental nature lies in the equal weight accorded to each vote and the equal dignity owed to each voter. The State, of course, after granting the franchise in the special context of Article II, can take back the power to appoint electors.

The right to vote is protected in more than the initial allocation of the franchise. Equal protection applies as well to the manner of its exercise. Having once granted the right to vote on equal terms, the State may not, by later arbitrary and disparate treatment, value one person's vote over that of another. See, *e.g., Harper v. Virginia Bd. of Elections* (1966). It must be remembered that "the right of suffrage can be denied by a debasement or dilution of the weight of a citizen's vote just as effectively as by wholly prohibiting the free exercise of the franchise." *Reynolds v. Sims* (1964).

There is no difference between the two sides of the present controversy on these basic propositions. Respondents say that the very purpose of vindicating the right to vote justifies the recount procedures now at issue. The question before us, however, is whether the recount procedures the Florida Supreme Court has adopted are consistent with its obligation to avoid arbitrary and disparate treatment of the members of its electorate.

Much of the controversy seems to revolve around ballot cards designed to be perforated by a stylus but which, either through error or deliberate omission, have not been perforated with sufficient precision for a machine to count them. In some cases a piece of the card—a chad—is hanging, say by two corners. In other cases there is no separation at all, just an indentation.

The Florida Supreme Court has ordered that the intent of the voter be discerned from such ballots. For purposes of resolving the equal protection challenge, it is not necessary to decide whether the Florida Supreme Court had the authority under the legislative scheme for resolving election disputes to define what a legal vote is and to mandate a manual recount implementing that definition. The recount mechanisms implemented in response to the decisions of the Florida Supreme Court do not satisfy the minimum requirement for non-arbitrary treatment of voters necessary to secure the fundamental right. Florida's basic command for the count of legally cast votes is to consider the "intent of the voter." *Gore v. Harris.* This is unobjectionable as an abstract proposition and a starting principle. The problem inheres in the absence of specific standards to ensure its equal application. The formulation of uniform rules to determine intent based on these recurring circumstances is practicable and, we conclude, necessary.

The law does not refrain from searching for the intent of the actor in a multitude of circumstances; and in some cases the general command to ascertain intent is not susceptible to much further refinement. In this instance, however, the question is not whether to believe a witness but how to interpret the marks or holes or scratches on an inanimate object, a piece of cardboard or paper which, it is said, might not have registered as a vote during the machine count. The factfinder confronts a thing, not a person. The search for intent can be confined by specific rules designed to ensure uniform treatment.

The want of those rules here has led to unequal evaluation of ballots in various respects. See *Gore v. Harris.* As seems to have been acknowledged at oral argument, the standards for accepting or rejecting contested ballots might vary not only from county to county but indeed within a single county from one recount team to another.

The record provides some examples. A monitor in Miami-Dade County testified at trial that he observed that three members of the county canvassing board applied different standards in defining a legal vote. And testimony at trial also revealed that at least one county changed its evaluative standards during the counting process. Palm Beach County, for example, began the process with a 1990 guideline which precluded counting completely attached chads, switched to a rule that considered a vote to be legal if any light could be seen through a chad, changed back to the 1990 rule, and then abandoned any pretense of a *per se* rule, only to have a court order that the county consider dimpled chads legal. This is not a process with sufficient guarantees of equal treatment.

An early case in our one person, one vote jurisprudence arose when a State accorded arbitrary and disparate treatment to voters in its different counties. *Gray v. Sanders* (1963). The Court found a constitutional violation. We relied on these principles in the context of the Presidential selection process in *Moore v. Ogilvie* (1969), where we invalidated a county-based procedure that diluted the influence of citizens in larger counties in the nominating process. There we observed that "the idea that one group can be granted greater voting strength than another is hostile to the one man, one vote basis of our representative government."

The State Supreme Court ratified this uneven treatment. It mandated that the recount totals from two counties, Miami-Dade and Palm Beach, be included in the certified total. The court also appeared to hold *sub silentio* that the recount totals from Broward County, which were not completed until after the original November 14 certification by the Secretary of State, were to be considered part of the new certified vote totals even though the county certification was not contested by Vice President Gore. Yet each of the counties used varying standards to determine what was a legal vote. Broward County used a more forgiving standard than Palm Beach County, and uncovered almost three times as many new votes, a result markedly disproportionate to the difference in population between the counties.

In addition, the recounts in these three counties were not limited to so-called undervotes but extended to all of the ballots. The distinction has real consequences. A manual recount of all ballots identifies not only those ballots which show no vote but also those which contain more than one, the so-called overvotes. Neither category will be counted by the machine. This is not a trivial concern. At oral argument, respondents estimated there are as many as 110,000 overvotes statewide. As a result, the citizen whose ballot was not read by a machine because he failed to vote for a candidate in a way readable by a machine may still have his vote counted in a manual recount; on the other hand, the citizen who marks two candidates in a way discernable by the machine will not have the same opportunity to have his vote count, even if a manual examination of the ballot would reveal the requisite indicia of intent. Furthermore, the citizen who marks two candidates, only one of which is discernable by the machine, will have his vote counted even though it should have been read as an invalid ballot. The State Supreme Court's inclusion of vote counts based on these variant standards exemplifies concerns with the remedial processes that were under way.

That brings the analysis to yet a further equal protection problem. The votes certified by the court included a partial total from one county, Miami-Dade. The Florida Supreme Court's decision thus gives no assurance that the recounts included in a final certification must be complete. Indeed, it is respondent's submission that it would be consistent with the rules of the recount procedures to include whatever partial counts are done by the time of final certification, and we interpret the Florida Supreme Court's decision to permit this. This accommodation no doubt results from the truncated contest period established by the Florida Supreme Court in *Bush I*, at respondents' own urging. The press of time does not diminish the constitutional concern. A desire for speed is not a general excuse for ignoring equal protection guarantees.

In addition to these difficulties the actual process by which the votes were to be counted under the Florida Supreme Court's decision raises further concerns. That order did not specify who would recount the ballots. The county canvassing boards were forced to pull together ad hoc teams comprised of judges from various Circuits who had no previous training in handling and interpreting ballots. Furthermore, while others were permitted to observe, they were prohibited from objecting during the recount.

The recount process, in its features here described, is inconsistent with the minimum procedures necessary to protect the fundamental right of each voter in the special instance of a statewide recount under the authority of a single state judicial officer. Our consideration is limited to the present circumstances, for the problem of equal protection in election processes generally presents many complexities.

The question before the Court is not whether local entities, in the exercise of their expertise, may develop different systems for implementing elections. Instead, we are presented with a situation where a state court with the power to assure uniformity has ordered a statewide recount with minimal procedural safeguards. When a court orders a statewide remedy, there must be at least some assurance that the rudimentary requirements of equal treatment and fundamental fairness are satisfied.

Given the Court's assessment that the recount process underway was probably being conducted in an unconstitutional manner, the Court stayed the order directing the recount so it could hear this case and render an expedited decision. The contest provision, as it was mandated by the State Supreme Court, is not well calculated to sustain the confidence that all citizens must have in the outcome of elections. The State has not shown that its procedures include the necessary safeguards. The problem, for instance, of the estimated 110,000 overvotes has not been addressed, although Chief Justice Wells called attention to the concern in his dissenting opinion.

Upon due consideration of the difficulties identified to this point, it is obvious that the recount cannot be conducted in compliance with the requirements of equal protection and due process without substantial additional work. It would require not only the adoption (after opportunity for argument) of adequate statewide standards for determining what is a legal vote, and practicable procedures to implement them, but also orderly judicial review of any disputed matters that might arise. In addition, the Secretary of State has advised that the recount of only a portion of the ballots requires that the vote tabulation equipment be used to screen out undervotes, a function for which the machines were not designed. If a recount of overvotes were also required, perhaps even a second screening would be necessary. Use of the equipment for this purpose, and any new software developed for it, would have to be evaluated for accuracy by the Secretary of State, as required by Fla. Stat. § 101.015 (2000).

The Supreme Court of Florida has said that the legislature intended the State's electors to "participate fully in the federal electoral process," as provided in 3 U.S.C. § 5. That statute, in turn, requires that any controversy or contest that is designed to lead to a conclusive selection of electors be completed by December 12. That date is upon us, and there is no recount procedure in place under the State Supreme Court's order that comports with minimal constitutional standards. Because it is evident that any recount seeking to meet the December 12 date will be unconstitutional for the reasons we have discussed, we reverse the judgment of the Supreme Court of Florida ordering a recount to proceed.

Seven Justices of the Court agree that there are constitutional problems with the recount ordered by the Florida Supreme Court that demand a remedy. [See SOUTER, J., dissenting; BREYER, J., dissenting.] The only disagreement is as to the remedy. Because the Florida Supreme Court has said that the Florida Legislature intended to obtain the safe-harbor benefits of 3 U.S.C. § 5, JUSTICE BREYER's proposed remedy—remanding to the Florida Supreme Court for its ordering of a constitutionally proper contest until December 18—contemplates action in violation of the Florida election code, and hence could not be part of an "appropriate" order authorized by Fla. Stat. § 102.168(8) (2000).

None are more conscious of the vital limits on judicial authority than are the members of this Court, and none stand more in admiration of the Constitution's design to leave the selection of the President to the people, through their legislatures, and to the political sphere. When contending parties invoke the process of the courts, however, it becomes our unsought responsibility to resolve the federal and constitutional issues the judicial system has been forced to confront.

The judgment of the Supreme Court of Florida is reversed, and the case is remanded for further proceedings not inconsistent with this opinion.

CHIEF JUSTICE REHNQUIST, with whom JUSTICE SCALIA and JUSTICE THOMAS join, concurring.

We join the *per curiam* opinion. We write separately because we believe there are additional grounds that require us to reverse the Florida Supreme Court's decision.

I

We deal here not with an ordinary election, but with an election for the President of the United States. In *Burroughs v. United States* (1934), we said:

"While presidential electors are not officers or agents of the federal government . . . they exercise federal functions under, and discharge duties in virtue of authority conferred by, the Constitution of the United States. The President is vested with the executive power of the nation. The importance of his election and the vital character of its relationship to and effect upon the welfare and safety of the whole people cannot be too strongly stated."

Likewise, in *Anderson v. Celebrezze* (1983) we said: "In the context of a Presidential election, state-imposed restrictions implicate a uniquely important national interest. For the President and the Vice President of the United States are the only elected officials who represent all the voters in the Nation."

In most cases, comity and respect for federalism compel us to defer to the decisions of state courts on issues of state law. That practice reflects our understanding that the decisions of state courts are definitive pronouncements of the will of the States as sovereigns. Of course, in ordinary cases, the distribution of powers among the branches of a State's government raises no questions of federal constitutional law, subject to the requirement that the government be republican in character. See U.S. Const., Art. IV, § 4. But there are a few exceptional cases in which the Constitution imposes a duty or confers a power on a particular branch of a State's government. This is one of them. Article II, § 1, cl. 2, provides that "each State shall appoint, in such Manner as the *Legislature* thereof may direct," electors for President and Vice President. (Emphasis added.) Thus, the text of the election law itself, and not just its interpretation by the courts of the States, takes on independent significance.

In *McPherson v. Blacker* (1892), we explained that Art. II, § 1, cl. 2, "conveys the broadest power of determination" and "leaves it to the legislature exclusively to define the method" of appointment. A significant departure from the legislative scheme for appointing Presidential electors presents a federal constitutional question.

3 U.S.C. § 5 informs our application of Art. II, § 1, cl. 2, to the Florida statutory scheme, which, as the Florida Supreme Court acknowledged, took that statute into account. Section 5 provides that the State's selection of electors "shall be conclusive, and shall govern in the counting of the electoral votes" if the electors are chosen under laws enacted prior to election day, and if the selection process is completed six days prior to the meeting of the electoral college. As we noted in *Bush v. Palm Beach County Canvassing Bd.*, "Since § 5 contains a principle of federal law that would assure finality of the State's determination if made pursuant to a state law in effect before the election, a legislative wish to take advantage of the 'safe harbor' would counsel against any construction of the Election Code that Congress might deem to be a change in the law."

If we are to respect the legislature's Article II powers, therefore, we must ensure that postelection state-court actions do not frustrate the legislative desire to attain the "safe harbor" provided by § 5.

In Florida, the legislature has chosen to hold statewide elections to appoint the State's 25 electors. Importantly, the legislature has delegated the authority to run the elections and to oversee election disputes to the Secretary of State (Secretary), Fla. Stat. § 97.012(1) (2000), and to state circuit courts, §§ 102.168(1), 102.168(8). Isolated sections of the code may well admit of more than one interpretation, but the general coherence of the legislative scheme may not be altered by judicial interpretation so as to wholly change the statutorily provided apportionment of responsibility among these various bodies. In any election but a Presidential election, the Florida Supreme Court can give as little or as much deference to Florida's executives as it chooses, so far as Article II is concerned, and this Court will have no cause to question the court's actions. But, with respect to a Presidential election, the court must be both mindful of the legislature's role under Article II in choosing the manner of appointing electors and deferential to those bodies expressly empowered by the legislature to carry out its constitutional mandate.

In order to determine whether a state court has infringed upon the legislature's authority, we necessarily must examine the law of the State as it existed prior to the action of the court. Though we generally defer to state courts on the interpretation of state law—see, e.g., Mullaney v. Wilbur (1975)—there are of course areas in which the Constitution requires this Court to undertake an independent, if still deferential, analysis of state law.

For example, in NAACP v. Alabama ex rel. Patterson (1958), it was argued that we were without jurisdiction because the petitioner had not pursued the correct appellate remedy in Alabama's state courts. Petitioners had sought a state-law writ of certiorari in the Alabama Supreme Court when a writ of mandamus, according to that court, was proper. We found this state-law ground inadequate to defeat our jurisdiction because we were "unable to reconcile the procedural holding of the Alabama Supreme Court" with prior Alabama precedent. The purported state-law ground was so novel, in our independent estimation, that "petitioner could not fairly be deemed to have been apprised of its existence."

Six years later we decided Bouie v. City of Columbia (1964), in which the state court had held, contrary to precedent, that the state trespass law applied to black sit-in demonstrators who had consent to enter private property but were then asked to leave. Relying upon NAACP, we concluded that the South Carolina Supreme Court's interpretation of a state penal statute had impermissibly broadened the scope of that statute beyond what a fair reading provided, in violation of due process. What we would do in the present case is precisely parallel: Hold that the Florida Supreme Court's interpretation of the Florida election laws impermissibly distorted them beyond what a fair reading required, in violation of Article II.

This inquiry does not imply a disrespect for state courts but rather a respect for the constitutionally prescribed role of state legislatures. To attach definitive weight to the pronouncement of a state court, when the very question at issue is whether the court has actually departed from the statutory meaning, would be to abdicate our responsibility to enforce the explicit requirements of Article II.

II

Acting pursuant to its constitutional grant of authority, the Florida Legislature has created a detailed, if not perfectly crafted, statutory scheme that provides for appointment of Presidential electors by direct election. Fla. Stat. § 103.011 (2000). Under the statute, "votes cast for the actual candidates for President and Vice President shall be counted as votes cast for the presidential electors supporting such candidates." The legislature has designated the Secretary of State as the "chief election officer," with the responsibility to "obtain and maintain uniformity in the application, operation, and interpretation of the election laws." § 97.012. The state legislature has delegated to county canvassing boards the duties of administering elections. § 102.141. Those boards are responsible for providing results to the state Elections Canvassing Commission, comprising the Governor, the Secretary of State, and the Director of the Division of Elections. § 102.111. Cf. *Boardman v. Esteva* (1975).

After the election has taken place, the canvassing boards receive returns from precincts, count the votes, and in the event that a candidate was defeated by .5% or less, conduct a mandatory recount. Fla. Stat. § 102.141(4) (2000). The county canvassing boards must file certified election returns with the Department of State by 5 p.m. on the seventh day following the election. § 102.112(1). The Elections Canvassing Commission must then certify the results of the election. § 102.111(1).

The state legislature has also provided mechanisms both for protesting election returns and for contesting certified election results. Section 102.166 governs protests. Any protest must be filed prior to the certification of election results by the county canvassing board. § 102.166(4)(b). Once a protest has been filed, "the county canvassing board may authorize a manual recount." § 102.166(4)(c). If a sample recount conducted pursuant to § 102.166(5) "indicates an error in the vote tabulation which could affect the outcome of the election," the county canvassing board is instructed to: "(a) Correct the error and recount the remaining precincts with the vote tabulation system; (b) Request the Department of State to verify the tabulation software; or (c) Manually recount all ballots," § 102.166(5). In the event a canvassing board chooses to conduct a manual recount of all ballots, § 102.166(7) prescribes procedures for such a recount.

Contests to the certification of an election, on the other hand, are controlled by § 102.168. The grounds for contesting an election include "receipt of a number of illegal votes or rejection of a number of legal votes sufficient to change or place in doubt the result of the election." § 102.168(3)(c). Any contest must be filed in the appropriate Florida circuit court, Fla. Stat. § 102.168(1), and the canvassing board or election board is the proper party defendant, § 102.168(4). Section 102.168(8) provides that "the circuit judge to whom the contest is presented may fashion such orders as he or she deems necessary to ensure that each allegation in the complaint is investigated, examined, or checked, to prevent or correct any alleged wrong, and to provide any relief appropriate under such circumstances." In Presidential elections, the contest period necessarily terminates on the date set by 3 U.S.C. § 5 for concluding the State's "final determination" of election controversies.

In its first decision, *Palm Beach Canvassing Bd. v. Harris* (Nov. 21, 2000) *(Harris I)*, the Florida Supreme Court extended the 7-day statutory certification deadline established by the legislature. This modification of the code, by lengthening the protest period, necessarily shortened the contest period for Presidential elections. Underlying the extension of the certification deadline and the shortchanging of the contest period was, presumably, the clear implication that certification was a matter of significance: The certified winner would enjoy presumptive validity, making a contest proceeding by the losing candidate an uphill battle. In its latest opinion, however, the court empties certification of virtually all legal consequence during the contest, and in doing so departs from the provisions enacted by the Florida Legislature.

The court determined that canvassing boards' decisions regarding whether to recount ballots past the certification deadline (even the certification deadline established by *Harris I*) are to be reviewed *de novo*, although the election code clearly vests discretion whether to recount in the boards, and sets strict deadlines subject to the Secretary's rejection of late tallies and monetary fines for tardiness. See Fla. Stat. § 102.112 (2000). Moreover, the Florida court held that all late vote tallies arriving during the contest period should be automatically included in the certification regardless of the certification deadline (even the certification deadline established by *Harris I)*, thus virtually eliminating both the deadline and the Secretary's discretion to disregard recounts that violate it.

Moreover, the court's interpretation of "legal vote," and hence its decision to order a contest-period recount, plainly departed from the legislative scheme. Florida statutory law cannot reasonably be thought to *require* the counting of improperly marked ballots. Each Florida precinct before election day provides instructions on how properly to cast a vote, § 101.46; each polling place on election day contains a working model of the voting machine it uses, § 101.5611; and each voting booth contains a sample ballot, § 101.46. In precincts using punch-card ballots, voters are instructed to punch out the ballot cleanly: "After voting, check your ballot card to be sure your voting selections are clearly and cleanly punched and there are no chips left hanging on the back of the card."

Instructions to Voters, quoted in *Touchston v. McDermott* (CA11) (Tjoflat, J., dissenting). No reasonable person would call it "an error in the vote tabulation," FLA. STAT. § 102.166(5), or a "rejection of legal votes," FLA. STAT. § 102.168(3)(c), when electronic or electromechanical equipment performs precisely in the manner designed, and fails to count those ballots that are not marked in the manner that these voting instructions explicitly and prominently specify. The scheme that the Florida Supreme Court's opinion attributes to the legislature is one in which machines are *required* to be "capable of correctly counting votes," § 101.5606(4), but which nonetheless regularly produces elections in which legal votes are predictably *not* tabulated, so that in close elections manual recounts are regularly required. This is of course absurd. The Secretary of State, who is authorized by law to issue binding interpretations of the election code, §§ 97.012, 106.23, rejected this peculiar reading of the statutes. See DE 00-13 (opinion of the Division of Elections). The Florida Supreme Court, although it must defer to the Secretary's interpretations, rejected her reasonable interpretation and embraced the peculiar one. See *Palm Beach County Canvassing Board v. Harris* (Dec. 11, 2000) *(Harris III).*

But as we indicated in our remand of the earlier case, in a Presidential election the clearly expressed intent of the legislature must prevail. And there is no basis for reading the Florida statutes as requiring the counting of improperly marked ballots, as an examination of the Florida Supreme Court's textual analysis shows. We will not parse that analysis here, except to note that the principal provision of the election code on which it relied, § 101.5614(5), was, as the Chief Justice pointed out in his dissent from *Harris II,* entirely irrelevant. See *Gore v. Harris* (Dec. 8, 2000). The State's Attorney General (who was supporting the Gore challenge) confirmed in oral argument here that never before the present election had a manual recount been conducted on the basis of the contention that "undervotes" should have been examined to determine voter intent. For the court to step away from this established practice, prescribed by the Secretary of State, the state official charged by the legislature with "responsibility to . . . obtain and maintain uniformity in the application, operation, and interpretation of the election laws," § 97.012(1), was to depart from the legislative scheme.

III

The scope and nature of the remedy ordered by the Florida Supreme Court jeopardizes the "legislative wish" to take advantage of the safe harbor provided by 3 U.S.C. § 5. December 12, 2000, is the last date for a final determination of the Florida electors that will satisfy § 5. Yet in the late afternoon of December 8th—four days before this deadline—the Supreme Court of Florida ordered recounts of tens of thousands of so-called "undervotes" spread through 64 of the State's 67 counties. This was done in a search for elusive—perhaps delusive—certainty as to the exact count of 6 million votes. But no one claims that these ballots have not previously been tabulated; they were initially read by voting machines at the time of the election, and thereafter reread by virtue of Florida's automatic recount provision. No one claims there was any fraud in the election. The Supreme Court of Florida ordered this additional recount under the provision of the election code giving the circuit judge the authority to provide relief that is "appropriate under such circumstances." Fla. Stat. § 102.168(8) (2000).

Surely when the Florida Legislature empowered the courts of the State to grant "appropriate" relief, it must have meant relief that would have become final by the cut-off date of 3 U.S.C. § 5. In light of the inevitable legal challenges and ensuing appeals to the Supreme Court of Florida and petitions for certiorari to this Court, the entire recounting process could not possibly be completed by that date. Whereas the majority in the Supreme Court of Florida stated its confidence that "the remaining undervotes in these counties can be [counted] within the required time frame," it made no assertion that the seemingly inevitable appeals could be disposed of in that time. Although the Florida Supreme Court has on occasion taken over a year to resolve disputes over local elections, see, *e.g.*, *Beckstrom v. Volusia County Canvassing Bd.* (1998) (resolving contest of sheriff's race 16 months after the election), it has heard and decided the appeals in the present case with great promptness. But the federal deadlines for the Presidential election simply do not permit even such a shortened process.

As the dissent noted: "In [the four days remaining], all questionable ballots must be reviewed by the judicial officer appointed to discern the intent of the voter in a process open to the public. Fairness dictates that a provision be made for either party to object to how a particular ballot is counted. Additionally, this short time period must allow for judicial review. I respectfully submit this cannot be completed without taking Florida's presidential electors outside the safe harbor provision, creating the very real possibility of disenfranchising those nearly 6 million voters who are able to correctly cast their ballots on election day." [See Wells, C. J., dissenting].

The other dissenters echoed this concern: "The majority is departing from the essential requirements of the law by providing a remedy which is impossible to achieve and which will ultimately lead to chaos." [See Harding, J., dissenting, Shaw, J. concurring].

Given all these factors, and in light of the legislative intent identified by the Florida Supreme Court to bring Florida within the "safe harbor" provision of 3 U.S.C. § 5, the remedy prescribed by the Supreme Court of Florida cannot be deemed an "appropriate" one as of December 8. It significantly departed from the statutory framework in place on November 7, and authorized open-ended further proceedings which could not be completed by December 12, thereby preventing a final determination by that date.

For these reasons, in addition to those given in the *per curiam*, we would reverse.

DISSENT: JUSTICE STEVENS, with whom JUSTICE GINSBURG AND JUSTICE BREYER join, dissenting.

The Constitution assigns to the States the primary responsibility for determining the manner of selecting the Presidential electors. See Art. II, § 1, cl. 2. When questions arise about the meaning of state laws, including election laws, it is our settled practice to accept the opinions of the highest courts of the States as providing the final answers. On rare occasions, however, either federal statutes or the Federal Constitution may require federal judicial intervention in state elections. This is not such an occasion.

The federal questions that ultimately emerged in this case are not substantial. Article II provides that "each *State* shall appoint, in such Manner as the Legislature *thereof* may direct, a Number of Electors" (emphasis added). It does not create state legislatures out of whole cloth, but rather takes them as they come—as creatures born of, and constrained by, their state constitutions. Lest there be any doubt, we stated over 100 years ago in *McPherson v. Blacker* (1892), that "what is forbidden or required to be done by a State" in the Article II context "is forbidden or required of the legislative power under state constitutions as they exist." In the same vein, we also observed that "the [State's] legislative power is the supreme authority except as limited by the constitution of the State." *Ibid.;* cf. *Smiley v. Holm* (1932). The legislative power in Florida is subject to judicial review pursuant to Article V of the Florida Constitution, and nothing in Article II of the Federal Constitution frees the state legislature from the constraints in the state constitution that created it. Moreover, the Florida Legislature's own decision to employ a unitary code for all elections indicates that it intended the Florida Supreme Court to play the same role in Presidential elections that it has historically played in resolving electoral disputes. The Florida Supreme Court's exercise of appellate jurisdiction therefore was wholly consistent with, and indeed contemplated by, the grant of authority in Article II. It hardly needs stating that Congress, pursuant to 3 U.S.C. § 5, did not impose any affirmative duties upon the States that their governmental branches could "violate." Rather, § 5 provides a safe harbor for States to select electors in contested elections "by judicial or other methods" established by laws prior to the election day. Section 5, like Article II, assumes the involvement of the state judiciary in interpreting state election laws and resolving election disputes under those laws. Neither § 5 nor Article II grants federal judges any special authority to substitute their views for those of the state judiciary on matters of state law.

Nor are petitioners correct in asserting that the failure of the Florida Supreme Court to specify in detail the precise manner in which the "intent of the voter," Fla. Stat. § 101.5614(5) (Supp. 2001), is to be determined rises to the level of a constitutional violation. We found such a violation when individual votes within the same State were weighted unequally, see, *e.g., Reynolds v. Sims* (1964), but we have never before called into question the substantive standard by which a State determines that a vote has been legally cast. And there is no reason to think that the guidance provided to the factfinders, specifically the various canvassing boards, by the "intent of the voter" standard is any less sufficient—or will lead to results any less uniform—than, for example, the "beyond a reasonable doubt" standard employed everyday by ordinary citizens in courtrooms across this country.

Admittedly, the use of differing substandards for determining voter intent in different counties employing similar voting systems may raise serious concerns. Those concerns are alleviated—if not eliminated—by the fact that a single impartial magistrate will ultimately adjudicate all objections arising from the recount process. Of course, as a general matter, "the interpretation of constitutional principles must not be too literal. We must remember that the machinery of government would not work if it were not allowed a little play in its joints." *Bain Peanut Co. of Tex. v. Pinson* (1931) (Holmes, J.). If it were otherwise, Florida's decision to leave to each county the determination of what balloting system to employ—despite enormous differences in accuracy—might run afoul of equal protection. So, too, might the similar decisions of the vast majority of state legislatures to delegate to local authorities certain decisions with respect to voting systems and ballot design.

Even assuming that aspects of the remedial scheme might ultimately be found to violate the Equal Protection Clause, I could not subscribe to the majority's disposition of the case. As the majority explicitly holds, once a state legislature determines to select electors through a popular vote, the right to have one's vote counted is of constitutional stature. As the majority further acknowledges, Florida law holds that all ballots that reveal the intent of the voter constitute valid votes. Recognizing these principles, the majority nonetheless orders the termination of the contest proceeding before all such votes have been tabulated. Under their own reasoning, the appropriate course of action would be to remand to allow more specific procedures for implementing the legislature's uniform general standard to be established.

In the interest of finality, however, the majority effectively orders the disenfranchisement of an unknown number of voters whose ballots reveal their intent—and are therefore legal votes under state law—but were for some reason rejected by ballot-counting machines. It does so on the basis of the deadlines set forth in Title 3 of the United States Code. But, as I have already noted, those provisions merely provide rules of decision for Congress to follow when selecting among conflicting slates of electors. They do not prohibit a State from counting what the majority concedes to be legal votes until a bona fide winner is determined. Indeed, in 1960, Hawaii appointed two slates of electors and Congress chose to count the one appointed on January 4, 1961, well after the Title 3 deadlines. Thus, nothing prevents the majority, even if it properly found an equal protection violation, from ordering relief appropriate to remedy that violation without depriving Florida voters of their right to have their votes counted. As the majority notes, "[a] desire for speed is not a general excuse for ignoring equal protection guarantees."

Finally, neither in this case, nor in its earlier opinion in *Palm Beach County Canvassing Bd. v. Harris* (Fla., Nov. 21, 2000), did the Florida Supreme Court make any substantive change in Florida electoral law. Its decisions were rooted in long-established precedent and were consistent with the relevant statutory provisions, taken as a whole. It did what courts do—it decided the case before it in light of the legislature's intent to leave no legally cast vote uncounted. In so doing, it relied on the sufficiency of the general "intent of the voter" standard articulated by the state legislature, coupled with a procedure for ultimate review by an impartial judge, to resolve the concern about disparate evaluations of contested ballots. If we assume—as I do—that the members of that court and the judges who would have carried out its mandate are impartial, its decision does not even raise a colorable federal question.

What must underlie petitioners' entire federal assault on the Florida election procedures is an unstated lack of confidence in the impartiality and capacity of the state judges who would make the critical decisions if the vote count were to proceed. Otherwise, their position is wholly without merit. The endorsement of that position by the majority of this Court can only lend credence to the most cynical appraisal of the work of judges throughout the land. It is confidence in the men and women who administer the judicial system that is the true backbone of the rule of law. Time will one day heal the wound to that confidence that will be inflicted by today's decision. One thing, however, is certain. Although we may never know with complete certainty the identity of the winner of this year's Presidential election, the identity of the loser is perfectly clear. It is the Nation's confidence in the judge as an impartial guardian of the rule of law.

I respectfully dissent.

JUSTICE SOUTER, with whom JUSTICE BREYER joins and with whom JUSTICE STEVENS and JUSTICE GINSBURG join with regard to all but Part C, dissenting.

The Court should not have reviewed either *Bush v. Palm Beach County Canvassing Bd.* (per curiam), or this case, and should not have stopped Florida's attempt to recount all undervote ballots, by issuing a stay of the Florida Supreme Court's orders during the period of this review, see *Bush v. Gore.* If this Court had allowed the State to follow the course indicated by the opinions of its own Supreme Court, it is entirely possible that there would ultimately have been no issue requiring our review, and political tension could have worked itself out in the Congress following the procedure provided in 3 U.S.C. § 15. The case being before us, however, its resolution by the majority is another erroneous decision.

As will be clear, I am in substantial agreement with the dissenting opinions of JUSTICE STEVENS, JUSTICE GINSBURG and JUSTICE BREYER. I write separately only to say how straightforward the issues before us really are.

There are three issues: whether the State Supreme Court's interpretation of the statute providing for a contest of the state election results somehow violates 3 U.S.C. § 5; whether that court's construction of the state statutory provisions governing contests impermissibly changes a state law from what the State's legislature has provided, in violation of Article II, § 1, cl. 2, of the national Constitution; and whether the manner of interpreting markings on disputed ballots failing to cause machines to register votes for President (the undervote ballots) violates the equal protection or due process guaranteed by the Fourteenth Amendment. None of these issues is difficult to describe or to resolve.

A

The 3 U.S.C. § 5 issue is not serious. That provision sets certain conditions for treating a State's certification of Presidential electors as conclusive in the event that a dispute over recognizing those electors must be resolved in the Congress under 3 U.S.C. § 15. Conclusiveness requires selection under a legal scheme in place before the election, with results determined at least six days before the date set for casting electoral votes. But no State is required to conform to § 5 if it cannot do that (for whatever reason); the sanction for failing to satisfy the conditions of § 5 is simply loss of what has been called its "safe harbor." And even that determination is to be made, if made anywhere, in the Congress.

B

The second matter here goes to the State Supreme Court's interpretation of certain terms in the state statute governing election "contests," Fla. Stat. § 102.168 (2000); there is no question here about the state court's interpretation of the related provisions dealing with the antecedent process of "protesting" particular vote counts, § 102.166, which was involved in the previous case, *Bush v. Palm Beach County Canvassing Board.* The issue is whether the judgment of the state supreme court has displaced the state legislature's provisions for election contests: is the law as declared by the court different from the provisions made by the legislature, to which the national Constitution commits responsibility for determining how each State's Presidential electors are chosen? See U.S. Const., Art. II, § 1, cl. 2. Bush does not, of course, claim that any judicial act interpreting a statute of uncertain meaning is enough to displace the legislative provision and violate Article II; statutes require interpretation, which does not without more affect the legislative character of a statute within the meaning of the Constitution. Brief for Petitioners 48, n. 22, in *Bush v. Palm Beach County Canvassing Bd.* (2000). What Bush does argue, as I understand the contention, is that the interpretation of § 102.168 was so unreasonable as to transcend the accepted bounds of statutory interpretation, to the point of being a nonjudicial act and producing new law untethered to the legislative act in question.

The starting point for evaluating the claim that the Florida Supreme Court's interpretation effectively re-wrote § 102.168 must be the language of the provision on which Gore relies to show his right to raise this contest: that the previously certified result in Bush's favor was produced by "rejection of a number of legal votes sufficient to change or place in doubt the result of the election." Fla. Stat. § 102.168(3)(c) (2000). None of the state court's interpretations is unreasonable to the point of displacing the legislative enactment quoted. As I will note below, other interpretations were of course possible, and some might have been better than those adopted by the Florida court's majority; the two dissents from the majority opinion of that court and various briefs submitted to us set out alternatives. But the majority view is in each instance within the bounds of reasonable interpretation, and the law as declared is consistent with Article II.

1. The statute does not define a "legal vote," the rejection of which may affect the election. The State Supreme Court was therefore required to define it, and in doing that the court looked to another election statute, § 101.5614(5), dealing with damaged or defective ballots, which contains a provision that no vote shall be disregarded "if there is a clear indication of the intent of the voter as determined by a canvassing board." The court read that objective of looking to the voter's intent as indicating that the legislature probably meant "legal vote" to mean a vote recorded on a ballot indicating what the voter intended. Gore *v. Harris* (Dec. 8, 2000). It is perfectly true that the majority might have chosen a different reading. See, *e.g.,* Brief for Respondent Harris et al. 10 (defining "legal votes" as "votes properly executed in accordance with the instructions provided to all registered voters in advance of the election and in the polling places"). But even so, there is no constitutional violation in following the majority view; Article II is unconcerned with mere disagreements about interpretive merits.

2. The Florida court next interpreted "rejection" to determine what act in the counting process may be attacked in a contest. Again, the statute does not define the term. The court majority read the word to mean simply a failure to count. That reading is certainly within the bounds of common sense, given the objective to give effect to a voter's intent if that can be determined. A different reading, of course, is possible. The majority might have concluded that "rejection" should refer to machine malfunction, or that a ballot should not be treated as "rejected" in the absence of wrongdoing by election officials, lest contests be so easy to claim that every election will end up in one. [See Wells, C. J., dissenting]. There is, however, nothing nonjudicial in the Florida majority's more hospitable reading.

3. The same is true about the court majority's understanding of the phrase "votes sufficient to change or place in doubt" the result of the election in Florida. The court held that if the uncounted ballots were so numerous that it was reasonably possible that they contained enough "legal" votes to swing the election, this contest would be authorized by the statute. While the majority might have thought (as the trial judge did) that a probability, not a possibility, should be necessary to justify a contest, that reading is not required by the statute's text, which says nothing about probability. Whatever people of good will and good sense may argue about the merits of the Florida court's reading, there is no warrant for saying that it transcends the limits of reasonable statutory interpretation to the point of supplanting the statute enacted by the "legislature" within the meaning of Article II.

In sum, the interpretations by the Florida court raise no substantial question under Article II. That court engaged in permissible construction in determining that Gore had instituted a contest authorized by the state statute, and it proceeded to direct the trial judge to deal with that contest in the exercise of the discretionary powers generously conferred by Fla. Stat. § 102.168(8) (2000), to "fashion such orders as he or she deems necessary to ensure that each allegation in the complaint is investigated, examined, or checked, to prevent or correct any alleged wrong, and to provide any relief appropriate under such circumstances." As JUSTICE GINSBURG has persuasively explained in her own dissenting opinion, our customary respect for state interpretations of state law counsels against rejection of the Florida court's determinations in this case.

C

It is only on the third issue before us that there is a meritorious argument for relief, as this Court's *Per Curiam* opinion recognizes. It is an issue that might well have been dealt with adequately by the Florida courts if the state proceedings had not been interrupted, and if not disposed of at the state level it could have been considered by the Congress in any electoral vote dispute. But because the course of state proceedings has been interrupted, time is short, and the issue is before us, I think it sensible for the Court to address it.

Petitioners have raised an equal protection claim (or, alternatively, a due process claim, see generally *Logan v. Zimmerman Brush Co.* (1982)), in the charge that unjustifiably disparate standards are applied in different electoral jurisdictions to otherwise identical facts. It is true that the Equal Protection Clause does not forbid the use of a variety of voting mechanisms within a jurisdiction, even though different mechanisms will have different levels of effectiveness in recording voters' intentions; local variety can be justified by concerns about cost, the potential value of innovation, and so on. But evidence in the record here suggests that a different order of disparity obtains under rules for determining a voter's intent that have been applied (and could continue to be applied) to identical types of ballots used in identical brands of machines and exhibiting identical physical characteristics (such as "hanging" or "dimpled" chads). I can conceive of no legitimate state interest served by these differing treatments of the expressions of voters' fundamental rights. The differences appear wholly arbitrary.

In deciding what to do about this, we should take account of the fact that electoral votes are due to be cast in six days. I would therefore remand the case to the courts of Florida with instructions to establish uniform standards for evaluating the several types of ballots that have prompted differing treatments, to be applied within and among counties when passing on such identical ballots in any further recounting (or successive recounting) that the courts might order.

Unlike the majority, I see no warrant for this Court to assume that Florida could not possibly comply with this requirement before the date set for the meeting of electors, December 18. Although one of the dissenting justices of the State Supreme Court estimated that disparate standards potentially affected 170,000 votes, *Gore v. Harris*, the number at issue is significantly smaller. The 170,000 figure apparently represents all uncounted votes, both undervotes (those for which no Presidential choice was recorded by a machine) and overvotes (those rejected because of votes for more than one candidate). But as JUSTICE BREYER has pointed out, no showing has been made of legal overvotes uncounted, and counsel for Gore made an uncontradicted representation to the Court that the statewide total of undervotes is about 60,000. To recount these manually would be a tall order, but before this Court stayed the effort to do that the courts of Florida were ready to do their best to get that job done. There is no justification for denying the State the opportunity to try to count all disputed ballots now.

I respectfully dissent.

JUSTICE GINSBURG, with whom JUSTICE STEVENS joins, and with whom JUSTICE SOUTER and JUSTICE BREYER join as to Part I, dissenting.

I

The CHIEF JUSTICE acknowledges that provisions of Florida's Election Code "may well admit of more than one interpretation." But instead of respecting the state high court's province to say what the State's Election Code means, THE CHIEF JUSTICE maintains that Florida's Supreme Court has veered so far from the ordinary practice of judicial review that what it did cannot properly be called judging. My colleagues have offered a reasonable construction of Florida's law. Their construction coincides with the view of one of Florida's seven Supreme Court justices. *Gore v. Harris* (Fla. 2000) [See Wells, C. J., dissenting]; *Palm Beach County Canvassing Bd. v. Harris* (Fla. 2000) (on remand) (confirming, 6-1, the construction of Florida law advanced in *Gore*). I might join THE CHIEF JUSTICE were it my commission to interpret Florida law. But disagreement with the Florida court's interpretation of its own State's law does not warrant the conclusion that the justices of that court have legislated. There is no cause here to believe that the members of Florida's high court have done less than "their mortal best to discharge their oath of office," *Sumner v. Mata* (1981), and no cause to upset their reasoned interpretation of Florida law.

This Court more than occasionally affirms statutory, and even constitutional, interpretations with which it disagrees. For example, when reviewing challenges to administrative agencies' interpretations of laws they implement, we defer to the agencies unless their interpretation violates "the unambiguously expressed intent of Congress." *Chevron U.S.A. Inc. v. Natural Resources Defense Council, Inc.* (1984). We do so in the face of the declaration in Article I of the United States Constitution that "All legislative Powers herein granted shall be vested in a Congress of the United States." Surely the Constitution does not call upon us to pay more respect to a federal administrative agency's construction of federal law than to a state high court's interpretation of its own state's law. And not uncommonly, we let stand state-court interpretations of *federal* law with which we might disagree. Notably, in the habeas context, the Court adheres to the view that "there is 'no intrinsic reason why the fact that a man is a federal judge should make him more competent, or conscientious, or learned with respect to [federal law] than his neighbor in the state courthouse.'" *Stone v. Powell* (1976).

No doubt there are cases in which the proper application of federal law may hinge on interpretations of state law. Unavoidably, this Court must sometimes examine state law in order to protect federal rights. But we have dealt with such cases ever mindful of the full measure of respect we owe to interpretations of state law by a State's highest court. In the Contract Clause case, *General Motors Corp. v. Romein* (1992), for example, we said that although "ultimately we are bound to decide for ourselves whether a contract was made," the Court "accords respectful consideration and great weight to the views of the State's highest court." And in *Central Union Telephone Co. v. Edwardsville* (1925), we upheld the Illinois Supreme Court's interpretation of a state waiver rule, even though that interpretation resulted in the forfeiture of federal constitutional rights. Refusing to supplant Illinois law with a federal definition of waiver, we explained that the state court's declaration "should bind us unless so unfair or unreasonable in its application to those asserting a federal right as to obstruct it."

In deferring to state courts on matters of state law, we appropriately recognize that this Court acts as an "'outsider' lacking the common exposure to local law which comes from sitting in the jurisdiction." *Lehman Brothers v. Schein* (1974). That recognition has sometimes prompted us to resolve doubts about the meaning of state law by certifying issues to a State's highest court, even when federal rights are at stake. Cf. *Arizonans for Official English v. Arizona* (1997). Notwithstanding our authority to decide issues of state law underlying federal claims, we have used the certification devise to afford state high courts an opportunity to inform us on matters of their own State's law because such restraint "helps build a cooperative judicial federalism." *Lehman Brothers.*

Just last Term, in *Fiore v. White* (1999), we took advantage of Pennsylvania's certification procedure. In that case, a state prisoner brought a federal habeas action claiming that the State had failed to prove an essential element of his charged offense in violation of the Due Process Clause. Instead of resolving the state-law question on which the federal claim depended, we certified the question to the Pennsylvania Supreme Court for that court to "help determine the proper state-law predicate for our determination of the federal constitutional questions raised." THE CHIEF JUSTICE's willingness to *reverse* the Florida Supreme Court's interpretation of Florida law in this case is at least in tension with our reluctance in *Fiore* even to interpret Pennsylvania law before seeking instruction from the Pennsylvania Supreme Court. I would have thought the "cautious approach" we counsel when federal courts address matters of state law, *Arizonans,* and our commitment to "building co-operative judicial federalism," *Lehman Brothers,* demanded greater restraint.

Rarely has this Court rejected outright an interpretation of state law by a state high court. *Fairfax's Devisee v. Hunter's Lessee* (1813), *NAACP v. Alabama ex rel. Patterson* (1958), and *Bouie v. City of Columbia* (1964), cited by THE CHIEF JUSTICE, are three such rare instances. But those cases are embedded in historical contexts hardly comparable to the situation here. *Fairfax's Devisee,* which held that the Virginia Court of Appeals had misconstrued its own forfeiture laws to deprive a British subject of lands secured to him by federal treaties, occurred amidst vociferous States' rights attacks on the Marshall Court. The Virginia court refused to obey this Court's *Fairfax's Devisee* mandate to enter judgment for the British subject's successor in interest. That refusal led to the Court's pathmarking decision in *Martin v. Hunter's Lessee* (1816). *Patterson,* a case decided three months after *Cooper v. Aaron* (1958), in the face of Southern resistance to the civil rights movement, held that the Alabama Supreme Court had irregularly applied its own procedural rules to deny review of a contempt order against the NAACP arising from its refusal to disclose membership lists. We said that "our jurisdiction is not defeated if the nonfederal ground relied on by the state court is without any fair or substantial support." *Bouie,* stemming from a lunch counter "sit-in" at the height of the civil rights movement, held that the South Carolina Supreme Court's construction of its trespass laws—criminalizing conduct not covered by the text of an otherwise clear statute—was "unforeseeable" and thus violated due process when applied retroactively to the petitioners.

THE CHIEF JUSTICE's casual citation of these cases might lead one to believe they are part of a larger collection of cases in which we said that the Constitution impelled us to train a skeptical eye on a state court's portrayal of state law. But one would be hard pressed, I think, to find additional cases that fit the mold. As JUSTICE BREYER convincingly explains, at 5-9 (dissenting opinion), this case involves nothing close to the kind of recalcitrance by a state high court that warrants extraordinary action by this Court. The Florida Supreme Court concluded that counting every legal vote was the overriding concern of the Florida Legislature when it enacted the State's Election Code. The court surely should not be bracketed with state high courts of the Jim Crow South.

THE CHIEF JUSTICE says that Article II, by providing that state legislatures shall direct the manner of appointing electors, authorizes federal superintendence over the relationship between state courts and state legislatures, and licenses a departure from the usual deference we give to state court interpretations of state law. ("To attach definitive weight to the pronouncement of a state court, when the very question at issue is whether the court has actually departed from the statutory meaning, would be to abdicate our responsibility to enforce the explicit requirements of Article II.") The Framers of our Constitution, however, understood that in a republican government, the judiciary would construe the legislature's enactments. See U.S.

Const., Art. III; The Federalist No. 78 (A. Hamilton). In light of the constitutional guarantee to States of a "Republican Form of Government," U.S. Const., Art. IV, § 4, Article II can hardly be read to invite this Court to disrupt a State's republican regime. Yet THE CHIEF JUSTICE today would reach out to do just that. By holding that Article II requires our revision of a state court's construction of state laws in order to protect one organ of the State from another, THE CHIEF JUSTICE contradicts the basic principle that a State may organize itself as it sees fit. See, *e.g., Gregory v. Ashcroft* (1991); *Highland Farms Dairy, Inc. v. Agnew* (1937). Article II does not call for the scrutiny undertaken by this Court.

The extraordinary setting of this case has obscured the ordinary principle that dictates its proper resolution: Federal courts defer to state high courts' interpretations of their state's own law. This principle reflects the core of federalism, on which all agree. "The Framers split the atom of sovereignty. It was the genius of their idea that our citizens would have two political capacities, one state and one federal, each protected from incursion by the other." *Saenz v. Roe* (1999) (citing *U.S. Term Limits, Inc. v. Thornton* (1995) (KENNEDY, J., concurring)). THE CHIEF JUSTICE's solicitude for the Florida Legislature comes at the expense of the more fundamental solicitude we owe to the legislature's sovereign. U.S. Const., Art. II, § 1, cl. 2 ("Each *State* shall appoint, in such Manner as the Legislature *thereof* may direct," the electors for President and Vice President) (emphasis added); [See STEVENS, J., dissenting]. Were the other members of this Court as mindful as they generally are of our system of dual sovereignty, they would affirm the judgment of the Florida Supreme Court.

II

I agree with JUSTICE STEVENS that petitioners have not presented a substantial equal protection claim. Ideally, perfection would be the appropriate standard for judging the recount. But we live in an imperfect world, one in which thousands of votes have not been counted. I cannot agree that the recount adopted by the Florida court, flawed as it may be, would yield a result any less fair or precise than the certification that preceded that recount. See, *e.g., McDonald v. Board of Election Comm'rs of Chicago* (1969) . . .

Even if there were an equal protection violation, I would agree with JUSTICE STEVENS, JUSTICE SOUTER, and JUSTICE BREYER that the Court's concern about "the December 12 deadline," is misplaced. Time is short in part because of the Court's entry of a stay on December 9, several hours after an able circuit judge in Leon County had begun to superintend the recount process. More fundamentally, the Court's reluctance to let the recount go forward—despite its suggestion that "the search for intent can be confined by specific rules designed to ensure uniform treatment,"—ultimately turns on its own judgment about the practical realities of implementing a recount, not the judgment of those much closer to the process.

Equally important, as JUSTICE BREYER explains [in his dissenting opinion], the December 12 "deadline" for bringing Florida's electoral votes into 3 U.S.C. § 5's safe harbor lacks the significance the Court assigns it. Were that date to pass, Florida would still be entitled to deliver electoral votes Congress *must* count unless both Houses find that the votes "had not been . . . regularly given." 3 U.S.C. § 15. The statute identifies other significant dates. See, *e.g.*, § 7 (specifying December 18 as the date electors "shall meet and give their votes"); § 12 (specifying "the fourth Wednesday in December"—this year, December 27—as the date on which Congress, if it has not received a State's electoral votes, shall request the state secretary of state to send a certified return immediately). But none of these dates has ultimate significance in light of Congress' detailed provisions for determining, on "the sixth day of January," the validity of electoral votes. § 15.

The Court assumes that time will not permit "orderly judicial review of any disputed matters that might arise." But no one has doubted the good faith and diligence with which Florida election officials, attorneys for all sides of this controversy, and the courts of law have performed their duties. Notably, the Florida Supreme Court has produced two substantial opinions within 29 hours of oral argument. In sum, the Court's conclusion that a constitutionally adequate recount is impractical is a prophecy the Court's own judgment will not allow to be tested. Such an untested prophecy should not decide the Presidency of the United States.

I dissent.

JUSTICE BREYER, with whom JUSTICE STEVENS and JUSTICE GINSBURG join except as to Part I-A-1, and with whom JUSTICE SOUTER joins as to Part I, dissenting.

The Court was wrong to take this case. It was wrong to grant a stay. It should now vacate that stay and permit the Florida Supreme Court to decide whether the recount should resume.

I

The political implications of this case for the country are momentous. But the federal legal questions presented, with one exception, are insubstantial.

A
1

The majority raises three Equal Protection problems with the Florida Supreme Court's recount order: first, the failure to include overvotes in the manual recount; second, the fact that *all* ballots, rather than simply the undervotes, were recounted in some, but not all, counties; and third, the absence of a uniform, specific standard to guide the recounts. As far as the first issue is concerned, petitioners presented no evidence, to this Court or to any Florida court, that a manual recount of overvotes would identify additional legal votes. The same is true of the second, and, in addition, the majority's reasoning would seem to invalidate any state provision for a manual recount of individual counties in a statewide election.

The majority's third concern does implicate principles of fundamental fairness.

The majority concludes that the Equal Protection Clause requires that a manual recount be governed not only by the uniform general standard of the "clear intent of the voter," but also by uniform subsidiary standards (for example, a uniform determination whether indented, but not perforated, "undervotes" should count). The opinion points out that the Florida Supreme Court ordered the inclusion of Broward County's undercounted "legal votes" even though those votes included ballots that were not perforated but simply "dimpled," while newly recounted ballots from other counties will likely include only votes determined to be "legal" on the basis of a stricter standard. In light of our previous remand, the Florida Supreme Court may have been reluctant to adopt a more specific standard than that provided for by the legislature for fear of exceeding its authority under Article II. However, since the use of different standards could favor one or the other of the candidates, since time was, and is, too short to permit the lower courts to iron out significant differences through ordinary judicial review, and since the relevant distinction was embodied in the order of the State's highest court, I agree that, in these very special circumstances, basic principles of fairness may well have counseled the adoption of a uniform standard to address the problem. In light of the majority's disposition, I need not decide whether, or the extent to which, as a remedial matter, the Constitution would place limits upon the content of the uniform standard.

2

Nonetheless, there is no justification for the majority's remedy, which is simply to reverse the lower court and halt the recount entirely. An appropriate remedy would be, instead, to remand this case with instructions that, even at this late date, would permit the Florida Supreme Court to require recounting *all* undercounted votes in Florida, including those from Broward, Volusia, Palm Beach, and Miami-Dade Counties, whether or not previously recounted prior to the end of the protest period, and to do so in accordance with a single-uniform substandard.

The majority justifies stopping the recount entirely on the ground that there is no more time. In particular, the majority relies on the lack of time for the Secretary to review and approve equipment needed to separate undervotes. But the majority reaches this conclusion in the absence of *any* record evidence that the recount could not have been completed in the time allowed by the Florida Supreme Court. The majority finds facts outside of the record on matters that state courts are in a far better position to address. Of course, it is too late for any such recount to take place by December 12, the date by which election disputes must be decided if a State is to take advantage of the safe harbor provisions of 3 U.S.C. § 5. Whether there is time to conduct a recount prior to December 18, when the electors are scheduled to meet, is a matter for the state courts to determine. And whether, under Florida law, Florida could or could not take further action is obviously a matter for Florida courts, not this Court, to decide . . .

By halting the manual recount, and thus ensuring that the uncounted legal votes will not be counted under any standard, this Court crafts a remedy out of proportion to the asserted harm. And that remedy harms the very fairness interests the Court is attempting to protect. The manual recount would itself redress a problem of unequal treatment of ballots. As JUSTICE STEVENS points out, the ballots of voters in counties that use punch-card systems are more likely to be disqualified than those in counties using optical-scanning systems. According to recent news reports, variations in the undervote rate are even more pronounced. Thus, in a system that allows counties to use different types of voting systems, voters already arrive at the polls with an unequal chance that their votes will be counted. I do not see how the fact that this results from counties' selection of different voting machines rather than a court order makes the outcome any more fair. Nor do I understand why the Florida Supreme Court's recount order, which helps to redress this inequity, must be entirely prohibited based on a deficiency that could easily be remedied.

B

The remainder of petitioners' claims, which are the focus of the CHIEF JUSTICE's concurrence, raise no significant federal questions. I cannot agree that the CHIEF JUSTICE's unusual review of state law in this case [See GINSBURG, J., dissenting opinion] is justified by reference either to Art. II, § 1, or to 3 U.S.C. § 5. Moreover, even were such review proper, the conclusion that the Florida Supreme Court's decision contravenes federal law is untenable.

While conceding that, in most cases, "comity and respect for federalism compel us to defer to the decisions of state courts on issues of state law," the concurrence relies on some combination of Art. II, § 1, and 3 U.S.C. § 5 to justify the majority's conclusion that this case is one of the few in which we may lay that fundamental principle aside. [See Opinion of REHNQUIST, C. J]. The concurrence's primary foundation for this conclusion rests on an appeal to plain text: Art. II, § 1's grant of the power to appoint Presidential electors to the State "Legislature." But neither the text of Article II itself nor the only case the concurrence cites that interprets Article II, *McPherson v. Blacker* (1892), leads to the conclusion that Article II grants unlimited power to the legislature, devoid of any state constitutional limitations, to select the manner of appointing electors. Nor, as JUSTICE STEVENS points out, have we interpreted the Federal constitutional provision most analogous to Art. II, § 1—Art. I, § 4—in the strained manner put forth in the concurrence . . .

The concurrence's treatment of § 5 as "informing" its interpretation of Article II, § 1, cl. [See REHNQUIST, C. J., concurring], is no more convincing. The CHIEF JUSTICE contends that our opinion in *Bush v. Palm Beach County Canvassing Bd.* (*Bush I*), in which we stated that "a legislative wish to take advantage of [§ 5] would counsel against" a construction of Florida law that Congress might deem to be a change in law, now means that *this Court* "must ensure that post-election state court ac-

tions do not frustrate the legislative desire to attain the 'safe harbor' provided by §
5." However, § 5 is part of the rules that govern Congress' recognition of slates of
electors. Nowhere in *Bush I* did we establish that *this Court* had the authority to enforce § 5. Nor did we suggest that the permissive "counsel against" could be transformed into the mandatory "must ensure." And nowhere did we intimate, as the
concurrence does here, that a state court decision that threatens the safe harbor
provision of § 5 does so in violation of Article II. The concurrence's logic turns the
presumption that legislatures would wish to take advantage of § 5's "safe harbor"
provision into a mandate that trumps other statutory provisions and overrides the
intent that the legislature *did* express.

But, in any event, the concurrence, having conducted its review, now reaches
the wrong conclusion. It says that "the Florida Supreme Court's interpretation of
the Florida election laws impermissibly distorted them beyond what a fair reading
required, in violation of Article II." [See REHNQUIST, C. J, concurring]. But what
precisely is the distortion? Apparently, it has three elements. First, the Florida court,
in its earlier opinion, changed the election certification date from November 14 to
November 26. Second, the Florida court ordered a manual recount of "undercounted" ballots that could not have been fully completed by the December 12 "safe harbor" deadline. Third, the Florida court, in the opinion now under review, failed to
give adequate deference to the determinations of canvassing boards and the Secretary.

To characterize the first element as a "distortion," however, requires the concurrence to second-guess the way in which the state court resolved a plain conflict in
the language of different statutes. Compare Fla. Stat. § 102.166 (2001) (foreseeing
manual recounts during the protest period) with § 102.111 (setting what is arguably
too short a deadline for manual recounts to be conducted); compare § 102.112(1)
(stating that the Secretary "may" ignore late returns) with § 102.111(1) (stating that
the Secretary "shall" ignore late returns). In any event, that issue no longer has any
practical importance and cannot justify the reversal of the different Florida court
decision before us now.

To characterize the second element as a "distortion" requires the concurrence to
overlook the fact that the inability of the Florida courts to conduct the recount on
time is, in significant part, a problem of the Court's own making. The Florida
Supreme Court thought that the recount could be completed on time, and, within
hours, the Florida Circuit Court was moving in an orderly fashion to meet the deadline. This Court improvidently entered a stay. As a result, we will never know
whether the recount could have been completed.

Nor can one characterize the third element as "impermissible distorting" once
one understands that there are two sides to the opinion's argument that the Florida
Supreme Court "virtually eliminated the Secretary's discretion." [See REHNQUIST,
C. J., concurring]. The Florida statute in question was amended in 1999 to provide

that the "grounds for contesting an election" include the "rejection of a number of legal votes sufficient to . . . place in doubt the result of the election." Fla. Stat. §§ 102.168(3), (3)(c) (2000). And the parties have argued about the proper meaning of the statute's term "legal vote." The Secretary has claimed that a "legal vote" is a vote "properly executed in accordance with the instructions provided to all registered voters." Brief for Respondent Harris. On that interpretation, punchcard ballots for which the machines cannot register a vote are not "legal" votes. The Florida Supreme Court did not accept her definition. But it had a reason. Its reason was that a different provision of Florida election laws (a provision that addresses damaged or defective ballots) says that no vote shall be disregarded "if there is a clear indication of the intent of the voter as determined by the canvassing board" (adding that ballots should not be counted "if it is impossible to determine the elector's choice"). Fla. Stat. § 101.5614(5) (2000). Given this statutory language, certain roughly analogous judicial precedent, *e.g.*, *Darby v. State ex rel. McCollough* (Fla. 1917) *(per curiam)*, and somewhat similar determinations by courts throughout the Nation . . . the Florida Supreme Court concluded that the term "legal vote" means a vote recorded on a ballot that clearly reflects what the voter intended. *Gore v. Harris* (2000). That conclusion differs from the conclusion of the Secretary. But nothing in Florida law requires the Florida Supreme Court to accept as determinative the Secretary's view on such a matter. Nor can one say that the Court's ultimate determination is so unreasonable as to amount to a constitutionally "impermissible distortion" of Florida law.

The Florida Supreme Court, applying this definition, decided, on the basis of the record, that respondents had shown that the ballots undercounted by the voting machines contained enough "legal votes" to place "the results" of the election "in doubt." Since only a few hundred votes separated the candidates, and since the "undercounted" ballots numbered tens of thousands, it is difficult to see how anyone could find this conclusion unreasonable—however strict the standard used to measure the voter's "clear intent." Nor did this conclusion "strip" canvassing boards of their discretion. The boards retain their traditional discretionary authority during the protest period. And during the contest period, as the court stated, "the Canvassing Board's actions [during the protest period] may constitute evidence that a ballot does or does not qualify as a legal vote." Whether a local county canvassing board's discretionary judgment during the protest period not to conduct a manual recount will be set aside during a contest period depends upon whether a candidate provides additional evidence that the rejected votes contain enough "legal votes" to place the outcome of the race in doubt. To limit the local canvassing board's discretion in this way is not to eliminate that discretion. At the least, one could reasonably so believe.

The statute goes on to provide the Florida circuit judge with authority to "fashion such orders as he or she deems necessary to ensure that each allegation . . . is *in-*

vestigated, examined, or checked, . . . and to provide any relief appropriate." Fla. Stat. § 102.168(8) (2000) (emphasis added). The Florida Supreme Court did just that. One might reasonably disagree with the Florida Supreme Court's interpretation of these, or other, words in the statute. But I do not see how one could call its plain language interpretation of a 1999 statutory change so misguided as no longer to qualify as judicial interpretation or as a usurpation of the authority of the State legislature. Indeed, other state courts have interpreted roughly similar state statutes in similar ways. See, *e.g., In re Election of U.S. Representative for Second Congressional Dist.,* 231 Conn. 602 (1994); *Brown v. Carr,* 130 W. Va. 455 (1947).

I repeat, where is the "impermissible" distortion?

II

Despite the reminder that this case involves "an election for the President of the United States," [See REHNQUIST, C. J., concurring] no preeminent legal concern, or practical concern related to legal questions, required this Court to hear this case, let alone to issue a stay that stopped Florida's recount process in its tracks. With one exception, petitioners' claims do not ask us to vindicate a constitutional provision designed to protect a basic human right. See, e.g., *Brown v. Board of Education* (1954). Petitioners invoke fundamental fairness, namely, the need for procedural fairness, including finality. But with the one "equal protection" exception, they rely upon law that focuses, not upon that basic need, but upon the constitutional allocation of power. Respondents invoke a competing fundamental consideration—the need to determine the voter's true intent. But they look to state law, not to federal constitutional law, to protect that interest. Neither side claims electoral fraud, dishonesty, or the like. And the more fundamental equal protection claim might have been left to the state court to resolve if and when it was discovered to have mattered. It could still be resolved through a remand conditioned upon issuance of a uniform standard; it does not require reversing the Florida Supreme Court.

Of course, the selection of the President is of fundamental national importance. But that importance is political, not legal. And this Court should resist the temptation unnecessarily to resolve tangential legal disputes, where doing so threatens to determine the outcome of the election.

The Constitution and federal statutes themselves make clear that restraint is appropriate. They set forth a road map of how to resolve disputes about electors, even after an election as close as this one. That road map foresees resolution of electoral disputes by *state* courts. See 3 U.S.C. § 5. But it nowhere provides for involvement by the United States Supreme Court.

To the contrary, the Twelfth Amendment commits to Congress the authority and responsibility to count electoral votes. A federal statute, the Electoral Count Act, enacted after the close 1876 Hayes-Tilden Presidential election, specifies that, after States have tried to resolve disputes (through "judicial" or other means), Congress is the body primarily authorized to resolve remaining disputes. See Electoral Count Act of 1887, 3 U.S.C. §§ 5, 6, and 15. The legislative history of the Act makes clear its intent to commit the power to resolve such disputes to Congress, rather than the courts: "The two Houses are, by the Constitution, authorized to make the count of electoral votes. They can only count legal votes, and in doing so must determine, from the best evidence to be had, what are legal votes. . . . The power to determine rests with the two Houses, and there is no other constitutional tribunal." H. Rep. No. 1638, 49th Cong., 1st Sess., 2 (1886).

The Member of Congress who introduced the Act added: "The power to judge of the legality of the votes is a necessary consequent of the power to count. The existence of this power is of absolute necessity to the preservation of the Government. The interests of all the States in their relations to each other in the Federal Union demand that the ultimate tribunal to decide upon the election of President should be a constituent body, in which the States in their federal relationships and the people in their sovereign capacity should be represented." 18 Cong. Rec. 30 (1886).

"Under the Constitution who else could decide? Who is nearer to the State in determining a question of vital importance to the whole union of States than the constituent body upon whom the Constitution has devolved the duty to count the vote?"

The Act goes on to set out rules for the congressional determination of disputes about those votes. If, for example, a state submits a single slate of electors, Congress must count those votes unless both Houses agree that the votes "have not been . . . regularly given." 3 U.S.C. § 15. If, as occurred in 1876, one or more states submits two sets of electors, then Congress must determine whether a slate has entered the safe harbor of § 5, in which case its votes will have "conclusive" effect. If, as also occurred in 1876, there is controversy about "which of two or more of such State authorities . . . is the lawful tribunal" authorized to appoint electors, then each House shall determine separately which votes are "supported by the decision of such State so authorized by its law." If the two Houses of Congress agree, the votes they have approved will be counted. If they disagree, then "the votes of the electors whose appointment shall have been certified by the executive of the State, under the seal thereof, shall be counted."

Given this detailed, comprehensive scheme for counting electoral votes, there is no reason to believe that federal law either foresees or requires resolution of such a political issue by this Court. Nor, for that matter, is there any reason to think that the Constitution's Framers would have reached a different conclusion. Madison, at least, believed that allowing the judiciary to choose the presidential electors "was out of the question." Madison, July 25, 1787 (reprinted in 5 Elliot's Debates on the Federal Constitution 363 (2d ed. 1876)).

The decision by both the Constitution's Framers and the 1886 Congress to minimize this Court's role in resolving close federal presidential elections is as wise as it is clear. However awkward or difficult it may be for Congress to resolve difficult electoral disputes, Congress, being a political body, expresses the people's will far more accurately than does an unelected Court. And the people's will is what elections are about.

Moreover, Congress was fully aware of the danger that would arise should it ask judges, unarmed with appropriate legal standards, to resolve a hotly contested Presidential election contest. Just after the 1876 Presidential election, Florida, South Carolina, and Louisiana each sent two slates of electors to Washington. Without these States, Tilden, the Democrat, had 184 electoral votes, one short of the number required to win the Presidency. With those States, Hayes, his Republican opponent, would have had 185. In order to choose between the two slates of electors, Congress decided to appoint an electoral commission composed of five Senators, five Representatives, and five Supreme Court Justices. Initially the Commission was to be evenly divided between Republicans and Democrats, with Justice David Davis, an Independent, to possess the decisive vote. However, when at the last minute the Illinois Legislature elected Justice Davis to the United States Senate, the final position on the Commission was filled by Supreme Court Justice Joseph P. Bradley.

The Commission divided along partisan lines, and the responsibility to cast the deciding vote fell to Justice Bradley. He decided to accept the votes by the Republican electors, and thereby awarded the Presidency to Hayes.

Justice Bradley immediately became the subject of vociferous attacks. Bradley was accused of accepting bribes, of being captured by railroad interests, and of an eleventh-hour change in position after a night in which his house "was surrounded by the carriages" of Republican partisans and railroad officials. C. Woodward, Reunion and Reaction 159-160 (1966). Many years later, Professor Bickel concluded that Bradley was honest and impartial. He thought that "'the great question' for Bradley was, in fact, whether Congress was entitled to go behind election returns or had to accept them as certified by state authorities," an "issue of principle." The Least Dangerous Branch 185 (1962). Nonetheless, Bickel points out, the legal question upon which Justice Bradley's decision turned was not very important in the contemporaneous political context. He says that "in the circumstances the issue of principle was trivial, it was overwhelmed by all that hung in the balance, and it should not have been decisive."

For present purposes, the relevance of this history lies in the fact that the participation in the work of the electoral commission by five Justices, including Justice Bradley, did not lend that process legitimacy. Nor did it assure the public that the process had worked fairly, guided by the law. Rather, it simply embroiled Members of the Court in partisan conflict, thereby undermining respect for the judicial process. And the Congress that later enacted the Electoral Count Act knew it.

This history may help to explain why I think it not only legally wrong, but also most unfortunate, for the Court simply to have terminated the Florida recount.

Those who caution judicial restraint in resolving political disputes have described the quintessential case for that restraint as a case marked, among other things, by the "strangeness of the issue," its "intractability to principled resolution," its "sheer momentousness, . . . which tends to unbalance judicial judgment," and "the inner vulnerability, the self-doubt of an institution which is electorally irresponsible and has no earth to draw strength from." Bickel at 184. Those characteristics mark this case.

At the same time, as I have said, the Court is not acting to vindicate a fundamental constitutional principle, such as the need to protect a basic human liberty. No other strong reason to act is present. Congressional statutes tend to obviate the need. And, above all, in this highly politicized matter, the appearance of a split decision runs the risk of undermining the public's confidence in the Court itself. That confidence is a public treasure. It has been built slowly over many years, some of which were marked by a Civil War and the tragedy of segregation. It is a vitally necessary ingredient of any successful effort to protect basic liberty and, indeed, the rule of law itself. We run no risk of returning to the days when a President (responding to this Court's efforts to protect the Cherokee Indians) might have said, "John Marshall has made his decision; now let him enforce it!" Loth, Chief Justice John Marshall and The Growth of the American Republic 365 (1948). But we do risk a self-inflicted wound—a wound that may harm not just the Court, but the Nation.

I fear that in order to bring this agonizingly long election process to a definitive conclusion, we have not adequately attended to that necessary "check upon our own exercise of power," "our own sense of self-restraint." *United States v. Butler* (1936) (Stone, J., dissenting). Justice Brandeis once said of the Court, "The most important thing we do is not doing." Bickel at 71. What it does today, the Court should have left undone. I would repair the damage done as best we now can, by permitting the Florida recount to continue under uniform standards.

I respectfully dissent.

Notes

Preface

1. "Parties, Politics, and the Law: Toward a More Representative Democracy," a conference sponsored by The University of Akron Ray C. Bliss Institute of Applied Politics and the Constitutional Law Center of the School of Law, was held on September 25, 1998, at the John S. Knight Center in Akron, Ohio.

Chapter 1. Superintending Democracy

1. 1 Cr. (5 U.S.) 137 (1803).

2. David M. O'Brien, "Judicial Review and American Politics: Historical and Political Perspectives," in *Judges on Judging: Views from the Bench*, ed. David M. O'Brien (Chatham, N.J.: Chatham House, 1997): 5.

3. David M. O'Brien, *Constitutional Law and Politics: Struggles for Power and Governmental Accountability*, 4th ed. (New York: W. W. Norton, 2000): 207–8.

4. Louis Henkin, "Is there a 'Political Question' Doctrine?" *Yale Law Journal* 85 (1976): 597–606.

5. O'Brien, *Constitutional Law and Politics,* 208.

6. 328 U.S. 549 (1946).

7. Samuel Issacharoff, Pamela S. Karlan, and Richard H. Pildes, *The Law of Democracy: Legal Structure of the Political Process* (Westbury, N.Y.: Foundation Press, 1998): 121.

8. 369 U.S. 186 (1962).

9. Issacharoff, Karlan, and Pildes, *The Law of Democracy,* 134–35. Justice Tom Clark wrote a concurring opinion in *Baker.*

10. See the Ethics in Government Act of 1978, 28 U.S.C. 591–98 (1978).

Chapter 2. The United States Supreme Court's Response to American Political Corruption

Epigraph source: James Madison, "Federalist No. 55," in *The Federalist Papers,* ed. Clinton Rossiter (New York: Mentor, 1961): 346.

1. Larry J. Sabato and Glenn R. Simpson, *Dirty Little Secrets: The Persistence of Corruption in American Politics* (New York: Random House, 1996): 10.

2. Bernard Bailyn, *The Ideological Origins of the American Revolution,* enlarged ed. (Cambridge, Mass.: Belknap Press, 1992): 51. See also James D. Savage, "Corruption and Virtue at the Constitutional Convention," *Journal of Politics* 56 (1992): 175.

3. Influential writings of the eighteenth century included *Cato's Letters* (John Trenchard and Thomas Gordon), *The Craftsmen* (Henry St. John, Viscount Bolingbroke), and

Two Treatises of Government (John Locke). Bailyn, *Ideological Origins of the American Revolution*, 22–54. See also Gordon S. Wood, *The Creation of the American Republic, 1776–1787* (New York: W. W. Norton and Company, 1972): 3–90; Savage, "Corruption and Virtue at the Constitutional Convention," 174–86.

4. Jack N. Rakove, *Original Meanings: Politics and Ideas in the Making of the Constitution* (New York: Vintage Books, 1996): 50–51.

5. Michael Kammen, "Introduction," in *The Origins of the American Constitution: A Documentary History*, ed. Michael Kammen (New York: Penguin Books, 1986.): xv.

6. Savage, "Corruption and Virtue at the Constitutional Convention," 177–82. See also John T. Noonan, Jr., *Bribes* (New York: Macmillan Publishing Company, 1984): 427–35.

7. Noonan, *Bribes*, 435–42; James C. Foster and Susan M. Leeson, *Constitutional Law: Cases in Context*, vol. 1 (Upper Saddle River, N.J.: Prentice Hall, 1998): 724–26. See also *Fletcher v. Peck*, 10 U.S. 87 (1810).

8. Foster and Leeson, *Constitutional Law*, 731–32.

9. Noonan, *Bribes*, 441. Representative Troup's remark is more interesting in light of the evidence (uncovered by Noonan) that Chief Justice John Marshall announced in open court that it was clear from the pleadings that Fletcher was aware of the defects in his title when he took the deed. Marshall's comments, which were made the first time *Fletcher* was considered by the Court on a procedural (and not on the merits) basis, are allegedly recorded in John Quincy Adams's memoirs. See ibid., 440 n. 44.

10. See, generally, David K. Ryden, *Representation in Crisis: The Constitution, Interest Groups, and Political Parties* (Albany, N.Y.: State University Press of New York Press, 1996).

11. Using the word "corruption" as a search term in the GenFed library and the U.S. file from LEXIS (the on-line legal research service that stores U.S. Supreme Court opinions), 360 case citations were generated from the beginning of the Court's first term up until the Court's 1996–97 term. A manual inspection of the citations produced a sample of sixty opinions that were selected for analysis. Of those sixty, three cases that were not on the master list generated by LEXIS were added to the sample; those cases (and the reasons for adding them) are identified in tables 2.3, 2.4, and 2.8. To be included in the sample, a case must meet one of two possible criteria: either (1) the facts of the case involve allegations of corrupt political activity of a governmental official who allegedly abused a position of trust in order to secure private gain, as in a bribery or conflict of interest case; or (2) the governmental interest in preventing the existence or the appearance of political corruption is a legal argument in a case, as in a campaign finance case, or a case concerning the regulation of campaigns or election procedures. Of course, the limitations of using the word "corruption" in a LEXIS search means that opinions dealing with corruption under the two criteria mentioned will not appear on the master list or sample. The master list (and the sample generated therefrom), however, is only intended to reflect a fair representation of the types of cases that the Court is likely to hear involving political corruption. It does not purport to pick up all political corruption cases.

12. Thomas Jefferson, "A Summary View of the Rights of British America," in *The Portable Thomas Jefferson*, ed. Merrill D. Peterson (New York: Penguin Books, 1977): 20–21.

13. "Political influence" cases include those with allegations of corruption by those persons holding an official position in government for the purpose of achieving private gain. They also include cases containing allegations that individuals in government (or about to enter government from the private sector) hold a conflict of interest in the

transaction (or event) at issue and should recuse themselves from having any involvement with the transaction or event.

14. The Court upheld an adverse ruling against the defendant in *In re Green*, 141 U.S. 325 (1891); *Burton v. U.S.*, 202 U.S. 344 (1906); *U.S. v. Russell*, 255 U.S. 138 (1921); *U.S. v. Hood*, 343 U.S. 148 (1952); *U.S. v. Shirey*, 359 U.S. 255 (1959); *Osborn v. U.S.*, 385 U.S. 323 (1966); *U.S. v. Brewster*, 408 U.S. 501 (1972); *Helstoski v. Meanor*, 442 U.S. 500 (1979); *U.S. v. Gillock*, 445 U.S. 360 (1980); and *Evans v. U.S.*, 504 U.S. 255 (1992). The Court ruled in favor of the defendant (or plaintiff, as in *Dennis*), in *U.S. v. Helstoski*, 442 U.S. 477 (1979); *Dennis v. Sparks*, 449 U.S. 24 (1980); *Brown v. Hartlage*, 456 U.S. 45 (1982); *McCormick v. U.S.*, 500 U.S. 257 (1991), *Bracy v. Gramley*, 117 S.Ct. 1793 (1997).

15. The Court refused to condone corruption in *Bartle v. Nutt*, 29 U.S. 184 (1830); *Marshall v. Baltimore & Ohio Railroad Co.*, 57 U.S. 314 (1850); *Trist v. Child*, 88 U.S. 441 (1874); *Meguire v. Corwine*, 101 U.S. 108 (1879); *Hazelton v. Sheckells*, 202 U.S. 71 (1906); *U.S. v. Carter*, 217 U.S. 286 (1910); *Mammoth Oil Co. v. U.S.*, 275 U.S. 13 (1927); *U.S. v. Harriss*, 347 U.S. 612 (1954); and *U.S. v. Mississippi Valley Generating Co.*, 364 U.S. 520 (1961). The litigant received a favorable holding in *Near v. Minnesota*, 283 U.S. 697 (1931); *U.S. v. Johnson*, 383 U.S. 169 (1966); *Powell v. McCormack*, 500 U.S. 257 (1969); *Crandon v. U.S.*, 494 U.S. 152 (1990); and *U.S. v. National Treasury Employees Union*, 513 U.S. 454 (1995).

16. See, e.g. *U.S. v. Helstoski*, 442 U.S. 477 (1979); *Brown v. Hartlage*, 456 U.S. 45 (1972); *Bracy v. Gramley*, 117 S.Ct. 1793 (1997); *Near v. Minnesota*, 283 U.S. 697 (1930); *U.S. v. Johnson*, 383 U.S. 169 (1966); *Powell v. McCormack*, 395 U.S. 486 (1969); and *U.S. v. National Treasury Employees Union*, 513 U.S. 454 (1995).

17. Art. I, Sec. 6, U.S. Constitution states that "[f]or any Speech or Debate in either House, they [Representatives or Senators] shall not be questioned in any other place."

18. *U.S. v. Brewster*, 408 U.S. 501 (1972): 524–25, 525.

19. Ibid., 532. See also *U.S. v. Johnson*, 383 U.S. 169 (1966): 179 (J. Harlan, opinion for the Court).

20. *Brewster*, 550.

21. Ibid., 556–60, 563.

22. With Justices Hugo Black and Byron White not participating, all the remaining Justices (Chief Justice Earl Warren and Justices William Douglas, Tom Clark, Abe Fortas, Potter Stewart, John Harlan, and William Brennan) agreed that the judicial inquiry into examining the authorship, motivation, and content of the senator's speech is barred by the Speech or Debate Clause. Justices Warren, Douglas, and Brennan dissented from that part of the Court's holding that refused to decide the validity of the senator's conviction under the conflict of interest counts of the indictment.

23. See Christopher P. Banks, "The Supreme Court and Precedent: An Analysis of Natural Courts and Reversal Trends," *Judicature* 75 (1992): 262–68.

24. Craig R. Ducat, *Constitutional Interpretation*, 6th ed. (Minneapolis, Minn.: West Publishing Company, 1996): 210–11. For a discussion of some of the Court's typical applications of the Speech or Debate Clause, see David M. O'Brien, *Constitutional Law and Politics: Struggles for Power and Governmental Accountability*, vol. 1, 4th ed. (New York: W. W. Norton and Co., 2000): 437–39.

25. Noonan, *Bribes*, 460–500, 621–28; Sabato and Simpson, *Dirty Little Secrets*, 10–18; Anthony Corrado, "Introduction [to] Money and Politics: A History of Federal Campaign Finance Law," in *Campaign Finance Reform: A Sourcebook*, ed. Anthony Corrado, et al. (Washington, D.C.: Brookings Institution, 1997): 27–35.

26. Corrado, "Introduction [to] Money and Politics," 28.

27. Ibid., 28–30.

28. Noonan, *Bribes*, 628; Corrado, "Introduction [to] Money and Politics," 31–32; Issacharoff, Karlan, and Pildes, *The Law of Democracy*, 618; Frank J. Sorauf, "Caught in a Political Thicket: The Supreme Court and Campaign Finance," *Constitutional Commentary* 3 (1986): 98.

29. Issacharoff, Karlan, and Pildes, *The Law of Democracy*, 618. See also Sorauf, "Caught in a Political Thicket," 98–99. See *Buckley v. Valeo*, 424 U.S. 1 (1976).

30. See Issacharoff, Karlan, and Pildes, *The Law of Democracy*, 616–18.

31. Art. I, Sec. 4, U.S. Const.

32. Art. I, Sec. 5, U.S. Const.

33. *Newberry v. U.S.*, 256 U.S. 232 (1921). Justice Joseph McKenna, who voted to reverse Newberry's conviction but reserved judgment on the question of the power that Congress had to regulate primary elections under the Seventeenth Amendment, cast a pivotal vote. See also Joan Biskupic and Elder Witt, *The Supreme Court and the Powers of the American Government* (Washington, D.C.: Congressional Quarterly, 1996): 156–57.

34. *Barry v. U.S.*, 279 U.S. 597 (1929).

35. In *Classic*, the commissioners of elections, who were conducting a primary election under Louisiana law held for the purpose of nominating a Democratic candidate for U.S. Congress, were criminally indicted for falsely counting and certifying the ballots of voters. *U.S. v. Classic*, 313 U.S. 299 (1941), overruling *Newberry v. U.S.*, 256 U.S. 232 (1921). See also Biskupic and Witt, *The Supreme Court*, 156 (suggesting that the majority ruling in *Newberry* was politically naive).

36. *Burroughs and Cannon v. U.S.*, 290 U.S. 534 (1934): 545.

37. Ibid, 545–47. See also ibid., 547, citing *Ex Parte Yarbrough*, 110 U.S. 651 (1884), 666–67.

38. *U.S. v. Congress of Industrial Organizations*, 335 U.S. 106 (1948): 107–24 (J. Reed, opinion for Court).

39. Ibid., 143, 145–46 (J. Rutledge, concurring in result only).

40. *U.S. v. International Union United Automobile, Aircraft, and Agricultural Implement Workers of America*, 352 U.S. 567 (1956): 77 (quoting Senator Bankhead during debate extending Hatch Act). According to Frankfurter, *CIO* did not control as precedent because the publication at issue there was only directed to the union's own membership. The message conveyed by the union in *International Union* was instead directed to the public at large. Ibid., 589. The dissent, written by Justice William O. Douglas and joined by Chief Justice Earl Warren and Justice Hugo Black, echoed Justice Rutledge's libertarian position in *CIO* that "money is speech." Ibid., 593–94 (J. Douglas, dissenting).

41. *Pipefitters Local Union No. 562 v. U.S.*, 407 U.S. 385 (1972).

42. *Barry* (1929), *Burroughs and Cannon* (1934), and *International Union* (1956) especially support Congress's power to regulate political money. Although the Court's dismissal of the indictment in *CIO* (1948) undercuts the power of the national government to control campaign finance, the limited nature of its holding and its refusal to consider the constitutionality of the Federal Corrupt Practices Act support a contrary view.

43. *Buckley v. Valeo*, 424 U.S. 1 (1976) (upholding $1,000 contribution limits by individuals and groups to candidates and authorized campaign committees), 23–25. In addition to the per curiam opinion, Chief Justice Warren Burger and Justices Byron White, Thurgood Marshall, William Rehnquist, and Harry Blackmun wrote separate partial con-

currences and dissents. See ibid., 235 (J. Burger, concurring and dissenting in part), 257 (J. White, concurring and dissenting in part), 286 (J. Marshall, concurring and dissenting in part), 290 (J. Blackmun, concurring and dissenting in part), 290 (J. Rehnquist, concurring and dissenting in part).

44. Ibid., 39–51 (striking down the $1,000 limitation on expenditures "relative to a clearly identified candidate"). See ibid., 19.

45. Ibid., 48–49.

46. The distinction is not directly applied in *Brown v. Socialist Workers '74 Campaign Committee*, 459 U.S. 87 (1982), which concerned the issue of whether a minor party must report the identity of campaign contributors or recipients of campaign expenditures to government under Ohio law. *Nixon v. Shrink Missouri Government PAC*, 120 S.Ct. 897 (2000) is not included in table 2.5 because the Lexis search predated the Court's ruling.

47. David Cole, "First Amendment Antitrust: The End of Laissez-Faire in Campaign Finance," *Yale Law and Policy Review* 9 (1991): 236–78; David Schultz, "Revisiting *Buckley v. Valeo*: Eviscerating the Line Between Candidate Contributions and Independent Expenditures," *Journal of Law and Politics* 14 (1998): 33–107; Bradley A. Smith, "Money Talks: Speech, Corruption, Equality, and Campaign Finance," *Georgetown Law Journal* 86 (1997): 45–99.

48. See, e.g., E. Joshua Rosenkranz, *Buckley Stops Here: Loosening the Judicial Stranglehold on Campaign Finance Reform* (New York: Century Foundation Press, 1998).

49. *Citizens Against Rent Control/Coalition for Fair Housing v. City of Berkeley*, 454 U.S. 290 (1981): 298 (quoting *First National Bank of Boston v. Bellotti*, 435 U.S. 765 [1978]: 790). See Cole, "First Amendment Antitrust": 249–52; L. A. Powe, "Mass Speech and the Newer First Amendment," *Supreme Court Review* 1982 (1982): 260.

50. *FEC v. National Conservative Political Action Committee*, 470 U.S. 480 (1985): 497.

51. *Austin v. Michigan State Chamber of Commerce*, 494 U.S. 652 (1990): 660. See Cole, "First Amendment Antitrust," 237, 264–71; Julian N. Eule, "Promoting Speaker Diversity: Austin and Metro Broadcasting," *Supreme Court Review* 1990 (1990): 106–17; Molly Peterson, "Reexamining Compelling Interests and Radical State Campaign Finance Reforms: So Goes the Nation?" *Hastings Constitutional Law Quarterly* 25 (1998): 431–33.

52. Law professor Bradley Smith lists seven problematic distinctions that the Court has wrestled with in its role as a judicial policeman. Smith, "Money Talks," 62 (distinguishing, for example, between spending by an ideological corporation versus spending by a nonideological one, as shown by *FEC v. Massachusetts Citizens for Life*, 479 U.S. 238 (1986).

53. *Colorado Republican Federal Campaign Committee v. FEC*, 116 S.Ct. 2309 (1996): 2316.

54. *Nixon v. Shrink Missouri Government PAC*, 120 S.Ct. 897 (2000).

55. See, e.g., Harold Leventhal, "Courts and Political Thickets," *Columbia Law Review* 77 (1977): 345–87; J. Skelly Wright, "Politics and the Constitution: Is Money Speech?" *Yale Law Journal* 85 (1976): 1001–21. See, generally, Daniel R. Ortiz, "The Reform Debate: Politics and the First Amendment," in *Campaign Finance Reform: A Sourcebook*, ed. Anthony Corrado et al. (Washington, D. C.: Brookings Institution, 1997): 95–97; Jamin B. Raskin and John C. Bonifaz, *The Wealth Primary: Campaign Fundraising and the Constitution* (Washington, D.C.: Center for Responsive Politics, 1994); Rosenkranz, *Buckley Stops Here*.

56. For a discussion of the obscenity jurisprudence after *Roth v. U.S.*, 354 U.S. 476 (1957) but before *Miller v. California*, 413 U.S. 15 (1973), see David M. O'Brien, *Constitu-*

tional Law and Politics: Civil Rights and Civil Liberties, vol. 2, 3rd ed. (New York: W. W. Norton and Company, 1997), 404–10.

57. See *Shrink* (J. Kennedy, dissenting and J. Thomas, joined by J. Scalia, dissenting; and J. Breyer, concurring). Notably, too, in *Shrink* Justice Breyer emphasized that contribution limits were constitutional because of their propensity to equalize the electoral playing field; and Justice John Paul Stevens in his concurrence asserted that "Money is property . . . [and] not speech," a distinction that runs counter to what some believe is the essence of *Buckley*, namely, that money is speech. See *Shrink* (J. Stevens, concurring).

58. *Colorado*, 2325 (J. Thomas, concurring in judgment and dissenting in part). Political scientist David Schultz states that eight different justices (Burger, Blackmun, White, Brennan, Marshall, Thomas, Ginsburg, and Stevens) have questioned the distinction since 1976. Schultz, "Revisiting *Buckley v. Valeo*," 70.

59. *Shrink* (J. Kennedy, dissenting).

60. *FEC v. Colorado Republican Federal Campaign Committee*, 41 F. Supp. 2d. 1197 (D. Colo. 1999), aff'd by 213 F.3d 1221 (10th Cir. 2000). The U.S. Supreme Court granted certiorari and will hear the oral argument on February 28, 2001. See http://www.supremecourtus.gov/calendar. For an analysis of some of the cutting-edge issues in campaign finance law that are being debated (and judicially challenged) in the states, see Peterson, "Reexamining Compelling Interests." Notably, too, the U.S. Supreme Court has summarily refused to let the City of Cincinnati impose campaign spending limits for city council elections in *Kruse v. City of Cincinnati*, 142 F.3d 907 (6th Cir. 1998), cert. denied, 119 S.Ct. 511 (1998). It also affirmed, without comment, the Sixth Circuit's ruling in *Suster v. Marshall*, 149 F.3d 523 (6th Cir. 1998), cert. denied (January 25, 1999), that spending limits are unconstitutional in judicial elections.

61. Issacharoff, Karlan, and Pildes, *The Law of Democracy*, 620.

62. Ibid., 187. See also Richard Hofstadter, *The Idea of a Party System* (Berkeley: University of California Press, 1969): 41–73.

63. James Madison, "Federalist No. 51," in *The Federalist Papers*, ed. Clinton Rossitor (New York: Mentor, 1961), 322. See ibid., "Federalist No. 10," 77–84.

64. See Michael J. Klarman, "Majoritarian Judicial Review: The Entrenchment Problem," *Georgetown Law Journal* 85 (1997): 491–553; Larry J. Sabato, *The Party's Just Begun: Shaping Political Parties for America's Future* (Glenview, Ill.: Scott, Foresman and Co., 1987): 5–25.

65. *Ex Parte Yarbrough*, 657–58. See also *Ex Parte Siebold*, 100 U.S. 371 (1879).

66. *U.S. v. Classic*, 313 U.S. 299 (1941).

67. Compare, for example, the opinion for the Court written by Justice William Brennan (supporting the First Amendment) with Justice Lewis Powell's dissent (defending patronage) in *Elrod*.

68. See Clifton McCleskey, "Parties at the Bar: Equal Protection, Freedom of Association, and the Rights of Political Organizations," *Journal of Politics* 46 (1984): 362; Glen S. Howard, "Patronage Dismissals: Constitutional Limits and Political Justifications," *University of Chicago Law Review* 41 (1974): 307.

69. *United Public Workers of America v. Mitchell*, 330 U.S. 75 (1947). See also *United States Civil Service Commission v. National Association of Letter Carriers*, 413 U.S. 548 (1973).

70. *United Public Workers of America; Elrod v. Burns*, 427 U.S. 347 (1976); *Branti v. Finkel*, 445 U.S. 507 (1980); *Rutan v. Republican Party of Illinois*, 497 U.S. 62 (1990); *Board of County Commissioners, Wabaunsee County, Kansas v. Umbehr*, 518 U.S. 668 (1996); *O'Hare Truck Service, Inc. v. City of Northlake*, 518 U.S. 712 (1996).

71. As Professor O'Brien points out, the Rehnquist Court extended the *Elrod* to *Rutan* line of rulings in the 1996 cases since a clear majority now supports adhering to *Elrod*, as the judicial philosophies of Justices Sandra Day O'Connor, Anthony Kennedy, and (perhaps) Chief Justice William Rehnquist have become more "centrist" (and less inclined to overrule controversial precedent, like *Rutan*, which extended *Elrod* and *Branti*). Only Justices Antonin Scalia and Clarence Thomas dissented in *Umbehr* and *O'Hare*. See David M. O'Brien, chapter 9 of this book.

72. See, e.g., Justice Lewis Powell's dissent in *Elrod* (1976), which acknowledged that patronage "entailed costs to governmental efficiency" (such as corruption) which led to civil service reform, the "course of [which] is of limited relevance to the task of constitutional adjudication [in *Elrod*]." See ibid., 379 (J. Powell, dissenting).

73. See, e.g., Justice Powell's dissent in *Elrod*, 376, and Justice Scalia's dissent in *Rutan*, 92.

74. *Eu v. San Francisco County Democratic Central Committee*, 489 U.S. 214 (1989): 233.

75. *McIntyre v. Ohio Elections Commission*, 514 U.S. 334 (1995): 381. For Justice White's views on *Buckley v. Valeo*, see his dissents in *Buckley* (concurring and dissenting in part), *First National Bank of Boston v. Bellotti, Citizens Against Rent Control/Coalition for Fair Housing v. City of Berkeley*, and *FEC v. National Conservative Political Action Committee*.

76. Troy L. Harris-Abbott, "Regulating Ballot Initiatives: How May a State Oversee Petition Circulators?" in *Preview of United States Supreme Court Cases, Issue No. 1* (September 25, 1998) (Chicago, Ill.: American Bar Association 1998): 22. See also *Buckley v. American Constitutional Law Foundation*, 525 U.S. 182 (1999); *Meyer v. Grant*, 486 U.S. 414 (1988).

77. *Buckley v. American Constitutional Law Foundation* (J. Ginsburg opinion for Court).

78. Harris-Abbott, "Regulating Ballot Initiatives," 23–26; *Buckley v. American Constitutional Law Foundation* (J. Rehnquist, dissenting).

79. *Buckley*, 262 (J. White, dissenting and concurring).

80. Carolyn Barta, "American Politics May Never Be the Same," *The Akron-Beacon Journal*, February 13, 1999, A10.

81. Sabato and Simpson, *Dirty Little Secrets*, 17. See also ibid., 14–17, concerning the authors' discussion of what they refer to as the "law of unintended consequences" in the context of campaign finance. Some scholars in public administration have captured a similar thought in the context of corruption reform: that is, striving to reach a "corruptfree government by means of more rules, procedures, and organizational shuffles" may contribute to the reason why government is "inefficient, wasteful, and unresponsive." See Frank Anechiarico and James B. Jacobs, *The Pursuit of Absolute Integrity: How Corruption Control Makes Government Ineffective* (Chicago: University of Chicago Press, 1996): xii.

82. Justice White made this remark in his dissent in *National Conservative Political Action Committee*, 518.

83. The assault on the judiciary by a number of reformers with different policy agendas illustrates this point well. See, for example, the discussion of campaign finance at the Web sites for the Center for Responsive Politics (http://www.opensecrets.org), the National Center for Policy Analysis (http://www.ncpa.org), Common Cause (http://www.commoncause.org), and the National Voting Rights Institute (http://www.nvri.org). For a vast array of information on campaign finance statistics, see the Web site of the Federal Elections Commission at http://www.fec.gov.

84. Alexander Hamilton, "Federalist No. 78," in *The Federalist Papers*, ed. Clinton Rossiter (New York: Mentor, 1961): 470.

Chapter 3. A Legal Strategy for Challenging
Buckley v. Valeo

1. Kevin Sack, "High Stakes and Higher Antes in Statehouse Races," *New York Times,* September 6, 1998, p. A1. See also *Buckley v. Valeo,* 424 U.S. 1 (1976); Ruth Marcus and Charles Babcock, "The System Cracks Under Weight of Cash; Candidates, Parties and Outside Interests Dropped a Record $2.7 Billion," *Washington Post,* February 9, 1997, p. A1; Don Van Natta, Jr. "Campaign Fundraising is at Record Pace," *New York Times,* October 3, 1999, p. A1.

2. Jamin Raskin and John Bonifaz, "Equal Protection and the Wealth Primary," *Yale Law and Policy Review* 11 (1993): 273, 293–97, 326–28. See also Fred Wertheimer and Susan Weiss Manes, "Campaign Finance Reform: A Key to Restoring the Health of Our American Democracy," *Columbia Law Review* 94 (1994): 1126–42; Charles Lewis and The Center for Public Integrity, *The Buying of the Congress: How Special Interests Have Stolen Your Right to Life, Liberty, and the Pursuit of Happiness* (New York: Avon, 1998); Vincent Blasi, "Free Speech and the Widening Gyre of Fund-Raising: Why Campaign Spending Limits May Not Violate the First Amendment After All," *Columbia Law Review* 94 (1994): 1281.

3. *Planned Parenthood of Southeastern Pennsylvania v. Casey,* 505 U.S. 833 (1992): 864.

4. *Nixon v. Shrink Missouri Government PAC,* 120 S. Ct. 897 (2000): 916, 913–14, 910. Notably, too, a major development emerged from Vermont in the movement to revisit *Buckley v. Valeo.* On August 10, 2000, the federal district court in Burlington, Vermont issued a decision which opened the door to a reconsideration of the constitutionality of campaign spending limits. In a ninety-page ruling upholding most of Vermont's sweeping campaign finance reform law but striking down mandatory campaign spending limits in Vermont state election, federal Judge William K. Sessions III stated clearly that the time had come to revisit *Buckley,* and he signaled that the matter should be reviewed by higher courts. The court cited the "substantial disagreement" over whether the U.S. Supreme Court in *Buckley* left open the possibility that such limits might be constitutionally justified based on governmental interests not directly addressed in *Buckley.* The disagreement includes recent statements of four sitting Supreme Court justices in the *Nixon v. Shrink Missouri Government PAC,* all of which indicate that Buckley may need to be reviewed. "Powerful, if not controlling, judicial commentary such as this," Judge Sessions stated, "reinforces the view that the constitutionality of expenditure limits bears review and reconsideration. Spending limits are an effective response to certain compelling governmental interests not addressed in *Buckley.*" See *Landell v. Sorrell,* 118 F. Supp. 2d 459 (D. Vt. 2000): 482. The defendant State of Vermont, represented by the Vermont attorney general's office, and the defendant-intervenors, represented by the National Voting Rights Institute, have appealed Judge Sessions' ruling striking down Vermont's campaign spending limits to the U. S. Court of Appeals for the Second Circuit.

5. *Breedlove v. Suttles,* 302 U.S. 277 (1937) and *Butler v. Thompson,* 341 U.S. 937 (1951) (per curiam).

6. *Harper v. Virginia Board of Elections,* 383 U.S. 663 (1966): 669.

7. *Buckley,* 7 (quoting *Buckley v. Valeo,* 519 F.2d 821 (D.C. Cir. 1975): 831.

8. *Buckley,* 424 U.S. 1, 11.

9. See "Judicial Review," 2 *United States Code* § 437h (Washington, D.C.: Government Printing Office, 2000).

10. *Buckley,* 519 F.2d 821 (D.C. Cir. 1975): 840–41.

11. Ibid, 841.

12. Justice John Paul Stevens did not participate in the *Buckley* ruling.

13. *Buckley,* 424 U.S. 1, 266.

14. See Brief in Support of Petition for Certiorari of the States of Arizona, Connecticut, Florida, Hawaii, Idaho, Indiana, Iowa, Kansas, Massachusetts, Michigan, Minnesota, Missouri, Montana, Nevada, New Hampshire, New Mexico, North Carolina, North Dakota, Ohio, Oklahoma, South Dakota, Texas, Utah, Vermont, Washington, and West Virginia as Amici Curiae in Support of Petitioners, *City of Cincinnati v. Kruse,* No. 98–454 (U.S. filed October 19, 1998); see also David Stout, "State Attorneys General Urge Limits on Campaign Spending," *New York Times,* January 28, 1997, p. A1 (noting that twenty-four state attorneys general joined statement in support of City of Cincinnati's spending limits while case was pending before United States district court). The secretaries of state or chief election officers of Arkansas, Connecticut, Georgia, Hawaii, Kentucky, Maine, Massachusetts, New Mexico, North Carolina, Oklahoma, Rhode Island, South Carolina, Tennessee, Washington, West Virginia, and Wisconsin joined the same statement.

15. See S. 1684, 98th Cong. §1 (1983); S. 1185, 98th Cong. §1 (1983); S. 59, 99th Cong. §1 (1985); H.R. 2473, 100th Cong. §1 (1987); H.R. 1456, 101st Cong. §1; H. Res. 168, 103rd Cong. §1 (1993); H.R. 3571, 103rd Cong. §1 (1993); H.R. 3651, 104th Cong. §2 (1996); H.R. 3658, 104th Cong. §2 (1996); S. 1057, 105th Cong. §1 (1997); H.R. 77, 105th Cong. §1 (1997).

16. James Bennett, "Clinton Pushes Spending Limits for Candidates," *New York Times,* June 16, 1997, p. A1.

17. See, e.g., Editorial, "Time to Rethink *Buckley v. Valeo,*" *New York Times,* November 12, 1998, p. A28. Editorial, "A Day in Court for Campaign Reform," *Boston Globe,* March 17, 1998, p. A12.

18. *Kruse v. City of Cincinnati,* 142 F.3d 907 (6th Cir. 1998), cert. denied, 119 S.Ct. 511 (1998). Notably, in *Suster v. Marshall,* 149 F.3d 523 (6th Cir. 1998), cert. denied, 525 U.S. 1114 (1999), the constitutionality of spending limits for judicial elections was considered, where twenty-two states joined an amicus brief (coauthored by the Iowa Attorney General's Office and the National Voting Rights Institute) arguing that judicial elections are distinguishable from legislative elections; or, that if *Buckley* is to be applied, the ruling should be reconsidered in light of new facts and circumstances. In July 1998, the United States Court of Appeals for the Sixth Circuit affirmed a district court judgment invalidating the judicial campaign spending limits, rejecting the argument that restrictions on judicial elections should be judged by different and more lenient standards than those applicable to elections for legislative and executive office. While the Supreme Court denied certiorari, the case raised important questions about the role of money in judicial elections and the potential need for campaign spending limits to protect the impartiality of a state judiciary. Given that the Supreme Court has yet to speak directly on this separate and distinct governmental interest, the door remains open in a jurisdiction under another federal circuit for a new test case on judicial campaign spending limits.

19. *Kruse,* 142 F.3d 907, 915–17.

20. Ibid., 920. While accepting the city's argument that *Buckley* permits proof of new facts and new compelling governmental interests that would justify campaign spending limits, Judge Cohn voted to affirm the district court's ruling, stating that the factual record was insufficient to uphold Cincinnati's limits. Judge Cohn did not explain why he

viewed the record as insufficient, and his ruling on this point appears inconsistent with the standards governing review of a grant of summary judgment. Of course, on a motion for summary judgment, a court may not weigh conflicting evidence; summary judgment is properly granted only "when there exists *no* genuine issues of material fact and the moving party is entitled to judgment as a matter of law." *Anderson v. Liberty Lobby, Inc.,* 477 U.S. 242 (1986): 248 (emphasis added). Cincinnati presented facts going directly to Judge Cohn's points concerning "the interest in freeing officeholders from the pressures of fundraising" and "the interest in preserving faith in our democracy." Having made this showing of genuine factual issues, the city should have been allowed the opportunity to go to trial to prove its case, and Judge Cohn's concurrence more logically should have been a dissent.

21. *Buckley,* 424 U.S. 1, 23–38.

22. Ibid., 27, citing *CSC v. National Association of Letter Carriers,* 413 U.S. 548 (1973): 565.

23. *Buckley,* 519 F.2d 817 (D.C. Cir. 1975): 859.

24. *Buckley,* 424 U.S. 1, 55–56.

25. District Court Record. No. 38, Deardourff Affidavit, 9–10: R. No. 38, Affidavit of Larry Mackinson, 6.

26. Public opinion survey conducted by Princeton Survey Research Associates on behalf of the Pew Research Center in conjunction with Public Broadcasting Service series, "The State of the Union" (November 1996) ("Politics, Morality, Entitlements Sap Confidence," at http://www.people-press.org/unionrpt.htm). The steady erosion of confidence in government is bolstered by numerous other polls: *The Gallup Poll: Public Opinion 1994,* (1994) (finding that 49% of the public believe Congress is more corrupt than in 1974) (see http://www.gallup.com/); Ronald G. Shafer, "Washington Wire: Fundraising Flaps Roil the Administration Even as Clinton Backs Overhaul," *Wall Street Journal,* January 31, 1997, p. A1 (citing survey results showing 68% of Americans believe politics more influenced by special interests today than twenty years ago); John R. Hibbing and Elizabeth Theiss-Morse, *Congress As Public Enemy: Public Attitudes Toward American Political Institutions* (New York: Cambridge University Press, 1995): 6–7, 31–39.

27. Public opinion poll conducted by Princeton Survey Research Associates on behalf of the Center for Responsive Politics; Center for Responsive Politics, *Money and Politics: A National Survey of the Public's View on How Money Impacts our Political System* (Washington D.C.: Center for Responsive Politics, 1997).

28. Public opinion poll commissioned by CNN/USA Today and performed by Gallup (February 1997) (reprinted in *Public Campaign, Pacs, Parties, and Potato Chips: Myths and Misconceptions About Reforming the Campaign Finance System* (Washington, D.C.: Public Campaign, 1998); and an additional 33% said contributions influenced officials a "moderate amount." See also Francis X. Clines, "Most Doubt a Resolve to Change Campaign Finance Reform, Poll Finds," *New York Times,* April 9, 1997, p. A1; Hibbing and Theiss-Morse, *Congress As Public Enemy,* 63–64 (indicating that 86% of the population believes that the government is controlled by special interests).

29. Public opinion poll commissioned by Public Campaign and conducted by The Mellman Group, Inc. (August 1998) (available at http://www.publicampaign.org/poll 9_3_98.html).

30. *Buckley,* 424 U.S. 1, 27–28, (quoting *United States Civil Service Commission. v. National Association of Letter Carriers,* 413 U.S. 548 (1973): 565). See *Buckley,* 424 U.S. 1,

55–56. See generally David Schultz, "Revisiting *Buckley v. Valeo:* Eviscerating the Line Between Candidate Contributions and Independent Expenditures," *Journal of Law and Politics* 14 (1998): 33, 93–100.

31. Marcus and Babcock; "Dawn to Dark/Chasing the Dollars: One Day on the Fundraising Trail," *Boston Globe*, May 16, 1997, p. A1, A12, quoting U.S. Senator Robert Byrd.

32. See, e.g., Wertheimer and Manes, "Campaign Finance Reform," 1126, 1140–42; Raskin and Bonifaz, "Equal Protection and the Wealth Primary," 326–27.

33. All information regarding MBNA bundling available from Center for Responsive Politics, "The Big Picture: The Money Behind the 1998 Elections" (available at http://www.opensecrets.org/pubs/bigpicture2000/).

34. *Kruse,* 142 F.3d 907, 916.

35. Center for Responsive Politics, "The Big Picture: Money Follows Power Shift in '96 Elections" (available at http://www.opensecrets.org/newsletter/ce46/ ce1115p1.html).

36. *Buckley,* 424 U.S. 1, 55 (emphasis added).

37. *Federal Election Commission v. National Conservative Political Action Committee,* 470 U.S. 480 (1985): 496–97 (emphasis added).

38. See District Court Record No. 38, Advisory Board Report at 4; District Court Record No. 38. Smith Affidavit 4: "[T]he high costs of City Council campaigns today causes our City Council members to spend too much time raising money for the next election, rather than focusing on their responsibilities on governing the city"; Record No. 38, League of Women Voters Report,1: "More time than is reasonable is spent raising money for campaigns, which may interfere with time for governing"; Blasi, "Free Speech and the Widening Gyre of Fund-Raising," 1283: "Legislators and aspirants for legislative office who devote themselves to raising money round-the-clock are not in essence representatives."

39. See Blasi, "Free Speech and the Widening Gyre of Fund-Raising," 1281: "Candidates for office spend too much time raising money. This is scarcely a controversial proposition" (citing sources on the burdens of fundraising in federal elections). See also Martin Schram, *Speaking Freely: Former Members of Congress Talk About Money in Politics* (Washington, D.C.: Center For Responsive Politics, 1995): 37–46 (former members of Congress discuss the enormous pressures of fundraising and its drain on their time for performing their official duties); Dan Clawson, Alan Neustadtl and Denise Scott, *Money Talks: Corporate PACs and Political Influence* (New York: Basic Books,1992): 7–8: "The quest for money is never ending. . . . To pay for an average winning campaign, representatives need to raise $3,700 and senators $12,000 during *every* week of their term of office" (emphasis in original); Philip M. Stern, *Still the Best Congress Money Can Buy* (Washington, D.C.: Gateway Regnery, 1992): 119 (quoting former congressman Bob Edgar, a Pennsylvania Democrat who resigned from the House to avoid another campaign fundraising cycle: "Eighty percent of my time, 80 percent of my staff's time, 80 percent of my events and meetings were fundraisers. Rather than go to a senior center, I would go to a party where I could raise $3,000 or $4,000"); *Congressional Record.* 100th Cong. 1st sess. 1987. Vol. 133, No. 1:S108. (statement of U.S. Senator Robert Byrd of West Virginia): "To raise the money, Senators start hosting fundraisers years before they next will be in an election. They all too often become fundraisers first, and legislators second."

40. *Kruse v. City of Cincinnati,* District Court Record No. 38, Affidavit of Jerry Galvin, 4–5.

41. Cincinnati, of course, would not have had the power to address the blackout phenomenon by imposing fairness requirements directly on the television stations, given the Federal Communication Commission's jurisdiction over regulation of broadcast media. See *Turner Broadcasting System, Inc. v. FCC,* 117 S.Ct. 1174 (1997): 1189.

42. *Kruse,* Appendix 31–32.

43. See Linda Greenhouse, "Justices Reject Appeals in Two Cases Involving Limits on Political Money," *New York Times,* November 17, 1998, p. A18; Edward Felsenthal, "High Court Demurs on Campaign Funds," *Wall Street Journal,* November 17, 1998, p. B12.

44. *Nixon v. Shrink Missouri Government PAC,* 120 S. Ct. 897 (2000): 910, 913–14, 916.

45. Vermont Statutes Annotated. 17, §2805a (effective November 4, 1998). See also *Landell v. Sorrell,* 188 F. Supp. 2d 459 (D. Vt. 2000) and accompanying discussion in note 4 of this chapter.

46. Dana Milbank, "Renewed Battle Brewing on Campaign Spending Caps," *Wall Street Journal,* March 24, 1998; Robert Zausner, "Campaign Spending Limit? In Albuquerque, It's Old Hat," *Philadelphia Inquirer,* October 23, 1998. See Albuquerque, New Mexico, Charter, art. XIII, § 4; *Murphy v. City of Albuquerque,* No. CV-97-7826 (Second Judicial District of New Mexico).

47. *Austin v. Michigan State Chamber of Commerce,* 494 U.S. 652 (1990): 660.

48. See, e.g., C. Lewis and the Center for Public Integrity, *The Buying of Congress;* see also Center for Responsive Politics, Influence Inc.: *Lobbyist Spending in Washington* (1998); "Congressional Committee Profiles", a searchable database maintained by the Center for Responsive Politics available at http://www.opensecrets.org/cmteprofiles/index.asp.

49. *Buckley,* 424 U.S. 1, 48–49. David A. Strauss, "Corruption, Equality, and Campaign Finance Reform," *Columbia Law Review* 94 (1994): 1369, 1383; J. Skelly Wright, "Money and the Pollution of Politics: Is the First Amendment an Obstacle to Political Equality?" *Columbia Law Review* 82 (1982): 609, 625. See also Alexander Meiklejohn, *Free Speech and Its Relation to Self-Government* (New York: Harper, 1948): 10–11; John Rawls, *A Theory of Justice* (Cambridge, Mass.: Belknap Press, 1971): 11–19, 205–7, 221–28; Thomas Scanlon, "A Theory of Freedom of Expression," *Philosophy and Public Affairs* 1 (1972): 204, 214; Alexis de Tocqueville, *Democracy in America,* eds. J. P. Mayer and M. Lerner (New York: Harper and Row, 1966): 59, 474.

50. James Madison, *The Papers of James Madison,* ed. R. A. Rutland, vol. 14 (Charlottesville, Va.: University Press of Virginia, 1983): 197; James Madison, "Federalist No. 57" in *The Federalist,* ed. Jacob E. Cooke (Middletown, Conn.: Wesleyan University Press, 1961): 305.

51. Madison, "Federalist No. 57," 385.

52. Rawls, *A Theory of Justice,* 221–28. Rawls' conclusion is particularly chilling when compared to the Court's own observation that "[o]ther rights, even the most basic, are illusory if the right to vote is undermined." See *Wesberry v. Sanders,* 376 U.S. 1 (1964): 17.

53. Evidence of popular sentiment is found in E. J. Dionne, "Democracy or Plutocracy?" *Washington Post,* op-ed, February 15, 1994, p. A17; Tom Fiedler, "Big Interests Spending Equally Big Bucks: Millions of Dollars Given to Campaigns of Influential Policy Makers," *Miami Herald,* May 21, 1995, p. 14A; Philip B. Heyman and Donald J. Simon, "Parties to Corruption," *Washington Post,* op-ed, June 25, 1998, p. A23; Albert R. Hunt, "The Best Congress Money Can Buy," *Wall Street Journal,* September 7, 1995, p. A15; Celinda Lake and Steve Cobble, "Voters Say Take 'Big Money' Out of Campaigns," *Milwaukee Journal Sentinel,* op-ed, April 16, 1995, p. 4A; Rodney A. Smith, "White House Auc-

tion," *Washington Post,* op-ed, April 14, 1995, p. A19; Howard Wilkinson, "No Campaign Money? Keep Your Mouth Shut About It," *Cincinnati Enquirer,* editorial, November 22, 1998, p. C1; "Political Scandal," *Boston Globe,* editorial, October 31, 1996, p. A26; "Time to Rethink *Buckley v. Valeo,"* *New York Times,* editorial, November 12, 1998, p. A22; "Unlimited Cash, Undue Influence," *St. Louis Post-Dispatch,* editorial, July 27, 1998, p. B6. The businessman's testimony is referred to in Edward Walsh, "Tamraz Defends Political Gifts for Clinton Access," *Washington Post,* September 19, 1997, p. A01. Research suggesting the effect of institutionalized influence peddling can be found in C. Lewis and the Center for Public Integrity, *The Buying of the Congress.*

54. See, e.g., *Kovacs v. Cooper,* 336 U.S. 77 (1949); *Cox v. Louisiana,* 379 U.S. 559 (1965); *City Council of Los Angeles v. Taxpayers for Vincent,* 466 U.S. 789 (1984); *Clark v. Community for Creative Non-Violence,* 466 U.S. 789 (1984); *City of Renton v. Playtime Theatres, Inc.,* 475 U.S. 41 (1986); *Ward v. Rock Against Racism,* 491 U.S. 781 (1989); *Barnes v. Glen Theatre,* Inc., 501 U.S. 560 (1991).

55. Ronald Dworkin, "The Curse of American Politics," *New York Review of Books,* October 16, 1996, pp. 19, 22, 23; John Rawls, *Political Liberalism* (New York: Columbia University Press, 1993): 356–63; Meiklejohn, *Free Speech and Its Relation to Self-Government,* 23.

56. Justice Stephen Breyer's remarks during oral argument are found in "Transcript of oral argument before the U.S. Supreme Court on October 5, 1999, in *Nixon v. Shrink Missouri Government PAC,* as prepared by Alderson Reporting Company, Inc.," 43–95 (on file with authors). See also *Nixon v. Shrink Missouri Government PAC,* 120 S. Ct. 897 (2000): 911–12 (J. Breyer, concurring); and, *Reynolds v. Sims,* 377 U.S. 533 (1964): 565.

57. *Nixon v. Shrink Missouri Government PAC,* 912.

58. *First National Bank of Boston v. Bellotti,* 435 U.S. 765 (1978): 803–812 (J. White, dissenting). See also ibid., 825–27 (J. Rehnquist, dissenting).

59. Daniel H. Lowenstein, "A Patternless Mosaic: Campaign Finance and the First Amendment after *Austin,"* *Capital University Law Review* 21 (1992): 381, 393. See *FEC v. Massachusetts Citizens for Life (MCFL),* 479 U.S. 238 (1986): 257–58; *Austin v. Michigan State Chamber of Commerce,* 494 U.S. 652 (1990): 659. *New York Times Company v. Sullivan,* 376 U.S. 254 (1964): 266, 269, quoting *Associated Press v. United States,* 326 U.S. 1 (1945): 20; and *Roth v. United States,* 354 U.S. 476 (1957): 484.

60. 383 U.S. 663 (1966).

61. *Bullock v. Carter,* 405 U.S. 134 (1972): 143.

62. See ibid., 144.

63. *Lubin v. Panish,* 415 U.S. 709 (1974): 717–18. Notably, in *M.L.B. v. S.L.J.,* 519 U.S. 102 (1996), the Court reaffirmed its landmark holdings in *Bullock, Lubin,* and *Harper* by stating "[t]he basic right to participate in political processes as voters and candidates cannot be limited to those who can pay for a license" (*M.L.B.,* 568, citing *Bullock, Lubin,* and *Harper*).

64. The red-baiting suggestion is found in Lillian R. BeVier, "Campaign Finance Reform: Specious Arguments, Intractable Dilemmas," *Columbia Law Review* 94 (1994): 1266 (emphasis in original). Commentators that make the *Lochner* comparison include John Rawls, *Political Liberalism,* 362–63; David A. J. Richards, *Toleration and the Constitution* (New York: Oxford University Press, 1986): 219; and, Cass R. Sunstein, *Democracy and the Problem of Free Speech* (New York Free Press, 1993): 97–98. See *Lochner v. New York,* 198 U.S. 45 (1905). Defenders of the plutocratic electoral system include BeVier, "Campaign

Finance Reform,"1258, 1262–66 (rejecting Professor Sunstein's imputation of state action in creating and preserving existing distributions of wealth); and, Bradley A. Smith, "Faulty Assumptions and Undemocratic Consequences of Campaign Finance Reform," *Yale Law Journal* 105 (1994): 1049.

65. The Court's holdings reveal a willingness to limit speech rights in favor of less crucial interests. See, e.g., *Members of the City Council of Los Angeles v. Taxpayers for Vincent*, 466 U.S. 789 (1984) (ban on signs on public property); *Metromedia, Inc., v. City of San Diego*, 453 U.S. 490 (1981) (ban on billboards); *Clark v. Community for Creative Non-Violence*, 468 U.S. 288 (1984) (upholding National Park Service anticamping regulation applied to demonstrators seeking to sleep in Lafayette Park and the Mall, "the American analogue to 'Speaker's Corner' in Hyde Park," despite acknowledgement that demonstration would contain "expressive activity" that would "enhance the message concerning the plight of the poor and homeless"). See also Lowenstein, "A Patternless Mosaic."

66. 424 U.S. 1, 21. See, generally, J. Skelly Wright, "Politics and the Constitution: Is Money Speech?" *Yale Law Journal* 85 (1976): 1001.

67. *United States v. O'Brien*, 391 U.S. 367 (1968). The *Buckley* Court rejected an *O'Brien* analysis of campaign finance reform extremely cursorily. By mistaking "suppressing communication" for suppressing a particular message, the Court ignored the fact that spending limits cap, but do not preclude, communication, as well as the fact that more campaign spending does not necessarily lead to more communication.

68. *Buckley*, 424 U.S. 1, 19. See also ibid., 18.

69. Wright, "Politics and the Constitution," 1004. See Dworkin, "The Curse of American Politics," 22.

70. Wright, "Politics and the Constitution," 1010–11, n. 41. See also *Buckley*, 424 U.S. 1, 18; *Kovacs v. Cooper*, 336 U.S. 77 (1949).

71. In her dissent in *Turner Broadcasting*, Justice O'Connor appears to acknowledge that the critical issue in the analysis of the First Amendment value of televised communication is viewership: "[w]hether cable poses a 'significant' threat to a local broadcast market . . . depends on whether viewers actually watch the stations that are dropped or denied carriage." *Turner Broadcasting System, Inc. v. Federal Communications Commission*, 520 U.S. 180 (1997) (J. O'Connor, dissenting). Analogously, whether wealthy candidates pose a significant threat to poor candidates depends on whether viewers actually watch the programming alongside which poorer candidates can afford to advertise.

72. *Red Lion Broadcasting Co. v. Federal Communications Commission*, 395 U.S. 367 (1969): 387–90. See also *National Broadcasting Company v. United States*, 319 U.S. 190 (1943): 227.

73. *Buckley*, 424 U.S. 1, 49, n. 55.

74. *Turner Broadcasting System, Inc. v. Federal Communications Commission*, 117 S. Ct. 1174 (J. O'Connor, dissenting). See ibid, (1997): 1189. (upholding the "must-carry" provisions of the Cable Television Consumer Protection and Competition Act of 1992: "Congress has an independent interest in preserving a multiplicity of broadcasters to ensure that all households have access to information and entertainment on an equal footing with those who subscribe to cable"). Cincinnati, of course, would not have the power to address this phenomenon by imposing "fairness" requirements directly on the television stations, given the Federal Communications Commission's jurisdiction over regulation of broadcast media.

75. *Nixon v. Shrink Missouri Government PAC*, 120 S. Ct. 897 (2000).

76. *Buckley,* 424 U.S. 1, 19 n. 18.
77. *First National Bank of Boston v. Bellotti,* 789.

Chapter 4. Dollars and Sense

1. *Buckley v. Valeo,* 424 U.S. 1 (1976).
2. Cass R. Sunstein, "Exchange; Speech in the Welfare State: Free Speech Now," *University of Chicago Law Review* 59 (1992): 255, 291; Owen M. Fiss, "Free Speech and Social Structure," *Iowa Law Review* 75 (1986): 1405. Although *Buckley* often is compared with the "discredited" *Lochner* doctrine, the decision is not without its defenders. See Lillian R. BeVier, "Campaign Finance Reform: Specious Arguments, Intractable Dilemmas," *Columbia Law Review* 94 (1994):1258; Kathleen M. Sullivan, "Political Money and Freedom of Speech," *University of California Davis Law Review* 30 (1997): 663; Bradley Smith, "Faulty Assumptions and Undemocratic Consequences of Campaign Finance Reform," *Yale Law Journal* 105 (1996): 1049, 1056. See *Lochner v. New York,* 198 U.S. 45 (1905).
3. *McIntyre v. Ohio Elections Commission,* 514 U.S. 334 (1995): 346
4. Ibid. at 346–347, quoting *Buckley v. Valeo,* 424 U.S. 1 (1976): 14–15 (citations omitted).
5. See *McIntyre,* 380, and cases cited therein.
6. See *United States v. National Committee for Impeachment,* 469 F.2d 1135 (2d Cir. 1972); see generally, Federal Election Campaign Act of 1971, 2 U.S.C. Section 431, et seq.
7. See, e.g. *Brandenburg v. Ohio,* 395 U.S. 444 (1969); *New York Times Co. v. United States,* 403 U.S. 713 (1971); *New York Times Co. v. Sullivan,* 376 U.S. 254 (1964); *Mills v. Alabama,* 384 U.S. 214 (1966); *Cohen v. California,* 403 U.S. 15 (1971).
8. The Federal Election Campaign Act of 1971, 2 U.S.C. 431, et. seq. Most of the more sweeping provisions that would be at issue in *Buckley* were passed three years later as the Federal Election Campaign Act Amendments of 1974.
9. See *United States v. National Committee for Impeachment,* 1142. That separate provision, operating directly on the press, but restraining both the press and the independent speakers, was directly challenged and found facially unconstitutional in *American Civil Liberties Union v. Jennings,* 366 F. Supp. 1041 (D.D.C. 1975) (three-judge court); and was vacated as moot, *Staats v. American Civil Liberties Union,* 422 U.S. 1030 (1975).
10. The McCain-Feingold bill is found in U.S. Congress. Senate. "Bipartisan Campaign Finance Reform Act of 1999." S. 26, 106th Cong. 1st sess., January 19, 1999. The bill would make two major changes in the law. First, it would outlaw soft money activity by national political parties. "Soft money" refers to contributions made not to candidates or their campaigns, but to political parties for general party activity not directly related to any candidate's campaign. Since the contributions do not underwrite specific campaigns, they can come from sources (like corporations and unions) and in amounts (more than $1,000) that would otherwise be prohibited. Currently, soft money is allowed. Second, the bill would severely restrain issue advocacy by any groups or individuals that mentions politicians and incumbents who are up for election within sixty days of the election. It would essentially force those groups to become partisan political organizations in order to comment on issues affecting politicians. Today, such issue advocacy, so long as it does not explicitly advocate the election or defeat of identified candidates, is wholly protected by the First Amendment from any government regulation. Although the bill exempts print media messages, it otherwise would reach precisely the kind of message contained in the impeachment ad case.

11. See *United States v. National Committee for Impeachment; American Civil Liberties Union v. Jennings.* The validity of the "major purpose" test as a constitutionally required or statutorily based limiting gloss on the applicability of the federal election campaign laws to nonpartisan groups was before the Court more recently in *Akins v. FEC*, 524 U.S. 11 (1998), but the Court did not decide the issue.

12. *Garrison v. Louisiana*, 379 U.S. 64 (1964): 74–75.

13. That law, the Federal Election Campaign Act of 1971, Public Law 92–255, 2 U.S.C. Sections 431, et. seq., was amended by the Federal Election Campaign Act Amendments of 1974, Public Law 93–443.

14. See Cass R. Sunstein, "Political Equality and Unintended Consequences," *Columbia Law Review* 94 (1994): 1390.

15. The act required covered political committees and organizations to disclose the names and addresses of all individuals who contributed more than $100 and to keep on file the names and addresses of all individuals who contributed as little as $11.

16. Although sustaining the disclosure provisions on their face, the *Buckley* Court indicated that where controversial political parties or groups could make a credible showing that disclosure would lead to harassment and disruption, they might be constitutionally immune from compliance with campaign reporting and disclosure rules. *Buckley*, 74. That principle would be applied six years later to hold that campaign committees formed by parties like the Socialist Workers' Party would be immune from effective disclosure. See *Brown v. Socialist Workers '74 Campaign Committee*, 459 U.S. 87 (1982).

17. That section was Section 437a of the Act, 2 U.S.C. 437a. Its rather clumsy language provided as follows:

> Any person (other than an individual) who expends any funds or commits any act directed to the public for the purpose of influencing the outcome of an election, or who publishes or broadcasts to the public any material referring to a candidate (by name, description, or other reference) advocating the election or defeat of such candidate, setting forth the candidate's position on any public issue, his voting record, or other official acts (in the case of a candidate who holds or has held Federal office), or otherwise designed to influence individuals to cast their votes for or against such candidate or to withhold their votes from such candidate shall file reports with the Commission as if such person were a political committee.

18. *Buckley v. Valeo*, 519 F.2d 821 (D.C. Cir. 1976) (en banc): 843–44.

19. Various bills like McCain-Feingold or Shays-Meehan seek to regulate issue advocacy in language virtually indistinguishable from Section 437a, which was roundly and conclusively condemned as unconstitutional in *Buckley*. They are virtually reincarnations of that flawed and condemned provision. As one commentator put it:

> Section 437a has the distinction of being the only section of the post-Watergate reforms struck down by what, at the time, was the most liberal pro-campaign finance regulation court in the country. Even to that naturally sympathetic court, Section 437a was beyond the constitutional pale. In fact, the section was so indefensible that its overturning was not appealed to the Supreme Court by any of its defenders, including the Department of Justice, the FEC, or their allied reform groups (including Common Cause). Even though the question was not presented directly, the Supreme Court's 1976 decision in *Buckley* . . . firmly enunciated the principles that led the D.C. Circuit to strike down Section 437a. Accordingly, the Supreme Court set forth in *Buckley* the holding, which is valid to this day, that only speech expressly advocating the election or defeat of clearly identified candidates may be subject-

ed to certain forms of regulation, including compulsory disclosure to the government. That court ruling calls into severe question many of the proposals today to control issue group spending and thereby speaking.

Jan Witold Baran, "The Reform That Cannot and Should Not Ever Happen," *Legal Times,* February 23, 1998, S.36.

20. *Buckley v. Valeo,* 39; quoting from Williams v. Rhodes, 393 U.S. 23 (1968) (emphasis added): 32.

21. Nancy Gibbs, "The Wake-Up Call: Clinton Makes Serious Noises About Campaign Reform, But That May Not Be Enough to Change a Cozy System That Loves Special-Interest Money," *Time,* February 3, 1997, p. 22.

22. For a particularly powerful and relatively contemporary salute to the wisdom of the *Buckley* decision, see L. A. Powe, "Mass Speech and the Newer First Amendment," *Supreme Court Review* 1982 (1982): 243.

23. An irony of the campaign finance reform debate is that those who attack the Court for "equating" money with speech do not hesitate to use (their own) often unlimited resources to argue that money is not speech. See Dierdre Shesgreen, "But Proliferation of Groups Doesn't Spur Progress in Curbing Political Cash," *Legal Times,* October 20, 1997, p. 1; Greg Pierce, "A Double Standard," *Washington Times,* June 18, 1997, p. A10; Ruth Marcus, "The Advocates Pipe Down the Ads," *Washington Post,* October 23, 1998, p. A10; Ira Glasser, "Campaign Reform Limits Speech," *New York Times,* September 9, 1998, p. A24.

24. The cases before *Buckley* include *New York Times Co. v. Sullivan,* 376 U.S. 254 (1964) (the fact that political advertisement is paid for does not justify depriving it of First Amendment protection); *Bigelow v. Virginia,* 421 U.S. 809 (1975) (the fact that abortion services advertisement is paid for does not justifying withdrawing First Amendment protection). Since *Buckley,* the Court has applied its principle numerous times to invalidate statutes and rules, which attempted to restrain speech by restraining the funding of that speech. See, e.g., *Buckley v. American Constitutional Law Foundation,* 119 S. Ct. 636 (1999) (invalidating rule that paid collectors of petition-signature had to disclose sources of funding); *United States v. National Treasury Employees Union,* 513 U.S. 454 (1995) (invalidating rule that federal employees could not be paid honorariums for giving speeches or writing articles while off duty); *Simon and Schuster, Inc. v. Members of New York State Crime Victims Board,* 502 U.S. 105 (1991) (invalidating rule that prevented criminal from receiving money for writing or speaking about his or her crime); *Meyer v. Grant,* 486 U.S. 414 (1988) (invalidating rule that prohibited paying people to circulate petitions to get signatures to put a voter initiative on the ballot).

25. In the more complex area of government efforts to control the speech uses of public funds, the Court has also recognized the important link between money and speech, but has been far too willing to let the government use its power of the purse to control the speech of those it patronizes. The issues were addressed most prominently by the Court in *National Endowment for the Arts v. Finley,* 524 U.S. 569 (1998), which upheld certain vague government restraints on governmentally funded art subsidized by the National Endowment for the Arts.

26. The quotations in the next few paragraphs can be found in *Buckley v. Valeo,* 424 U.S.1, 57; ibid., 48–49 (emphasis added), 14, 42, 45 (emphasis added).

27. Ibid., 14, 35, 27.

28. *National Black Police Association v. District of Columbia Board of Election and Ethics,*

924 F. Supp. 270 (D.D.C. 1996); *California Profile Council PAC v. Scully*, 989 F. Supp. 1282 (N.D. Cal. 1998), on appeal, 164 F.3d. 1189 (9th Cir. 1999). But see *Kentucky Right to Life, Inc. v. Terry*, 108 F.3d 637 (6th Cir. 1997), 645–51.

29. See *Shrink Missouri Government PAC v. Adams*, 161 F.3d 519 (8th Cir. 1998), reversed by *Nixon v. Shrink Missouri Government PAC*, 120 S. Ct. 897 (2000).

30. Often overlooked in the *Buckley* debate is that the Court also upheld the Act's sweeping and overbroad disclosure requirements. The Court, though acknowledging that compelled disclosure can substantially interfere with freedom of association, sustained the wide-sweeping disclosure that invades an extremely broad area of political privacy without any sufficient justification. The Court felt that the low disclosure levels were reasonable attempts to detect patterns of giving and to discourage violations of the contribution limits. Though the Court did show some sensitivity to the plight of controversial minor parties, which would lead to a later ruling that such groups did not have to disclose their contributors and supporters (see *Brown v. Socialist Workers '74 Campaign Committee*, 459 U.S. 87 [1982]), the Court nonetheless upheld the facial validity of the disclosure rules.

31. 120 S. Ct. 897 (2000), reversing *Shrink Missouri Government PAC v. Adams*, 161 F. 3d 519 (8th Cir. 1998).

32. *Buckley v. Valeo*, 424 U.S. 1, 99. The ruling prompted Justice Rehnquist to remark that the funding disparities enshrined the Republican and Democratic parties in a permanently preferred position. Ibid. at 293.

33. Kathleen M. Sullivan, "Reply: Political Money and Freedom of Speech: A Reply to Frank Askin," *University of California Davis Law Review* 31 (1998): 1083; *Gable v. Patton*, 142 F.3d 940 (6th Cir. 1998) (upholding triggered public funding).

34. Michael Janofsky, "Gore Building Network in California," *New York Times*, February 23, 1999, sec. 1, p. 24. See also Bernard Weinraub, "Hollywood Raises Curtain on 2000," *New York Times*, February 20, 1999 (noting that both Democratic and Republican Presidential hopefuls "troop in almost every week to gather support from the rich and super-rich" among the Hollywood and entertainment industry moguls). Compare the remark in *Buckley* that public financing of presidential elections would be "a means of eliminating the improper influence of large private contributions . . ." (424 U.S. 1, 96).

35. Some scholars even think that controls on wealthy media owners or other speakers in the service of campaign finance reform and equalization would justify restraints. See Richard Hasen, "Campaign Finance Laws and the Rupert Murdoch Problem," *Texas Law Review* 77 (1999): 1627 (arguing that it would be permissible to cover media under campaign finance laws, especially if the theme of equality of political opportunity rejected in *Buckley* were adopted by the Court); Richard L. Hasen, "Clipping Coupons for Democracy: An Egalitarian/Public Choice Defense of Campaign Finance Vouchers," *California Law Review* 84 (1996): 1; Scott E. Thomas, "Corporate Funds' Use in Campaign Banned," editorial, *Wall Street Journal*, March 12, 1999, p. A15 (letter to *Wall Street Journal* from Scott Thomas, commissioner of the Federal Election Commission, justifying the proceeding [later dropped] against Steve Forbes for that portion of his monthly magazine column deemed partisan and not issue oriented).

36. George Santayana, *The Life of Reason*, vol. I, *Reason in Common Sense*, quoted in *Bartlett's Familiar Quotations* (1982): 703.

37. U.S. Congress. Senate. "Bipartisan Campaign Finance Reform Act of 1999." S. 26, 106th Cong. 1st sess., January 19, 1999. The Shays-Meehan parallel bill in the House is

U.S. Congress. House. "bipartisan Campaign Finance Reform Act of 1999." H. R. 417, 106th Cong. 1st sess., January 19, 1999.

38. The quotations in the next few paragraphs are from *Buckley*, 424 U.S. 1, 14, 42, and 44.

39. Ibid., 45 (emphasis added). For almost twenty-five years, the Federal Election Commission has repeatedly attempted to expand the concept of express advocacy well beyond what the courts have permitted. And the courts have consistently rebuffed the commission in cases ranging from *Federal Election Commission v. Central Long Island Tax Reform Immediately Committee*, 616 F.2d 45 (2d Cir. 1980) (enbanc) to *Right to Life of Dutchess County v. Federal Election Committee*, 6 F. Supp. 2d. 248 (S.D.N.Y. 1998). In one case, the Fourth Circuit even awarded costs and attorneys' fees to an organization harassed by the commission for what was clearly and purely issue speech. See *Federal Election Commission v. Christian Action Network, Inc.*, 110 F.3d 1049 (4th Cir. 1997).

40. As the Court said a decade before *Buckley* in *Mills v. Alabama*, 384 U.S. 214 (1966): 220 ("No test of reasonableness can save a state statute from invalidation as a violation of the First Amendment if that law makes it a crime for a newspaper editor to do no more than urge people to vote one way or another in a publicly held election").

41. *Monitor Patriot Co. v. Roy*, 401 U.S. 265 (1971): 272.

42. U.S. Congress. Senate. "Bipartisan Campaign Finance Reform Act of 1999." S. 26., 101(B)(2).

43. Richard Briffault, "Campaign Finance, The Parties and the Court: A Comment on *Colorado Republican Federal Campaign Committee v. Federal Election Commission*," *Constitutional Commentary* 14 (1997): 91: Bradley Smith, "The Current Debate Over Soft Money: Soft Money, Hard Realities, The Constitutional Prohibition on a Soft Money Ban," *Journal of Legislation* 24 (1998): 179.

44. The dismissed FEC enforcement action against Steve Forbes for writing his monthly column in his magazine seems to have gotten the attention of the editorial board of the *New York Times*, which, despite their persistent support for analytically indistinguishable controls on issue advocacy in campaign finance reform legislation, condemned the FEC action as violative of the First Amendment. "The Election Commission Goes Astray," *New York Times*, September 3, 1998, p. A30; "U.S. Decides that Columns By Forbes Were Not Gifts," *New York Times*, February 19, 1999, p. A17.

45. "Stirrings on Campaign Finance," *Washington Post*, March 19, 1999, p. A28; "Time to Reform Campaign Reforms," *Chicago Tribune*, March 7, 1999, p. 20; Paul Merrion, "Biz Backs Bid to Curb Soft Money: A New Corporate-Led Bid for Campaign Reform," *Crain's Chicago Business*, April 5, 1999, p. 3.

46. In this regard, the Court's decision in *Timmons v. Twin Cities Area New Party*, 520 U.S. 351 (1997), which allowed broad government regulation of political third-party choices regarding the fusion tickets, was a disappointment, as was the Court's decision allowing public broadcasting stations broad discretion to exclude a "non-serious" congressional candidate from publicly sponsored televised candidate debates. See *Arkansas Educational Television Commission v. Forbes*, 118 U.S. 1633 (1998); Joel M. Gora, "Finley, Forbes, and the First Amendment: Does He Who Pays the Piper Call the Tune," *Touro Law Review* 15 (1999): 965.

47. Jonathan Rauch, "Give Pols Free Money, No Rules," *U.S. News and World Report*, December 29, 1997/January 5, 1998.

48. For a strong argument against the constitutionality of requiring broadcasters to

provide free time for politicians, see Lillian R. BeVier, *Is Free TV For Federal Candidates Constitutional?* (Washington, D.C.: American Enterprise Institute, 1998).

Chapter 5. The Role of Disclosure in Campaign Finance Reform

1. See, e.g., H.R. 965, 105th Cong., 1st sess. 1997 (the Doolittle bill); H.R. 3582, 105th Cong., 2nd sess., 1998 (the revised Shays-Meehan bill). See generally 144 Cong. Rec., (daily ed., March 30, 1998) at H1756 (debate on Campaign Reporting and Disclosure Act of 1998). Campaign finance experts favoring a deregulation approach nonetheless favor disclosure. See, e.g., Larry J. Sabato and Glenn R. Simpson, *Dirty Little Secrets: The Persistence of Corruption in American Politics* (New York: Random House, 1996): 230. So do proregulation reformers. See e.g., Center for Responsive Politics, *Plugging In the Public: A Model for Campaign Finance Disclosure* (Washington, D. C.: Center for Responsive Politics, 1996).

2. 424 U.S. 1 (1976).

3. 514 U.S. 334 (1995).

4. 424 U.S. 1 (1976).

5. Federal Election Campaign Act of 1971, 86 Stat. 3, as amended by the Federal Election Campaign Act of 1974, 88 Stat. 1263.

6. 2 U.S.C. §434(e) (1974).

7. 290 U.S. 534 (1934).

8. 43 Stat. 1070.

9. 290 U.S. 534.

10. 357 U.S. 449 (1958).

11. *Buckley v. Valeo,* 424 U.S. 1 (1976): 64.

12. Ibid., 66–67.

13. Ibid., 66.

14. *NAACP v. Alabama,* 357 U.S. 449 (1958): 462, 464.

15. In a footnote, the Court suggested that mere unwillingness of potential donors to give because their names would be disclosed was not sufficient. *Buckley,* 424 U.S. 1 n. 88.

16. *Brown v. Socialist Workers '74 Campaign Committee,* 459 U.S. 87 (1982): 96, 99–100. See also *Buckley v. American Constitutional Law Foundation,* 119 S. Ct. 636 (1999).

17. *Federal Election Commission v. Massachusetts Citizens for Life,* 479 U.S. 238 (1986): 254. See ibid., 238 n. 7.

18. Ibid., at 255. Notably, in *Republican National Committee v. FEC,* 76 F.3d 400 (D.C. Cir. 1996), the Republican National Committee (RNC) challenged the FEC's disclosure regulations regarding the duty of political committees to make "best efforts" to collect disclosure information from contributors. The D.C. Circuit rejected the RNC's assertion that this requirement imposed such large administrative burdens and costs that it constituted an unconstitutionally severe restriction on First Amendment rights, noting in particular the proportionally small financial burden imposed by the regulation.

19. *Buckley,* 424 U.S. 1, 82. The disclosure threshold under FECA for individual contributions is $200. 2 U.S.C. 434(b)(3).

20. *Buckley,* 424 U.S. 1, 79.

21. Ibid., 80 n.52.

22. See, generally, *House Committee on the Judiciary, Hearings on the First Amendment*

and Restrictions on Issue Advocacy before the Subcommittee on the Constitution of the House Comm. on the Judiciary, 105th Cong., 1st sess., September 19, 1997.

23. In *MCFL,* the Court found the communications in question constituted "express advocacy." In a number of other cases involving issue advocacy, the Court has declined certiorari review of lower court decisions raising the issue. In *Colorado Republican Federal Campaign Committee v. Federal Election Commission,* 116 S.Ct. 2309 (1996), a case that centered on the question of whether the Colorado Republican Party's political advertising at issue was "express advocacy," the Court vacated the 10th Circuit's decision (which found express advocacy) but never addressed the issue itself in the case.

24. 2 U.S.C §437a (1974) (emphasis added).

25. *Buckley v. Valeo,* 519 F.2d 821 (D.C. Cir. 1975): 873 (emphasis added).

26. *North Carolina Right to Life Inc. v. Bartlett,* 3 F. Supp. 2d 675 (E.D. N.C. 1998): 679–80.

27. *West Virginians for Life, Inc. v. Smith,* 919 F. Supp. 954 (S.D. W.Va. 1996): 959 (granting preliminary injunction); ibid., 952 F. Supp. 342, 348 (awarding fees and costs); ibid., 960 F. Supp. 1036, 1039–40 (decision on summary judgment motion). But see *Buckley,* 424 U.S. 1, 79 (Court did not hold that issue advocacy can never be subject to disclosure provisions, but rather that the statute in question was unconstitutionally vague *as drafted*).

28. *FEC v. Survival Education Fund, Inc.,* 65 F.3d 285 (1995): 288.

29. Ibid., 295.

30. Ibid., 293, 297.

31. *Elections Board v. Wisconsin Mfrs. & Commerce,* No. 97-CV-1729 (Wisc. Cir. Ct., Dane Cty., Jan. 16, 1997). See also "Memorandum from George A. Dunst to Election Board members, Mar. 13, 1997" (staff analysis of advertisements) (Exh. B., Resp. Br., *Elections Bd. v. Wisconsin Mfrs. & Commerce,* No. 98-0596 (Wisc. Ct. App. Dist. IV)).

32. *First National Bank of Boston v. Bellotti,* 435 U.S. 765 (1978): 792 n. 3.

33. *Citizens Against Rent Control/Coalition for Fair Housing v. City of Berkeley,* 454 U.S. 290 (1981): 298, 298 n. 4. See also FCC sponsor identification rules, 47 C.F.R. 73.1212(e).

34. *McIntyre v. Ohio Elections Commission,* 514 U.S. 334 (1995): 346–47.

35 Ibid., 348.

36. Ibid., 349, 352. *McIntyre* did not explicitly address whether its analysis extended to contributions. *Citizens Against Rent Control/Coalition for Fair Housing* indicated in dicta that legislatures are capable of enacting a ban on anonymous contributions. See *Citizens Against Rent Control/Coalition for Fair Housing,* 300.

37. *Buckley v. American Constitutional Law Foundation,* 119 S. Ct. 636 (1999). The Court also reviewed a nondisclosure provision of the statute requiring that all petition circulators be registered Colorado voters. The six-justice majority struck down the registration requirement on free speech grounds, with Chief Justice Rehnquist and Justices O'Connor and Breyer dissenting. Ibid., 644–45. In addition, a portion of the Colorado statute unchallenged by the petitioners in *American Constitutional Law Foundation* requires persons or groups filing initiative petitioners to register with the state, and report the amount they spend to qualify the initiative for the ballot.

38. *Buckley v. American Constitutional Law Foundation,* 646.

39. Ibid., Justices David Souter, Anthony Kennedy, John Paul Stevens, and Antonin Scalia. Justice Clarence Thomas concurred in the holding but not the reasoning of the disclosure decision.

40. Ibid., 647–49.

41. Ibid., 649.

42. *Buckley v. American Constitutional Law Foundation,* 656 (J. O'Connor, concurring). See ibid., 658.

43. *McIntyre,* 334 n. 3.

44. *Vermont Right to Life Committee, Inc. v. Sorrell,* 19 F. Supp. 2d 204 (D. Vt. 1998): 208, 213.

45. *KVUE, Inc. v. Moore,* 709 F.2d 922 (1983): 926, 937. See also *Anderson v. Celebrezze,* 460 U.S. 780 (1983); *Storer v. Brown,* 415 U.S. 724 (1974).

46. For an excellent discussion about the legislative history and early administration of the political identification statute and regulations, see *Loveday v. Federal Communications Commission,* 707 F.2d 1443 (D.C. Cir. 1983): 1449.

47. Code of Federal Regulations §73.1212 (1998) (emphasis added).

48. See U.S. Congress. House. Committee on the Judiciary. Subcommittee on the Constitution. *The First Amendment and Restrictions on Issue Advocacy: Hearing Before the Subcommittee on the Constitution of the Committee on the Judiciary.* 105th Congress. 1st Sess. Sept. 18, 1997 (testimony of James Bopp, conceding broadcast disclosure regulations have never been subject to court challenge). But see *KVUE, Inc.* (upholding requirements against constitutional challenge).

49. *Loveday,* 707 F.2d 1443 (D.C. Cir.), certiorari denied, 464 U.S. 1008 (1983). See *Loveday,* 1448–49, 1457–58.

50. FCC Rcd. 20415, 1996 WL 635821 (October 29, 1996).

51. *United States v. Harriss,* 347 U.S. 612 (1954): 620–21, 625–26. See also "Federal Regulation of Lobbying Act," 2 U.S.C. §§261 et. seq.

52. See *Florida League of Professional Lobbyists, Inc. v. Meggs,* 87 F.3d 457 (11th Cir. 1996); *Minnesota State Ethical Practices Board v. Nat'l Rifle Ass'n,* 761 F.2d 509 (8th Cir. 1985); *Associated Industries of Kentucky v. Commonwealth,* 912 S.W.2d 947 (Ky. 1995); *Fair Political Practices Commission v. Superior Court of Los Angeles,* 599 P.2d 46 (Cal. 1979).

53. *Florida League of Professional Lobbyists, Inc.,* 460–61.

54. *Minnesota State Ethical Practices Board,* 511–13.

55. *Associated Industries of Kentucky v. Commonwealth,* 952–53. See ibid., 953 distinguishing *NAACP v. Alabama,* 357 U.S. 449 (1958) and *Bates v. Little Rock,* 362 U.S. 516 (1960).

56. *United States v. Peace Information Center,* 97 F. Supp. 255 (D.D.C. 1951): 262. Compare *McIntyre,* 378 (J. Scalia, dissenting, where he said "[Disclosure] forbids . . . the expression of no idea, but merely requires identification of the speaker"). See also *Peace Information Center,* 259–63.

57. Ibid., 262, distinguishing *Thomas v. Collins,* 323 U.S. 516 (1945): 540 (holding that a "requirement that one must register [for a labor union organizer's card] before he undertakes to make a public speech to enlist support for a lawful movement is quite incompatible with the requirements of the First Amendment").

58. *Plante v. Gonzalez,* 575 F.2d 1119 (5th Cir. 1978): 1132–33.

59. Ibid., 1134.

60. Ibid., 1136.

61. *Igneri v. Moore,* 898 F. 2d 870 (2d Cir. 1990): 877.

62. *Slevin v. City of New York,* 551 F. Supp. 917 (S.D.N.Y. 1982): 921. See also ibid., 922; *Barry v. City of New York,* 712 F.2d 1554 (2d Cir. 1983) (affirming *Slevin* in relevant part

and upholding the constitutionality of full public disclosure of the information). In *Barry*, intermediate scrutiny was also applied to the litigants' claim that the law violated their rights under the Equal Protection Clause, by burdening one class of public employees. *Barry*, 1563. See also *Eisenbund v. Suffolk County*, 841 F.2d 42 (2d Cir. 1988).

63. *County of Nevada v. MacMillen*, 522 P.2d 1345 (Cal. 1974): 1350.

64. *Falcon v. Alaska Public Offices Commission*, 570 P.2d 469 (Alaska 1977): 480.

65. *NAACP v. Alabama*, 357 U.S. 449 (1958): 452, 460.

66. *Barenblatt v. United States*, 360 U.S. 109 (1959): 112, 126.

67. *Gibson v. Florida Legislation Investigation Committee*, 372 U.S. 539 (1963): 546–47. See also *DeGregory v. New Hampshire Attorney General*, 383 U.S. 825 (1966): 829; *Bates v. Little Rock*, 361 U.S. 516, 224 (1960); *Barenblatt*, 127–28; *NAACP*, 463–66.

68. *Federal Election Commission v. Akins*, 524 U.S. 11 (1998).

69. The RNC was denied certiorari by the Supreme Court in *Republican National Committee v. Federal Election Commission*, 117 S. Ct. 682 (1997). See also *Republican National Committee v. Federal Election Commission*, 76 F.3d 400 (D.C. Cir. 1996).

70. The FECA requires disclosure of all independent expenditures (communications expressly advocating the election or defeat of a candidate) of more than $250 a year, and the identification of each person who made a contribution in excess of $200 to the person or organization filing such statement that was made for the purpose of furthering the independent expenditure. 2 U.S.C. §434(c).

Chapter 6. Splitting the Difference

1. *Baker v. Carr*, 369 U.S. 186 (1962): 270.

2. Hannah Pitkin, *The Concept of Representation* (Westport, Conn.: Greenwood Press, 1967): 61.

3. Frederick C. Mosher, *Democracy and the Public Service*, 2nd ed. (New York: Oxford University Press, 1982): 12–17.

4. Lani Guinier and Gerald Torres, "The Geography of Race in Elections: Color-blindness and Redistricting," remarks made at the American Bar Association Presidential Showcase Program, *Journal of Law and Politics* 14 (1998): 109–35.

5. Guinier and Torres, "The Geography of Race in Elections," 109–35.

6. Steven A. Light, "Too (Color)blind to See: The Voting Rights Act of 1965 and the Rehnquist Court," *George Mason University Civil Rights Law Journal* 8 (1997–1998): 1–63.

7. Charles D. Hadley, "Blacks and Southern Politics: An Agenda for Research," *Journal of Politics* 56 (1994): 585–600; Elisabeth R. Gerber, Rebecca B. Morton, and Thomas A. Reitz, "Minority Representation in Multimember Districts," *American Political Science Review* 92 (1998): 127–44. See *Shaw v. Reno*, 509 U.S. 630 (1993).

8. Hadley, "Blacks and Southern Politics," 587–91.

9. *United Jewish Organization v. Carey*, 430 U.S. 30 (1977).

10. Henry J. Abraham and Barbara A. Perry, *Freedom and the Court: Civil Rights and Liberties in the United States*, 7th ed. (New York: Oxford University Press, 1998): 382. See *Mobile v. Bolden*, 446 U.S. 55 (1980).

11. David Lubin and D. Stephen Voss, "The Partisan Impact of Voting Rights Law: A Reply to Pamela S. Karlan," *Stanford Law Review* 50 (1998): 765–77; John Hart Ely, "Gerrymanders: The Good, the Bad, and the Ugly," *Stanford Law Review* 50 (1998): 607–41. See *Thornburg v. Gingles*, 478 U.S. 30 (1986).

12. Frank R. Parker, "Predominant Factors and Narrow Tailoring: Can Racial Districts

Be Justified by Incumbent Protection and the Voting Rights Act," *Preview* 3 (1995): 137–44.

13. Bernard Grofman, "*Shaw v. Reno* and the Future of Voting Rights," *PS* 28 (1995): 27–36; Timothy G. O'Rourke, "*Shaw v. Reno* and the Hunt for Double Cross-Overs," *PS* 28 (1995): 27–36.

14. Pamela Karlan, quoting *Shaw v. Reno,* 509 U.S. 630 (1993), in Guinier and Torres, "The Geography of Race in Elections," 109–35.

15. Jim Morrill, "The Shaw of *Shaw v. Hunt:* Lead Plaintiff in District Case Pays a Price for Her Stand," *Charlotte Observer,* June 14, 1996, 10A.

16. Nancy Maveety, *Justice Sandra Day O'Connor: Strategist on the Court* (Lanham, Md.: Rowman and Littlefield, 1996).

17. *Holder v. Hall,* 512 U.S. 874 (1994); *Johnson v. De Grandy,* 512 U.S. 997 (1994).

18. *United States v. Hays,* 515 U.S. 737 (1995).

19. *Miller v. Johnson,* 515 U.S. 900 (1995): 916.

20. Linda Greenhouse, "Justices, in 5–4 Vote, Reject Districts Drawn with Race the 'Predominant Factor,'" *New York Times,* June 30, 1995, pp. A1, A33. Ely, "Gerrymanders," 607–41.

21. *Miller v. Johnson,* 928–29 (J. O'Connor, concurring).

22. Ibid., 929.

23. *Shaw v. Hunt,* 517 U.S. 899 (1996).

24. *Bush v. Vera,* 517 U.S. 952 (1996).

25. *Vera v. Richards,* 861 F. Supp. 1304 (S.D. Tex. 1994); Joan Biskupic, "'Majority-Minority' House Districts Face Court Test," *Washington Post,* December 5, 1995, p. A32.

26. *Bush v. Vera,* 985. See also *"Bush v. Vera* and *Shaw v. Hunt,"* *Washington Post,* June 14, 1996, p. A33.

27. *Bush v. Vera,* 969. See also Biskupic, "'Majority-Minority' House Districts Face Court Test."

28. *Bush v. Vera,* 993 (J. O'Connor, concurring).

29. *Bush v. Vera,* 1011. See also Biskupic, "'Majority-Minority' House Districts Face Court Test."

30. *"Bush v. Vera; Shaw v. Hunt."*

31. *Abrams v. Johnson,* 521 U.S. 74 (1997).

32. Ibid., 91. See also Joan Biskupic, "New Georgia Voting Map Upheld by High Court," *Washington Post,* June 20, 1997, p. A9.

33. *Abrams v. Johnson,* 119 (J. Breyer, dissenting). See also Biskupic, "'Majority-Minority' House Districts Face Court Test."

34. Guy Gugliatta, "Back to the Drawing Board in North Carolina," *Washington Post,* April 8, 1998, p. A4.

35. *Hunt v. Cromartie,* 526 U.S. 541 (1999).

36. Marvin L. Overly and Kenneth M. Cosgrove, "Unintended Consequences? Racial Redistricting and the Representation of Minority Interests," *Journal of Politics* 58 (May 1996): 540–50; Charles Cameron, David Epstein, and Sharyn O'Halloran, "Do Majority-Minority Districts Maximize Substantive Black Representation in Congress?" *American Political Science Review* 90 (December 1996): 794–812.

37. Alan Gerber, "African Americans' Congressional Careers and the Democratic House Delegations," *Journal of Politics* 58 (August 1996): 831–45.

Chapter 7. The Right to Party

1. Daniel Hays Lowenstein, *Election Law: Cases and Materials* (Durham, N.C.: Carolina Academic Press, 1995).

2. See Justice White's comments in *United States v. Robel*, 389 U.S. 258 (1967); John W. Epperson, *The Changing Legal Status of Political Parties in the United States* (New York: Garland, 1986).

3. Jerome M. Mileur, "Legislative Responsibility: American Political Parties and the Law," in *Challenges to Party Government*, ed. John K. White and Jerome M. Mileur (Carbondale, Ill.: Southern Illinois University Press, 1992). This essay owes a great deal to Mileur's clear exposition. Also see Jack W. Peltason, "Constitutional Law for Political Parties," in *On Parties: Essays Honoring Austin Ranney*, eds. Nelson W. Polsby and Raymond E. Wolfinger, (Berkeley, Calif.: Institute of Government Studies Press, University of California, Berkeley, 1999): 9–42; and Leon D. Epstein, "The American Party Primary," in *On Parties: Essays Honoring Austin Ranney*, eds. Nelson W. Polsby and Raymond E. Wolfinger, (Berkeley, Calif.: Institute of Government Studies Press, University of California, Berkeley, 1999): 43–72.

4. See Austin Ranney, *The Doctrine of Responsible Government* (Urbana: University of Illinois Press, 1954); also *Challenges to Party Government*, eds. John Kenneth White and Jerome M. Mileur (Carbondale: Southern Illinois University Press, 1992).

5. Mileur, "Legislative Responsibility," 183–84.

6. Daniel H. Lowenstein, "Associational Rights of Major Political Parties: A Skeptical Inquiry," *Texas Law Review* 71 (1993): 1741–92. Also see Daniel H. Lowenstein, "Associational Rights of the Major Political Parties: A Political and Jurisprudential Dead End," *American Review of Politics* 16 (Winter 1995): 351–70. This essay owes a great deal to the logic of Lowenstein's argument.

7. See Morris P. Fiorina, *The Decline of Collective Responsibility in American Politics* (St. Louis, Mo.: Center for the Study of American Business, Washington University, 1980).

8. Paul A. Beck, *Party Politics in America*, 8th ed. (New York: Longman, 1997): 38–39.

9. E. E. Schattschneider, *Party Government* (New York: Farrar and Rinehardt, 1942): 124–26.

10. John H. Aldrich, *Why Parties? The Origin and Transformation of Political Parties in America* (Chicago: University of Chicago Press, 1995): 287–96.

11. Beck, *Party Politics in America*, 24–25.

12. Leon D. Epstein, *Political Parties in the American Mold* (Madison: University of Wisconsin Press, 1986).

13. John W. Bibby, "Party Organizations, 1946–1996" in *Partisan Approaches to Postwar American Politics*, ed. Bryon E. Shafer (Chatham, N.J.: Chatham House, 1998): 142–85.

14. See Charles Merriam and Louise Overacker, *Primary Elections* (Chicago: University of Chicago Press, 1928): 120.

15. Mileur, "Legislative Responsibility," 171–72 and Epstein, *Political Parties in the American Mold*, 174–79. Key cases were *Grovey v. Townsend*, 295 U.S. 45 (1935); *United States v. Classic*, 313 U.S. 299 (1941); *Smith v. Allwright*, 321 U.S. 649 (1944); and *Terry v. Adams*, 345 U.S. 461 (1953).

16. Austin Ranney and Willmoore Kendall, *Democracy and the American Party System* (New York: Harcourt, Brace and World, 1956): 218–20.

17. See Kay Lawson, "How State Laws Undermine Parties," in *Elections American Style*,

ed. James Reichley (Washington, D.C.: Brookings Institution, 1987); also see Committee on Political Parties, American Political Science Association, "Toward a More Responsible Two–Party System," *American Political Science Review* 44 (Supplement): 1950.

18. Mileur, "Legislative Responsibility," 173.

19. See Bibby, "Party Organizations, 1946–1996," 160–74.

20. Aldrich, *Why Parties?;* Beck, *Party Politics in America,* 96–98.

21. Bibby, "Party Organizations, 1946–1996," 151–54.

22. Aldrich, *Why Parties?,* 24–25.

23. John C. Green and Daniel M. Shea, eds. *The State of the Parties,* 2nd ed. (Lanham, MD: Rowman and Littlefield, 1995): 1–10; also see Paul S. Herrnson and Diana Dwyre, "A Party Issue Advocacy in Congressional Campaigns," in *The State of the Parties,* eds. John C. Green and Daniel M. Shea, 3rd ed., (Lanham, Md.: Rowman and Littlefield, 1999): 86–104.

24. William Crotty, *Party Reform* (New York: Longman, 1983).

25. Nelson W. Polsby, *The Consequences of Reform* (Oxford: Oxford University Press, 1983).

26. Bibby, "Party Organizations, 1946–1996," 168–74.

27. Daniel M. Shea, *Transforming Democracy* (Albany, N.Y.: SUNY Press, 1995); also see chapters 22 and 23 in Green and Shea, *The State of the Parties.*

28. See Epperson, *The Changing Legal Status of Political Parties in the United States.* For a general picture of the politics within service parties, see Joseph A. Schlesinger, *Political Parties and the Winning of Office* (Ann Arbor: University of Michigan Press, 1991).

29. Lowenstein, "Associational Rights of the Major Political Parties: A Political and Jurisprudential Dead End"; Lowenstein, "Associational Rights of Major Political Parties: A Skeptical Inquiry".

30. *NAACP v. Alabama,* 357 U.S. 449 (1958).

31. Mileur, "Legislative Responsibility," 174.

32. *Sweezy v. New Hampshire,* 357 U.S. 234 (1957).

33. Lowenstein, "Associational Rights of the Major Political Parties: A Political and Jurisprudential Dead End," 357–60.

34. *Cousins v. Wigoda,* 419 U.S. 477 (1974).

35. Bruce A. Harris, "National Political Party Conventions: State's Interest Subordinate to Party's in Delegate Selection Process," *University of Miami Law Review* 29 (1975): 800–15.

36. *Democratic Party of U.S. v. La Follette,* 450 U.S. 107 (1980).

37. Christopher J. Martin, "*Democratic Party v. Wisconsin ex. rel. LaFollette:* May States Impose Open Primary Results Upon National Party Conventions?" *Denver Law Review* 59 (1982): 624–25.

38. See Jerome M. Mileur, "Massachusetts: The Democratic Party Charter Movement," in *Party Renewal in America,* ed. Gerald M. Pomper (New York: Praeger, 1980): 159–75.

39. *Opinion of the Justices to the Governor,* 385 Mass. 1201, p.1930. The court was quoting a statement by Harvard Law Professor Laurence Tribe. The U.S. Supreme Court affirmed the state court decision in *Bellotti v. Connolly,* 460 U.S. 1057 (1983).

40. *Tashjian v. Republican Party of Connecticut,* 479 U.S. 208 (1986).

41. David K. Ryden, *Representation in Crisis* (Albany: State University of New York Press, 1996): 155–58.

42. 530 U.S. 567 (2000), rev'd, 169 F.3d 646 (9th Cir. 1999). See Epstein, "The American Party Primary," 61–65.

43. *Eu v. San Francisco County Democratic Central Committee,* 489 U.S. 214 (1989). In this case, the plaintiffs also alleged that the state violated the party's freedom of speech by prohibiting endorsements of candidates in primaries. The Supreme Court supported the plaintiffs in this matter, but not on the basis of associational rights.

44. Kay Lawson, "Questions Raised by Recent Attempts at Local Party Reform," in *Machine Politics, Sound Bites, and Nostalgia,* ed. Michael Margolis and John Green (Landam, Md.: University Press of America, 1993): 38–45.

45. Roy Christman and Barbara Norrander, "A Reflection on Political Party Deregulation via the Courts: The Case of California," *Journal of Law and Politics* 6 (1990): 723–42.

46. 517 U.S. 186 (1996). See David K. Ryden, "The Good, the Bad and the Ugly: The Judicial Shaping of Party Activities", in *The State of the Parties,* ed. John C. Green and Daniel M. Shea, 3rd ed. (Lanham, Md.: Rowman and Littlefield, 1999): 58–60.

47. Lowenstein, "Associational Rights: A Political and Jurisprudential Dead End," 361–63. See *Morse v. Republican Party of Virginia,* 517 U.S. 186 (1996).

48. Lowenstein, "Associational Rights," 363–65.

49. On this point, see Charles G. Geyh, "It's My Party and I'll Cry If I Want to: State Intrusions Upon the Associational Freedoms of Political Parties," *Wisconsin Law Review* 1983 (1983): 211–40. Also see Stephen Gottlieb, "Rebuilding the Right of Association: The Right to Hold a Convention as a Test Case," *Hostra Law Review* 11 (1982): 191–247.

50. See Ryden in this volume (chapter 8) on *Timmons.* See also *Timmons v. Twin Cities Area New Party,* 520 U.S. 351 (1997).

51. Although not always with great success. A good example is redistricting; see Ryden, *Representation in Crisis,* 127–42.

52. See Lowenstein, "Associational Rights of the Major Political Parties: A Political and Jurisprudential Dead End," for good examples of the paths such litigation has already taken.

Chapter 8. The United States Supreme Court as Obstacle to Political Reform

1. *Timmons v. Twin Cities Area New Party,* 137 L. Ed. 2d 589 (1997).

2. William J. Keefe, *Parties, Politics, and Public Policy in America,* 7th ed. (Washington, D.C.: Congressional Quarterly, 1994): 319.

3. Bradley Smith, "Judicial Protection of Ballot Access Rights: Third Parties Need Not Apply," *Harvard Journal on Legislation* 28 (1991): 178–93.

4. Daniel Hays Lowenstein, *Election Law: Cases and Materials* (Durham, N.C.: Carolina Academic Press, 1995): 199; Laurence H. Tribe, *American Constitutional Law,* 2nd ed. (Mineola, N.Y.: Foundation Press, 1998): 1102.

5. *Williams v. Rhodes,* 393 U.S. 23 (1968): 30.

6. *Jenness v. Fortson,* 403 U.S. 431 (1971).

7. *Lubin v. Panish,* 415 U.S. 709 (1974): 716.

8. David K. Ryden, *Representation in Crisis: The Constitution, Interest Groups, and Political Parties* (Albany: State University of New York Press, 1996): 148.

9. *Storer v. Brown,* 415 U.S. 767 (1974).

10. Ryden, *Representation in Crisis,* 149.

11. *Anderson v. Celebrezze,* 460 U.S. 780 (1983).

12. Ryden, *Representation in Crisis,* 151.

13. Ibid., 147–48.

14. *Burdick v. Takushi,* 112 S. Ct. 2059 (1992).

15. Ryden, *Representation in Crisis,* 152–53.

16. Ibid., 144.

17. *Timmons* (1997).

18. *Timmons,* 592.

19. Lowenstein, *Election Law,* 298.

20. Dean McSweeney and John Zvesper, *American Political Parties* (London: Routledge, 1991): 38–44.

21. Keefe, *Parties, Politics, and Public Policy,* 3.

22. McSweeney and Zvesper, *American Political Parties,* 66.

23. Nancy Maveety, *Representation Rights and the Burger Years* (Ann Arbor: University of Michigan Press, 1991): 147.

24. Maveety, *Representation Rights and the Burger Years,* 187.

25. Samuel Issacharoff, Pamela S. Karlan, and Richard H. Pildes, *The Law of Democracy: Legal Structures of the Political Process* (Westbury, N.Y.: The Foundation Press, 1998): 187.

26. James Madison, "Federalist No. 10," in *The Federalist Papers,* ed. Clinton Rossiter, (New York: Mentor, 1961).

27. *Timmons,* 605.

28. Michael J. Klarman, "Majoritarian Judicial Review: The Entrenchment Problem," *Georgetown Law Journal* 85 (1997): 498.

29. Maveety, *Representation Rights and the Burger Years,* 183.

30. *Timmons,* 610–11.

31. These dynamics have led other commentators to the opposite conclusion, that indeed the Court should show more deference to state legislatures in ballot access cases. Todd J. Zywicki, "Federal Judicial Review of State Ballot Access Regulations: Escape from the Political Thicket," *Thurgood Marshall Law Review 20* (1994): 87.

32. Ryden, *Representation in Crisis,* 30.

33. Peter Argersinger catalogues in detail the historical significance of fusion balloting practices and their impact on elections. Such practices were especially commonplace in the late 1880s, which were the heyday of minor party activity and electoral success. Peter H. Argersinger, "A Place on the Ballot: Fusion Politics and Antifusion Laws," *American History Review* 85 (1980): 287.

34. Theodore J. Lowi, "Toward a Responsible Three–Party System: Prospects and Obstacles," in *The State of the Parties: The Changing Role of Contemporary American Parties,* eds. John C. Green and Daniel M. Shea, 2nd ed. (Lanham, Md.: Rowman and Littlefield, 1996); Argersinger, "A Place on the Ballot," 287; Lowenstein, *Election Laws,* 405.

35. Maveety, *Representation Rights and the Burger Years,* 187.

36. Ibid., 149.

37. Note, "Fusion and the Associated Rights of Minor Political Parties," *Columbia Law Review* 95 (1995): 713.

38. Maveety, *Representation Rights and the Burger Years,* 6–7.

39. David E. Price, *Bringing Back the Parties* (Washington, D.C.: Congressional Quarterly, 1984): 123.

40. Charles R. Kesler, "Political Parties, the Constitution, and the Future of American

Politics," in *American Political Parties and Constitutional Politics*, eds. Peter W. Schramm and Bradford P. Wilson, (Lanham, Md.: Rowman and Littlefield, 1993): 244–46.

41. Leon D. Epstein, *Political Parties in the American Mold* (Madison: University of Wisconsin Press, 1986): 173.

42. *Timmons* (J. Stevens, dissenting.)

43. Smith, "Judicial Protection of Ballot Access Rights," 193.

44. Ryden, *Representation in Crisis*, 6.

45. Maveety, *Representation Rights and the Burger Years*, 187.

46. Ibid., 4, 156, 171.

47. *Timmons*, 599–601.

48. Ibid., citing *Eu v. San Francisco County Democratic Central Committee*, 489 U.S. 214 (1989): 224.

49. Ryden, *Representation in Crisis*, 150.

50. Ibid., 145.

51. *Eu*, 224.

52. *Tashjian v. Republican Party of Connecticut*, 479 U.S. 208 (1986): 216.

53. Ryden, *Representation in Crisis*, 247.

Chapter 9. Ironies Abound in the United States Supreme Court's Rulings Limiting Political Patronage

1. *Elrod v. Burns*, 427 U.S. 347 (1976).

2. *Branti v. Finkel*, 445 U.S. 507 (1980).

3. *Rutan v. Republican Party of Illinois*, 497 U.S. 62 (1990).

4. *O'Hare Truck Service, Inc. v. City of Northlake*, 518 U.S. 712 (1996).

5. See Justice Powell's dissenting opinion in *Elrod v. Burns*, 376–90; and Justice Scalia's dissenting opinion in *Rutan v. Republican Party of Illinois*, 92–66.

6. For criticisms and defenses of political patronage see Robert Maranto, "Thinking the Unthinkable in Public Administration: A Case of Spoils in the Federal Bureaucracy," *Administration and Society* 29 (1998): 623; and Ronald Johnson and Gary Libecap, "Courts, A Protected Bureaucracy, and Reinventing Government," *Arizona Law Review* 37 (1995): 791. See, generally, Frank Sorauf, "Patronage and Party," *Midwest Journal of Political Science* 3 (1959): 115; Frank Sorauf, "The Silent Revolution in Patronage," *Public Administration Review* 20 (1960): 28; and Clifton McCleskey, "Parties at the Bar: Equal Protection, Freedom of Association, and the Rights of Political Organizations," *Journal of Politics* 46 (1984): 347.

7. *Jenkins v. Medford*, 119 F.3d 1156 (4th Cir. 1997) (en banc), *certiorari denied*, 118 S.Ct. 881 (1998).

8. See James Q. Wilson, *Amateur Democrat: Club Politics in Three Cities* (Chicago: University of Chicago Press, 1950).

9. See n. 61 and the discussion in the text that follows.

10. An exception is *United States v. National Treasury Employees Union*, 115 S.Ct. 1003 (1995) (striking down a provision in the Ethics Reform Act of 1989 banning federal employees from receiving honoraria for speeches and publications unrelated to their work).

11. See, generally, Leon Epstein, *Political Parties in the American Mold* (Madison: University of Wisconsin Press, 1986); and Martin Tolchin and Susan Tolchin, *To the Victor: Political Patronage from the Clubhouse to the Whitehouse* (New York: Random House, 1971).

12. See, generally, Ari Arthur Hoogenboom, *Outlawing the Spoils: A History of the Civil Service Reform Movement, 1865–1883* (Urbana: University of Illinois Press, 1968); and Paul P. Van Riper, *History of the United States Civil Service* (Evanston, Ill.: Row, Peterson, 1958).

13. See "Federal Employees Political Activities," *Congressional Digest* 195–225 (August/September 1993); and Karl T. Thurber, "Big, Little, Littler: Synthesizing Hatch Act–Based Political Activity Legislation Research," *Review of Public Personnel Administration* 13 (1993): 38–51.

14. *United Public Workers of America v. Mitchell*, 330 U.S. 75 (1947).

15. *United States Civil Service Commission v. National Association of Letter Carriers*, 413 U.S. 548 (1973).

16. James W. Fesler, *The 50 States and Their Local Governments*, (New York: Alfred Knopf, 1967): 586.

17. No single model or code appears to have been followed in the state and local regulations. For example, while forty-one states permit employees to participate while off duty in political campaigns, thirty-four states allow their employees to become candidates in partisan elections. See Thurber, "Synthesizing Hatch Act–Based Political Activity Legislation Research," 45–47; Council of State Governments, *The Book of the States* (Lexington, Ky.: Council of State Governments, 1992); and William M. Pearson, and David S. Castle, "Liberalizing Restrictions on Political Activities of State Employees: Perceptions of High–Level State Executives," *American Review of Public Administration* 21 (1991): 91–104.

18. For a major study of political patronage in the 1980s and 1990s, see Anne Freedman, *Patronage: An American Tradition* (Chicago: Nelson-Hall, 1994). See also Michael Johnston, "Patrons and Clients, Jobs and Machines: A Case Study of the Uses of Patronage," *American Political Science Review* 73 (1979): 385.

19. Larry Sabato, *The Party's Just Begun: Shaping Political Parties for America's Future* (Glenview, Ill.: Scott, Foresman and Co., 1987): 231.

20. See Mike Causey, "Patronage Is Potluck," *Washington Post,* January 25, 1998, p. B1; and "Sour Plums," *Maclean's* 109, December 9, 1996, p. 16.

21. See, e.g., *Adler v. Board of Education*, 342 U.S. 485 (1952) (upholding New York's Feinberg law barring from employment in public schools any person who advocated the overthrow of the government).

22. *McAuliff v. Mayor of New Bedford*, 155 Mass. 216 (1892).

23. See, generally, Gordon Baker, *The Reapportionment Revolution* (New York: Random House, 1966).

24. See, generally, William Van Alstyne, "The Demise of the Right-Privilege Distinction in Constitutional Law," *Harvard Law Review* 87 (1968): 1439.

25. *Colegrove v. Green*, 328 U.S. 549 (1946).

26. *Baker v. Carr*, 369 U.S. 186 (1962).

27. *Wesberry v. Sanders*, 376 U.S. 1 (1964).

28. For a discussion and summary of the Court's rulings extending the principle of "one person, one vote," see David M. O'Brien, *Constitutional Law and Politics*, vol. 1, *Struggles for Power and Governmental Accountability*, 4th ed. (New York: Norton, 2000): 790–814.

29. See, e.g., *Williams v. Rhodes*, 393 U.S. 23 (1969) (holding that overly restrictive ballot access requirements violate the First and Fourteenth Amendments); and *Moore v. Ogilvie*, 394 U.S. 814 (1969) (striking down an Illinois law requiring independent candi-

dates to secure petition signatures from citizens in at least half of the counties in the state in order to be placed on the ballot).

30. See *Shelton v. Tucker,* 364 U.S. 479 (1960); *Cramp v. Board of Education,* 368 U.S. 278 (1961); and *Baggett v. Bullitt,* 377 U.S. 360 (1964).

31. *Keyishian v. Board of Regents,* 385 U.S. 589 (1967).

32. *Keyishian* overruled *Adler v. Board of Education,* 342 U.S. 485 (1952), which had upheld New York's Feinberg law, barring from employment in public schools anyone who advocated the overthrow of government, and struck down New York's Feinberg law as unconstitutionally vague and over broad.

33. *Pickering v. Board of Education of Township High School District,* 391 U.S. 563 (1968).

34. Ibid., 568, and reaffirmed in *Connick v. Myers,* 461 U.S. 138, 154 (1983); *Rankin v. McPherson,* 483 U.S. 378, 384 (1987); and *Board of County Commissioners, Wabaunsee County, Kansas v. Umbehr,* 518 U.S. 668 (1996).

35. See *Rankin v. McPherson,* 483 U.S. 378 (1987); and *United States v. National Treasury Employees Union,* 115 S.Ct. 1003 (1995).

36. *Connick v. Myers,* 461 U.S. 138 (1983).

37. See also *Waters v. Churchill,* 114 S.Ct. 1878 (1994).

38. See *Jenkins v. Medford,* 119 F.3d 1156, 1166 (J. Motz, dissenting).

39. One of the most notable cases involved a challenge brought by a candidate for the position of delegate to Illinois's 1970 Constitutional Convention against Cook County's patronage system in *Shakman v. Democratic Organization of Cook County,* 310 F. Supp. 1398 (N.D. Ill.1969), reversed, 435 F.2d 267 (7th Cir. 1970), cert. denied, 402 U.S. 909 (1971); *Shakman v. Democratic Organization of Cook County,* 533 F.2d 344 (7th Cir. 1976), cert. denied, 429 U.S. 858 (1976); *Shakman v. Democratic Organization of Cook County,* 481 F. Supp. 1315 (N.D. Ill. 1979); *Shakman v. Dunne,* 829 F.2d 1387 (7th Cir. 1987). The Shakman litigation is recounted in C. Richard Johnson, "Successful Reform Litigation: The Shakman Patronage Case," *Chicago-Kent Law Review* 64 (1988): 479. See also David A. Strauss, "Legality, Activism, and the Patronage Case," *Chicago-Kent Law Review* 64 (1988): 585.

40. *Elrod v. Burns,* 374 (J. Stewart and J. Blackmun, concurring).

41. Ibid., 386 (J. Powell, dissenting).

42. Ibid., 363.

43. Ibid., 367.

44. *Branti v. Finkel,* 445 U.S. 507 (1980).

45. Ibid., 518.

46. *Rutan v. Republican Party of Illinois,* 497 U.S. 62 (1990).

47. Ibid., 74.

48. Ibid., 93 (J. Scalia, dissenting).

49. Ibid.

50. *Payne v. Tennessee,* 501 U.S. 808 (1991).

51. *Board of County Commissioners, Wabaunsee County, Kansas v. Umbehr,* 518 U.S. 668 (1996).

52. *O'Hare Truck Service, Inc. v. City of Northlake,* 518 U.S. 712 (1996).

53. *Umbehr,* 685 (citations omitted).

54. For further discussion, see David M. O'Brien, "Charting the Rehnquist Court's Course: How the Center Folds, Holds, and Shifts," *New York School Law Review* 40 (1996): 981.

55. See, e.g., Justice Kennedy's opinion for the Court in *Rosenberger v. The Rector and Visitors of the University of Virginia,* 515 U.S. 819 (1995). See also *Reno v. American Civil Liberties Union,* 117 S.Ct. 2329 (1997); and *National Endowment for the Arts v. Finley,* 118 S.Ct. 2168 (1998).

56. See, e.g., Justice Kennedy's concurrence in *Texas v. Johnson,* 491 U.S. 397 (1989): 420.

57. See, e.g., Justice Souter's dissenting opinion in *National Endowment for the Arts v. Finley,* 2185.

58. *Roe v. Wade,* 410 U.S. 113 (1973).

59. *Planned Parenthood of Southeastern Pennsylvania v. Casey,* 505 U.S. 833 (1992).

60. Further discussed in David M. O'Brien, *Storm Center: The Supreme Court in American Politics,* 5th ed. (New York: W. W. Norton and Co., 2000): 208–13. See also Christopher P. Banks, "The Supreme Court and Precedent: An Analysis of Natural Courts and Reversals Trends," *Judicature* 75 (1992): 262.

61. See "Recent Cases," *Harvard Law Review* 111 (1998): 1596.

62. *Jenkins v. Medford,* 1166 (J. Motz, dissenting).

63. *Jones v. Dodson,* 727 F.2d 1329 (4th Cir. 1984).

64. Ibid., 1168 (J. Motz, dissenting).

65. For a further discussion see David M. O'Brien, *Judicial Roulette,* (New York: Twentieth Century Fund, 1988); and Sheldon Goldman, *Picking Federal Judges: Lower Court Selection from Roosevelt Through Reagan* (New Haven: Yale University Press, 1997).

66. For a further discussion see David M. O'Brien, "The Reagan Judges: His Most Enduring Legacy," in *The Reagan Legacy: Promise and Performance,* ed. Charles O. Jones (Chatham, N.J.: Chatham House, 1988).

67. For a further discussion see David M. O'Brien, "Clinton's Legal Policy and the Courts: Rising from Disarray or Turning Around and Around?" in *The Clinton Presidency: First Appraisals,* ed. Colin Campbell and Bert A. Rockman (Chatham, N.J.: Chatham House, 1996): 126.

68. Judges J. Harvie Wilkinson, L. Michael Luttig, Paul V. Niemeyer, William W. Wilkins, Clyde H. Hamilton, and Karen J. Williams.

69. Judge Kenneth K. Hall.

70. President Carter appointed Judges Sam J. Ervin III and Francis D. Murnaghan, Jr. President Clinton named Judges Diana Motz and M. Blane Michael.

71. *Jenkins v. Medford,* 1166 (J. Motz, dissenting).

72. See, e.g., *Upton v. Thompson,* 930 F.2d 1209 (7th Cir. 1991); and *Terry v. Cook,* 866 F.2d 373 (11th Cir. 1989).

73. The Court's denial of review does not, technically, indicate that it approves of a lower court's decision. Moreover, the Rehnquist Court's plenary docket has been shrinking and the current justices, compared with those on the Burger Court, do not appear as concerned about correcting errors in the lower courts. See David M. O'Brien, "The Rehnquist Court's Shrinking Plenary Docket," *Judicature* 81 (1997): 58. Still, the Court generally grants cases in order to reverse a lower court's decision. In the 1996–97 term, for instance, the Court reversed 75 percent of the lower courts' decisions in cases granted plenary review. See David M. O'Brien, *Supreme Court Watch 1997* (New York: W. W. Norton and Co., 1998): 16.

74. See Walter Dean Burnham, "The End of American Political Parties," *Society* 35 (Jan.–Feb. 1998): 68; L. Sandy Maisel, ed., *The Parties Respond,* (Boulder, Colo.: Westview

Press, 1992); Frank J. Sorauf and Paul Allen Beck, *Political Parties in America,* 6th ed. (Glenview, Ill.: Scott, Foresman, 1988); Van Riper, *History of the United States Civil Service;* and Freedman, *Patronage.*

75. See Freedman, *Patronage,* and L. Stein, *Holding Bureaucrats Accountable,* (Tuscaloosa: University of Alabama Press, 1991).

76. See Michael J. Klarman, "Rethinking the Civil Rights and Civil Liberties Revolution," *Virginia Law Review* 82 (1996): 1.

77. See, e.g., S. P. Erie, *Rainbow's End* (Berkeley: University of California Press, 1988).

78. See Cynthia Grant Bowman, "The Law of Patronage at a Crossroads," *Journal of Law and Politics* 12 (1996): 341; and Cynthia Grant Bowman, "Public Policy: 'We Don't Anybody Sent': The Death of Patronage Hiring in Chicago," *Northwestern University Law Review* 86 (1991): 57.

79. Freedman, *Patronage,* 171–83.

80. See, e.g., *Shaw v. Reno,* 509 U.S. 630 (1993); *Miller v. Johnson,* 512 U.S. 622 (1995); *Bush v. Vera,* 517 U.S. 952 (1996); *Shaw v. Hunt,* 517 U.S. 899 (1996); and David M. O'Brien, *Constitutional Law and Politics,* vol. 1, 828–61.

Chapter 10. Whitewater, Iran-Contra, and the Limits of the Law

1. 28 U.S.C. 591–98 (Public Law 95–521) (1978). In 1982 the name was changed to "independent counsel" in order to try to remove some of the Watergate stigma associated with "special prosecutor."

2. See, for example, Lloyd Cutler, "A Proposal for a Continuing Public Prosecutor," *Hastings Constitutional Law Quarterly* 2 (1975): 21–25. The concern about conflict of interest and the need to promote public confidence in the impartiality of these investigations were central arguments in the legislative debate. See House of Representatives, Committee on the Judiciary, *Special Prosecutor and Watergate Grand Jury Legislation Hearings Before the Subcommittee on Criminal Justice,* 93rd Cong., 1st sess., 1973; and U.S. Senate, Committee on the Judiciary, *Special Prosecutor,* 93rd Cong., 1st sess., 1973.

3. Michael Schudson, *Watergate in American Memory* (New York: Basic Books, 1992): 100.

4. *U.S. v. Nixon,* 418 U.S. 683 (1974).

5. See for example, the prepared statement of Rep. John Culver, House, Comm. On Judiciary, *Special Prosecutor and Watergate Grand Jury,* 66–67. In urging his fellow congressman to support prompt creation of a judicially appointed special prosecutor, he argued that they were "responding to an unmistakable and deeply felt public determination to restore full rule of law."

6. Kenneth Starr's jurisdiction was expanded to include many allegations unrelated to the initial investigation into business dealings associated with the Whitewater land development deal. I use "Whitewater" to refer to the investigation of all of these allegations since the phrase "Whitewater, FBI files, Travelgate, Interngate investigation" seems overly cumbersome.

7. *Report of the Congressional Committees Investigating the Iran-Contra Affair with the Minority Views,* abridged edition (New York: Times Books, 1988): 347.

8. Lawrence Walsh, *Firewall: The Iran-Contra Conspiracy and Cover-up* (New York: W. W. Norton, 1997): xv.

9. Jeffrey Toobin, "Starr Can't Help It," *New Yorker,* May 18, 1998, p. 33.

10. *Morrison v. Olson,* 487 U.S. 654 (1988).

11. Most, but not all, of the independent counsel investigations have involved the empanelling of grand juries as part of the investigative process. There have been, or will be, trials in the investigations of Michael Deaver, Lyn Nofziger, the Iran-Contra scandal, Mike Espy, Whitewater, and Henry Cisneros.

12. There have been appellate court rulings, including decisions by the U.S. Supreme Court, in the Nofziger, Iran-Contra, Espy, Whitewater, and Cisneros cases. Finally, the special court panel that appoints the independent counsel has issued a number of rulings related to jurisdictional questions and the awarding of attorneys fees to targets of the investigations.

13. Katy J. Harriger, *Independent Justice: The Federal Special Prosecutor in American Politics* (Lawrence: University Press of Kansas, 1992): 13–39.

14. Ibid., 39–72.

15. Katy J. Harriger, "The History of the Independent Counsel Provisions: How the Past Informs the Current Debate," *Mercer Law Review* 49 (Winter 1998): 489.

16. 28 U.S.C.A. sec. 591–592.

17. 28 U.S.C.A. sec. 49 (establishing special division of court); 28 U.S.C.A. sec. 593 (establishing duties of special division).

18. 28 U.S.C.A. sec. 596.

19. 487 U.S. 654 (1988).

20. Ibid., 695–96.

21. Ibid., 677–84.

22. Ibid., 685–96.

23. Ibid., (J. Scalia, dissenting): 697–734.

24. Lawrence Walsh, *Iran-Contra: The Final Report* (New York: Times Books, 1994): xiv–xv; xxiii–xxv.

25. Ibid., 555.

26. "Don't Wallow in the Iran Scandal," *New York Times,* March 11, 1987, p. 26.

27. Ruth Marcus, "The World Series of White-Collar Crime," *Washington Post National Weekly Edition,* May 4, 1987, p. 13.

28. Ibid.

29. Walsh, *Final Report,* p. 555.

30. *U.S. v. North,* 910 F.2d 843 (D.C. Cir. 1990).

31. *U.S. v. Poindexter,* 951 F.2d 369 (D.C. Cir. 1991).

32. Walsh, *Final Report,* p. 558.

33. Ibid.

34. Glen Craney, "Access to Secret Papers Snarls Iran Contra Case," *Congressional Quarterly Weekly Report* 46, April 30, 1988, pp. 1157–58; Ann Pelham, "Walsh Clashes with Justice Department over Secrets," *Legal Times,* July 31, 1989, p. 2.

35. Public Law No. 96–456, 94 Stat. 2025 (codified at 18 U.S.C. app.).

36. Brian Z. Tamanaha, "A Critical Review of the Classified Information Procedure Act," *American Journal of Criminal Law* 13 (Summer 1986): 280.

37. Ann Pelham, "Can North Be Tried? Who's To Be Trusted?" *Legal Times,* February 20, 1989, p. 11.

38. Harold Hongju Koh, *The National Security Constitution: Sharing Power After the Iran–Contra Affair* (New Haven: Yale University Press, 1990): 31.

39. Gerald Craney, "Judge Won't Derail North's Iran–Contra Trial," *Congressional Quarterly Weekly Report* 46, November 26, 1988, p. 3403.

40. "Secrecy Spat Jeopardizes Iran-Contra Trial," *Congressional Quarterly Weekly Report* 46, December 3, 1988, p. 3455.

41. Glen Craney, "Iran-Contra Case May Drop Two Counts," *Congressional Quarterly Weekly Report* 47, January 7, 1989, pp. 28–29; and "Two Iran-Contra Charges Against North Dismissed," *Congressional Quarterly Weekly Report* 47, January 14, 1989, p. 99.

42. Koh, *National Security Constitution*, p. 26.

43. See for example, Gordon Crovitz, "The Criminalization of Politics," in *The Imperial Congress: Crisis in the Separation of Powers*, eds. Gordon S. Jones and John A. Marini, (New York: Pharos Books, 1988): 239–67.

44. William S. Cohen and George J. Mitchell, *Men of Zeal* (New York: Viking Press, 1988); and Lawrence Walsh, *Firewall: The Iran-Contra Conspiracy and Cover-Up* (New York: W. W. Norton, 1997): 27.

45. Theodore Draper, " How Not to Deal with the Iran-Contra Crimes," *New York Review of Books*, June 14, 1990, pp. 39–44.

46. Walsh, *Final Report*, p. 559.

47. Ibid., 563–564.

48. Ibid., 564.

49. An analysis of news coverage of earlier appointments demonstrates that until the Iran-Contra case none of the Ethics Act cases generated enough coverage to create public awareness. Harriger, *Independent Justice*, 168–98.

50. Helen Dewar and Ann Devroy, "Fiske, Hill Negotiate on Hearings," *Washington Post*, March 10, 1994, p. A1; Stephen Labaton, "D'Amato Bows to Prosecutor, Delaying Whitewater Hearing," *New York Times*, December 14, 1994, p. B8.

51. Letter from Robert Fiske to Democratic and Republican Leaders of the House and Senate Banking Committees, dated March 7, 1994, in *Congressional Quarterly Weekly Report* 52, p. 627.

52. Ronald Wright, "Congressional Use of Immunity Grants After Iran-Contra," *Minnesota Law Review* 80 (December 1995): 407, 410; and Larry Sabato and Robert Lichter, *When Should the Watchdogs Bark? Media Coverage of the Clinton Scandals* (Washington, D.C.: Center for Media and Public Affairs, 1994): 7–9.

53. Toobin, "Starr Can't Help It," p. 32.

54. Evan Thomas and Daniel Klaidman, "A Break in the Clouds," *Newsweek*, April 13, 1998, p. 29.

55. Sue Kirchhoff, "Starr Report Hits Capitol Hill, Drawing Outrage and Trepidation," *Congressional Quarterly Weekly Report* 56, September 12, 1998, pp. 2387–89; Dan Carney, "GOP Looks for Impeachment Course by the Light of a Single Starr," *Congressional Quarterly Weekly Report* 56, November 14, 1998, p. 3096.

56. Karen Foerstel, "Voters' Plea for Moderation Unlikely to Be Heeded," *Congressional Quarterly Weekly Report* 56, November 7, 1998, pp. 2980–84; Jeffrey L. Katz and Andrew Taylor, "House Accuse Clinton of Perjury, Obstruction," *Congressional Quarterly Weekly Report*, December 22, 1998, pp. 3320–25.

57. "The Gallup Top Ten," available on-line at http://www.gallup.com.

58. *In Re Grand Jury Proceeding*, 5 F. Supp. 2d 21 (D.D.C. 1998); *In Re Lindsay*, 148 F.3d 1100 (D.C. Cir. 1998); and *Swidler and Berlin v. U.S.*, 524 U.S. 399 (1998).

59. *In Re Sealed Case*, 148 F.3d 1073 (D.C. Cir. 1998).

60. Lisa E. Toporek, "Bad Politics Makes Bad Law: A Comment on the Eighth Circuit's Approach to the Governmental Attorney-Client Privilege," *The Georgetown Law Journal* 86 (July 1998): 2421.

61. Kenneth Mann, *Defending White Collar Crime* (New Haven: Yale University Press, 1985).

62. Starr accused the president of abuse of power for, among other things, obstructing the investigation by "invoking executive privilege." "Independent Counsel's Report: The President Lied under Oath and Obstructed Justice," *Congressional Quarterly Weekly Report,* September 12, 1998, p. 2420. Article IV of the impeachment articles accused the president of "abuse of power" for a "pattern of deceit and obstruction of duly authorized investigations." This article was rejected by a vote of 148–285. "The Articles of Impeachment Considered By the House," *Congressional Quarterly Weekly Report,* December 22, 1998, p. 3323.

63. Lori Nitschke, "Would the Case Against Clinton Hold Up in Court?" *Congressional Quarterly Weekly Report,* December 22, 1998, p. 3328.

64. Frank Anechiarico and James B. Jacob, *The Pursuit of Absolute Integrity: How Corruption Control Makes Government Ineffective* (Chicago: University of Chicago Press, 1996): xi, 12.

65. Ibid., 12.

66. Wright, "Congressional Use of Immunity Grants," 464–68.

67. Norman J. Ornstein, "Doing Congress's Dirty Work," *Georgetown Law Journal* 86 (July 1998): 2179.

Chapter 11. The Influence of the NAACP Legal Defense Fund

Epigraph source can be found in Lani Guinier, "A Development of the Franchise: 1982 Voting Rights Amendments," in *Voting Rights America: Continuing the Quest for Full Participation,* eds. Karen McGill Arrington and William L. Taylor (Washington, D.C.: Joint Center for Political and Economic Studies, 1992): 107.

1. *Shelley v. Kraemer,* 334 U.S. 1 (1948); Clement Vose, *Caucasians Only: The Supreme Court, The NAACP, and the Restrictive Covenant Cases* (Berkeley: University of California Press, 1959). See also David Truman, *The Governmental Process: Political Interest and Public Opinion* (New York: Alfred A. Knopf, 1951): 479.

2. See for example: Richard Corner, "Strategies and Tactics of Litigants in Constitutional Cases," *Journal of Public Law* 17 (1968): 287–307; Richard Kluger, *Simple Justice: The History of* Brown v. Board of Education *and Black America's Struggle for Equality* (New York: Alfred A. Knopf, 1975); David R. Manwaring, *Render Unto Caesar: The Flag Salute Controversy* (Chicago: University of Chicago Press, 1962); Michael Melstner, *Cruel and Unusual: The Supreme Court and Capital Punishment* (New York: Random House, 1973); Karen O'Connor, *Women's Organizations' Use of the Court* (Lexington, Mass.: Lexington Books, 1980).

3. Some examples of research highlighting extralegal influences on judicial decision making include Lincoln Caplan, *The Tenth Justice* (New York: Alfred A. Knopf, 1987); Tracy E. George and Lee Epstein, "On the Nature of Supreme Court Decision Making," *American Political Science Review* 86 (1992): 323–37; Rebecca Salokar, *The Solicitor General: The Politics of Law* (Philadelphia: Temple University Press, 1992); David W. Rohde and Harold J. Spaeth, *Supreme Court Decision Making* (San Francisco: W. H. Freeman, 1986); Jeffrey A. Segal and Albert D. Cover, "Ideological Values and the Votes of U.S. Supreme Court Justices," *American Political Science Review* 83 (1989): 557–65; Jeffrey A. Segal, Lee Epstein,

Charles Cameron, and Harold Spaeth, "Ideological Values and the Votes of U.S. Supreme Court Justices Revisited" *Journal of Politics* 57 (1995): 812–23; Jeffrey A. Segal and Harold J. Spaeth, *The Supreme Court and the Attitudinal Model* (Cambridge: Cambridge University Press, 1993); C. Neal Tate, "Personal Attribute Models of the Voting Behavior of U.S. Supreme Court Justices: Liberalism in Civil Liberties and Economics Decisions, 1946–1978," *American Political Science Review* 75 (1981): 355–67.

4. The following list includes some of this more recent interest group litigation research focusing on a group's litigation campaign over the long term, and on the extent that extralegal factors limit a group's efficacy: Lee Epstein and C. K. Rowland, "Debunking the Myth of Interest Group Invincibility in the Courts," *American Political Science Review* 86 (1991): 323–; Lee Epstein and Joseph Kobylka, *The Supreme Court and Legal Change: Abortion and the Death Penalty* (Chapel Hill: University of North Carolina Press, 1992); Gregg Ivers, *To Build A Wall: American Jews and the Separation of Church and State* (Charlottesville: University Press of Virginia, 1995); Steven C. Tauber, "The NAACP-LDF and the U.S. Supreme Court's Racial Discrimination Decision Making," *Social Science Quarterly* 80 (1999): 325–34; Steven C. Tauber, "On Behalf of the Condemned: The Impact of the NAACP Legal Defense Fund on Capital Punishment Decision Making in the U.S. Courts of Appeals," *Political Research Quarterly* 51 (1998): 191–219; Stephen L. Wasby, *Race Relations Litigation in an Age of Complexity* (Charlottesville: University Press of Virginia, 1995).

5. *United States v. Reese*, 92 U.S. 214 (1876).

6. *United States v. Cruikshank*, 92 U.S. 542 (1876).

7. *Giles v. Harris*, 189 U.S. 475 (1903).

8. Jack Greenberg, *Crusaders in the Court: How a Dedicated Band of Lawyers Fought for the Civil Rights Revolution* (New York: Basic Books, 1994): 14–15; James Marlise, *The People's Lawyers* (New York: Holt, Rinehart, and Winston, 1973): 259–71.

9. *Guinn and Beal v. United States*, 238 U.S. 347 (1915); See Gregory A. Caldeira, "Litigation, Lobbying, and the Voting Rights Law," in *Controversies in Minority Voting: The Voting Rights Act in Perspective*, eds. Bernard Grofman and Chandler Davidson (Washington, D.C.: The Brookings Institution, 1992): 232–35; Clement Vose, *Constitutional Change: Amendment Politics and Supreme Court Litigation* (Lexington, Mass.: Lexington Books, 1972): 31–44.

10. *Love v. Griffith*, 266 U.S. 32 (1924); see Vose, *Constitutional Change*, 288–91.

11. *Nixon v. Herndon*, 273 U.S. 536 (1927).

12. Vose, *Constitutional Change*, 296–307.

13. *Nixon v. Condon*, 386 U.S. 573 (1932); see also Vose, *Constitutional Change*, 309–14.

14. *Grovey v. Townsend*, 295 U.S. 45 (1935); see also Alan Robert Burch, "The NAACP Before and After *Grovey v. Townsend*" (master's thesis, University of Virginia, 1994); Greenberg, 10. *Crusaders in the Court*, 39; Vose, *Constitutional Change*, 314–16.

15. Greenberg, *Crusaders in the Court*, 19–21; Vose, *Constitutional Change*, 317–18.

16. *United States v. Classic*, 313 U.S. 299 (1941).

17. *Smith v. Allwright*, 321 U.S. 649 (1944).

18. Greenberg, *Crusaders in the Court*, 108–09; Vose, *Constitutional Change*, 317–22.

19. Literacy tests were upheld as constitutional in *Lassiter v. Northampton Election Board*, 360 U.S. 45 (1959).

20. Chandler Davidson, "Minority Vote Dilution: An Overview," in *Minority Vote Dilution*, ed. Chandler Davidson (Washington, D.C.: Howard University Press, 1984): 4.

21. *Mobile v. Bolden*, 446 U.S. 55 (1980)

22. For more on the passage of the 1982 amendments to the Voting Rights Act of 1965, consult Drew Days and Lani Guinier. "Enforcement of Section 5 of the Voting Rights Act," in *Minority Vote Dilution*, ed. Chandler Davidson (Washington, D.C.: Howard University Press, 1984); Greenberg, *Crusaders in the Court*, 475–76; Guinier, "A Development of the Franchise."

23. *Thornburg v. Gingles,* 478 U.S. 30 (1986).

24. Bernard Grofman, "The Supreme Court, The Voting Rights Act, and Minority Representation," in *Affirmative Action and Representation:* Shaw v. Reno *and the Future of Voting Rights,* ed. Anthony Peacock (Durham, N.C.: Carolina Academic Press, 1997); Paula D. McClain and Joseph Stewart, Jr. *Can We All Get Along?: Racial and Ethnic Minorities in American Politics* (Boulder, Colo.: Westview Press, 1995): 107–08.

25. *Chisom v. Roemer,* 501 U.S. 380 (1991).

26. *Shaw v. Reno,* 509 U.S. 630 (1993).

27. While many, like the dissenters in *Shaw v. Reno,* believe that the case reversed precedent, not everyone agrees that it did. Some have argued that *Shaw* was consistent with the meaning of the Court's previous minority vote dilution rulings; see Timothy G. O'Rourke, *"Shaw v. Reno:* The Shape of Things to Come," in *Affirmative Action:* Shaw v. Reno *and the Future of Voting Rights,* ed. Anthony Peacock (Durham, N.C.: Carolina Academic Press, 1997).

28. *Miller v. Johnson,* 515 U.S. 900 (1995)

29. *Shaw v. Hunt,* 517 U.S. 899 (1996).

30. *Bush v. Vera,* 517 U.S. 952 (1996). For a discussion of *Shaw v. Reno* and its progeny, see Barbara Perry's discussion in chapter 6 of this book.

31. Caplan, *The Tenth Justice;* Salokar, *The Solicitor General.*

32. Michael Belknap, ed. *Civil Rights, the White House, and the Justice Department, 1945–1968,* vols. 1 and 2 (New York: Garland Publishing Company, 1991): 348–49.

33. The Reagan Justice Department opposed the LDF's position in *Thornburg v. Gingles,* 478 U.S. 30 (1986), although the LDF prevailed in this case; see also Wasby, *Race Relations Litigation,* 24–25.

34. John Dunne, "Protection of Minority Voting Rights." *Presidential Studies Quarterly* 22 (1991): 697–702.

35. For more on the extent that ideology influences judicial decision making, consult George and Epstein, "On the Nature of Supreme Court Decision Making"; Segal and Cover, "Ideological Values and the Votes of U.S. Supreme Court Justices"; Segal, Epstein, Cameron, and Spaeth, "Ideological Values and the Votes of U.S. Supreme Court Justices Revisited"; Segal and Spaeth, *The Supreme Court and the Attitudinal Model.*

36. See Henry J. Abraham, *Justices and Presidents: A Political History of Appointments to the Supreme Court,* 3rd ed. (New York: Oxford University Press, 1992): 208–40.

37. Ibid., 13–23, 296–373.

38. NAACP-Legal Defense Fund, *1988–1989 Annual Report* (New York: NAACP Legal Defense Fund, 1989): 2.

39. Lexis, an on-line legal research program, identified the applicable decisions.

40. Table 11.1 displays these results in more detail. The chi-square of 0.304 is not statistically significant at the .1 level, which indicates that there is no demonstrable relationship between the LDF's participation and the outcome minority voting rights cases.

41. Table 11.2 displays these results in more detail. The chi-square of 6.044 is statistically significant at the .05 level, which demonstrates a statistical relationship between

the LDF's participation and the outcome minority voting rights cases in cases where the Justice Department also participates.

42. Table 11.3 displays these results in more detail. Neither chi-square was statistically significant.

43. *Holder v. Hull*, 512 U.S. 874 (1994); *Shaw v. Hunt*, 517 U.S. 899 (1996); *Bush v. Vera*, 517 U.S. 952 (1996); *Abrams v. Johnson*, 521 U.S. 74 (1997).

44. From the NAACP Legal Defense Fund Web site, http://www.ldfla.org/ldf.html, visited on February 19, 2000.

45. See LDF associate director-counsel Theodore Shaw's statement in Theodore Shaw, "Rebuttal: Wrong About Racism, Columnist Misses Point When He Blames Blacks for Racism," *American Lawyer*, December 19, 1996.

46. *United States v. Hays*, 515 U.S. 737 (1995); *Bush v. Vera*, 517 U.S. 952 (1996); *Lopez v. Montgomery County, California*, 519 U.S. 9 (1996).

47. Mike Magan, " 'Boh' Knows Leadership as NAACP President," *Indiana Lawyer*, November 1, 1995, p. 9.

48. Days and Guinier, "Enforcement of Section 5 of the Voting Rights Act," 174–76; Greenberg, *Crusaders in the Court*, 475–76.

Chapter 12. "A December Storm over the U.S. Supreme Court"

Epigraph sources can be found in Associated Press, "Bush Ally Opposes Role for Courts in Elections," *Washington Post* (February 18, 2001): A27; David Von Drehle, Peter Slevin, Dan Balz, and James V. Grimaldi, "Anxious Moments in the Final Stretch: High Court Stepped In and Wrote Stirring Finish," *Washington Post* (February 3, 2001): A01; *Bush v. Gore*, 121 S. Ct. 525 (2000) (J. Ginsburg, dissenting): 549.

1. *Bush v. Gore*, 121 S. Ct. 525 (2000) (J. Stevens, joined by J. Ginsburg and J. Breyer, dissenting): 542; ibid. (J. Breyer, joined by J. Stevens and J. Ginsburg, except as to Part I-A-1, and joined by J. Souter, as to Part I, dissenting): 551. See Ruth Bader Ginsburg, "Remarks on Judicial Independence: The Situation of the U.S. Federal Judiciary," delivered at University of Melbourne Law School on February 1, 2001: 11 (on file with the author).

2. See Alexander Bickel, *The Least Dangerous Branch: The Supreme Court at the Bar of Politics* (Indianapolis: Bobbs-Merrill, 1962).

3. See Barry Friedman, "Dialogue and Judicial Review," *Michigan Law Review* 91 (1993): 577 (arguing that constitutional interpretation is a process of dialogue involving all segments of society); Barry Friedman, "The History of the Countermajoritarian Difficulty, Part Four: Law's Politics," *University of Pennsylvania Law Review* 148 (2000): 971 ("law and politics are intertwined, but at a remove").

4. Associated Press, "Rehnquist Says Courts Severely Tested in Election Dispute," posted on-line on January 1, 2001 and available at http://www.cnn.com/2001/LAW/01/01/rehnquist.election.ap/index.html (viewed January 3, 2001).

5. The description here and in the next few paragraphs of the key events of Campaign 2000 is derived from an eight-part series the *Washington Post* published between January 28, 2001, and February 4, 2001. See "Series: Deadlock: The Inside Story of America's Closest Election," at http://washingtonpost.com/wp-srv/onpolitics/elections/deadlockmain.htm (viewed February 23, 2001); and a chronology of election events outlined by the Brookings Institution's Web Companion to the institute's coedited book, *Bush v. Gore: The Court Cases and the Commentary*, eds., E. J. Dionne, Jr. and William Kristol (Washington, D.C.: Brookings Institution Press, 2001), at http://www.brook.edu/

press/ books/ bush_v_gore.htm (viewed February 24, 2001). The judicial opinions and all of the supporting motions and pleadings referred to in the ensuing text and notes are taken from the Jurist Law Professor Network Web site at http://jurist.law.pitt.edu/election2000.htm (viewed February 26, 2000).

6. See *Siegel v. LePore*, 120 F. Supp.2d 1041 (S.D. Fla. 2000); *Siegel v. LePore*, 234 F.3d 1163 (11th Cir. 2000) (en banc), rehearing denied, 234 F.3d 1218 (11th Cir. 2000). See also *Touchston v. McDermott*, 234 F.3d 1133 (11th Cir. 2000) (affirming denial of a preliminary injunction by U.S. District Court Judge John Antoon II, from the Middle District of Florida); see ibid., 120 F. Supp.2d 1053 (M.D. Fla. 2000). The Eleventh Circuit Court also considered, and denied en banc, an emergency motion for injunction pending appeal in *Siegel v. LePore*, 234 F.3d 1162 (11th Cir. 2000); *Touchston v. McDermott*, 234 F.3d 1130 (11th Cir. 2000); *Touchston v. McDermott*, 234 F.3d 1161 (11th Cir. 2000). Other federal courts were part of the 2000 presidential campaign. The Robert Crown Law Library of Stanford law school has a comprehensive listing of the cases and their relevant litigation documents, collected at http://election2000.stanford.edu. See also *Palm Beach County Canvassing Board v. Harris*, 772 So.2d 1220 (Fla. 2000).

7. The circuit court observed that a presumption of irreparable injury is limited to claims that the right to privacy or certain free speech rights were deprived. Also, the court found that finding irreparable harm was dubious since the U.S. Supreme Court (at that point) had vacated the Florida Supreme Court's decision that allowed the recount to continue. See *Siegel v. LePore*, 234 F.3d 1163 (11th Cir. 2000) (en banc): 1177.

8. Ibid., 234 F.3d 1163, 1179 (C. J. Anderson, concurring specially): 1181, 1182–90.

9. Ibid., 234 F.3d 1163, 1190 (J. Birch, dissenting): 1191–93; ibid., 1193 (J. Dubina, dissenting).

10. Ibid., 234 F.3d 1163, 1194 (J. Carnes, dissenting). Judge Tjoflat dissented in *Siegel* but wrote extensively as to the reasons why in *Touchston v. McDermott*, 234 F.3d 1133, 1134 (11th Cir. 2000). The data on appointing the president was compiled from the Federal Judicial Center Web site at http://www.fjc.gov/ (viewed March 2, 2001).

11. *Palm Beach County Canvassing Board v. Harris*, 772 So.2d 1220 (Fla. 2000): 1229–30, 1238, 1240.

12. However, it was reported that law clerks inside the Court were more optimistic that the Court would hear the case. David Von Drehle, Dan Balz, James V. Grimaldi, and Susan Schmidt, "For Gore, Reasons to Hope Dwindled: Blows Came from Supreme Court, Florida Judge," from Part V, Ballot Battle in "Series: Deadlock: The Inside Story of America's Closest Election," available at http://washingtonpost.com/wp-dyn/articles/A10382-2001Jan31.html (viewed February 26, 2001).

13. Michael A. Carvin et al., "Petition for a Writ of Certiorari," in *Bush v. Palm Beach County Canvassing Board* (November 22, 2000): 10, 12, 20.

14. Laurence H. Tribe et al., "Brief in Opposition of Respondents Al Gore, Jr., and Florida Democratic Party" in *Bush v. Palm Beach County Canvassing Board* (November 23, 2000): 1–3, 8, 15, 25, and 29.

15. *Bush v. Palm Beach County Canvassing Board*, 121 S.Ct. 471 (2000) (per curiam): 474; *McPherson v. Blacker*, 146 U.S. 1 (1892). See also Roger J. Magnuson et al., "Brief of the Florida Senate and House of Representatives as *Amici Curiae* in Support of Neither Party," in *Bush v. Palm Beach County Canvassing Board* (November 27, 2000).

16. *Gore v. Harris*, 772 So.2d 1243 (Fla. 2000): 1253, 1256–57, 1260–62. Notably, the four-justice majority did not explain or reconcile its conclusion with the U.S. Supreme

Court's reliance on *McPherson v. Blacker,* 146 U.S. 1, 25 (1892) in *Bush v. Palm Beach County Canvassing Board* (its December 4 ruling), where the Court quoted *Blacker* in saying "Article II, 1, cl. 2 does not read that the people or the citizens shall appoint, but that each State shall . . ."

17. *Gore v. Harris,* 772 So.2d 1243, 1263 (Fla. 2000) (C. J. Wells, dissenting): 1263, 1264, 1267–69.

18. Ibid., 1268.

19. Michael A. Carvin et al., "Emergency Application for a Stay of Enforcement of the Judgment Below Pending the Filing and Disposition of a Petition for a Writ of Certiorari to the Supreme Court of Florida," in *Bush v. Gore* (December 8, 2000); Ronald A. Klain et al., "Opposition of Respondent Albert Gore, Jr. to Emergency Motion for a Stay Pending Certiorari," in *Bush v. Gore* (December 8, 2000).

20. *Bush v. Gore,* 121 S.Ct. 512 (2000) (J. Scalia, concurring). See also Klain et al., "Opposition of Respondent Albert Gore, Jr. to Emergency Motion for a Stay Pending Certiorari," 7.

21. *Bush v. Gore,* 121 S.Ct. 512 (2000) (J. Scalia, concurring): 512.

22. Ibid., (J. Stevens, dissenting): 512–13.

23. *Bush v. Gore,* 121 S. Ct. 525 (2000) (per curiam): 530–32.

24. Ibid., 533 (J. Rehnquist, concurring, joined by J. Scalia and J. Thomas): 533–39.

25. Ibid., 539 (J. Stevens dissenting): 539–42. See also Judge Birch's dissent in *Siegel v. LePore,* 234 F.3d 1163, 1190 (11th Cir. 2000).

26. *Bush v. Gore,* 121 S.Ct. 525, 542 (2000) (J. Souter, dissenting): 542–46.

27. Ibid., 546 (J. Ginsburg, dissenting): 546–50.

28. Ibid., 550 (J. Breyer, dissenting): 550–58.

29. Ibid., 555–58.

30. *Bush v. Gore,* 121 S.Ct. 525 (2000) (per curiam): 533.

31. *Marbury v. Madison,* 1 Cr. (5 U.S.) 137 (1803): 170.

32. Erwin Chemerinsky, "Cases Under the Guarantee Clause Should Be Justiciable," *Colorado Law Review* 65 (1994): 849, 858–59.

33. See, e.g., ibid., 852–53; J. Peter Mulhern, "In Defense of the Political Question Doctrine," *University of Pennsylvania Law Review* 137 (1988): 97; Martin H. Redish, "Judicial Review and the 'Political Question,'" *Northwestern University Law Review* 79 (1984–85): 1031; Louis Henkin, "Is There a 'Political Question' Doctrine?" *Yale Law Journal* 85 (1976): 597; Herbert Wechsler, "Toward Neutral Principles of Constitutional Law," *Harvard Law Review* 73 (1959): 1.

34. Chemerinsky, "Cases Under the Guarantee Clause Should Be Justiciable," 853.

35. See ibid., 853.

36. *Colegrove v. Green,* 328 U.S. 549 (1946): 550–56.

37. *Baker v. Carr,* 396 U.S. 186, 217 (1962).

38. Justice Black cited *McPherson v. Blacker,* 146 U.S. 1, 23–24, *Baker v. Carr,* 369 U.S. 186, 208–37 (1962) and *Wesberry v. Sanders,* 376 U.S. 1, 5–7 (1964) in saying they "raise a justiciable controversy under the Constitution and cannot be relegated to the political arena." *Williams v. Rhodes,* 393 U.S. 23 (1968): 28.

39. Chemerinsky, "Guaranteeing a Republican Form of Government," 870–74.

40. Magnuson et al., "Brief of the Florida Senate and House of Representatives as Amici Curiae in Support of Neither Party," 7–8.

41. Bickel, *The Least Dangerous Branch*, 184.

42. See ibid., 186–88, 191.

43. See Roger J. Magnuson et al., "Brief of the Florida Senate and House of Representatives as Amici Curiae in Support of Neither Party."

44. The Gallup Organization, "Election Controversy Apparently Drove Partisan Wedge into Attitudes towards Supreme Court," available at http://gallup.com/poll/releases/pr010116.asp (poll of January 10–14 showing that the public is sharply divided along party lines when evaluating the U.S. Supreme Court, a pattern that was markedly different from several months earlier); The Gallup Organization, "Opinion of U.S. Supreme Court Has Become More Politicized," available at http://gallup.com/poll/releases/pr010103b.asp (poll of December 15–17, 2000, showing that 49% of Americans had either a "great deal" or "quite a lot" of confidence in the U.S. Supreme Court, but that confidence increased sharply for Republicans, from 48% to 67%, but not Democrats, shortly after *Bush v. Gore* was decided); The Gallup Organization, "Eight in Ten Americans to Accept Bush as 'Legitimate' President," available at http://gallup.com/poll/releases/pr001214.asp (poll of December 13, 2000, showing that while 66% of national adults did not lose confidence in the U.S. Supreme Court because of *Bush v. Gore*, 30% did; and 62% of those Americans who disagreed with the decision say they have lost confidence); The Gallup Organization, "Public Willing to Accept Supreme Court as Final Arbiter of Election Dispute," available at http://gallup.com/poll/releases/pr001212.asp (poll of December 10, 2000, showing that 51% of the public believes that the personal political views of the justices are influencing their decision in *Bush v. Gore*). See also Linda Greenhouse, "Court's Action Brings Confusion, Not Clarity," reprinted in *36 Days: The Complete Chronicle of the 2000 Presidential Election Crisis* (New York: Times Books, 2001): 314–16; Samuel Issacharoff, "OpEd: Court May Have Expanded Voting Rights," reprinted in ibid., 316–17; Larry D. Kramer, "No Surprise, It's an Activist Court," reprinted in ibid., 317–18; William Glaberson, "Legal Scholars Question Supreme Court's Role," reprinted in ibid., 346–47.

45. Bickel, *The Least Dangerous Branch*, 24.

46. Bickel, *The Least Dangerous Branch*, 20.

47. *Marbury*, 170 (emphasis provided).

48. Linda Greenhouse, "Election Case a Test and Trauma for Justices," *New York Times* (February 20, 2001), available at: http://www.nytimes.com (viewed February 20, 2001); Associated Press, "Rehnquist Says Courts Severely Tested in Election Dispute" (reporting that in the Annual Report on the U.S. Judiciary Chief Rehnquist wrote "This presidential election . . . tested our Constitutional system in ways it has never been tested before. The Florida state courts, the lower federal courts and the Supreme Court of the United States became involved in a way that one hopes will seldom, if ever, be necessary in the future"): 1; Joan Biskupic, "Election Decision Still Splits Court," *USA Today* (January 22, 2001), available at http://usatoday.com (viewed on January 22, 2001) (reporting that internal conflict between Justices has increased following *Bush v. Gore,* with Justice Sandra Day O'Connor telling people close to her that she has never seen so much anger over a case in twenty years on Court); Ginsburg, "Remarks on Judicial Independence," 5 (observing that initial commentary on *Bush v. Gore* has been mixed).

49. Charles Levendosky, "Will Court Rue the Day It Decided '*Bush v. Gore,*'" *Akron Beacon Journal* (February 8, 2001): 12. See also *Nixon v. Shrink Missouri Government PAC*, 120 S.Ct. 897 (2000): 906, citing *United States v. Mississippi Valley Generating Co.*, 364 U.S. 520, 562 (1961).

Bibliography

Abraham, Henry J. *Justices and Presidents: A Political History of Appointments to the Supreme Court.* 3rd ed. New York: Oxford University Press, 1992.

Abraham, Henry J., and Barbara A. Perry. *Freedom and the Court: Civil Rights and Liberties in the United States.* 7th ed. New York: Oxford University Press, 1998.

Aldrich, John H. *Why Parties? The Origin and Transformation of Political Parties in America.* Chicago: University of Chicago Press, 1995.

Anechiarico, Frank, and James B. Jacobs. *The Pursuit of Absolute Integrity: How Corruption Control Makes Government Ineffective.* Chicago: University of Chicago Press, 1996.

Argersinger, Peter H. "A Place on the Ballot: Fusion Politics and Antifusion Laws." *American History Review* 85 (1980).

Bailyn, Bernard. *The Ideological Origins of the American Revolution.* Enlarged ed. Cambridge, Mass.: Belknap Press, 1992.

Baker, Gordon. *The Reapportionment Revolution.* New York: Random House, 1966.

Banks, Christopher P. "The Supreme Court and Precedent: An Analysis of Natural Courts and Reversal Trends." *Judicature* 75 (1992).

Beck, Paul A. *Party Politics in America.* 8th ed. New York: Longman, 1997.

Belknap, Michael. *Civil Rights, the White House, and the Justice Department, 1945–1968.* Vols. 1 and 2. New York: Garland Publishing Company, 1991.

BeVier, Lillian R. "Campaign Finance Reform: Specious Arguments, Intractable Dilemmas." *Columbia Law Review* 94 (1994).

———. *Is Free TV For Federal Candidates Constitutional?* Washington, D.C.: American Enterprise Institute, 1998.

Bibby, John W. "Party Organizations, 1946–1996." In *Partisan Approaches to Postwar American Politics,* edited by Bryon E. Shafer. Chatham, N.J.: Chatham House, 1998.

Bickel, Alexander. *The Least Dangerous Branch: The Supreme Court at the Bar of Politics.* Indianapolis: Bobbs-Merrill, 1962.

Biskupic, Joan, and Elder Witt. *The Supreme Court and the Powers of the American Government.* Washington, D.C.: Congressional Quarterly, 1996.

Blasi, Vincent. "Free Speech and the Widening Gyre of Fund-Raising: Why Campaign Spending Limits May Not Violate the First Amendment After All." *Columbia Law Review* 94 (1994).

Bowman, Cynthia Grant. "The Law of Patronage at a Crossroads." *Journal of Law and Politics* 12 (1996).

———. "Public Policy: 'We Don't Anybody Sent': The Death of Patronage Hiring in Chicago." *Northwestern University Law Review* 86 (1991).

Briffault, Richard. "Campaign Finance, the Parties and the Court: A Comment on *Col-*

orado Republican Federal Campaign Committee v. Federal Election Commission." Constitutional Commentary 14 (1997).

Burch, Alan Robert. "The NAACP Before and After *Grovey v. Townsend.*" (unpublished) Master's Thesis, University of Virginia, 1994.

Burnham, Walter Dean. "The End of American Political Parties." *Society* 35 (January–February 1998).

Caldeira, Gregory A. "Litigation, Lobbying, and the Voting Rights Law." In *Controversies in Minority Voting: The Voting Rights Act in Perspective,* edited by Bernard Grofman and Chandler Davidson. Washington, D.C.: Brookings Institution, 1992.

Cameron, Charles, David Epstein, and Sharyn O'Halloran. "Do Majority-Minority Districts Maximize Substantive Black Representation in Congress?" *American Political Science Review* 90 (December 1996).

Caplan, Lincoln. *The Tenth Justice.* New York: Alfred A. Knopf, 1987.

Center for Responsive Politics. *Plugging in the Public: A Model for Campaign Finance Disclosure.* Washington, D.C.: Center for Responsive Politics, 1996.

———. *Money and Politics: A National Survey of the Public's View on How Money Impacts our Political System.* Washington, D.C.: Center for Responsive Politics, 1997.

Chemerinsky, Erwin. "Cases Under the Guarantee Clause Should Be Justiciable." *Colorado Law Review* 65 (1994).

Christman, Roy, and Barbara Norrander. "A Reflection on Political Party Deregulation via the Courts: The Case of California." *Journal of Law and Politics* 6 (1990).

Clawson, Dan, and Alan Neustadtl, and Denise Scott. *Money Talks: Corporate PACs and Political Influence.* New York: Basic Books, 1992.

Cohen, William S. and George J. Mitchell. *Men of Zeal.* New York: Viking Press, 1988.

Cole, David. "First Amendment Antitrust: The End of Laissez-Faire in Campaign Finance." *Yale Law and Policy Review* 9 (1991).

Committee on Political Parties, American Political Science Association. "Toward a More Responsible Two-Party System." *American Political Science Review* 44 (Supplement) (1950).

Corner, Richard. "Strategies and Tactics of Litigants in Constitutional Cases." *Journal of Public Law* 17 (1968).

Corrado, Anthony. "Introduction [to] Money and Politics: A History of Federal Campaign Finance Law." In *Campaign Finance Reform: A Sourcebook,* edited by Anthony Corrado et al. Washington, D.C.: Brookings Institution, 1997.

Council of State Governments. *The Book of States.* Lexington, Ky.: Council of State Governments, 1992.

Crotty, William. *Party Reform.* New York: Longman, 1983.

Crovitz, Gordon. "The Criminalization of Politics." In *The Imperial Congress: Crisis in the Separation of Powers,* edited by Gordon S. Jones and John A. Marini. New York: Pharos Books, 1988.

Cutler, Lloyd. "A Proposal for a Continuing Public Prosecutor." *Hastings Constitutional Law Quarterly* 2 (1975).

Davidson, Chandler. "Minority Vote Dilution: An Overview." In *Minority Vote Dilution,* edited by Chandler Davidson. Washington, D.C.: Howard University Press, 1984.

Days, Drew, and Lani Guinier. "Enforcement of Section 5 of the Voting Rights Act." In *Minority Vote Dilution,* edited by Chandler Davidson. Washington, D.C.: Howard University Press, 1984.

Dionne, E. J., Jr. and William Kristol, eds. *Bush v. Gore: The Court Cases and the Commentary.* Washington, D.C.: Brookings Institution Press, 2001.

Ducat, Craig R. *Constitutional Interpretation.* 6th ed. Minneapolis, Minn.: West Publishing Company, 1996.

Dunne, John. "Protection of Minority Voting Rights." *Presidential Studies Quarterly* 22 (1991).

Ely, John Hart. "Gerrymanders: The Good, the Bad, and the Ugly." *Stanford Law Review* 50 (1998).

Epperson, John W. *The Changing Legal Status of Political Parties in the United States.* New York: Garland, 1986.

Epstein, Lee, and C. K. Rowland. "Debunking the Myth of Interest Group Invincibility in the Courts." *American Political Science Review* 86 (1991).

Epstein, Lee, and Joseph Kobylka. *The Supreme Court and Legal Change: Abortion and the Death Penalty.* Chapel Hill: University of North Carolina Press, 1992.

Epstein, Leon D. "The American Party Primary." In *On Parties: Essays Honoring Austin Ranney,* edited by Nelson W. Polsby and Raymond E. Wolfinger. Berkeley, Calif.: Institute of Government Studies Press, University of California, Berkeley, 1999.

———. *Political Parties in the American Mold.* Madison: University of Wisconsin Press, 1986.

Erie, S. P. *Rainbow's End.* Berkeley: University of California Press, 1988.

Eule, Julian N. "Promoting Speaker Diversity: Austin and Metro Broadcasting." *Supreme Court Review* (1990).

"Federal Employees' Political Activities." *Congressional Digest.* (August/September 1993).

"Fusion and the Associated Rights of Minor Political Parties." *Columbia Law Review* 95 (1995).

Fesler, James W. *The 50 States and Their Local Governments.* New York: Alfred Knopf, 1967.

Fiorina, Morris P. *The Decline of Collective Responsibility in American Politics.* St. Louis, Mo.: Center for the Study of American Business, Washington University, 1980.

Fiss, Owen M. "Free Speech and Social Structure." *Iowa Law Review* 75 (1986).

Foster, James C., and Susan M. Leeson. *Constitutional Law: Cases in Context.* Vol. 1. Upper Saddle River, N. J.: Prentice Hall, 1998.

Freedman, Anne. *Patronage: An American Tradition.* Chicago: Nelson-Hall, 1994.

Friedman, Barry. "Dialogue and Judicial Review." *Michigan Law Review* 91 (1993).

———. "The History of the Countermajoritarian Difficulty, Part Four: Law's Politics." *University of Pennsylvania Law Review* 148 (2000).

George, Tracy E., and Lee Epstein. "On the Nature of Supreme Court Decision Making." *American Political Science Review* 86 (1992).

Gerber, Alan. "African Americans' Congressional Careers and the Democratic House Delegations." *Journal of Politics* 58 (August 1996).

Gerber, Elisabeth R., Rebecca B. Morton, and Thomas A. Reitz. "Minority Representation in Multimember Districts." *American Political Science Review* 92 (1998).

Geyh, Charles G. "It's My Party and I'll Cry If I Want to: State Intrusions Upon the Associational Freedoms of Political Parties." *Wisconsin Law Review* 1983 (1983).

Glaberson, William "Legal Scholars Question Supreme Court's Role." In *36 Days: The Complete Chronicle of the 2000 Presidential Election Crisis.* New York: Times Books, 2001.

Goldman, Sheldon. *Picking Federal Judges: Lower Court Selection from Roosevelt Through Reagan.* New Haven: Yale University Press, 1997.

Gora, Joel M. "Finley, Forbes and The First Amendment: Does He Who Pays the Piper Call the Tune." Touro Law Review 15 (1999).

Gottlieb, Stephen. "Rebuilding the Right of Association: The Right to Hold a Convention as a Test Case." Hostra Law Review 11 (1982).

Green, John C., and Daniel M. Shea, eds. The State of the Parties. 2nd ed. Lanham, Md.: Rowman and Littlefield, 1995.

Greenberg, Jack. Crusaders in the Court: How a Dedicated Band of Lawyers Fought for the Civil Rights Revolution. New York: Basic Books, 1994.

Greenhouse, Linda. "Court's Action Brings Confusion, Not Clarity." In 36 Days: The Complete Chronicle of the 2000 Presidential Election Crisis. New York: Times Books, 2001.

Grofman, Bernard. "Shaw v. Reno and the Future of Voting Rights." PS 28 (1995).

————. "The Supreme Court, The Voting Rights Act, and Minority Representation." In Affirmative Action and Representation: Shaw v. Reno and the Future of Voting Rights, edited by Anthony A. Peacock. Durham, N.C.: Carolina Academic Press, 1997.

Guinier, Lani. "A Development of the Franchise: 1982 Voting Rights Amendments." In Voting Rights America: Continuing the Quest for Full Participation, edited by Karen McGill Arrington and William L. Taylor. Washington, D.C.: Joint Center for Political and Economic Studies, 1992.

Guinier, Lani, and Gerald Torres. "The Geography of Race in Elections: Color-blindness and Redistricting." Journal of Law and Politics 14 (1998).

Hadley, Charles D. "Blacks and Southern Politics: An Agenda for Research." Journal of Politics 56 (1994).

Hamilton, Alexander. "Federalist No. 78." In The Federalist Papers, edited by Clinton Rossiter. New York: Mentor, 1961.

Harriger, Katy J. "The History of the Independent Counsel Provisions: How the Past Informs the Current Debate." Mercer Law Review 49 (Winter 1998).

————. Independent Justice: The Federal Special Prosecutor in American Politics. Lawrence, Kansas: The University Press of Kansas, 1992.

Harris, Bruce A. "National Political Party Conventions: State's Interest Subordinate to Party's in Delegate Selection Process." University of Miami Law Review 29 (1975).

Harris-Abbott, Troy L. "Regulating Ballot Initiatives: How May a State Oversee Petition Circulators?" In Preview of United States Supreme Court Cases. Issue No. 1. (September 25, 1998) Chicago, Ill.: American Bar Association, 1998.

Hasen, Richard. "Campaign Finance Laws and the Rupert Murdoch Problem." Texas Law Review 77 (1999).

————. "Clipping Coupons for Democracy: An Egalitarian/Public Choice Defense of Campaign Finance Vouchers." California Law Review 84 (1996).

Henkin, Louis. "Is there a 'Political Question' Doctrine?" Yale Law Journal 85 (1976).

Herrnson, Paul S., and Diana Dwyre. "A Party Issue Advocacy in Congressional Campaigns." In The State of the Parties, 3rd ed. edited by John C. Green and Daniel M. Shea. Lanham, Md.: Rowman and Littlefield, 1999.

Hibbing, John R., and Elizabeth Theiss-Morse. Congress as Public Enemy: Public Attitudes Toward American Political Institutions. New York: Cambridge University Press, 1995.

Hofstadter, Richard. The Idea of a Party System. Berkeley: University of California Press, 1969.

Hoogenboom, Ari Arthur. Outlawing the Spoils: A History of the Civil Service Reform Movement, 1865–1883. Urbana: University of Illinois Press, 1968.

Howard, Glen S. "Patronage Dismissals: Constitutional Limits and Political Justifications." *University of Chicago Law Review* 41 (1974).

Issacharoff, Samuel. "OpEd: Court May Have Expanded Voting Rights." In *36 Days: The Complete Chronicle of the 2000 Presidential Election Crisis.* New York: Times Books, 2001.

Issacharoff, Samuel, Pamela S. Karlan, and Richard H. Pildes. *The Law of Democracy: Legal Structures of the Political Process.* Westbury, N.Y.: Foundation Press, 1998.

Ivers, Gregg. *To Build A Wall: American Jews and the Separation of Church and State.* Charlottesville: University Press of Virginia, 1995.

Jefferson, Thomas. "A Summary View of the Rights of British America." In *The Portable Thomas Jefferson,* edited by Merrill D. Peterson. New York: Penguin Books, 1977.

Johnson, C. Richard. "Successful Reform Litigation: The Shakman Patronage Case." *Chicago-Kent Law Review* 64 (1988).

Johnson, Ronald and Gary Libecap. "Courts, A Protected Bureaucracy, and Reinventing Government." *Arizona Law Review* 37 (1995).

Johnston, Michael. "Patrons and Clients, Jobs and Machines: A Case Study of the Uses of Patronage." *American Political Science Review* 73 (1979).

Kammen, Michael. "Introduction." In *The Origins of the American Constitution: A Documentary History,* edited by Michael Kammen. New York: Penguin Books, 1986.

Keefe, William J. *Parties, Politics, and Public Policy in America.* 7th ed. Washington, D.C.: Congressional Quarterly, 1994.

Kesler, Charles R. "Political Parties, the Constitution, and the Future of American Politics." In *American Political Parties and Constitutional Politics,* edited by Peter W. Schramm and Bradford P. Wilson. Lanham, Md.: Rowman and Littlefield, 1993.

Klarman, Michael J. "Majoritarian Judicial Review: The Entrenchment Problem." *Georgetown Law Journal* 85 (1997).

———. "Rethinking the Civil Rights and Civil Liberties Revolution." *Virginia Law Review* 82 (1996).

Kluger, Richard. *Simple Justice: The History of* Brown v. Board of Education *and Black America's Struggle for Equality.* New York: Alfred A. Knopf, 1975.

Koh, Harold Hongju. The National Security Constitution: *Sharing Power After the Iran-Contra Affair.* New Haven: Yale University Press, 1990.

Kramer, Larry D. "No Surprise, It's an Activist Court." In *36 Days: The Complete Chronicle of the 2000 Presidential Election Crisis.* New York: Times Books, 2001.

Lawson, Kay. "How State Laws Undermine Parties." In *Elections American Style,* edited by James Reichley. Washington, D.C.: Brookings Institution, 1987.

———. "Questions Raised by Recent Attempts at Local Party Reform." In *Machine Politics, Sound Bites, and Nostalgia,* edited by Michael Margolis and John Green. Lanham, Md.: University Press of America, 1993.

Leventhal, Harold. "Courts and Political Thickets." *Columbia Law Review* 77 (1977).

Lewis, Charles, and The Center for Public Integrity. *The Buying of Congress: How Special Interests Have Stolen Your Right to Life, Liberty, and the Pursuit of Happiness.* New York: Avon, 1998.

Light, Steven A. "Too (Color)blind to See: The Voting Rights Act of 1965 and the Rehnquist Court." *George Mason University Civil Rights Law Journal* 8 (1997–1998).

Lowenstein, Daniel H. "Associational Rights of Major Political Parties: A Skeptical Inquiry." *Texas Law Review* 71 (1993).

——. "Associational Rights of the Major Political Parties: A Political and Jurisprudential Dead End." *American Review of Politics* 16 (Winter 1995).

——. *Election Law: Cases and Materials.* Durham, N.C.: Carolina Academic Press, 1995.

——. "A Patternless Mosaic: Campaign Finance and The First Amendment After *Austin.*" *Capital University Law Review* 21 (1992).

Lowi, Theodore J. "Toward a Responsible Three-Party System: Prospects and Obstacles." In *The State of the Parties: The Changing Role of Contemporary American Parties.* 2nd ed., edited by John C. Green and Daniel M. Shea. Lanham, Md.: Rowman and Littlefield, 1996.

Lubin, David, and D. Stephen Voss. "The Partisan Impact of Voting Rights Law: A Reply to Pamela S. Karlan." *Stanford Law Review* 50 (1998).

Madison, James. "Federalist No. 57." In *The Federalist,* edited by Jacob E. Cooke. Middletown, Conn.: Wesleyan University Press, 1961.

——."Federalist No. 10." In *The Federalist Papers,* edited by Clinton Rossitor. New York: Mentor, 1961.

——. "Federalist No. 51." In *The Federalist Papers,* edited by Clinton Rossitor. New York: Mentor, 1961.

——. "Federalist No. 55." In *The Federalist Papers,* edited by Clinton Rossiter. New York: Mentor, 1961.

——. *The Papers of James Madison,* edited by R. A. Rutland. Vol. 14. Charlottesville, Va.: University Press of Virginia, 1983.

Maisel, L. Sandy, ed. *The Parties Respond.* Boulder, Colo.: Westview Press, 1992.

Mann, Kenneth. *Defending White Collar Crime.* New Haven: Yale University Press, 1985.

Manwaring, David R. *Render Unto Caesar: The Flag Salute Controversy.* Chicago: University of Chicago Press, 1962.

Maranto, Robert. "Thinking the Unthinkable in Public Administration: A Case of Spoils in the Federal Bureaucracy." *Administration and Society* 29 (1998).

Marlise, James. *The People's Lawyers.* New York: Holt, Rinehart, and Winston, 1973.

Martin, Christopher J. "*Democratic Party v. Wisconsin ex. rel. LaFollette:* May States Impose Open Primary Results Upon National Party Conventions?" *Denver Law Review* 59 (1982).

Maveety, Nancy. *Justice Sandra Day O'Connor: Strategist on the Court.* Lanham, Md.: Rowman and Littlefield, 1996.

——. *Representation Rights and the Burger Years.* Ann Arbor: University of Michigan Press, 1991.

McClain, Paula D., and Joseph Stewart. *Can We All Get Along?: Racial and Ethnic Minorities in American Politics.* Boulder, Colo.: Westview Press, 1995.

McCleskey, Clifton. "Parties at the Bar: Equal Protection, Freedom of Association, and the Rights of Political Organizations." *Journal of Politics* 46 (1984).

McSweeney, Dean, and John Zvesper. *American Political Parties.* London: Routledge, 1991.

Meiklejohn, Alexander. *Free Speech and Its Relation to Self-Government.* New York: Harper, 1948.

Melstner, Michael. *Cruel and Unusual: The Supreme Court and Capital Punishment.* New York: Random House, 1973.

Merriam, Charles, and Louise Overacker. *Primary Elections.* Chicago: University of Chicago Press, 1928.

Mileur, Jerome M. "Legislative Responsibility: American Political Parties and the Law." In

Challenges to Party Government, edited by John K. White and Jerome M. Mileur. Carbondale: Southern Illinois University Press, 1992.

———. "Massachusetts: The Democratic Party Charter Movement." In *Party Renewal in America,* edited by Gerald M. Pomper. New York: Praeger, 1980.

Mosher, Frederick C. *Democracy and the Public Service.* 2nd ed. New York: Oxford University Press, 1982.

Mulhern, J. Peter. "In Defense of the Political Question Doctrine." *University of Pennsylvania Law Review* 137 (1988).

NAACP-Legal Defense Fund. *1988–1989 Annual Report.* New York: NAACP Legal Defense Fund, 1989.

Noonan, Jr., John T. *Bribes.* New York: Macmillan Publishing Company, 1984.

O'Brien, David M. "Charting the Rehnquist Court's Course: How the Center Folds, Holds, and Shifts." *New York School Law Review* 40 (1996).

———. "Clinton's Legal Policy and the Courts: Rising from Disarray or Turning Around and Around?" In *The Clinton Presidency: First Appraisals,* edited Colin Campbell and Bert A. Rockman. Chatham, N.J.: Chatham House, 1996.

———. *Constitutional Law and Politics: Civil Rights and Civil Liberties.* Vol. 2. 4th ed. New York: W. W. Norton and Co., 2000.

———. *Constitutional Law and Politics: Struggles for Power and Governmental Accountability.* Vol. 1. 4th ed. New York: W. W. Norton and Co., 2000.

———. "Judicial Review and American Politics: Historical and Political Perspectives." In *Judges on Judging: Views from the Bench,* edited by David M. O'Brien. Chatham, N.J.: Chatham House, 1997.

———. *Judicial Roulette.* New York: Twentieth Century Fund, 1988.

———. "The Reagan Judges: His Most Enduring Legacy." In *The Reagan Legacy: Promise and Performance,* edited by Charles O. Jones. Chatham, N.J.: Chatham House, 1988.

———. "The Rehnquist Court's Shrinking Plenary Docket." *Judicature* 81 (1997).

———. *Storm Center: The Supreme Court in American Politics.* 5th ed. New York: W. W. Norton and Co., 2000.

———. *Supreme Court Watch 1997.* New York: W. W. Norton and Co., 1998.

O'Connor, Karen. *Women's Organization's Use of the Court.* Lexington, Mass.: Lexington Books, 1980.

O'Rourke, Timothy G. "*Shaw v. Reno* and the Hunt for Double Cross-Overs." *PS* 28 (1995).

———. "*Shaw v. Reno:* The Shape of Things to Come." In *Affirmative Action:* Shaw v. Reno *and the Future of Voting Rights,* edited by Anthony Peacock. Durham, N.C.: Carolina Academic Press, 1997.

Ornstein, Norman. "Doing Congress's Dirty Work." *Georgetown Law Journal* 86 (July 1988).

Ortiz, Daniel R. "The Reform Debate: Politics and the First Amendment." In *Campaign* Finance Reform: A *Sourcebook,* edited by Anthony Corrado et al. Washington, D.C.: Brookings Institution, 1997.

Overly, Marvin L., and Kenneth M. Cosgrove. "Unintended Consequences? Racial Redistricting and the Representation of Minority Interests." *Journal of Politics* 58 (May 1996).

Parker, Frank R. "Predominant Factors and Narrow Tailoring: Can Racial Districts Be Justified by Incumbent Protection and the Voting Rights Act?" *Preview* 3 (1995).

Pearson, William M., and David S. Castle. "Liberalizing Restrictions on Political Activities of State Employees: Perception of High-Level State Executives." *American Review of Public Administration* 21 (1991).

Peltason, Jack W. "Constitutional Law for Political Parties." In *On Parties: Essays Honoring Austin Ranney,* edited by Nelson W. Polsby and Raymond E. Wolfinger. Berkeley: Institute of Government Studies Press, University of California, Berkeley, 1999.

Peterson, Molly. "Reexamining Compelling Interests and Radical State Campaign Finance Reforms: So Goes the Nation?" *Hastings Constitutional Law Quarterly* 25 (1998).

Pitkin, Hannah. *The Concept of Representation.* Westport, Conn.: Greenwood Press, 1967.

Polsby, Nelson W. *The Consequences of Reform.* Oxford: Oxford University Press, 1983.

Powe, L. A. "Mass Speech and the Newer First Amendment." *Supreme Court Review* 1982 (1982).

Price, David E. *Bringing Back the Parties.* Washington, D.C.: Congressional Quarterly, 1984.

Public Campaign. *Pacs, Parties, and Potato Chips: Myths and Misconception About Reforming the Campaign Finance System.* Washington, D.C.: Public Campaign, 1998.

Rakove, Jack N. *Original Meanings: Politics and Ideas in the Making of the Constitution.* New York: Vintage Books, 1996.

Ranney, Austin. *The Doctrine of Responsible Government.* Urbana: University of Illinois Press, 1954.

Ranney, Austin, and Willmoore Kendall. *Democracy and the American Party System.* New York: Harcourt, Brace and World, 1956.

Raskin, Jamin, and John Bonifaz. "Equal Protection and the Wealth Primary." *Yale Law and Policy Review* 11 (1993).

———. *The Wealth Primary: Campaign Fundraising and the Constitution.* Washington, D.C.: Center for Responsive Politics, 1994.

Rawls, John. *Political Liberalism.* New York: Columbia University Press, 1993.

———. *A Theory of Justice.* Cambridge, Mass.: Belknap Press, 1971.

"Recent Cases." *Harvard Law Review* 111 (1998).

Redish, Martin H. "Judicial Review and the 'Political Question.'" *Northwestern University Law Review* 79 (1984–85).

Report of the Congressional Committees Investigating the Iran-Contra Affair: with the Minority View. Abridged ed. New York: Times Books, 1988.

Richards, David A. J. *Toleration and the Constitution.* New York: Oxford University Press, 1986.

Rohde, David W. and Harold J. Spaeth. *Supreme Court Decision Making.* San Francisco: W. H. Freeman, 1986.

Rosenkranz, E. Joshua. *Buckley Stops Here: Loosening the Judicial Stranglehold on Campaign Finance Reform.* New York: Century Foundation Press, 1998.

Ryden, David K. "The Good, the Bad and the Ugly: The Judicial Shaping of Party Activities." In *The State of the Parties,* 3rd ed., edited by John C. Green and Daniel M. Shea. Lanham, Md.: Rowman and Littlefield, 1999.

———. *Representation in Crisis: The Constitution, Interest Groups, and Political Parties.* Albany: State University Press of New York Press, 1996.

Sabato, Larry J. *The Party's Just Begun: Shaping Political Parties for America's Future.* Glenview, Ill.: Scott, Foresman and Co., 1987.

Sabato, Larry, and Robert Lichter. *When Should the Watchdogs Bark? Media Coverage Of the Clinton Scandals.* Washington, D.C.: Center for Media and Public Affairs, 1994.

Sabato, Larry J., and Glenn R. Simpson. *Dirty Little Secrets: The Persistence of Corruption in American Politics*. New York: Random House, 1996.

Salokar, Rebecca. *The Solicitor General: The Politics of Law*. Philadelphia: Temple University Press, 1992.

Savage, James D. "Corruption and Virtue at the Constitutional Convention." *Journal of Politics* 56 (1992).

Scanlon, Thomas. "A Theory of Freedom of Expression." *Philosophy and Public Affairs* 1 (1972).

Schattschneider, E. E. *Party Government*. New York: Farrar and Rinehardt, 1942.

Schlesinger, Joseph A. *Political Parties and the Winning of Office*. Ann Arbor: University of Michigan Press, 1991.

Schram, Martin. *Speaking Freely: Former Members of Congress Talk About Money in Politics*. Washington, D.C.: Center For Responsive Politics, 1995.

Schudson, Michael. *Watergate in American Memory*. New York: Basic Books, 1992.

Schultz, David. "Revisiting *Buckley v. Valeo:* Eviscerating the Line Between Candidate Contributions and Independent Expenditures." *Journal of Law and Politics* 14 (1998).

Segal, Jeffrey A., and Albert D. Cover. "Ideological Values and the Votes of U.S. Supreme Court Justices." *American Political Science Review* 83 (1989).

Segal, Jeffrey A., and Harold J. Spaeth. *The Supreme Court and the Attitudinal Model*. Cambridge: Cambridge University Press, 1993.

Segal, Jeffrey A., Lee Epstein, Charles Cameron, and Harold Spaeth. "Ideological Values and the Votes of U.S. Supreme Court Justices Revisited." *Journal of Politics* 57 (1995).

Shaw, Theodore. "Rebuttal: Wrong About Racism, Columnist Misses Point When He Blames Blacks for Racism." *American Lawyer* (December 19, 1996).

Shea, Daniel M. *Transforming Democracy*. Albany, N.Y.: SUNY Press, 1995.

Smith, Bradley. "The Current Debate Over Soft Money: Soft Money, Hard Realities, The Constitutional Prohibition on a Soft Money Ban." *Journal of Legislation* 24 (1998).

———. "Faulty Assumptions and Undemocratic Consequences of Campaign Finance Reform." *Yale Law Journal* 105 (1996).

———. "Judicial Protection of Ballot Access Rights: Third Parties Need Not Apply." *Harvard Journal on Legislation* 28 (1991).

———. "Money Talks: Speech, Corruption, Equality, and Campaign Finance." *Georgetown Law Journal* 86 (1997).

Sorauf, Frank J. "Caught in a Political Thicket: The Supreme Court and Campaign Finance." *Constitutional Commentary* 3 (1986).

———. "Patronage and Party." *Midwest Journal of Political Science* 3 (1959).

———. "The Silent Revolution in Patronage." *Public Administration Review* 20 (1960).

Sorauf, Frank J., and Paul Allen Beck. *Political Parties in America*. 6th ed. Glenview, Ill.: Scott, Foresman, 1988.

Stein, L. *Holding Bureaucrats Accountable*. Tuscaloosa: University of Alabama Press, 1991.

Stern, Philip M. *Still the Best Congress Money Can Buy*. Washington, D.C.: Regnery Gateway, 1992.

Strauss, David A. "Corruption, Equality, and Campaign Finance Reform." *Columbia Law Review* 94 (1994).

———. "Legality, Activism, and the Patronage Case." *Chicago-Kent Law Review* 64 (1988).

Sullivan, Kathleen M. "Political Money and Freedom of Speech." *University of California at Davis Law Review* 30 (1997).

———. "Reply: Political Money and Freedom of Speech: A Reply to Frank Askin." *University of California at Davis Law Review* 31 (1998).

Sunstein, Cass R. *Democracy and the Problem of Free Speech.* New York: Free Press, 1993.

———. "Exchange; Speech in the Welfare State: Free Speech Now." *University of Chicago Law Review* 59 (1992).

———. "Political Equality and Unintended Consequences." *Columbia Law Review* 94 (1994).

Tamanaha, Brian Z. "A Critical Review of the Classified Information Procedure Act." *American Journal of Criminal Law* 13 (Summer 1986).

Tate, C. Neal. "Personal Attribute Models of the Voting Behavior of U.S. Supreme Court Justices: Liberalism in Civil Liberties and Economics Decisions, 1946–1978." *American Political Science Review* 75 (1981).

Tauber, Steven C. "The NAACP-LDF and the U.S. Supreme Court's Racial Discrimination Decision Making." *Social Science Quarterly* 80 (1999).

———. "On Behalf of the Condemned: The Impact of the NAACP Legal Defense Fund on Capital Punishment Decision Making in the U.S. Courts of Appeals." *Political Research Quarterly* 51 (1998).

Thurber, Karl T. "Big, Little, Littler: Synthesizing Hatch Act–Based Political Activity Legislation Research." *Review of Public Personnel Administration* (1993).

Tocqueville, Alexis de. *Democracy in America,* edited by J. P. Mayer and Max Lerner. New York: Harper and Row, 1966.

Tolchin, Martin, and Susan Tolchin. *To the Victor: Political Patronage from the Clubhouse to the Whitehouse.* New York: Random House, 1971.

Toporek, Lisa E. "Bad Politics Makes Bad Law: A Comment on the Eighth Circuit's Approach to the Governmental Attorney-Client Privilege." *The Georgetown Law Journal* 86 (July 1998).

Tribe, Laurence H. *American Constitutional Law.* Mineola, N.Y.: Foundation Press, 1988.

Truman, David. *The Governmental Process: Political Interest and Public Opinion.* New York: Alfred A. Knopf, 1951.

U.S. Congress. House. Committee on the Judiciary. Subcommittee on the Constitution. *The First Amendment and Restrictions on Issue Advocacy: Hearing Before the Subcommittee on the Constitution of the Committee on the Judiciary.* Committee Serial No. 43. 105th Cong., 1st sess., 18 September 1997.

U.S. Congress. House. Committee on the Judiciary. *Special Prosecutor and Watergate Grand Jury Legislation Hearings Before the Subcommittee on Criminal Justice.* 93rd Cong., 1st sess., 1973.

U.S. Congress. Senate. Committee on the Judiciary. *Special Prosecutor.* 93rd Cong., 1st sess., 1973.

U.S. Federal Communications Commission. *FCC Record : a Comprehensive Compilation Decisions, Reports, Public Notices and Other Documents of the Federal Communications Commission of the United States.* Washington, D.C.: GPO, 1986.

U.S. Federal Communications Commission. *FCC Rules and Regulations.* Washington, D.C.: GPO, 1998.

Van Alstyne, William. "The Demise of the *Right-Privilege Distinction in Constitutional Law." *Harvard Law Review* 87 (1968).

Van Riper, Paul P. *History of the United States Civil Service Reform Movement, 1865–1883.* Evanston, Ill.: Row, Peterson, 1958.

Vose, Clement. *Caucasians Only: The Supreme Court, The NAACP, and the Restrictive Covenant Cases*. Berkeley, Calif.: University of California Press, 1959.

———. *Constitutional Change: Amendment Politics and Supreme Court Litigation*. Lexington, Mass.: Lexington Books, 1972.

Walsh, Lawrence. *Firewall: The Iran-Contra Conspiracy and Cover-up*. New York: W. W. Norton and Co., 1997.

———. *Iran-Contra: The Final Report*. New York Times Books, 1994.

Wasby, Stephen L. *Race Relations Litigation in an Age of Complexity*. Charlottesville: University Press of Virginia, 1995.

Wechsler, Herbert. "Toward Neutral Principles of Constitutional Law." *Harvard Law Review* 73 (1959).

Wertheimer, Fred, and Susan Weiss Manes. "Campaign Finance Reform: A Key to Restoring the Health of Our American Democracy." *Columbia Law Review* 94 (1994).

White, John K., and Jerome M. Mileur. *Challenges to Party Government*. Carbondale, Ill.: Southern Illinois University Press, 1992.

Wilson, James Q. *Amateur Democrat: Club Politics in Three Cities*. Chicago: University of Chicago Press, 1950.

Wood, Gordon S. *The Creation of the American Republic, 1776–1787*. New York: W. W. Norton and Co., 1972.

Wright, J. Skelly. "Money and the Pollution of Politics: Is the First Amendment an Obstacle to Political Equality?" *Columbia Law Review* 82 (1982).

———. "Politics and the Constitution: Is Money Speech?" *Yale Law Journal* 85 (1976).

Wright, Ronald. "Congressional Use of Immunity Grants After Iran-Contra." *Minnesota Law Review* 80 (December 1995).

Zywicki, Todd J. "Federal Judicial Review of State Ballot Access Regulations: Escape from the Political Thicket." *Thurgood Marshall Law Review* 20 (1994).

About the Contributors

Christopher P. Banks is an associate professor of political science at The University of Akron. His research interests include studying political the behavior of the U.S. Supreme Court and the U.S. Courts of Appeals. In addition to serving as the university and departmental pre-law advisor, he teaches courses in constitutional law, civil rights and liberties, criminal justice, the judicial process, and American political ideas. Before receiving his doctorate, he practiced law in civil and criminal litigation and was active in state and local politics. He is the author of *Judicial Politics in the D.C. Circuit Court* (1999) and has published several articles and book reviews on public law topics in *Judicature, Southeastern Political Review, Social Science Quarterly,* the *Journal of Law and Politics, Seattle University Law Review,* and the *University of Akron Law Review.*

John C. Bonifaz, Gregory G. Luke, and Brenda Wright are, respectively, the executive director, staff attorney, and managing attorney for the National Voting Rights Institute in Boston, Massachusetts. The Institute (http://www.nvr.org) is a nonprofit organization dedicated to challenging the constitutionality of the current campaign finance system across the United States. Through litigation and public education the institute has redefined campaign finance as a basic voting rights issue. The Institute is leading a new legal movement to revisit *Buckley v. Valeo* (1976).

Joel M. Gora is a professor of law at Brooklyn Law School and has served as staff counsel and associate legal director at the American Civil Liberties Union from 1969–78. He was also cocounsel for the plaintiffs in *Buckley v. Valeo,* 424 U.S. 1 (1976).

John C. Green is the director of the Ray C. Bliss Institute of Applied Politics, a bipartisan research and teaching institute at The University of Akron dedicated to the nuts and bolts of practical politics. Green is a widely known observer of Ohio and national politics. His research interests include American political parties, campaign finance, and religion and politics. He is the coauthor of *The State of the Parties: The Changing Role of Contemporary Party Politics* (1999); *Multiparty Politics in America* (1996); and *The Politics of Ideas: Intellectual Challenges to the Major Parties* (1995). He

381

is the editor of the *Vox Pop,* the newsletter of the Political Organizations and Parties Section of the American Political Science Association. He has published numerous articles in scholarly journals and edited books on campaign finance, including *Financing the 1996 Elections* (1999). Green has focused on religion and politics and is the coauthor of *The Bully Pulpit: The Politics of Protestant Clergy* (1997), and *Religion and the Culture Wars: Dispatches From the Front* (1996).

Katy J. Harriger is an associate professor of politics at Wake Forest University. She is the author of *Independent Justice: The Special Prosecutor in American Politics* (2nd ed. 2000). She has published articles in *Publius: The Journal of Federalism, Mercer Law Review, Review of Politics,* and *Georgetown Law Review.* Her professional focus is on American constitutional law, independent counsel, and government ethics.

David M. O'Brien is the Leone Reaves and George W. Spicer Professor of Government and Foreign Affairs at the University of Virginia. He is the author of several books including *Storm Center: The Supreme Court in American Politics* (5th ed., 2000), winner of the American Bar Association's Silver Gavel Award. His other publications include *Supreme Court Watch* (Annual), *Constitutional Law and Politics: Struggles for Power and Governmental Accountability* Vol. 1 (4th ed., 2000), *Constitutional Law and Politics: Civil Rights and Civil Liberties* Vol. 2 (4th ed., 2000), *To Dream of Dreams: Religious Freedom and Constitutional Politics in Postwar Japan* (1996), numerous articles, and co-edited books. He has also served as a Judicial Fellow at the Supreme Court of the United States, a Russell Sage Foundation Visiting Fellow and a Fulbright Lecturer at Oxford University.

Barbara Perry is a professor of government at Sweet Briar College and the author of *A "Representative" Supreme Court? The Impact of Race, Religion, and Gender on Appointments* (1991). She is the coauthor with Henry J. Abraham of *Freedom and the Court: Civil Rights and Liberties in the United States* (7th ed. 1998). She is author of *The Priestly Tribe: The Supreme Court's Image in the American Mind* (1999) and *The Supremes: Essays on the Current Justices of the Supreme Court of the United States* (1999). She served as the 1994–95 Judicial Fellow at the Supreme Court in the Office of the Administrative Assistant to the Chief Justice and received the Tom C. Clark Award as the outstanding fellow.

Trevor Potter was a commissioner of the Federal Election Commission from 1991 to 1995, and chairman of the FEC in 1994. He has served as the Merrill Lecturer at the University of Virginia School of Law, and as chair of the Administrative Law Section of the American Bar Association's Election Law Committee. He is partner in the Washington, D.C., law firm of Wiley, Rein, and Fielding, and a senior fellow in government studies at the Brookings Institution.

David K. Ryden is an assistant professor and Towsley Research Scholar at Hope College. He also has a law degree and has practiced law in the area of civil litigation. His research focuses on matters of law and politics and he teaches courses concerning rights and civil liberties, the judicial process, and law and society. He is author of *Representation in Crisis* (1996), and an editor and contributor to *The U.S. Supreme Court and the Electoral Process* (2000).

Steven C. Tauber received his Ph.D. in government from the University of Virginia in 1995, and is an assistant professor of government and international affairs at the University of South Florida. He has published articles in *Political Research Quarterly* and *Social Science Quarterly* and presented many papers on NAACP-LDF's impact on judicial decision making. He is also a codirector of a project that studies inter–minority group socioeconomic and political competition in urban areas. Professor Tauber is currently developing a database of decision making by the justices on the Supreme Court of Florida.

Subject Index

Numbers in italics indicate information that appears in tables within the text.

Case Index

Numbers in italics indicate information that appears in tables within the text.

About the Book

Superintending Democracy: The Courts and the Political Process was designed and typeset on a MacIntosh in QuarkXPress by Kachergis Book Design of Pittsboro, North Carolina. The typeface, ITC Stone Serif, was designed by Sumner Stone in 1987. Mr. Stone has been very influential in digital type, and from 1984 to 1991 was the Director of Typography at Adobe.

Superintending Democracy: The Courts and the Political Process was printed on 60-pound Writers Offset and bound by Thomson-Shore, Inc., of Dexter, Michigan.